INTRODUCTION TO COMPARATIVE PHILOSOPHY

by

P. T. RAJU

SOUTHERN ILLINOIS UNIVERSITY PRESS
Carbondale and Edwardsville

Feffer & Simons, Inc.
London and Amsterdam

ARCTURUS
BOOKS ®

Arcturus Books Edition April 1970
This edition printed by offset lithography
in the United States of America
SBN 8093-0419-8
Library of Congress Catalog Card Number 62-7870

Preface

Comparative philosophy is a field of inquiry that has been little explored. It could not have come into existence before intellectually significant contacts among the philosophical traditions. China had such a contact with India during the early centuries of the Christian era, mainly through Buddhism; but India remained unaffected. Between Greece and India the encounter was sporadic and short-lived; neither made a deliberate attempt to study the other. But the world situation has now changed. The East and the West have come once for all into intimate contact on a vast scale. Each feels the necessity for mutual understanding and even for assimilating whatever in the other is true and useful. This need to understand is no longer a matter of mere intellectual curiosity but of survival. The eastern and western minds need to be integrated. It has been asserted and is still being maintained today that each has a different kind of soul. But if the two are to be integrated, we have to assume a deeper soul comprehending the manifest souls of both. This common soul must always have been, without either component being conscious of its presence. The encompassing soul has to be discovered and understood; and in its terms the separate souls have to be reappraised.

There have been works useful for the study of comparative philosophy, such as source books, treatises on philosophical beginnings, separate histories, evaluations of cultures, and some syntheses. However, they have not presented the philosophical traditions with a unified perspective from which they can be studied comparatively. Comparative philosophy must have a philosophical aim. Only when the aim is clarified can the work be given a definite shape. The aim has to illuminate the perspective; then the traditions thrown into perspective take on a definite meaning and significance. The aim of comparative philosophy is the elucidation of the nature of man and his environment in order that a comprehensive philosophy of life and a plan for thought and action may be obtained. It is with this end in view that the present work has been written. Many who know western philosophy know very little of the Indian and the Chinese; even the Indians who are acquainted with both western and Indian philosophies have little knowledge of the Chinese. Similarly, many Chinese know very little of the western and the Indian except Buddhism. Moreover, each has many wrong notions about the other philosophies and cannot get the feel of them. There is therefore a need for a book in which all three traditions are given in outline. From this book the reader can learn the general trends and central ideas of each.

In comparing and evaluating, the reader should be allowed to draw his own conclusions. He need not accept those given by authors, not even by the present writer. But he can draw his own conclusions only if the traditions are presented according to a single plan and if he is given some insight into them. He should know fairly well *what* he is to compare before he does compare.

There are many standard works on the separate histories of the philosophical traditions. But often they are so detailed that it is difficult to understand the main trends and interests. One cannot easily rise above the minutiae in order to view all the traditions together. There are also briefer histories of philosophy. But they have not been written from any single point of view, not even according to any single plan, with the result that one becomes confused when attempting to get a comparative view. The reader belonging to any one tradition should get an understandable impression of the others. This purpose can be achieved only if all the traditions can be presented according to a generally common plan and common concepts. This volume undertakes to do this in a modest fashion by introducing the western, Indian, and Chinese readers to each others' philosophies.

A few books have been written about the world's philosophies, but often without an adequate grasp or exposition of their natures. The result is that the reader finds the unfamiliar traditions strange and outlandish, and is unable to form an opinion about them. Some of the authors treat several different philosophies sympathetically. Yet sympathy, though essential, is not enough, unless it leads to deeper understanding. That is why their interpretations are often curious, and not very helpful. If reason is the same everywhere and many of life's problems are shared, this strangeness ought to be minimized. Any presentation of all philosophies together should lessen this strangeness and increase understandability.

One great hurdle in preparing a work on comparative philosophy is the difficulty of learning all the languages involved. The project could have taken the form of a symposium by a number of specialists. Nevertheless, even when a uniform plan is outlined, it is hard to obtain uniformity of treatment, since the minds of individual investigators operate along different lines.

How long, then, are we to wait till a master of all languages and philosophies offers the world a work on comparative philosophy? Some one has to start the task, and the author, along with a few others before him, has ventured to begin, even though aware of the perils. He accepts dependence on translations as inevitable for any treatment of comparative philosophy. One who attempts to master several languages as well as the philosophies written in them risks shallowness. The language barrier is likely to confront every writer on comparative philosophy who wishes to base his work entirely on original sources. But any defect that may result from the difficulty will rectify itself in course of time, as thinkers of different traditions, interested in comparative philosophy, cooperate with one another through mutual criticism.

Usually the important philosophical traditions of the world are regarded as four: the Greek, the Jewish, the Chinese, and the Indian. But the Jewish tradition has become part of the western, and so the author has included it there. In an introductory work this is not improper. Were this a comparative treatment of some philosophical subject, particularly ethics, Jewish thought would be given special consideration.

No separate section is allotted to Islamic philosophy. That philosophy is alternatively Platonism, Aristotelianism, a mixture of the two, or a union of the two with Neo-Platonism. The entry of Islamic philosophy into Europe via North Africa is practically a forerunner of the Renaissance of the sixteenth century, and is considered by some to be an earlier renaissance. This indicates the closeness of Islamic to ancient Greek and Hellenistic thought.

This survey does not aim at comparing religions. Western scholars have done much work on comparative religion, and many of them have treated eastern religions with sympathy and appreciation. When a reference to religion is made in the present study, it is not to religion as such, but only to the philosophy underlying or imbedded in it.

In an introductory book, which may be used as a textbook in

comparative philosophy, many details and technicalities have to be eschewed. The first three sections may be treated, not only as brief summaries of the histories of the traditions, but also as running commentaries on them from the standpoint of man. No particular historian has been followed. The author has utilized several authorities to supplement his own knowledge of individual philosophers. Care has been taken to avoid preconceived opinions and oversimplifications. But in a work like this, covering the histories of the philosophies of the world, the reader may find that some ideas which he considers to be important are not included. This seems to be unavoidable when each tradition is concisely presented. This cannot be a work on philosophers and their systems, but on trends of thought; and the names of philosophers are introduced only as they represent the trends. Detailed accounts are available in separate histories of philosophy. Each tradition has a history of thirty centuries or more. Only the central ideas can be given in a work of this kind.

This book grew out of the "Sir Hari Singh Gaur Foundation Lectures" on comparative philosophy, delivered at the Saugor University during December, 1955. A few changes were incorporated later. The author thanks the university for providing him with the occasion to prepare the book. The lectures were intended for generally educated audiences, and the introductory nature of the presentation has been retained in this volume.

I have to express my thanks to H. E. Dr. S. Radhakrishnan for the constant help he has given me in my work on comparative philosophy; to Professors E. A. Burtt, W. H. Sheldon, H. W. Schneider, C. A. Moore, and Brand Blanshard for encouraging me in preparing this book; to Dr. W. T. Chan, not only for his friendly suggestions, but also for going through the chapter on Chinese thought in manuscript; and to my research students for checking the typescript.

My most grateful thanks are due to Professor H. W. Schneider, Director, Blaisdell Institute, Claremont, California, and to its members, Dr. T. M. Greene, Dr. S. Y. Ch'en, and others, who held a seminar during 1959–60 on my manuscript and made several important comments and suggestions. I am grateful to Dr. M. H. Fisch of the University of Illinois and Dr. Virgil C. Aldrich of Kenyon College, Gambier, Ohio, who also read the manuscript and offered helpful criticisms. Professor John D. Goheen and Dr. David Nivison of Stanford University also reviewed the manuscript; and I am particularly obliged to them for their encouraging reaction to my method of approach and treatment and for their valuable contributions. Finally my sincere thanks are extended to the Asia Foundation for its generous grant, which enabled me to spend some time at the Blaisdell Institute and hold discussions with its members, and to the Committee on International Cooperation of the American Philosophical Association for cooperating with the Blaisdell Institute in sponsoring my work, and last but not least to Professor W. H. Werkmeister, who has been a constant source of encouragement and help for my work on comparative philosophy. I also thank Professor J. Hutchison of Claremont College for checking the proofs.

Philosophisches Seminar
Johannes Gutenberg University of Mainz
Mainz, West Germany

Contents

GENERAL INTRODUCTION

General Introduction

It is the author's conviction and conclusion that, for the comparison of philosophical traditions, philosophy should start with man. Dissatisfied with approaches from Spirit, philosophers started with physical nature or matter in order to have a sure foundation for philosophy. Unable to explain life, man's ethical nature, and spiritual experience from the side of matter, some started with life, thinking that it was a less intangible foundation than Spirit. But they were unable to explain matter and Spirit from the side of life. Faith in the supernatural sometimes got the upper hand. But then man lost confidence in reason, experience, and action, even so far as this world was concerned. Why not start with man, for whom philosophy is meant as a guide to life and for whom life, mind, and Spirit have meaning and significance? In man all have met and been integrated. Philosophy has to clarify the nature of this integrality and give man a picture of what he is. It must also suggest to him how he is, and is to be, motivated in his thought and action, and how he is to be guided. Even for comparative philosophy man has to be the central idea, the common denominator, for understanding and evaluating the varied tableaux of philosophical traditions.

Even a single tradition is a vast panorama. The three important traditions, when observed from a philosophical height, constitute one of the most impressive and exciting creations of human activity—with changes of values and interests, shiftings of emphases on forms of experience, variations of methods and standpoints, and crisscrossings of all—showing how man struggled hard in different parts of the world to understand himself and his environment, to discover the meaning of his life, to frame its ideals, and to regulate his thought and activity. Most of the problems which confronted thinking men of the past are problems for contemporary man also, though in contexts modified by changes and differences in the human situation and by the increase in knowledge. Moreover, when educated men see that men in the other parts of the globe have the same aspirations, are guided by identical or similar motives, and think and act like themselves, the strangeness of other cultures and apathy towards them is bound to be lessened, and a sense of the oneness of humanity will be strengthened. This is wanted urgently in the present-day world situation. Even when the governments are at loggerheads, so long as the common man of one country feels for the common man of another, we may hope that humanity will not be lost.

The author hopes that, in addition to serving as an introduction to comparative philosophy, this book will help the growth of the sense of the basic oneness of all humanity, the human solidarity, in spite of differences. Differences there are and there will be. But whether man is an emanation of Spirit or a product of matter or an evolute of the *élan vital,* or life force, he ought basically to be the same, and dissimilarities need explanation. The same factors contributing to differences may appear where so far they have not, produce changes in cultures, and make men depart from their traditional ways of thought and action. History furnishes enough evidence to show that people of the same culture react to their environment otherwise during various periods of their history. Acquaintance with diverse traditions makes men more tolerant, more understanding, more accommodating, sympathetic, and cooperative than unfamiliarity, provided of course there is good will. To foster this concord is the hope of the author and many others who have been advocating comparative philosophy. More fruitful results may emerge, but this at least can be the minimum.

Mention of religion in this study is confined to its relevance to the main purpose. Such reference has been unavoidable, not only because in the beginning philosophy and religion were not distinguished, but also because the influence of religion on philosophic thought continued to be considerable even after the distinction had been made. If reference to faith is made, it is because faith affected reason's clarification of the experience of God, that is, communion with Him, so much so that reason has tended to reject God, and all that was considered to be of high spiritual value has come to be ignored. The result is that spiritual values have suffered. At the same time, Indian philosophy, which has all along been religious except for the Cārvāka school, tended to overemphasize spiritual values, sometimes even as against the ethical. If such difficulties are pointed out, it is not to undervalue religion, but because of the necessity of showing that both spiritual and ethical values are equally important for a full and meaningful life of man.

Every religion has made immense contributions to the good of humanity, of which the author is not unaware. The ethical zeal preached by Judaism, the neighborly love, the brotherhood of man, and the fatherhood of God taught by Christianity, the compassion advocated by Buddha, the *ahimsā* (noninjury and respect for every life) upheld above every other virtue by Jainism, the social solidarity taught by Islam, and the divine communion advocated by the Upaniṣads are some of the greatest contributions made by religion to the good life of man on earth. So long as man adheres to these teachings sincerely, thoughtfully, and wholeheartedly, the future of humanity can be safe. These religions differ from each other; but their differences are outside the scope of this work.

Materialism has its importance as well, for man needs material values too. But materialism will be one-sided; for a consistently thoroughgoing materialist has to deny the reality and objectivity of ethical and spiritual values, including the freedom of man. A new tendency has appeared even among the materialists, some of whom react as strongly to any criticism of materialism as others react to a criticism of their religion. The author thinks that materialism has one truth in it, namely, that man's existence is rooted not only in the nonmaterial but in matter also. But the word "also" is important, and the materialist will not accept this reservation. It is the author's opinion that a philosophy based on the concept of matter alone or of life alone or of spirit alone cannot be adequate. It must be based upon man, in whom all the three are found to meet. In the growing atmosphere of science and technology, spiritual values are in the greatest danger.

Very few important philosophies now emphasize the reality of spirit and the necessity of recognizing spiritual values as being objective. Any new defense of spiritual values may be received as a good old philosophical story. The next casualty may be ethical values themselves. As Russell W. Davenport[1] asks: If materialism is true, whatever be the nature of its determinism, whether dialectical or mechanistic, and if man belongs entirely to the world of such matter, then what is the point in speaking of, and fighting for, the freedom of man? If

[1] Russell W. Davenport, *The Dignity of Man* (New York: Harper and Brothers, 1955).

man belongs entirely to the deterministic world of matter, it is nonsense to speak of his freedom. Freedom is meaningful if we accept the freedom, and therefore the reality, of spirit. Yet we cannot ex cathedra say that spirit is real. It is working in matter; and the materially embodied spirit is man. Philosophy has to show that man is embodied spirit and how spirit is embodied in him. If it cannot, our reason and experience get baffled. So in the context of the world's present outlook, spiritual values can be saved by philosophy only if it starts with man's conscious being spread out in the two directions, outwardly towards matter and inwardly towards spirit. The concept of matter cannot explain spirit, and the concept of spirit cannot explain matter; but the concept of man must be able to explain both. The present work expresses no disrespect for materialism, much less for any spiritual religion.

There is a real need now, however difficult and ambitious the task, to present both eastern and western philosophies together, not merely a few of their outstanding rounded-out systems, but the traditions in their development and in their connection with life. This has to be done first, not as a fully detailed account, but as movements, trends, currents—which sometimes flowed parallel to each other, sometimes crossed each other, combining and separating, but always reflecting the widening and deepening outlook and ideals of life. One thus gets a bird's-eye or aerial view, an overall picture, of the traditions as totalities, and can understand the peculiarities of their interests, standpoints, and achievements. This bird's-eye view the book attempts to give; and for obtaining it, it is hoped, the first three sections, apart from the last one, will be useful. The final section gives a general comparative résumé and some reflections, assuming acquaintance with the preceding discussions. The reader can make his own comparisons and draw his own conclusions. The last section will then serve as a stimulus, a sort of guide, for reflecting on the three traditions, for recognizing their significance and evaluating them.

All the three traditions are thrown into one perspective, the perspective that develops from the standpoint of man as a conscious being with two directions, the inward and the outward. This seems to be the only proper and useful standpoint from which all the traditions can be viewed as philosophies of life, inspiring ways of life, which are not and cannot be antagonistic when rightly viewed. None of the traditions is only inward or only outward in outlook, interests, and aims. So the reader who expects only pure materialism in the West or only pure spiritualism in India or only pure humanism in China will be disappointed. Nor is it fair to compartmentalize the traditions, which have long histories, several systems, and even their amalgamations. The differences are of emphases leading to intense development of thought in some spheres of life and to underdevelopment in some other spheres.

The author felt it necessary to present the central ideas and trends for the additional reason that they form the real clues for understanding the philosophies; and if some of them are omitted, the reader gets an inaccurate picture. For instance, while the Indian writers say that the survival of the Indian culture and civilization is due to the spiritual philosophy of the Vedānta, some western thinkers wonder how Indian culture could survive in spite of the Vedānta, which demands renunciation of action, is too idealistic, and treats the world as of secondary importance. Without activism no culture can survive, because it has to survive in the world of action. Then from where does Indian culture get its activism? Certainly from the Mīmāmsā. So in expounding Indian philosophy, it is as necessary to bring out the importance of the Mīmāmsā as that of the Vedānta. Whether the two philosophies can be reconciled is another question. But whether reconciled or not, India has been living both philosophies, sometimes balanced and other times unbalanced; and any competent representation of Indian philosophy requires that both trends be displayed in equal light, though the Vedānta may have become dominant later. Similarly, though Confucianism dominates Chinese thought, the other currents require an adequate presentation for a full view.

For the same reason—that is, for exhibiting an adequate picture—the author is not following some recent attempts to interpret eastern philosophies. The pictures can be evaluated only if they are presented as complete wholes. If they are torn into parts and analyzed, appreciation becomes impossible. Later one may do the analysis, and inquire about the colors used, the nature of the canvas, how all were obtained, what ingredients were used, and so on. Some moderns are approaching the eastern philosophies with a number of preconceived ideas of linguistic analysis and logical positivism, abandoning the definitions given to terms by the easterners themselves and attaching new meanings depending mainly on etymology. The result is that certain of their interpretations are new to the Indians themselves.

We should not forget that all philosophies in their beginnings have something elemental about their nature—a reference, in a naive form, to life, experience, and existence; not too logically, epistemologically, or linguistically analyzed; with a strong ontological sense even in the analyses that followed subsequently. It is safer, therefore, to understand and interpret their ideas with that background than to read new meanings into them with the help of new methods. Otherwise, even Plato and Aristotle, if alive today, might not understand our interpretations of their philosophies. It will be more understandable to interpret their notions and categories as people of the time and subsequent expounders of Greek thought understood them than to say what the Greeks should or could have meant, after applying our logical and linguistic analysis. It is true, as Kant said, that what is in the depths of a philosopher's mind is sometimes better understood by his expounders than by himself. Etymological and linguistic analysis helps us to some extent in revealing some inner meanings of his ideas. The deeper meaning of a concept, again, may be discovered by observing its relations to other concepts of the system. But the system itself gets its meaning with reference to other systems, particularly the rival. Again, the same concept with the same name may be used by rival systems with more or less difference in meaning. For instance, the word *dharma,* with the same etymological meaning, is used by both the Mīmāmsā and Buddhism. But the difference in the import it acquired in the two schools, as the reader will see, is enormous. Further, different terms may be used in the same sense by two schools.

In addition, the meanings of words and concepts diverge, if the systems grow along different lines. Thus there are several complexities, and the mere adoption of linguistic and etymological methods is likely to mislead. Words were generally used by philosophers with some primary meanings that had common acceptance. That is why these meanings and the development of theories based on them were capable of being criticized by rival philosophers. Otherwise, they would not have understood each other. All philosophies started with words and concepts referring to aspects and parts of existence recognized by the philosophers of the time. Though a thinker cannot avoid understanding another system, ancient or modern, in terms of his own ideas, he will attain more objectivity in explanation and interpretation if he observes the meanings attached to words by a philosopher, taking into consideration how they were understood by contemporaneous critics. Afterwards the interpreter can use his own methods and criticize the ideas from his own point of view. He will then not render the interpreted system strange to its originator. In an introductory book, the use of linguistics would only confuse and even mislead the reader, who may form strange notions about the philosophies interpreted.

Therefore, the doctrines of the traditions are approached as philosophies of life—as inspiring ways of life, and hence as referring to existence which we also experience—not simply as hypothetico-deductive systems to be interpreted by means of some linguistic devices. The author hesitated to make the section on Indian philosophy as long as it is. But misunderstandings about Indian philosophy had been so many that he felt obliged to counteract them with a balanced and connected presentation, in which some aspects of Indian thought not given proper emphasis previously could be specifically mentioned and illuminated. Again, a Chinese scholar could perhaps have given less space to the section on Chinese philosophy. But our ideas about it have been so vague and amorphous—in India it has been particularly so—that the philosophy requires a coordinated exposition of all its trends if its nature is to be properly appreciated. Even then the treatment can give only the central ideas.

In the author's opinion none of the traditions is self-sufficient. That contention may be taken as disparaging to all. But no disrespect is meant for any, either for the intellectualism and humanism of the West or for the immediatistic and humanistic pragmatism of China or for the intuitive spiritualism of India.[2] As the reader will find, each is deficient, tending to be one-sided and incomplete. Each tradition started with some philosophy and, as an antithesis in reaction against its one-sidedness, developed opposite philosophies that were absorbed into the thesis, the dominant trend, which did not lose its peculiar color and tone. The thesis indeed became richer, but still remained incomplete. This, in the opinion of the author, is due to the persistence of the standpoint determining the nature and formulation of the thesis, which in its turn determines the nature and formulation of the antithesis. This one-sidedness cannot completely be overcome, unless all the three traditions are made to complement one another, with the wealth of valid detail each accumulated in its development through a sort of dialectical process, starting with a certain standpoint as the

[2] See P. T. Raju, *Idealistic Approaches: Eastern and Western* (Baroda, India: M. S. University, 1957).

thesis and giving rise to another, distinct, contrary or contradictory, as the case may be, and absorbing it. The three important traditions are not incompatible with one another but complementary, distinct but not necessarily opposed.

The main characteristics of the three traditions are characteristics of life—not of different species of life, but of the same species placed in cultural situations posing disparate problems. Western philosophy, on the whole, is first and primarily rationalistic and intellectualistic; and since reason finds itself more at home with the expanse of matter and quantity, it has become overwhelmingly scientific and outward-looking. This aspect becomes obvious if we survey its growth from Heraclitus and Pythagoras to logical positivists, physicalists, and analysts. So we may say that this tradition succeeded in the emancipation of the object more than the subject, of matter more than spirit, although it would be wrong at the same time to say that the tradition has had no spiritual philosophies and leaders. The one-sided emphasis can be traced to the original Greek conception that the essence of man, of his soul, is reason; there is practically nothing tangible beyond and above, though there are indications of something beyond in a few philosophies, including that of Plato. But the importance of that something has not been worked out philosophically. Second, the western tradition is humanistic; and its humanism has the tendency to be rational and scientific. But the predominance of reason and science, again, have done some injustice to man and his values; thus humanism has become a secondary characteristic, not the primary.

In contrast, the Chinese tradition is primarily humanistic; the hard facts for philosophy are man and society, they are the first implicit affirmations and final goals. What I discovered in Chinese philosophy is that human nature is made the basic concept and is called by the unqualified term "nature." The concept of human nature is the concept of nature for Chinese thought. Human nature is as basic and real for the Chinese as matter is for the physical scientist. All intellectual efforts, all theories, are meant for immediate application to man and society for their benefit. Thus the tradition exhibits a pragmatic immediatism, and is impatient with mere intellectual questions. One finds in it an anxious human-mindfulness, not mindfulness of spirit but of man, not of man's reason but of his individual and social life. No Chinese philosopher need be apologetic for this characteristic; for the other traditions have to answer the question, What is all the philosophical toil worth, if it is not for the good of man as man? If the Upaniṣadic philosophy started by saying that the Ātman, Spirit, first affirmed itself as "I am"; if western philosophy started with reason first affirming itself as "I am"; then Chinese philosophy would start with man affirming himself as "I am." These three are important standpoints for any philosophy of life, necessary for one another in order to present a total picture of human life.

The main contribution of the Indian tradition is the explication of the inwardness of man, the freedom of his spirit. As a philosophy of the whole life of man, it also exhibits a one-sidedness by not working out in positive detail how inwardness and outwardness are related. It was not unaware of outwardness, but did not attach much importance to it. Its main interest lay in inwardness. It is rational like the western tradition, but it applied all its intellectual energies to explaining inwardness. Just as reason can get absorbed in matter—for instance, in physicalism in the West—it gets absorbed in Spirit in India.[3] Reason is not the highest in man as it is in Greek philosophy, but only the second highest. Just as outwardness, matter, can be the content of reason, inwardness, Spirit, also can be its content. In both directions there are limits to reason, the limit of outwardness and the limit of inwardness, or matter and spirit.[4]

In interrelating inwardness and outwardness, several problems arise. The present work is not meant for raising and solving them. But the author believes that, for any comprehensive philosophy, the reality and importance of both the directions have to be maintained and defended. He found that, as soon as he framed the concept of man with two directions, some took the cue and began saying that outwardness is illusory and deceptive and thus false and unimportant. But the reader should not equate the author's view with those of others. However, the traditions have been placed in the perspective of man with the two directions of his being. If we consider the dominant trends and achievements of the three traditions, it can become clear how each needs the others for obtaining both breadth and depth as a philosophy of life. This consideration will also enable us to evaluate the cultures as expressed and focused in their philosophies.

[3] "Matter" is used in a general sense. It may be space-time, energy, or events.

[4] Cf. Heisenberg's principle of indeterminacy. Just as reason cannot explain why spirit is as it is, it cannot explain why the ultimate constituents of matter behave as they do. At each end reason encounters a limit.

A word may be said here about the use of the definite article before terms like East and West, Brahman, Tao, Advaita. Even in the ordinary language the usage is not fixed. For instance, we say, "Man is an animal" and "The cow is an animal." Doubt arises, therefore, about the use of the definite article before philosophical terms. So I have followed one rule: If the word East refers only to culture, I have not used the definite article; but if the word has a geographical import also, I have used "the." Similarly, when the Brahman, Tao, Śūnya mean "the Absolute," I have used "the," following the western usage. I also think that the usage is right, as there is only one Absolute, one Brahman, one Tao, and one Śūnya. In other cases, as for instance when *śūnya* means the adjective "void," the definite article is omitted. Again, when "Advaita" refers to Śaṅkara's philosophy, which is a definite system, it is called "the Advaita." There are other Advaitas; and when the word is used to refer to them generally, the definite article is omitted. I think that this usage is likewise correct, for it avoids confusion.

1. WESTERN PHILOSOPHY *and the* Struggle for the Liberation of the Outward

Introduction

In the oft-quoted words of Pope, "The proper study of Mankind is Man." Man has two dimensions, which are also the directions of his conscious being, a being never static but directed outwards towards the objects of sensation, perception, emotion, feeling, and thought or inwards and through his very core to something which is variously called the Universal Spirit, God, and so forth. Men have always believed that the limit of their outward consciousness is something common to all; it is the common world composed of matter. Similarly, they believed that the limit of their inward consciousness is the same for all; God or the Universal Spirit is one, not many. In between the two limits, men are many and separate from each other. This is a very complex situation; and the philosophies of the world, Indian, Chinese, and western, have attempted to understand it in various ways.

Of the three main philosophical traditions, the western has the most diverse and complicated development. In the childhood of humanity the consciousness of the inward and the outward could not have been very clear and definite. Each was taken for the other in different degrees. The methods for understanding each and the position of man with reference to them were first crudely and naively grasped; it was only as the thought of mankind matured that the methods also developed with the resulting conceptions. Sometimes the outward was regarded as primary, and even as the only reality; at other times primacy was assigned to the inward. In between there were various degrees of overemphasis or underemphasis on one or the other, according to the temperament, stimuli, and urgency of the problems offered by the social, political, and natural environment of the philosopher. In the West, one system grew out of another, as development or as criticism or as both. Because of the Greek legacy of free thought, and because of the purely rational and human approach to the problem of understanding the universe of man, every age and often every philosopher in the West developed a somewhat distinct standpoint and system, thereby contributing to the total understanding of man. And with the advance of philosophy, as we may expect, the understanding of man also grew. In this chapter we shall try to delineate the attempts of the West to understand the nature of man and his environment. When man is understood in the two dimensions of outwardness and inwardness, matter and Spirit—the limits of the two dimensions—become determinants of his nature, which tends to be reinterpreted in terms of either or both.

Greek Philosophy

Western philosophy is generally divided into three periods: the ancient or the Greek, the medieval or the Christian, and the modern. In between the ancient and the medieval, there is a period of transition, which is called the Hellenistic, during which Jewish thought was blended with the Greek and taken over into the Christian. Similarly, in between the medieval and the modern periods, there is a period of transition, in which Greek thought was studied more systematically in order to make it a more useful handmaid to Christianity than was possible by understanding Plato and Aristotle through the Neo-Platonists and the Arabs; but in the attempt thought was so much liberated from dogma that it boldly became scientific. Yet thought so freed did not become antireligious or antispiritual, but human and humanistic, and attempted to approach the problems of spirit also independently of established religious dogmas. There were indeed antitheistic and atheistic philosophers; but, though their influence on the general environment was not negligible, the belief in God was still quite strong in the general run of mankind.

Among the historians of philosophy, there is a tendency to end modern philosophy with Hegel and classify the later philosophers as belonging to the contemporary period, the marked feature of which is the scientific outlook and dependence on logic and science for solving the problems of man and the world. Along with the recognition of the importance of logic and science, there is also an increasing realization that these two disciplines are not enough to solve our problems.

Like every other philosophical tradition in the world, Greek philosophy grew out of religion. This development is generally divided into two periods, the pre-Socratic and the post-Socratic. There are some writers on Greek thought who consider the former period the more important, because it was more scientific in that the philosophers adopted a kind of naturalistic or even mechanistic view of the world, treating the source of the world as water, air, fire, atoms, etc., thus laying the foundations of science, while the later period introduced much confusion into thought by mixing up ethical and religious problems with the scientific.[1] Bertrand Russell also says that the ethical and religious preoccupations, which are noticeable in Pythagoras, Socrates, and the post-Socratics including Plato, "brought an obscurantist bias into Greek philosophy." [2] However, if philosophy is to show a way of life, one cannot see how ethical and religious preoccupations can be excluded from philosophy. The question of value cannot be isolated entirely from questions about truth and reality. One of the great achievements of Plato is his establishment of an intimate relation between the two, which has not been given up as completely false even today by many.

The origins of Greek religion can be traced to Egypt, Asia Minor, and Greece and its surrounding countries in Europe. By the time Greek philosophy began with Thales (7th century B.C.), Greek religion had developed two distinct strands, the Olympian and the Dionysian, or the Apollonian and the Orphic.[3] The former was outward-looking, finding its gods in natural objects and forces like the sun, wind, and fire; the latter was inward-looking, mystic in character, endeavoring to find the origin of the world within the consciousness of man.

It is often said that the Orphic religion is oriental and the Apollonian occidental. But it is time that this identification be given up. Everywhere man feels the presence of reality both within himself and outside himself.[4] Some may feel the presence of the external more strongly than that of the internal; others the presence of the internal

[1] Warbecke, *The Searching Mind of Greece,* pp. 94–95. See also Scoon, *Greek Philosophy before Plato,* pp. 114 ff.

[2] Bertrand Russell, *A History of Western Philosophy* (New York: Simon & Schuster, 1945), p. 63.

[3] Marvin, *A History of European Philosophy* (1920 ed.), chap. viii.

[4] Cf. modern existentialism, esp. Kierkegaard.

more strongly than that of the external. But there are people of both types everywhere in the world. So everywhere both types of philosophy can be present. And both have elements of truth. But in some cultures, and at some times, one may be so dominating and pressing that the other is suppressed or ignored; and philosophical inquiry develops as if the other does not exist or is only of secondary importance. Further, the tendency to interpret what offers less pressing problems in terms of that which is more pressing becomes strong. The best philosophies, however, should be those that give equal recognition to both the inward and the outward.

Naturally, because the outward depends on man's experience of external objects, it encourages a scientific and observational attitude and a primitive kind of ethics based upon somehow—through science, magic, or sacrifice—controlling the forces of nature and controlling oneself according to them, often treating the forces as so many gods. But the inward develops a psychological religion and a technique of inward self-control. These two attitudes and the two forms of self-control may be intermingled in various degrees of unbalance when man loses confidence in himself and his thought, for some reason or other. When he has the confidence, he may be able to balance the two. Also, when this confidence is one-sided because of preoccupation with the outward or the inward, the resulting philosophical synthesis may be defective, and, when followed as a way of life, may lead to disaster, individual or social. For man fitted into an imperfect conceptual framework will either himself break or break the mold. Usually after the destruction and sacrifice of some individuals, humanity will break the mold and reconstruct another.

The earliest important philosophers of the pre-Socratic period are Thales (7th century B.C.), according to whom water was the origin of the world; Anaximander (6th century B.C.), who maintained that the origin was the Indefinite, unlike the concrete element of water; and Anaximenes (6th century B.C.), who maintained that air was the source of the world. All three conceived of the principle of the universe in terms of something outward, though Anaximander rose to the idea of the indefinite. Russell says of him that he is the most interesting of the Milesian triad, scientific and rationalistic. His thought could rise above the concrete in that he could see that what is universal cannot be any of the particulars to which it can give rise.

Pythagoras (6th century B.C.) and the Pythagorean school represent the next important movement. They maintained that the origin of the universe is number. The Pythagoreans considered this discovery a secret doctrine. They might have thought that the world was ultimately due to some numerical relation between the ultimate parts of the world, whatever they might be. Russell thinks that, according to Pythagoras, these constituents might be atomic. The Pythagorean conception of number was crude and naive, being that of shapes.[5] The name of Pythagoras comes down to us, however, as that of the discoverer of the Pythagorean theorem about the right-angled triangle.

In the doctrine that number is the source of the concrete universe is involved the idea that what is given to reason but not to sense is the truth about the world: so the Pythagoreans believed. Reason, therefore, is the source of the world, for mathematics is the subject of pure reason apart from sense. Reason is thus truer than sense. But this reason, like number, was understood in a mystical way by Pythagoras. Number, for him, is not an abstract concept, divorced from existence, as it is for the modern philosophy of mathematics. Numbers exist; hence mathematics, like primitive geometry, was an existential science. And as it is the science of pure reason also for Pythagoras, reason is existential. However much modern philosophers of mathematics admire the genius of Pythagoras, they would not accept these conclusions.

Though Pythagoras was one of the founders of mathematics, he belonged to the mystic Orphic tradition. The Pythagoreans believed that through mathematics one could release himself from the wheel of birth. This idea sounds very strange to us. But mathematics lifts man above sense. In this connection, Cornford refers to the derivation of the word "theory," which at first had a theological sense. It meant "passionate sympathetic contemplation," in which "the spectator is identified with the suffering God, dies in his death, and rises again in his new birth." [6] In the terminology of later philosophers, it is surrender of one's lower self to the higher, the Logos, Universal Reason. And the technique of self-surrender must have been taught to those who were newly initiated into the sect. Hence comes the association of

[5] Russell, *op. cit.*, p. 35.

[6] *Ibid.*, pp. 33, 35. Similarly, "orgy" meant for the Orphics "sacrament" intended to purify the soul and lift it above the wheel of birth (p. 24).

mathematics with mysticism. For this reason, Russell says, Pythagoras is one of the most important intellectuals that ever lived, both when he is wise and when he is unwise; unwise, particularly, according to Russell, when Pythagoras mixed up mathematics with ethical and spiritual discipline, and thought of the subject as existential.[7] However, Russell is right when he says that, but for Pythagoras, the Christian doctrine of the Word and the proofs for the existence of God would not have appeared in the history of philosophy.

One aspect of the doctrine which is given a passing reference by the historians of philosophy, but which, to a student of Indian philosophy, appears striking, is that reason, which is essentially mathematical, is treated as an existential entity by the Pythagoreans. It has something in it of the doctrine of the Word-Brahman of Indian thought, which corresponds to the Logos doctrine of the pre-Christian West. If the lower self in us is to surrender itself, it does so to the higher, which is reason: which reminds one of the exhortation that reason should control our instincts. Man can rise to God through his higher self, which is reason. This doctrine with all its implications was not clearly before the mind of Pythagoras. But he seems to be the first in the West to have had a glimpse of its importance.

It is now easy for us to see that what apparently are purely philosophical inquiries for us constituted a religious quest for even the earliest of the Greek philosophers, including the Milesians—Thales, Anaximander, and Anaximenes. Water for Thales, the Indefinite for Anaximander, and Air for Anaximenes were the God for each. But He was a depersonified cosmic principle. The Number of Pythagoras also was similar. God was not yet conceived in the fullest spirituality, akin to the spirit in man and lying somewhere deep within it. For the first three philosophers mentioned, He was naturalistic and mechanistic. Even for Pythagoras, He was nothing more than reason as found in mathematical numbers. He was not yet the Ultimate Spirit or Self, one of whose expressions is reason. This conception could not be attained, because the human self was not yet adequately grasped. The difference between mind and matter, man and his environment, was not yet sharply felt. In Pythagoras there is much of the inward, but it is not yet clearly grasped. He could see that reason is higher than sense, but not clearly that it is inward. The outlook was still cosmic

[7] *Ibid.*, p. 29.

and outward. Yet it was religious, a search for God, the creator of the world. Even the Water of Thales was the primitive living stuff.[8]

Heraclitus (5th century B.C.) was the next great Greek philosopher. He maintained that change, or becoming, is the source of the world. Yet the essence of the world is everlasting Fire, which is the moral judge as well.[9] "Fire coming upon us will judge and convict all things." He believed that thought is universal, common to all. He propounded the doctrine of the Word, or Logos, saying that it is one and everlasting. Fire and the Word are one and the same.[10] Heraclitus says, "I have searched myself," and after the search he must have found the truth.[11] Cornford says that Fire, Thought, and Logos were one and the same and were identified with the thunderbolt of Zeus.[12]

Heraclitus seems to be a mystic of a peculiar kind. He is a rationalistic mystic, for the Ultimate is still the Logos—Reason, Word. He seems to have arrived at this conception by searching within himself. Yet by calling the Ultimate by the name Fire, he retains a kinship with the early cosmologists, although fire is not conceived by them as one of the elements. However, it was for him God Himself, like Water and Air for Thales and Anaximenes.

There is another interesting idea in Heraclitus' philosophy. According to him, sleep is better than life and death. "Night has been called *Euphrone,* because at that time the soul has rest from the perceptions of sense, turns in upon itself and has a greater share of wisdom (*phronesis*)." [13] This reminds us of the *Māṇḍūkya Upaniṣad,* which says that the soul becomes *prajña* in deep sleep, consciousness solid and integrated, and is full of bliss (*ānanda*).

Heraclitus seems beyond doubt to have reached an inwardness, quite deep, in his search within himself. One does not expect a more systematic explanation of inwardness in an atmosphere the general outlook of which was cosmological and outward. It is very likely that Heraclitus mistook the inner light of his conscious rational self for

[8] F. M. Cornford, *Greek Religious Thought* (London: J. M. Dent & Sons Ltd., 1923), p. xxi.

[9] G. Misch, *The Dawn of Philosophy* (London: Routledge, 1926), p. 259.

[10] It is interesting to note that in the early philosophical speculations of India, Fire is called the god of Speech.

[11] Misch, *op. cit.,* p. 259.

[12] *Op. cit.,* p. 79.

[13] *Ibid.,* p. 81.

physical fire.[14] In spite of this inwardness, it is very remarkable that he took the world of change and sense to be real, saying that "eyes are trustier witnesses than the ears." [15]

As a cosmologist, however, Heraclitus did not notice the peculiar opposition between the inward and the outward, between man and his environment. Anaxagoras (5th century B.C.) was the first in the West to think of mind, *nous,* as an entity distinct from the rest of the universe. "Mind is unlimited and self-ruled and is not mixed up with anything, but is just alone by itself." [16] It enters all living things and distinguishes them from dead matter. But Anaxagoras seems to have made very little further use of his discovery. To *nous* is traced the source of all motion.

The tendency to find the source of the world in some principle which is outward is found in a more explicit form in the atomism of Democritus (5th century B.C.). There were other atomists; but Democritus said that the atoms have no secondary qualities and differ from each other only in size and shape. Cornford says that, according to Democritus, soul is a sort of fire or heat.[17] The tendency of the time seems to have been to associate soul with fire, perhaps because of the light-giving nature of both and also perhaps because heat disappears from the body when it is dead. We read that Empedocles jumped into the crater of Mt. Etna, because he thought that Fire was God and the source of the world. However, he believed that the atoms are qualitatively different and are brought together and separated by Love and Hate.

The doctrine of Heraclitus that change is the ultimate nature of the universe was opposed by Parmenides (5th century B.C.), who maintained that changelessness is the nature of ultimate reality. In the controversy between change and changelessness, becoming and being, a new philosophical approach is noticeable. Earlier philosophers were in search of some concrete entity like water or air for an explanation of the universe. But by the time of Heraclitus and Parmenides, philosophers were looking for an abstract universal feature. The intricate questions and the confusion which these abstractions raise do not

[14] Even the Upaniṣads call it *tejas,* which in the physical sense means fire and light and in the mental sense psychic force.

[15] Misch, *op. cit.,* p. 260.

[16] Cornford, *op. cit.,* p. 124.

[17] *Ibid.,* p. 139.

appear to have been distinctly noticed by them. For instance, "Which is reality?" is a different question from "What is the nature of reality?" The latter again may mean "What is the nature of reality originally?" and also "What is the nature of reality as we perceive it?" Such questions were all mixed up and led to long controversies. Parmenides believed that not only was being changeless, but also it was one, not many. He distrusted sense, and gave all importance to reason.

In the doctrines of all the above-named philosophers, the distinction between inwardness and outwardness, soul and the material world, man and his environment, is not clearly noticed and worked out. Anaxagoras framed the concept of *nous,* but did not work out its relation to the world; neither did he inquire into the nature of its structure. The first attempts were made in this direction by the Sophists and the post-Socratics. The subject-object distinction little troubled the earlier philosophers. Heraclitus had some idea of man's soul, which he regarded as part of the universal Fire. The *nous* of Anaxagoras seems to be the cosmic Mind rather than that of the individual, and he even speaks of it as the most rarefied matter.[18] The pre-Socratic philosophers, we may say, were vaguely after two principles, both of which were cosmic: the supreme creative principle of the universe and the supreme rational principle of the universe. In other words, they were after the cause of the world as well as after the reason in the world, and often mixed up the two. Heraclitus had some intimations that these principles, which he identified as Fire and Logos, were to be found within man. The quest for either principle was a religious quest.

Greek philosophy seems to have taken a rather abrupt turn with the rise of the Sophists by about the end of the fifth century B.C. It was an age of enlightenment. A peculiar kind of individualism and relativism and the consequent subjectivism were introduced. Interest shifted from cosmology, cosmogony, and theogony to man and humanism, and a certain belittling of the former came into vogue. Aristophanes ridicules the earlier philosophers in his *Clouds,* saying: "Long live King Vortex, who has dethroned Zeus." "If no human advantage could possibly be derived from a study of evolution, or of atomic theories, why should one be bothered by them?" [19] Philosophy has to be a philoso-

[18] Frank Thilly and Ledger Wood, *A History of Philosophy* (New York: Henry Holt & Co., 1951), p. 45.

[19] Warbecke, *The Searching Mind of Greece,* p. 113.

phy of life, has to solve ethical and political problems, which are of more immediate concern for man than questions about the cosmos. Protagoras in his theory of knowledge and Thrasymachus and Callicles, among others, in their ethics unsettled the old beliefs. Here again Aristophanes complains that the old discipline is gone, religion is ridiculed, and men have become selfish and sensual, because of the teachings of the Sophists.[20] But this unsettling of institutions based upon traditional philosophies, religion, morals, and customs had its advantage: a demand was made that they should justify themselves before human reason and experience. It seems, however, that the Sophists, in placing man at the center of philosophy, did not think of the universal man as a norm, but individual men, whose opinions and motives differ from each other's. This individualistic standpoint gave rise to a kind of subjectivism and skepticism, the defects of which some of the later philosophers sought to remove.

The result of the Sophistic teachings is the recognition of the individuality of man and his liberation, in philosophy, from the rest of the cosmos. The Logos, or Universal Reason, reveals the structure of the world; but this Reason has to work through human reason, and it is human reason that has to reveal the Logos and the world for us. This recognition on the part of humanity was made possible by the work of the Sophists, however one-sided.

Protagoras (*c.* 5th century B.C.) is well known for his enunciation that "man is the measure of all things; of that which is, that is; and of that which is not, that is not." Hegel writes:

> Now Protagoras' assertion is in its real meaning a great truth, but at the same time it has a certain ambiguity, in that as man is the undetermined and many-sided, either he may in his individual particularity, as this contingent man, be the measure, or else self-conscious reason in man, man in his rational nature and his universal substantiality, is the absolute measure. If the statement is taken in the former sense, all is self-seeking, all self-interest, the subject with his interests forms the central point; and if man has a rational side, reason is still something subjective, it is "he." [21]

That the Sophists, including Protagoras himself, seem to have taken man in the particularist sense, not as the universal man, is made evi-

[20] Thilly and Wood, *op. cit.*, p. 55.

[21] Hegel, *History of Philosophy* (Eng. tr.; Routledge, 1955), I, 374.

dent in the second doctrine attributed to Protagoras, which he expresses as: "Truth is a manifestation for consciousness. Nothing is in and for itself one, but everything has a relative truth only." [22]

Gorgias (4th century B.C.) maintained that (1) there is nothing; (2) even if there is something, we cannot know it; and (3) even if it is and can be known, we cannot communicate our knowledge of it to others. Thus he went beyond Protagoras and formally enunciated skepticism. Both he and Protagoras held that moral precepts, and consequently virtue, were not the same for all. Then what about natural right? Later Callicles said that might was right, and Thrasymachus maintained that it was not even might but accident that made an action right, for the superior who came to power and dictated what is right came only by accident.

Thus the Sophists, in spite of the bad name they earned, introduced a tremendous change into Greek thought. The philosophical interest was shifted from the world as a whole externally viewed to man and what was within man. Some of the Sophists were even iconoclasts in religion. One has to say that, on the whole, the universality of the inwardness of man was missed by them.

Socrates (born *c.* 470 B.C.) was the first to introduce universality into the doctrines of the Sophists, by evolving universal judgments and discovering a method for evolving them. Thus relativism, subjectivism, and skepticism were put an end to, and a basis for universal ethics was laid. The method he adopted was that of the dialectic, which at first assumed ignorance and, through question and answer and by taking opposite views one after another into consideration, developed conceptual definitions of principles universally applicable. The wrong definition was rejected by drawing certain conclusions from it which were contrary to facts and so unacceptable. Thus universal truths were obtained both in logic and ethics.

Thus confidence in human reason was restored and objectivity and universality were conferred on it. The aim of Socrates was to restore the foundations of morality and the state, which were threatened by the Sophists. But in his attempt to build morality and the state on universal foundations, Socrates came into conflict with the existing institutions, was finally condemned and compelled to take the hemlock.

The interest of Socrates was more in ethics than in science and cosmology. But even for ethics, a theory of knowledge was necessary in

[22] *Ibid.*, p. 375.

order to obtain universally valid judgments. And his faith in knowledge was so strong that he maintained the doctrine that "virtue is knowledge." Knowledge is the necessary and sufficient condition of the good.

Another side of Socrates' philosophy, which scientifically minded historians of western philosophy are apt to underrate, is its inwardness. Socrates was a great mystic, but his mysticism was rationalistic. He accepted that truth is discovered in the subject's reason, but only so far as it is identical with Universal Reason, thereby reaffirming its cosmic character, which Heraclitus discovered in the Logos. Thus the Logos exists in each man and is common to everyone. Socrates took up the study of Anaxagoras with great hopes, thinking that he would find an explanation of how Mind works in the universe, but was greatly disappointed to find only that the *nous* had nothing more to do than to set the vortical movement going.[23] Anaxagoras did not discover it for explaining the universal ordering of things. Socrates was so much impressed by the inward universal reason that he called it the "daimon," giving him prohibitory messages and warnings. In a campaign he was once sunk in deep meditation and stood immovable at one spot for a whole day and night. Hegel writes:

> From this physical setting free of the inward abstract self from the concrete bodily existence of the individual, we have, in the outward manifestation, a proof of how the depths of his mind worked within him. In him we see pre-eminently the inwardness of consciousness that in an anthropological way existed in the first instance in him, and became later on a usual thing.[24]

Socrates was a remarkable man, an out-and-out rationalist, and yet a mystic, one who, we may say, felt that the "daimon" in him was the universal objective reason. And because the Logos was within each man, Socrates thought that knowledge was within each and that his task was not to impart knowledge but to bring it out—like a midwife—from within each man. Thus, to a certain extent, he anticipated Leibniz' doctrine of innate ideas. But actually in the dialectic, all the particular judgments were taken by him from experience to be marshaled as theses and antitheses, objections and counterobjections, in order that universal judgments might be derived. Thus subjective rea-

[23] F. Copleston, *A History of Philosophy,* I, 97.
[24] *Op. cit.,* I, 391.

son was given objective content and made universally valid. When treated as inner to man, the universal was an object of recollection; but when treated as objective, outside of and transcending the individual, the universal is the truth common to all individuals, the particular subjective truths canceling each other's particularity in the process of the dialectic and leading up to the universal. It must have been a wonder of all wonders to Socrates that the universal could be discovered within man and not outside him. The universality of the inner rational being of man was once for all established in Greek thought by Socrates.

It is this aspect of reason which a modern scientific philosopher would call obscurantist. But it is a peculiar aspect of our experience, which may need an explanation, but cannot be denied.

In this combination of the doctrine of recollection and dialectic, Socrates could have pointed out that, though the Divine Universal Reason works through man in ordering the world, man, because of his finitude, has laboriously to collect particular facts from experience, which is to constitute the content to be ordered. And though Socrates spoke of the "inner voice," or "daimon," as an agent, he did not philosophically clarify how it works through man. Inwardness was recognized, but not philosophically worked out. The object recollected was a static entity, not an active agent, and recollection was made possible by the particulars marshaled with reference to each other.

Plato (born 427 B.C.) was an enthusiastic disciple of Socrates. In fact, much that we know about Socrates is known through Plato's writings. Scholars distinguish between the dialogues written by Plato in which he gives Socrates' views and those in which Plato puts his own views in the mouth of Socrates. Such distinction is beyond the scope of the present chapter, which can barely present even Plato's doctrines. It is said that the doctrine of reminiscence, recollection, belongs to Plato; Socrates expounded only the dialectic. But it is a corollary of Socrates' view that he does not impart knowledge, but only draws out what is already present in man's mind. However, Plato, like Socrates, was interested in discovering stable foundations for morals and politics. For that purpose not only political philosophy, but also epistemology, cosmology, and psychology were needed. Taking the field of interest into consideration, one cannot but admit that Plato is the first of the greatest philosophical synthesizers of the world, including China and India. Indian epics constitute stupendous world syntheses; but they are not systematic philosophies, though they include every aspect of life and thought of the times, cosmology, cosmogony, theogony, psychology, religion, ethics and political thought, statecraft, and so forth. Hence Plato's right to be called the first great philosophical synthesizer cannot be controverted.

With Plato is associated the idea that only philosophers ought to be kings. He even tried to apply his utopian theory to Syracuse by converting the two tyrants, Dionysius I and his son, Dionysius II, to his views, but with very little success. His *Republic*, however, is one of the most widely read books even today, not only by philosophers but also by students of ethics and politics.

Plato was greatly influenced by the doctrines of Pythagoras, Parmenides, Heraclitus, and Socrates. The respect for mathematics, the intellectual mysticism, otherworldliness, transmigration, immortality of the soul, all the implications of the doctrine of the cave, and so on, which constitute the Orphic strand of Plato's philosophy, are Pythagorean. He incorporated Parmenides' idea that reality is eternal and changeless and that therefore change is illusory. With Heraclitus he maintained that the world of sense is a continual change. But because reality is changeless, he said, knowledge cannot be derived from the senses. From Socrates he derived the doctrine of the universals, of the dialectic, of the good, and of teleology.

The mysticism of reason, which is so prominent in the thought of Socrates, Heraclitus, and the Pythagoreans is clearly found in Plato. It is true that the Ideas, which Plato postulated, are reached through a dialectical criticism of sense experience, but they are not derived from sense experience. When they are actually reached, sense experience is found to be an imitation of the realm of Ideas. It is only a stimulus for the recollection of Ideas, which are within the reason of man. Hence the real world, the world of the Logos or thought, is, in a sense, within man. The inwardness of man's being, reaching up to reason, or the Logos, is therefore clearly recognized by Plato. As the Ideas are not the copies of the objects of perception, but the objects of perception are imperfect copies of the world of reason, the higher world is within man, in his reason, not outside him. The world of reason, which is the inner world, is not merely the world of the intellect, but also the world of norms, the realm of the Good, and thus the ethical world, with which are connected ethical retribution, immortality, and transmigration. Whether these doctrines are demonstrably true or not, it is difficult to say. Jewish and Christian religious thought, which started with the idea of the chance of only one life for man to justify his deeds before God, treated them as false. At least the Greek philosophers were more humane in giving man several chances. But a very important and interesting point is that the concept of reason as not merely intellectual but also ethical and axiological is common to Plato and most of Indian thought: the corresponding Indian concepts of *buddhi* and *mahat* not only perform the functions of the intellect but also carry *dharma* (merit) and *adharma* (demerit) in the Upaniṣads and the Sāṅkhya. The ground for associating merit and demerit with reason is not epistemological in Indian thought. But the great philosophical achievement of Plato is to show that epistemology also needs their association. The true is also the good; and both are found within the higher rational nature of man.

Philosophically, Plato could reach only as much inwardness as Socrates could. Is there something deeper within man than the Logos, or reason, which works through it? The question may be called obscurantist. But if man's conscious being points to something in its outward direction, it is certainly reasonable and necessary to ask: What is that to which it points in its inward direction? It is not justifiable to interpret man's being in terms of something reached in the outward direction only; for then we shall be doing violence to the nature of man, who, however vaguely and inadequately, knows that his being has an inward direction also. Only when the world experienced in both the directions is articulated and interrelated can philosophy succeed in interrelating science, ethics, and religion. The task may not be easy, and may take several centuries to accomplish. But it has to be done; and until it is done, it will be foolish not to recognize the two directions, like the man who does not eat until he knows the physiology of the digestive processes.

One feels that the inquiry into inwardness could have been pushed further by Plato. The Idea of the Good is the highest, nearly as important as God, and is deep within man's being. Yet, God is higher than the Logos. How does He create the world? Plato held that the Ideas are creative; but how? His answer is not clear. We are told that, by being remembered, they confer being on the sense objects. But when the sense objects are needed as the stimuli for remembering Ideas, the former become prior to the latter; where, then, is the occasion for conferring being on them, a fortiori for creating them? And in explaining reminiscence Plato lapses into myth making. At this point of inwardness, his philosophy stopped.

Aristotle (born *c.* 384 B.C.) was a pupil of Plato; though he was more realistic and had more faith in sense experience than Plato, he placed a more contemplative ideal before man than Plato. God is "thought of thought," pure contemplation. He was the first mover of the universe, the cause to introduce the first motion. Thereafter God's connection with the world ends. In Plato's philosophy neither inwardness nor outwardness was carried to the extreme. On the one side, matter, although called nonbeing, was the limit of outwardness; and on the other side, reason as the repository of the Good was the limit. How it could be creative was, indeed, not explained. Aristotle refused to regard matter as nonbeing and called it potentiality. Actuality is due to Forms, or Ideas, but they exist in matter and the sensible world. Thus reason is located in the sensible world itself. But what becomes of the reason in man? Aristotle maintained that it is immortal. But how can it be immortal, if it cannot exist without matter?

Aristotle, like Plato, finds three divisions in the soul. For Plato, they are the rational, the irascible, and the sensuous. The rational is indivisible and immortal. This is, on the whole, similar in kind to the World Soul. It is in contact with the world of Ideas. The lowest part, the sensuous, is in contact with the world of sense. We can see that Plato's epistemology is related to his conception of the soul. Aristotle is averse to dividing the soul into parts, but says that it has three aspects. As a biologist, he calls them vegetative, sensitive, and rational—corresponding to plant life, animal life, and human life. In his cosmology, therefore, he places human existence higher than every other of the mundane world. Though he treats the three aspects as inseparable, he calls the rational aspect immortal. Of course, the universal is beyond time and is immortal. But it is difficult to understand how this immortal aspect can be separated from the mortal, though consistently Aristotle treats the Idea as inseparable from the particular object. It is easy to understand Plato's conception of immortality as the identification of individual reason with Universal Reason; but it is difficult to understand how, according to Aristotle, the individual reason, which is inseparable from the rest of his soul, can become immortal at all. This is not only a difficulty for philosophy of religion but also for epistemology. In fact, for both Plato and Aristotle the starting point is epistemology. Immortality is the attainment of universality through liberation from particularity: this cannot be allowed by Aristotle's epistemology, though he accepted it as a religious idea.

We have, therefore, to conclude that Aristotle toned down the inwardness achieved by Plato and, to a certain degree, turned it into outwardness. Reason is made to dwell in the outward objects and tied down to the physical and sensuous nature of man. The inwardness of the Logos of the pre-Socratic philosophers also is in a way spread out and tied down to outwardness. And it was rescued by the Jewish and Christian philosophers in certain peculiar circumstances.

By the time of Aristotle, Greece had been conquered by Macedon; and Alexander the Great, a pupil of Aristotle, was the Emperor of the vast territories from the Punjab in the east to Greece and Egypt in the west. The political supremacy and leadership not only of Athens but also of the rest of Greece was lost. It was an age of despair, of loss of nerve, of decadence. Man lost confidence in the powers of his reason to improve himself and his society; and therefore the tendency of self-centeredness grew. A peculiar individualism developed, which is alien to the general spirit of Greek philosophy. After the loss of independence, pessimism and a kind of inner misery entered the minds of Greek thinkers and expressed itself in the later Greek schools.[25]

That political and social events influenced the general outlook of the Greek thinkers is supported by the fact that the major and important part of Greek philosophy—namely, that of Socrates, Plato, and Aristotle—was primarily interested in ethical and political questions, which initiated their inquiries; and the metaphysical, religious, and cosmological questions came in to clarify, substantiate, and complement them. So long as the ethical and political situations were hopeful, the philosophical inquiries did not have a pessimistic tone. But when that situation was changed, the tone of philosophy changed.

Even immediately after Socrates, three schools of thought arose. Antisthenes (4th century B.C.) and Diogenes (4th century B.C.), who is known for living in a tub, belonged to the school of Cynics, who drew inspiration from the independent nature and self-control of Socrates and preached extreme disregard for worldly happiness. "Virtue itself was happiness." The school of Cyrenaics, started by Aristippus (5th century B.C.), reversed the principle and said that "happiness is virtue" and taught pleasure as the good. Neither school accepted the realism of the universals. The Magaraics, whose leader was Euclid,

[25] Erdmann, *A History of Philosophy* (Eng. tr.), I, 181.

took "Virtue is knowledge" literally and preached contemplation as the highest good, which they identified with the Being of Parmenides. During the period of decadence Cynicism gave rise to Stoicism, and Cyrenaicism to Epicureanism. The Skeptics, of whom Pyrrho is the best known, belonged to this period.

In all these tendencies—subjectivism, individualism, asceticism, hedonism, skepticism—we see that the human being is more and more isolating himself from society. Even in the cosmopolitanism of the Stoics, the individual feels his reality more than the vague and intangible whole, the cosmos, with which he is asked to be one. Human society and community is a more tangible reality than the cosmos as a whole, and demands more concrete acts for establishing oneness than the intangible, ethereal cosmos. There was an ethical interest in all these schools, even in skepticism. Skepticism was originally as much an ethical doctrine as an epistemological one. Pyrrho, it is said, accompanied Alexander the Great up to India, and very probably came across the Indian skeptics. He might have found the differing customs and morals of the peoples conquered by Alexander and might have felt that the question as to which of them were right could not be answered affirmatively or negatively. Hence, arose the ethical skepticism, which found its analogue in epistemological skepticism. But the ethical interest of these schools is individual-centered, not society-centered, which shows that, philosophically, though in a pessimistic atmosphere, man began to recognize his existence apart from society and the world.

But the inwardness reached was not deep and, because subjective, was even false. For Heraclitus, Pythagoras, and Plato, the inward Logos was identical with cosmic universality. But such a universality was not admitted by the Epicureans and the Skeptics. The Stoics held a peculiar position. They adopted the Heraclitean doctrine that Fire is the stuff of the universe, that it is God and absolute reason. The soul of the individual is of the same stuff; but in itself it has no value. This idea fits in with their ascetic ethical doctrine. Curiously enough, the ultimate Fire was at first materialistically conceived by them. We may say therefore that, for the Stoics, the self-centeredness of man ended in negating itself, so that he ceased to be of any value. The reality of the universal accepted by Plato was rejected by the Stoics, so that the way epistemologically opened by him to reach the Logos was closed. Rational inwardness, which was the only inwardness clearly understood by the Greek philosophers, was given up, and the way to become one with the universal Fire was understood in terms of outwardness, as the material destruction of one's individuality. It looks as though asceticism was not an instrument but the end itself. However, whatever we say philosophically about Stoicism, the noble spirit of endurance, self-control, and self-surrender, often approaching self-annihilation, which it preached, appealed to the times so much that a good deal of the Stoic ethical teaching was assimilated by Christianity, and some of the greatest souls were stoic by temperament. And further, as Russell says, Stoicism was not the same philosophy throughout its history. The materialism of Zeno (3rd century B.C.) disappeared as Stoicism developed during the later centuries.[26]

Hellenistic and Neo-Platonic Philosophies

The loss of hope characterizing the philosophies of post-Aristotelian Greek thought was counteracted by the entry of Jewish thought into the West. The original Jews of Israel do not seem to have been a remarkably reflective race, but were endowed with an intense ethical sense, which, through an unwavering faith in Yahweh, the One God, produced in them a sense of discipline, understood by them as unquestioning obedience to God's commands. The Jews offered a peculiar contrast to the Greeks. The latter were reflective and wanted to know the why and how of things, even of ethical laws. There was little that was sacrosanct about ethical imperatives except so far as they were warranted by the nature of man, society, and the cosmos. The Jews were quite the opposite. They were not interested in questions of cosmology and were satisfied with the belief that Yahweh created the world for man. Their ethics consisted in unswerving obedience to the commandments of God as given through Moses. Their faith in God was so strong that political and other catastrophes were interpreted

[26] *Op. cit.*, p. 252.

by them as due to His wrath on account of man's ethical transgressions. Yahweh was a personal God, and a very jealous God, who would not tolerate the worship of other gods. Provided man followed His commands, he could be sure of the best life on earth. For had not Yahweh led them to the promised land from captivity in Egypt, because of unswerving faith in Him? History, therefore, was eminently real and had a divine purpose, the goal of which was the final deliverance through faith. For the Greeks, on the other hand, history was mainly human; it was the history of human, social, and national endeavors. But when those endeavors failed, philosophy became pessimistic, and confidence in man, in his reason and his powers, also failed. Faith admits no failures; but reason does.

The God of the Jews was beyond everything, even reason, and was completely transcendent. We cannot even reason about Him; much less can we have an image of Him. Hence the repudiation of all idol worship. But the God of the Greeks was rational: He was Reason itself. Man can grasp Him through his own reason. The Jewish God was not philosophical, would not tolerate any philosophy: He was the creator of the world and the commander of men, rewarding them for implicit obedience and punishing them for the slightest deviation from His commands.

When reason in Greek philosophy lost self-confidence and was failing, faith came to support man.

But the Jews, in spite of all their faith, were several times conquered by rival peoples and even dispersed. It was in Alexandria that this strong Jewish faith mixed with reflective Greek thought and gave birth to the philosophy of the Neo-Platonists, which later became an integral part of Christian philosophy.

Neo-Platonism combined Jewish thought with Platonic elements. Again, it was not so much the reflective outwardness of Platonism that was considered to be important and taken over, but its reflective inwardness. Jewish thought had at first very little of inwardness. The early Jews did not even think of the soul surviving death and leaving the body in order to have another existence. Much less did they believe in transmigration, which is still a taboo to both Christian and Islamic religions through the influence of Jewish associations. Yet the Jews of Alexandria, when they came into contact with the cultured Greeks there, found that they could combine their thought with that of the Greeks without detriment, as they thought, to their transcendent God.

There were several such thinkers, of whom Philo and Plotinus are the most important.[27] Plato's philosophy gave their thought inwardness and rationality, over which they could superpose their transcendent God, who thereby became inward to man. Yet as He transcends reason, which is possessed by man also, He retains His transcendence. Have not Plato and Aristotle declared that the highest part or aspect of man's soul is reason? If so, man can reach only up to the Cosmic Reason, and God beyond can be transcendent. Still, He is inwardly transcendent—an idea in line with the mysticism of Plato, but going deeper.

Philo (*c.* 25 B.C.–*c.* 40 A.D.) of Alexandria, says the Reverend E. R. Bevan, was rather a religious preacher than a philosopher.[28] His God was not the "thought of thought" of Aristotle, but the Jewish God, creating the world and issuing commands. He created the world out of nothing, a conception which was opposed to the Greek idea that nothing could come out of nothing. He was personal and yet Pure Being. He could be attained through contemplation, as Aristotle taught. However, this contemplation was not scientific understanding or reason, as the Greeks would understand it, but intuition. Reason thus had to be transcended. The importance of reason in Philo's philosophy was much less than in Greek thought. For Philo as a Jewish teacher, first was needed action in obedience to God's commands, and then contemplation in which moral action was transcended. Bevan writes:

> God is for him [Philo] an essentially righteous and beneficent Will who does mighty acts, but the mighty acts which Philo cares about are not done in the broad field of history, but in the Soul. God "plants virtues" in the Soul. The precepts of the Law which warn the children of Israel not to take any credit to themselves for the conquest of the land of Canaan are transferred by Philo from the literal fields of the Holy Land to the inner life.[29] It is the supreme sin when a man says of his virtues "I planted these." Because Philo remains Hebrew all the time, he takes all that man attains in the inner life to be concrete acts of God's gracious Will, and prostrates

[27] Many historians of philosophy do not call Philo a Neo-Platonist, but consider him a forerunner of Neo-Platonism.

[28] Bevan and Singer, *The Legacy of Israel* (Oxford, 1948), p. 45.

[29] Cf. the teachings of the *Bhagavadgītā*.

> himself in adoration and gratitude and confession of his own nothingness in a way quite foreign to the Greek man of virtue.[30]

Mystic knowledge is not necessarily extension of real knowledge; it may be produced by drugs even. Philo's mysticism was not of that type. It was knowledge reached after inwardness was attained through moral action. Bevan says that Philo transcribes psychology into metaphysics, which means that the ultimate can be found not only outwardly but also inwardly.[31] It is after Aristotle that the idea that the ultimate reality lies beyond physics has been made fashionable. But there is no reason why it should not be reached after psychology. If there is metaphysics, there can be metapsychology also.

Logos, or World Reason, therefore, is lower than God for Philo. It is said to be the first-born of God. Philo distinguishes two aspects or functions of the Logos, the first consisting of the immaterial world of Ideas and the second of the material world of things, which are copies of Ideas.[32] There are other intermediary beings than the Logos, coming between God and man.

For our purpose, we need not go into further details. One point is evident: Philo was not satisfied with the rationalism of the Greeks, and felt it necessary to transcend it. Even Plato did not regard the Logos as the highest and called it the first-born son of God.[33] But the Greeks did not show the way how inwardly man could reach God, and their faith in reason was too overwhelming. They might have had an idea of the way, but it was not clearly worked out in philosophy. Only Judaism, combined with Greek thought, could work the way out.

Again, Philo became the first great philosopher to expound the doctrine of the emanation of the world out of God, though he also clung to the idea that God created the world out of nothing. The Christians did not like the doctrine of emanation, for it contradicted the other idea. In emanation, God creates the world out of Himself: but this view may lead to pantheism and may come into conflict with the supreme transcendence of God. However, the doctrine of emana-

[30] Bevan and Singer, *op. cit.*, pp. 50–51.

[31] *Ibid.*, p. 59.

[32] Copleston, *op. cit.*, I, 460.

[33] Erdmann, *op. cit.*, I, 219. Plato is not very clear as to whether the Logos, Demiurge, and God are the same or different.

tion brought with it the concept of the degrees of Being.[34] Another idea which Jewish thought introduced is that of the necessity of moral action for attaining spiritual inwardness. Ethical action is necessary for inward knowledge. It cannot be said that the Greeks were not men of action; they showed intense interest in questions of ethics. But their epistemology had few activistic elements. Only Jewish thought could remove this defect, though it took some centuries for activism as a system of philosophy to appear.

The greatest contribution that Philo made to Jewish thought was to tell man that the significance of ethical conduct does not lie in the realm of politics and society but in the inward being of man. The discipline of the soul needed psychology, which the Jews did not possess, and so Philo borrowed it from the Greeks and laid the foundation for understanding the spiritual significance of ethical discipline. In the polytheistic atmosphere of Greek philosophy, the gods of the outer world were allegorically interpreted as psychological forces.

Most of the historians of philosophy do not classify Philo under the Neo-Platonists. But it cannot be denied that he is at least the most important of the forerunners of Neo-Platonism, which is generally associated with Plotinus (born *c.* 204 A.D.). Porphyry was one of the pupils of Plotinus. Plotinus, unlike Philo, did not care for the Jewish conception of God as personal, transcendent, and commanding, but represented the highest reality as the One—the Ineffable and the Good. Transcendence is retained, but personality is given up, and everything is expressed in Platonic terminology, so far as available. The One certainly is beyond reason and unattainable by reason. Because transcendent, the One cannot be the One Being of Parmenides. The world is due to emanation, the overflowing of the One's Being. The first emanation is *nous*—or Reason, Mind—the nature of which is intuition or immediate apprehension of itself and the One. It contains the whole world of Ideas, and is identified with the Demiurge of Plato's *Timaeus.* The Ideas are not distinct from the Nous, but are its parts. Plurality, therefore, appears first in the Nous. From Nous is born the World Soul, corresponding to the World Soul of the *Timaeus.* It is of two kinds, the higher and the lower, the former being nearer to the Nous and uncontaminated by the material world, the latter being the phenomenal world. Individual human souls issue forth from

[34] *Ibid.*

the World Soul. Each individual soul has three parts. The highest is uncontaminated by matter and is rooted in the world of Ideas. The lowest is connected with the body and is therefore contaminated by matter. The middle one makes the ethical ascent.

Below the soul is the material world, the last emanation from God. Though a manifestation from God, it is evil. So man, under the impulse of the Eros, has to purify and free himself from the body. Next, the soul must rise above sense perception. The third stage is the union with the Nous, and the last union with God or the One in an ecstasy devoid of all duality. Then the soul realizes that, in essence, it is God.

Philo, as a Jewish philosopher, would not go the length to which Plotinus did in the search for inwardness. Plotinus would show and proclaim boldly that God, realized through inwardness, was the limit of inwardness itself and so in some way one and continuous with the inwardness in man, just as a modern materialist philosopher would now as boldly proclaim that man is one with matter, the limit of his outwardness. In an age of dominant outwardness, the philosophy of Plotinus may look superstitious, not merely mystical but also misty. It may be that much in the thought of Plotinus that is misty is due to the incorporation of some of the current superstitious beliefs in angels and spirits. Neither can we say that pure materialism, as a philosophy of unmixed outwardness, is satisfactory as a philosophy of life. If, as recent science has shown in the works of Heisenberg and Schrödinger, pure determinism fails at the extreme limit of matter, there is nothing absurd in the idea that pure rationalism fails at the extreme limit of inwardness. The Nous, Logos, or objective universal reason has to be transcended; the One becomes the transcendent entity. The transcendence that the Jewish religion demanded was thus preserved; but because the transcendent One had become inward to man, intuition replaced faith. Another important point to be noticed is that this One is reached after the Nous, or Reason, is reached. Hence, the One is not irrational but suprarational.

Thus only via the path of reason is the transcendence of reason advocated. If the realm of outwardness is gradually divested of superstitious personifications, as it is in modern science, by rejecting the equation of material forces to the forces of man's lower nature, a similar depersonification of the deeper inward elements could have weeded out all superstitions from philosophy, which could have been as scientific as the science of pure outwardness has now become. But inwardness is mixed up more easily with man's imagination than outwardness. And the tendency of man has been to avoid and ignore what is difficult to do. We should not forget that privacy reaches up to sensations, and imagination and image-building up to perception. But this fact has not deterred man from eliciting what is objective from sensations and perception with the help of reason, in which almost from the beginnings of the history of science and philosophy man has reposed faith as the power capable of giving the objective and universally true. Why it should deter man from doing the same with regard to inwardness can be explained only by the assumption that he is made naturally to look outward and not inward. That is why the people who have gained true inwardness are very few in the world. Again, if depersonification is essential for science and rational understanding, just as matter is depersonified and is not called the Devil or Satan now, the ultimately inward also will have to be depersonified and treated as the Universal Spirit, and not as the fulminating King of Heaven.

Medieval Philosophy

The foregoing line of thinking, however, did not become strong in western thought; and because of the peculiar atmosphere prevailing at the time of Plotinus and immediately after him, such questions did not primarily engage the thoughts of men. Man was indeed isolated from society and nature; nature was little cared for and was condemned. But the isolation brought about by external adverse circumstances created a sense of alienation from nature and society, produced a loneliness and despair, which could be removed only by a sense of companionship with God, the inward Ultimate, from which man could expect help and derive hope, which Jewish-Hellenistic thought and Neo-Platonism supplied and Christian philosophy tried to work out in its own way. From this time up to the dawn of modern philosophy, which restored man's confidence in the outward and in his reason as capable of assimilating and appropriating it and removing its alien features, the preoccupation of western thought was with the inward.

The peculiar form in which the philosophical problems were handed down to the Middle Ages made reason hesitant, timid, non-assertive, because it was taken as axiomatic that reason had to subserve faith. Whenever it asserted itself, it was apologetic. The supremacy of reason was never a tenet of the Jewish religion, out of which Christianity grew. Nor did inwardness and experience of God belong to Jewish origins; they were supplied by Greek thought. Had reason been made subservient to experience rather than to faith, it could have been more bold. But experience of God through man's inwardness was made a taboo by the peculiar transcendence accepted of God. So those few who accepted such an experience became suspect. The medieval philosophers reasoned very keenly and vehemently. But their reason was circumscribed and often snubbed whenever it transgressed its supposed limits. It appeared as though they were arguing in a vacuum. Inwardness was treated as if it were outwardness; arbitrary limits were put on it, and it was asked to move within them.

Bevan writes that the essential elements of Christianity are: "(1) the belief in a mighty creative and redemptive act of God; (2) in a world-plan initiated and carried out by such acts and leading up to a great future consummation; and (3) in connecting the world-plan with a Divine Community, whose perfection in a heavenly bliss is the end to which the whole creation moves." [35] Burlitt says that the creed of Christianity is belief in the Trinity and salvation through Christ. It has also a ritual like the Eucharist. The doctrine of the Trinity was foreign to the original Jewish thought. The Jews in the beginning did not accept Christ at all even as a religious leader, much less as the Son of God. However, the Platonic idea that the Logos or the Demiurge was the first-born of God was akin to the idea of Christ as the Son of God and was taken over. But other difficulties arose. There was the Holy Ghost. Were the three separate or one? If three, then polytheism follows, which was opposed to the monotheism of Judaism accepted by Christianity. Here the Platonic and the Aristotelian doctrines of the universal and the particular helped the Christians. Hence the keen interest taken by them in the doctrine of the universal and the particular, some maintaining that all the three have the same universal, which exists prior to them but manifests it-

[35] Bevan and Singer, *op. cit.*, p. 52.

self as the three, others saying that it actually exists in the three. The earlier Christians, following Augustine, adopted Plato; the later, following St. Thomas Aquinas, adopted Aristotle. There were nominalists like Roscelin and William of Ockham, and also conceptualists like Abelard.

Again, there was the problem of the person of Christ. If Christ was the Son of God and consubstantial with Him, he could not have been crucified like an ordinary mortal. Some held that there were two persons, the lower person only being physical; others held that there was only one person. Such controversies appear to be empty and valueless to a scientific philosopher, but they were of the utmost importance to the people of the time, when the natures of the inward and the outward were mixed up. There was another burning topic. Both the Jews and the Greeks were politically minded. The Kingdom of God for the early Jews was a kingdom on earth; but it was a Kingdom in Heaven, the other world, for the early Christians. The idea of the Kingdom of God on earth entered Christian thought also, particularly when Christianity became a state religion, and the question as to what attitude the Christians should take to the kings and emperors of the earth came to the forefront. Was the emperor superior to the pope or vice versa? Heated controversies arose; and after a long and unsuccessful attempt to combine the two, the kingdom of God was separated from the kingdom of the secular monarch. Further, when the distinction was settled, the other world was understood not as the world of inwardness transcending space and time, but as a world existing somewhere else in space and time. Ethics was not plainly presented as the pathway to real inwardness, but as leading to another world, which was somehow spatio-temporal. Medieval thought thus became a peculiar mixing up of inwardness and outwardness, faith and reason, enlightenment and superstition, dogma and argument, and otherworldliness as preached by the Church and this-worldliness as practiced by the claimants that the kingdom of God was to be on earth. There were thinkers who presented spiritual life as pure inwardness, but they were on the whole not influential.

Christian religion consists of three elements: first, the philosophical beliefs of Plato, Aristotle, the Stoics, and the Neo-Platonists; second, morals and history derived from the Jews; and third, rites and theories of salvation traceable to Orphic and kindred cults. The Greeks were not obsessed by the sense of sin; but the Jews were, and they transmitted that sense to the Christians. It is within these philosophical and religious ideas that Christian philosophy moved. It showed little or no interest in actual outwardness or the world of nature.

Of all the medieval philosophers, St. Augustine (born 354) and St. Thomas Aquinas (born 1227) are the greatest. From about the fourth century to the twelfth, Platonism, mixed with Neo-Platonism and Stoicism, was the philosophy. From the twelfth onwards, Aristotle was the philosopher, and he became Christianized. Not that Platonism was completely rejected; but Aristotle was utilized more. St. Augustine was a Platonist and St. Thomas an Aristotelian.

Augustine was first a Manichean dualist; and it is said that he became a Catholic after reading the *Enneads* of Plotinus.[36] If sense is evil, then Plato's theory that senses cannot give truth is more akin to the Christian doctrine than Aristotle's contention that truth (Idea) is found in sense knowledge. Augustine used a kind of causal argument to prove the existence of God. God created the world out of nothing. In enunciating this doctrine, Augustine differed from the Greeks in general, though Plato would support him in a way with his doctrine that matter is nonbeing. If nonbeing is turned into this world, then "nothing" can be transformed into the world. Further, the world is evil, and evil, according to Augustine, is not a positive entity. Evil has no *efficient* cause, but only a *deficient* cause.[37] He adopted the Platonic doctrine of the Logos to explain that "the Word was made flesh and dwelt among us." But he did not know that the doctrine of Incarnation and salvation existed among the Orphics and other mystic religions. He was greatly obsessed by the sense of sin, and attacked the Pelagians for rejecting the doctrine of the original sin. Time was purely subjective, not objective. History was not cyclic, as the Greeks thought, but proceeded in a straight line. "Christ died once for our sins." Augustine was inclined towards predestination and foreordination. So free will in man was difficult to defend.

Curiously enough, Augustine used the same argument for the existence of the soul as that used by Descartes: "I doubt, therefore I am." Error is due to Adam's fall and our inheriting the original sin from him. Our reason is therefore obscured: hence the need of revelation through Christ's Incarnation. Thus Christianity tended to destroy confidence in human reason and powers—which was characteristic of the

[36] B. A. G. Fuller, *A History of Philosophy* (New York: Henry Holt, 1945), p. 353.
[37] Russell, *op. cit.*, p. 359.

Greeks. Inwardness was accepted, but at the sacrifice of reason. The Greeks accepted the identity of human reason with that of the Logos; Augustine would reject it, as otherwise such an identity would imply some identity of the human being with the Son of God, who alone can have the revelation of truth.

The philosophers of the time of Augustine knew little of Aristotle except what was written by Porphyry, namely, the *Predicables*. But by about the twelfth century much of Aristotle was made available to Europe through the Latin translations of the Arabic versions of the original Greek works. So St. Thomas Aquinas was in a better position to know about Aristotle than Augustine could be. Further, Aristotle's doctrine of the universal was more useful than Plato's in solving the problem of the Trinity according to Christian belief—which was one of the reasons for the greater popularity of Aristotle with the Christian philosophers of the time of St. Thomas.

St. Thomas uses about five proofs for the existence of God: first, He is the unmoved mover; second, He is the first cause; third, He is the ultimate source of all necessity; fourth, He is the highest perfection of the various grades of perfection; fifth, He is the purpose of everything, living and nonliving. St. Thomas rejects Anselm's metaphysical argument. Though we can know that God exists, we cannot know His nature. We can know only what He is not, but not what He is. He is His own essence, goodness itself, delight, joy, and love. God knows not only universals but also particulars. But none of them have any distinct being in Him.

Aquinas criticizes Plato's theory of the universals and accepts Aristotle's in a Christian form. Like Abelard, he tries to avoid the extremes of nominalism and realism. He adopts the Aristotelian distinction of form and matter to explain the hierarchy of beings. Again, Aquinas, like Aristotle, maintains that active reason is immortal, whereas the sensitive and vegetative functions of the soul perish with the body. It is difficult to understand how this doctrine could be reconciled with personality and resurrection.

Modern Philosophy

Except for the Jewish factor introduced into philosophy, it does not seem that medieval philosophy contributed very much to the growth of western thought. So long as human reason was identified with Universal Reason, or the Logos, loss of confidence in man brought loss of confidence in Universal Reason also. But when the Logos was made transcendent, failures could be attributed to human reason, and faith and hope in the Universal Reason could be retained. This is what the Jewish element could do in the Middle Ages.

But this absolute transcendence, with faith only as the path to it, could not satisfy man long enough. When in Neo-Platonism reason and intuitive experience were substituted for faith, philosophy became too inward. Being was found in what transcended reason inwardly; man's worldly existence was considered to be of little value, and he was exhorted not to trust it. Explanations of the world were given from the purely inward point of view, in which the outward and the inward were confused, each being taken for the other, as in the enunciation, for example, of the world's being created in 4004 B.C., or that man is the center of the universe—which is true for inwardness but not for outwardness—and so the earth he inhabits is the center of the planetary system, which later reflective outwardness of science could not support. The realization of the reality of the inward in days when science made little progress and the world was peopled with many beings like angels and devils led to the justification of many superstitions. The condemnation of the world, whether regarded as real or unreal, being or nonbeing, produced in man not only disgust with the world and lack of confidence in it, but also an intense subjectivism and preoccupation with his self or soul.

But it was at this time that events happened which shook man's self-centeredness and subjectivism. Copernicus, and later Galileo, proved that the earth is not the center of the planetary system, but the sun. Should it not follow that man is not the center of the outward universe? Constantinople was conquered by the Turks, and more and more of Greek learning spread to western Europe as Greek scholars fled from the east. Along with Greek learning, interest in man and confidence in his reason also were revived. They would not perhaps have been revived, had it not been that scientific progress also started as a kind of reassertion of the value of man and his reason. Before the sixteenth century Renaissance there was another renaissance brought about by the Arabs of Spain; but it was not so powerful and significant in its results as the later one. Along with the Renaissance, the Reformation precipitated by Luther gave greater dignity to man by justifying the right of the individual's conscience and thereby gave him greater confidence in himself. The Reformation was still Christian and was still unwilling to recognize the right of reason. Luther is said to have remarked when he heard of the theory of Copernicus: "This fool wishes to reverse the entire science of astronomy; but sacred scripture tells us that Joshua commanded the sun to stand still, and not the earth." [38]

Yet the general atmosphere and the outlook of the time were changing. Man wanted to break the shackles by which his mental and physical faculties were tied down. Ability to conquer nature with the help of reason gave him greater confidence in his reason and led to greater interest in the outside world. Man could have, after all, a reasonable amount of happiness in this world, contrary to what the Church had been teaching him so long. He began to be outward-looking with a vengeance. The result of the Renaissance was a new enlightenment and a new kind of humanism, not yet expressed as a system of philosophy, but manifest in general outlook and activity. Man regained his individuality, dignity, and faith in himself. The age became an age of individualism and a new kind of subjectivism. Reason was the reason of the individual, not of the Logos, though it could give truth; and experience also was the experience of the individual: interest centered in the individual's reason and experience with reference to the external world. Theological questions were to be derivative and secondary.

It is not meant that orthodox Christian thought came to an abrupt end by the sixteenth century. It still continued, sometimes making compromises and other times existing in uncompromising hostility; and it still continues to the present day. But those who advocated orthodox Christian thought were by degrees pushed to the background.

[38] *Ibid.*, p. 528.

They had little new to express that could satisfy the changing times.

One peculiarity of the Renaissance that an orthodox Christian, however liberal and scientific, may not notice may be pointed out here. What was revived was not Greek religious thought, the reflective and rational religion of the philosophers, but Greek rationalism, humanism, and logic; and they were not utilized rigorously and boldly to reinterpret religion, but only man and nature. Reflective penetration of spiritual depths, apart from dogmatics and theology, was rare. The Church was too strong and potent for the philosophers to make such an attempt. Descartes, after dividing reality into mind and matter, gave matter to the philosopher and the scientist, and left mind for faith and theology. Even then he had to flee from France and die in the cold of Sweden. Copernicus escaped persecution by dying a natural death before the Church started to take action. The fate of Galileo and even of theologians who dared to differ from the Church was a warning to all thinkers who wanted to be seriously rational about religion. After St. Thomas made his ideas the philosophy of the Church, none would tackle religious problems without fear. Reason was practically forbidden to light up religious experience even so far as it could. Thus Greek religious thought, branded as paganism, was left out. If reliance on reason and experience had been allowed to inward experience, as it was allowed to outward experience by the philosophers from the time of the Renaissance, materialistic communism might not have been born. But the intolerance not only of other religions but also of any deviation from the established dogma made inwardness a stranger to man, who by degrees was led to believe that it was not true. And this intolerance became intolerance of all reason and also characterizes materialistic communism, to which it gave rise.[39] Had religious thought also been revived at the time of the Renaissance and not been branded as paganism, there might have been less scope for intolerant materialistic communism to appear.

Modern philosophy began with the restoration of confidence in the reason and experience of the human individual, who began searching for more experience and greater rationality in the outward world. This confidence tended to express itself with overemphasis either on reason or on experience. Right from the time of Heraclitus and Pythagoras, reason or thought has been considered to be universal,

[39] Alexander Zielinski, *The Religion of Ancient Greece* (Eng. trans.; Oxford, 1926), p. 215.

not only in the sense of being common to all men but also in that of having an objective significance and therefore as being common to both man and nature. The Logos, in other words, expresses the universal structure not only of man's being but also of nature. Plato had the same faith in reason, and Ideas are not merely concepts in our mind but also real objects, of which the physical objects are imitations. For Aristotle, Ideas are even constituent parts of real objects. Now, reason attains self-certainty in mathematics. So faith in reason, for those who had it, meant making mathematics the ideal of explanation and the key to the secrets of existence. The belief of some of the medieval philosophers that reason can say nothing about God was given up, and as philosophies developed it was thought that even He could be brought down into the structure of reason.

There grew, on the other hand, a certain doubt as to whether reason by itself contains all the secrets of nature. Reason can order and organize; but it has to order and organize some material which it does not contain within itself. The study of pure reason itself can tell us little about the world. Man has reason, which is the key to the structure of the world. But the content of the world has to be obtained from experience. Thus the idea that the Logos contains both the form and being of the world was abandoned. Nay, this reaction against absolute reliance on reason was pushed to the extreme; it was said that all knowledge, of both form and content, had to be obtained through experience of objects lying outside man. When it is accepted that all knowledge has to be obtained from outside, induction as a method of logic becomes primary and deduction secondary. Aristotle was the logician up to the end of the Middle Ages; he had to be pulled down from the high pedestal on which he had been placed.

Modern rationalism starts with René Descartes (1596–1650), who asserted as his first proposition, *"cogito ergo sum,"* "I think, therefore I am." It is thinking that confers existence on the "I," and therefore has self-certainty and existence. Its essence is thought; thought is not distinct from the "I," it is the "I" itself. Had not Plato said that the highest part of the soul is reason itself? Descartes' conception of the "I" is in line with the Platonic tradition. What the western philosopher would not notice, but what appears to the Indian philosopher to be a reasonable question to raise, is: Why should thinking confer existence on the "I" and not vice versa? Why should we not argue: I think, therefore thinking exists? This question does not seem to have been raised, however, by any western philosopher, not even by those who maintained that God transcended reason and was beyond the Logos. Augustine anticipated Descartes in enunciating *cogito ergo sum,* but he also thought that reason conferred existence on the "I." The existence of the "I" was self-certain only so far as it was identical with reason; but is the "I" as universal as reason?

In the western tradition, on the whole, the "I," the ego or the soul, in its highest aspects, is identified with reason. In the mystical trend, the tendency to place the soul above reason is not absent. When Plotinus said that man has to rise above reason in order to realize God, he admitted that the soul in its purity is above reason. Then why should this transcendence not be felt and recognized in the lower forms of experience? There is a particularity in the "I"; but reason is pure universality. Western philosophy and psychology did not care to work out this transcendence in detail except Kant and a few of the post-Kantians.

Further, if from "I think" we are to take that the "I" and thought are the same, then why should we not infer from "I act" that the "I" and action are the same? What is lacking in western thought and what appears peculiar to the Indian is the analysis of the "I-consciousness." Indeed, by the time of Descartes, inwardness was very much pushed out of philosophy. But even during the Middle Ages, the inwardness, which was quite intense, especially in the philosophers who followed the Neo-Platonic mystic trend, did not give rise to a systematic analysis of the "I-consciousness."

The weakness of Descartes' argument for the existence of God in this connection has been noticed by many. Pure reason without any empirical content can of course have clear and distinct ideas, if it can have any. Then clear and distinct ideas are true. These can be of pure mathematics, and for Descartes, geometry of the Euclidean space. Then space or extension became matter. To have clear ideas of matter meant to have clear ideas of geometry. When once the Euclidean geometry and the intuition of its axioms were accepted, Descartes would say that the nature of the world of matter could be deduced from a study of reason itself. Such seems to be the idea at the back of Descartes' mind. But he here allowed a confusion in his thought in order to accommodate theology. The existence of God could not be denied and was accepted by the traditional faith. And so Descartes argued: I have clear ideas of things including God; so he exists. And my clear ideas must be true, because they are caused by God, who is a benevolent being and who does not deceive His creatures. Here there is mixing up of "God produces clear and distinct ideas in me" and "reason produces clear and distinct ideas in me." But reason was originally given an external function, the function of deducing the geometrical truths of outwardness, extension. But how can reason, mind, which is opposed to extension and is separated from it, give truths about extension? One way out of this confusion would have been to say: God produces reason in me and reason externalizes itself into extension. Thus rationalism would have been made theological. Then, of course, the question about the relation of God and reason would be raised, in which Descartes did not show much interest. In answering this question God would have been made inward or outward. But the spirit of the time was in favor of the latter alternative, as evidenced in Deism.

Descartes' dualism of mind and matter, thought and extension, poses another problem. Even accepting that matter is extension, a thoroughgoing rationalism requires that extension be the innate content of reason, and so cannot be opposed to reason, as Descartes thought. If it is opposed, how can reason get any content at all? Then how is extension innate to reason? If it is not innate to reason, how can the study of reason disclose the structure of matter? How can one pass from the self-certainty of reason to the certainty of ideas about matter, however clear and distinct they be? Descartes furnished no satisfactory solution of these difficulties and gave rise to the psycho-physiological body-mind problem, and also to the epistemological problem as to how mind knows any object at all. The main defect of rationalism is the nonrecognition of the fact that the content of reason cannot be determined by our reason itself and that human reason is not capable of comprehending the Logos in its entirety as it can comprehend a triangle or square, but only by bits, and so the total content of the Logos cannot be known simply by studying the structure of human reason.

In this connection, we can appreciate the doctrine of innate ideas, started by Descartes and systematized by Leibniz (1646–1716), which is the result of inwardness expressed as outwardness. If the study of reason can give us detailed knowledge of the world, then every possible perception must already be contained in reason and within a rational structure. That we do not know everything when we look within is due to confusion and ignorance, which are removed as mind becomes mature. Many of the upholders of the doctrine and their opponents do not seem to have held absolutely extreme views. But Leibniz with his doctrine of windowless monads could not but have held it, and Locke, in his refutation, must have taken the opposite extreme position, though certain innate tendencies of mind were accepted by him. This acceptance is interpreted by some recent students of Locke as the admission of some innate ideas. But the position of Leibniz is in line with the Platonic tradition: has not Socrates said that he does not impart knowledge but, like a midwife, brings out what is already present in the mind of man?

Spinoza (1632–77) tried to overcome the dualism of Descartes by saying that mind and matter are attributes of a single entity, which he called Substance and identified with God. God indeed possesses an infinite number of attributes of which we know only two, thought and extension. Again, thought knows extension and so in a way includes extension and is the higher of the two. But this inclusion seems to be only an incidental admission, which is not philosophically worked out; for the activities of the mind and body are parallel to each other, neither including the other. That they are not often parallel does not seem to have bothered Spinoza very much. The recognition that thought is higher than extension places human reason in a privileged position; for it may be that, through human reason, a way can be opened to God as the most inward of man's being. In fact, Spinoza had something like this idea in mind when he spoke of the intellectual love of God. It reminds us of the Orphic doctrine that reason in mathematics lifts man towards God. But the doctrine of parallelism not only pulled human reason down to the level of matter, but also did not explain why parallelism is absent in some cases like error. Further, the concept of Substance is not adequate to understand God, who is the limit of inwardness in man. This limit, which is spiritual and transcends thought, as Spinoza himself says, cannot be mere substance, but has also to be self-conscious, conscious of other things, whether they are its attributes or created by it.

Hegel's criticism, therefore, that the absolute substance is not the whole truth is justified. "In order to be this it must also be thought of as in itself active and living, and by that very means it must determine itself as mind." But Spinoza's difficulty would then be that mind is already one of the attributes of Substance; and he thought that Substance could transcend mind and not vice versa. Yet as he admitted that thought was in a privileged position, he could have said that it could mediate between the Absolute Mind and extension. But such a view would have struck at the roots of parallelism which he advocated in order to get over the difficulties of Descartes' dualism.

The prevalent attitude of the time seems to have been that, if mind and matter were separated and placed on the same level, the study of the material world could be facilitated; but the difficulties it raised led philosophy in perhaps unanticipated directions. Hegel also did not notice a difficulty in raising substance to the level of mind. Mind is reason, thought; it faces extension or matter; but the Absolute must transcend this opposition of both reason and matter. So a concept higher than reason was needed. Such words as spirit, mind, *geist* are used in western thought, but vaguely, without proper distinctions of meaning. Spirit also is little more than reason in western thought. Following the general Greek tradition, Hegel treated reason as the highest and said that it could comprehend itself and matter. But this Spinoza also said about thought, and yet felt that it ought to be transcended.

Leibniz was not satisfied with Spinoza's solution of the dualism left over by Descartes. As the author of monadology, he adopted an inward point of view, and reduced matter to mind by calling material monads undeveloped monads, which would realize their mental nature when they matured. Descartes maintained that the nature of mind was activity and that of matter passivity. But Leibniz contended that the inertia of matter was not passivity. Inertia is resistance, and resistance is activity. So the difference between matter and mind is not of kind but of degree. If so, even the nature of the material world will be spiritual in essence. But the question of how there can be a common world and how it can be cognized as common when the monads are windowless and all knowledge innate became difficult for Leibniz, who said that the harmony in all our perceptions is due to the principle of pre-established harmony, according to which God created the world. But the monads, being simple, infinitesimal, and infinite, are eternal; and so the problem of their creation according to the principle should really have no place in Leibniz' philosophy. Then the inwardness which Leibniz wanted to maintain consistently would break down at either limit: God, who should have been the common center of all monads in the inward direction in order to make pre-established harmony work was external to the monads and was only one among them; and the world of nature which we suppose to be one and the same for all of us could not be common to all the monads, being internal to each one separately. A way out of this difficulty was shown later by Kant.

While on the Continent of Europe, faith in reason remained strong and philosophers were striving hard to elicit the content of the universal or objective reason from a study of human reason itself and brought the line of thinking to its end in the philosophy of Leibniz, according to which all knowledge is internal and develops from within mind itself, the philosophers of England developed a distrust in the method and contended that mind has to obtain its content from outside. In other words, knowledge is derived from experience. The credit for starting the empirical school goes to Francis Bacon (1561–1626), who held strongly that knowledge is obtained from experience through careful and patient observation of what nature contains and through cautious generalization on that basis, and who was also mainly responsible for the growth of distrust in Aristotle's logic as the sole instrument for obtaining knowledge, and even forestalled J. S. Mill in the formulation of inductive methods. The first recognized empirical philosopher was John Locke (1632–1704), who still retained rationalism to the extent that he wanted to make ethics as systematic a subject as mathematics—this aim seems to have been common to many philosophers of the time both in England and on the Continent—but at the same time tried to be a consistent empiricist in method. But as the initiator of a new line of philosophical thought, he could not be as consistent as his successors. Besides, the problem of faith versus reason was also a burning issue of the time. Philosophers, moreover, wanted to be certain about the limits which human knowledge, both rational and empirical, could reach; for what is beyond human knowledge can at the most be a matter of faith. Even then, the objects of faith, like God, soul, and immortality, were brought within the limits of reason, and philosophers inquired how far they could be justified by human knowledge. Thus some kind of belief in inwardness was not lost; but philosophers sought to tackle the problems of inwardness as if they were problems of outwardness, as evinced in the deistic conception of God.

The opposite extreme to Leibniz' inwardness, as contained in his doctrine of innate ideas and windowless monads, is found in the extreme outwardness of Locke's standpoint and view that mind is a *tabula rasa,* thereby implying complete denial of mind's contribution from the inward to human knowledge and the rejection of innate ideas. Mind by itself is completely blank and obtains whatever knowledge it can through impressions produced on it by objects external to it. There is also an implied dualism, like that of Descartes, in Locke's philosophy. Though Locke was an empiricist, and though according to empiricism mind can know only the primary and secondary qualities that it perceives but not the substance underlying them, he did not categorically reject it, but accepted it as "something we know not what." And this dualism gave rise to the correspondence theory of truth with all its difficulties, which is generally attributed to Locke. Neither did he say, as Hume did, that mind is not a substance. Locke thus externalized both mind and matter, and philosophically mind ceased to be the mediating link between God at the inward extreme and matter at the outward. God of course was the cause of the world; but having once created it and set it to work according to mechanical laws, He placed himself outside His creation: such seems to have been the general attitude of the time to God. With this idea Locke mixed up a number of religious ideas of the faith current at the time, like the immateriality of God, revelation, and immortality, maintaining of course that faith should not contradict reason and was to be accepted where reason could not reach.

Berkeley (1685–1753), who was more religiously minded than Locke, but who at the same time belonged to the empirical tradition, saw the difficulty in accepting external substance from the empirical standpoint, which he could not overcome. Besides, he was afraid that the recognition of matter as an eternal substance would lead to materialism in that strong empirical atmosphere. How can matter be coeternal with God? It has, therefore, to be rejected as a fabrication of human mind. From the empirical point of view Berkeley rejected the reality of the external substance. Perception discloses to us only secondary and primary qualities. Both of them, he contended, were mind-dependent. He made no special concession to primary qualities; for even extension and movement are perceived only along with secondary qualities, without which they cannot be perceived at all. No one can see an uncolored object. But if secondary qualities are mind-dependent, then primary qualities also must be. And this dependence on mind meant, for Berkeley, being mental. Hence, the *esse* of all things is their *percipi*. This view is pure subjective idealism.

Then, how is the stability of things to be explained? Objects are lasting for some time; we see things today which we saw yesterday. If they are not the same, material objects will be momentary like our perceptions; even if not momentary, they can exist only so long as someone perceives them. Berkeley then shifted the basis of their self-identity from the mind of man to the mind of God. The mind, whether of man or God, is not the same as reason, but the experiencing mind. Ideas also are not rational universals like the Ideas of Plato but concrete particulars. All empiricists, including Berkeley, are opposed to the reality of universals. For universals as such and by themselves are perceived and experienced by none. They are only abstractions made by our mind.

Thus physical objects became ideas in the mind of God. The objects we see, therefore, are ideas in the mind of God. As the mind of God is one, not many, its ideas constitute our common world. Thus an empiricist theological idealism was founded by Berkeley.

Rationalists like Plato attempt to establish the universality of our experience, its commonness to all men, by postulating a universal reason, or Logos, of which men partake. Berkeley ends by postulating a similar universal spirit, except that this spirit is not reason but akin to our perceptual mind, having objects as its particular images or percepts. Universals, of course, are ruled out by the empirical point of view. How we can partake of the Logos, however, was easier for the rationalists to explain; for human reason has that required universality, though it is limited. But this participation becomes difficult for an empiricist to explain, because the ideas he speaks of are concrete particulars. Reason is the highest part of the human mind and is akin to the divine; but we cannot as confidently say that having images or pictures of particular objects is the highest function of even our mind, much less that it is that of the divine. Indeed, most of the empiricists left the meaning of "idea" vague; but on the whole they tended to use the word in the sense of sense-impressions, images, mental pictures, and even abstractions. So the problem of participation in the nature of God through perceiving His ideas was left unsolved and confused, which is due to the nonrecognition of the real nature of man's inwardness. Empiricism indeed need not be outwardness alone; but the empiricists of the time understood it mainly as outwardness.

There is another point. If man partakes of God in every perception, then the object and the mind perceiving the object must be consubstantial with God. One may suspect pantheism or something like it here; but it cannot be avoided. The being of God must somehow be continuous with our being; otherwise, the same object cannot be perceived in the same way by both man and God. For Berkeley's philosophy it is therefore necessary to recognize the inwardness of God to man; God's idea can be man's idea if the mind of God works through man's mind.

Though Berkeley rejected material substance, he retained mental substance for theological purposes. But Hume (1711–76), coming after Berkeley in the empirical tradition, applied the empirical method to mind also and rejected it. If, for the reason that we perceive qualities only, matter is to be rejected, then for the reason that we perceive ideas, emotions, and feelings only, mental substance also is to be rejected. We never perceive mental substance but only ideas, and so on, which we wrongly think are the manifestations of a substance behind. Hume went even further. Empirically the reality of universals cannot be accepted, nor the reality of universal laws; then the law of causality also goes with them. Locke made use of the law of causality to prove the existence of God. But if causality itself cannot be accepted, the existence of God cannot be proved. Immortality also shares the same fate. Ethics is to be based upon sentiments like sympathy and upon desire for pleasure. Nothing of a universal nature can be established; for every universal, either idea or law, has to be traced back to a particular experience, that is, an impression. But no universal can be an impression. Hence no knowledge of universal significance can be defended. The result was skepticism, sensationalism, or phenomenalism. Some students of Hume say that it can be naturalism. It can be so, provided naturalism does not include belief in natural laws universally valid, but only probabilities.

The impasse into which Leibniz' rationalism led on the Continent and Hume's empiricism led in England set Kant thinking about the problem, and he took upon himself the task of reconciling rationalism with empiricism. Both rationalism and empiricism made the possibility of human knowledge difficult. If each one of us is shut up within his own mind and knowledge is to be had from within only, how can we have knowledge of the external common world? Whence does our knowledge get its content? If, on the other hand, all knowledge is to be obtained from sensations, how can we have any knowledge of universal necessary laws? In fact, we believe that we have knowledge of both, the common world and universal laws. This belief, therefore, has to be justified. For this purpose, Kant developed his critical philosophy.

Kant (1724–1804) has been differently interpreted and differently made use of by subsequent philosophers and writers. But we shall present his ideas in the perspective we have adopted. Kant's importance lies in bringing together again the inward and the outward attitudes and explanations which the rationalists and empiricists adopted and gave; and they were brought together through man as the medium. Sensations are different for different individuals. Why they are similar and are believed to refer to the same common world of objects can be explained only by men having the same mechanism of knowledge and by the sensations being produced by the same objects, which Kant called things-in-themselves. Things in themselves are causes of sensations and are not groups of sensations; groups of sensations fall within experience, but things in themselves fall outside experience. The latter are not even substances: we do not know what they are, except that our sensations are due to them. In fact, we have no justification even to call them causes, for causation belongs to what is experienced, but they lie outside our experience. They are posited only to explain why we have sensations.

As soon as sensations appear, human mind begins to work on them by imposing on them its own forms, which are innate to it. First, it arranges them according to the two forms of intuition: space and time. Next, it brings them under the categories of understanding: quality, quantity, relation, and modality. Thus we get all objects of our experience, which we consider to be substances with attributes, causes and effects, positive and negative, possible, actual and necessary, and so on. These categories are innate to understanding, as space and time are to intuition. Understanding, again, is different from reason. The function of reason is to build up ideal unities, the unity of the synthetic activity of mind, the unity of the world as a whole which is the result of this activity, and the unity of these two unities. The first is the transcendental self, or the ego; the second is the world as a whole, which more or less corresponds to the *natura naturata* of the earlier hinkers; and the third is the Supreme Being, or God, required for xplaining the conformity of the transcendental activity of the ego to he equally transcendental activity of the things in themselves. Thus he transcendental ego and the things in themselves become unified n God, just as the two attributes are unified in God in Spinoza's hilosophy. Otherwise, if the sensations produced by the things in hemselves and the activity of the transcendental ego do not conform o each other, the world of experience will not be possible. These three deal unities cannot be experienced; and so we cannot know whether hey exist or not. Hence, they are only regulative principles of ex- erience, not constitutive. Thus, in theory of knowledge, we cannot be ure of the existence of God. According to some interpreters of Kant ike Caird, who follows the Hegelian tradition, the explanation of the onformity of sensations to the activity of the ego is to be found in od, who is ultimately the source of both the sensations and the orms of mind and so must include both the transcendental ego and he things in themselves. His knowledge, therefore, must be of the orm of intuitive understanding or intellectual intuition, in which orms and sensations are one.

God thus becomes, in Kant's philosophy, inward to man, because Ie acts through man's transcendental ego in imposing the forms on he manifold of sensations; and yet He remains outward to man in hat He, as the thing in itself external to man, produces sensations in is mind from outside. Thus Berkeley's God as the retainer of all and indry objects of perception is changed into the active agent of ra- onal and sensuous activity in man. God becomes both the Logos nd the content of the Logos. But approaching God from man's ex- erience, which alone has existential validity for Kant, he thought of od only as a regulative ideal. However, at this point, Kant's line of ought led him to the position of Plato, except for the reality of the ings in themselves, the phenomenalism and the regulative nature of e Idea of God. And it was, in a way, richer than Plato's philosophy. lato made no distinction between the ideas of empirical objects and leas of universal applicability in his discussion of the theory of Ideas. ut Kant did. Plato did not explain how the Logos works through the uman mind, though he showed how human reason reaches the Logos. he Logos creates the world; but how it creates the world is not nown. But Kant showed how God works through man and how the orld can be created through human mind. Again, Kant had a stronger sense of realism: matter for Plato was nonbeing, but for Kant it can be the sensations or the things in themselves, though he is not very clear on the point.

If we compare Spinoza and Kant, another point of significance comes to the surface. Spinoza started with God and attempted to deduce man and ethics from Him; but Kant started with human experience and wanted to know its implications. Thus the two attributes of Spinoza's God, mind and matter, become the two postulates of human experience in Kant, the transcendental ego and the transcendental object. The mental and material modes of Spinoza become the empirical ego and the phenomenal object in Kant. God ceases to be substance and becomes the Intuitive Understanding, akin to the Logos, or Objective Reason, of the Greeks. But Kant was not sure of the existence of God, theoretically, as an object of pure reason. The certainty of God is possible only at the ethical level, as an object of practical reason, not for thought but for activity. The truth of an ideal can be tested only in activity, not in theory, in which an opposed ideal can also be proved. Pragmatism is necessary for testing the validity of ideals.

If the three ultimate unities or Ideas of Reason are really necessary for regulating our ideas, and if our experience is existential, how can one maintain that the regulative principles necessary for experience cannot be constitutive? This is an old question leading to an ancien view: reason, both of the Logos and man, is an entity constitutive o the world. Second, if God can be the unity of both the transcendenta ego and the thing in itself—which indeed Kant did not assert in sc many words but which seems to be logically implied in his philosophy —and if His intellect is intuitive and intuition intellectual, wha need is there for the thing in itself to produce sensations and of a tran scendental ego to organize them? God Himself can do both the func tions. In the third place, if God acts through the forms of intuitio and the categories of understanding, are they eternal or just what ma has taken them to be? Almost all the post-Kantian idealists asked th first question and regarded God or the Absolute as constitutive of ou experience.

Fichte (1762–1814) and others who came immediately after Kan raised the second question also and dispensed with the thing in itsel and philosophically identified the transcendental ego with God. Thu the distinction between the two vanishes, or at least becomes thir

Some, like Fichte, treated will as primary in the constitution of the transcendental ego; for, as Kant said, it is only in the processes of the will that we are sure of the constitutive function of the Ideas of Reason in our experience. Others, like Schelling (1775–1854), considered intuition primary; and some others, like Hegel, reason. Again, some, like Fichte and Schopenhauer (1788–1860), treated the transcendental ego as the subject; others, like Schelling and Hegel (1770–1831), as inclusive of both the subject and the object.

One important feature of the philosophical outlook after the Renaissance is the attempt to understand God in terms of man, because man has become more confident of himself and of his existence than of the outer world and God. Instead of understanding man as the image of God, it has become the vogue to understand God as the perfected image of man. Man is now clear that philosophy has to start with himself, not with God. Human reason is not an imperfect imitation of the Logos, but the Logos is the perfection and completion of human reason. We do not know the Logos as such so that we can realize that our reason is its imperfect copy. On the contrary, so far as man goes, we have gradually, bit by bit, to build up our conception of the Logos with the help of our own reason. Hence the importance of the doubt about the ontological argument: the perfection of human reason is our idea; can it be the idea of an existent entity? The question thus put makes the entity different from the idea and brings the entity down to the common world. So the idea itself must have existence in this case. Indeed, Anselm (1033–1109) is said to have formulated this argument first; he had to formulate it because even for him reason started with the self-certainty of itself, not of God. But after the Renaissance, the importance of the argument became all the greater.

From the standpoint of man's experience Kant could not treat the regulative idea as constitutive and rejected the ontological argument. But Hegel had to defend it, because his standpoint was that of the Absolute and its consciousness, in which understanding is at the same time intuitive. That is the reason for his not accepting the distinction between Reason as regulative and Understanding as constitutive. When Kant tried to keep up the balance between the inward and the outward from the side of man's experience, he had to reject God as constitutive. But when Hegel tried to keep God as a constitutive principle, he had to give up the standpoint of man for the Absolute's standpoint. He felt that reason is the highest and is objective; when man rises to the level of the universality of reason, he rises to the level of the Absolute. But he did not see that, although every human being tries to rise to the level of reason and its universality, not even the greatest philosopher can rise to it in all its aspects and totality. All that we can do is to get glimpses of the objective reason. That is the reason for the Greeks and the Neo-Platonists placing the Logos above the world and man, for Spinoza saying that man's mind is not even the attribute of God but only a mode of the attribute, and for Kant distinguishing between the spontaneous activity of the transcendental ego and the activities of the empirical ego. In the processes of the transcendental ego, there must have already been established the conformity between the forms of the mind on the one side and the manifold of intuition on the other; and this conformity can be intuitively experienced, if at all, by the transcendental ego, not by us.

We cannot once for all rise to the level of the Logos and view the world from its height. Hence the dialectic of the Absolute Consciousness became defective, unwarranted, mistaken, and surreptitious in its empirical references. Yet Hegel's is perhaps the grandest attempt in western philosophy to view the world as a logically interrelated cosmos from the standpoint of the Absolute Consciousness as the Logos, or Universal Reason. In Hegel's philosophy the standpoint of the finite man is given up; in this he is in line with Plotinus and Spinoza, who attempted to derive the world from the Absolute.

Moreover, inwardness and outwardness have significance only for man. The Absolute, or God, is inward to man; but when man imagines himself to be one with the Absolute Consciousness, and yet remains man, this inwardness disappears and is spread out as outwardness, because he cannot so completely universalize himself as to lose his own particularity. The Greek philosophers and some of the medieval philosophers maintained that God is above the Logos even and is still inward to the Logos. In Hegel's philosophy this further inwardness is canceled, and the Absolute as Objective Reason becomes practically one with the Logos. Though dynamism is introduced into Hegel's dialectic, in which one category evolves and passes into another, this dynamism is only logical dynamism, not creative dynamism, or the dynamism of a reason or ground, not of cause. Hence William James was justified in calling the universe of the Hegelians a block universe. Real creativity or dynamism is not the evolution of one category out of another through the triads of thesis, antithesis, and synthesis, even if the categories can be marshaled in that way. Evolution of categories is one thing; and evolution of reality is another. The concept of evolution was utilized by Schelling in the latter sense.

Indeed, this inwardness was retained in a subjectivist application of Kant by Fichte and Schopenhauer, the pessimist who said that, as the world is evil, salvation lies in destroying the will to live. But the distinction between the transcendental ego and the empirical ego is not clear. Fichte, for instance, said that the transcendental ego posits the external world as its field of moral activity. But moral activity belongs to the empirical ego and not to the transcendental ego. It is not, therefore, clear why the latter posits the world at all. And again, why should it posit the outside world with so much of the undesirable in it? It is possible to build up a grand system of philosophy, self-consistent and closed, by adopting either Fichte's or Hegel's point of view. But then man, with his vast number of difficulties and problems and greater certainty of himself than of the transcendental ego, or the Absolute, is left out. The charm of Kant's philosophy, though difficult and left with unsolved problems, lies in this: he did not claim to give us a grand system, but approached philosophical problems from the modest viewpoint of man and his experience. The student who reads him knows where and how he stands and, though not without difficulty, can trace his way inwards and outwards. But Fichte and Hegel ask him to cease to be man and become the transcendental ego, or the Absolute, which he cannot. Kant's great contribution to western philosophy is that he pointed out the necessity for man to look both inwards and outwards for understanding reality and his conclusion that ultimately the two limits meet at a point or can possibly meet. He warns us that we should not start with the meeting point to derive and explain the world of subject and object.

Post-Hegelian and Contemporary Trends

Kant's philosophy, with its background of the conflict between rationalism and empiricism, brings to the forefront a peculiar philosophical possibility, the significance of which does not seem to have been noticed: philosophy may try to explain everything in terms of the most inward or in terms of the most outward. The former attempt will lead to some spiritual monism and the latter to some materialistic monism. Indeed, there can be various modifications and compromises. In the former case, matter would be an emanation, a manifestation of the inward spirit; in the latter case, everything else would be a transformation of the outward matter. Kant, having started with man and his experience, did not adopt either extreme. Both are possibilities, however, and there have been philosophers who followed each. But both, in their extreme form, can do little justice to man. It is impossible to refer to all the different lines of thought which originated in Kant's philosophy.

The third question we referred to above: namely, whether the categories of the human mind, through which God acts spontaneously, are coeternal with God and so absolute, was raised particularly by the scientific philosophers. Man can understand the universe with the help of a different set of categories: how then can they be absolutely true? What is the harm in understanding objects as mere groups of sensations or systems of events instead of as substances? If we can, why should substance be treated as a category universally applicable? Why should space and time be two forms of intuition and not relations between things? Further, as the doctrine of relativity has shown, things themselves may be spatio-temporal configurations. Causation need not be a universal law, but only an expression of probability or correlation between two kinds of events. Thus every category which Kant accepted as absolute and innate to mind can be understood differently, and some of them may even be dismissed;

and all of them can be reinterpreted in terms of outwardness. Again, can we not understand the so-called categories as the ways engendered by the culture of the time for comprehending the universe? Is not culture a changing phenomenon? Then why should the categories be absolute and necessary elements in our experience?

After Darwin (1809–82) published his *Origin of Species,* the concept of evolution was systematically worked out and applied to all spheres of thought. Not only was the Christian Church shocked, but also every attempt by it to explain the world obtained a setback. At first Christianity viewed the doctrine as an enemy, for, if evolution is accepted, God will not be considered to have breathed spirit into matter, but matter will be considered as having evolved spirit. Then how can spirit obtain salvation if dependent on matter? Christianity later became reconciled to the new theory and treated it as a friend; for that matter evolved mind may be interpreted as a sign of God's purpose running through matter and of matter being subservient to God's will. But the outward explanation remained and, I believe, still remains. For instead of matter being an emanation or evolute of God through Cosmic Reason, which is akin to man's reason and works through it, man's reason becomes an evolute out of matter.

In fact, evolution can be applied both ways. What the ancients called creation and emanation may be called a kind of evolution: but this will be evolution of the outward many from the inward one. Evolution from the outward, on the other hand, will be evolution ultimately of the inward one out of the outward many. Which of the two will be more workable and acceptable? Philosophers have taken opposite sides in the history of philosophy. And from a detached theoretical point of view, we may say that it is a matter of theoretical convenience and rational workability.

Then again, Fichte, rejecting the conclusions of Kant's *Critique of Pure Reason* and accepting those of his *Critique of Practical Reason,* enunciated that the essential nature of the ego is will. For the former *Critique* this essential nature would be reason or thought; and for thought both a transcendental subject and a transcendental object are necessary, and it cannot be known, except as a matter of faith, why the processes of each will conform to the activities of the other. But moral action presupposes that the object which is to be reshaped by human action is by nature conformatory to the moral will. And if morality is an undeniable truth, then this conformation also is an undeniable truth. Then, any object, if it is true, must be capable of being confirmed by human action. That is, action becomes a test of truth and reality, for the world is created for action. With this discovery of the epistemological implication of activity arose various forms of activism, including pragmatism.

Kant said that the Ideas of Reason, though necessary, are only regulative, but not constitutive, of experience; but the categories of the understanding and the forms of intuition are both regulative and constitutive. A systematic approach from outwardness, it was later contended, shows that not even the categories and forms of intuition have a priori absoluteness. If so, they can only be regulative, neither necessary nor a priori. Hence, they are logical fictions and conventions, expedients of scientific thought, which man creates in order to organize his experience. Thus arose certain forms of fictionalism and conventionalism.

Right from the time of Pythagoras to the present day there have been many philosophers who believed that mathematics is the clue to the understanding of existence. Kant treated mathematical judgments as synthetic and a priori and as constituting our experience. In Pythagoras and Plato mathematics led up to mysticism. But modern researches have shown that mathematical propositions are purely analytic and so cannot be a guide to inward existence or outward existence, in short, to any existence. Mathematics is only a part of logic, or, according to some, logic is a part of mathematics. Neither pure mathematics nor pure logic says anything about existence. What philosophy can do is to combine this a priori with experience and reconstruct the world. This experience may be pure sensations or the entities accepted by physics, which has become almost a rounded-out system of discipline. This line of thinking is called logical empiricism or more generally the school of analysis, which is one of the most important schools of the present day.

While for logical empiricism, logical analysis is primary, for existentialism existence is primary. Ideas or concepts, also called essences, are secondary. It was Hegel who treated the concepts as primary; for only when freed from existence can thought move freely within the realm of concepts. But how can thought get its content, when liberated and then shut off from existence? Thus while logical empiricism is an offshoot of rationalism, existentialism is an offshoot of empiricism. Yet logical empiricism wants to incorporate something from empiricism also. For logic can tell us very little about the world, and so experience, or that part of it of which we have the greatest certainty, has to be added to it in order to reconstruct the world.

Again, the reaction against the Berkeleyan form of idealism resulted in a number of realistic schools. Berkeley, it is contended, was wrong in thinking that the objects we see are only our ideas. The objects are there, not merely as ideas in the mind of God, but as natural entities existing in their own right. A physical object like a stone cannot be said to be our idea or God's idea. Then two possibilities are found to be open; for it may be said that the object is either directly presented to our mind or indirectly through an idea or essence that intervenes between the object and mind, both the essence and the object being real. Some realists held the former view, and some others the latter.

Another line of thinking is that of phenomenology, which is a philosophy based upon the investigation of the phenomena of experience. The transcendental subject and the transcendental object, which, even according to Kant, are not objects of experience, are left out of phenomenology, which therefore distinguishes itself from the phenomenalism of Kant. The reconstruction of the world is a reconstruction out of what falls within experience. Phenomenology combines the method of Descartes, which excludes everything that can be doubted, Kant's method of analyzing our experience, and Hegel's phenomenology, which works as though everything which philosophy treats falls within rational experience. In any case the transcendental is given up.

The transcendental can be given up in absolute idealism also, but only if the transcendence of the Absolute is canceled. Hegel's Absolute, whatever he may have said about it, is really beyond human consciousness. But it can be treated as falling within human consciousness, for, after all, man cannot know what lies beyond in order to interpret his experience in its terms. What lies within him is history, which marches through his consciousness. The Absolute can be history, which is the sum total of the motive forces of individual minds, expressing itself in each and making each its vehicle. The Absolute can thus be made immanent, experienceable, exerting a pressure on each mind as if from beyond, but not really transcendent. The consciousness of man has come to its own; and so what is generally called the transcendent God, or the Absolute, must fall within man.

Then, if the Absolute is humanized and brought down as history to the level of man, why should we not humanize matter and interpret the world in its terms? Matter is the field of human activity, and can best be understood in its terms. So, instead of starting with the dead matter of the early materialists, who understood it in static terms, we should understand it as a dynamic entity, the matter of economic activity, which can be substituted for the Absolute Spirit of Hegel's philosophy. Then, if history is the Absolute, we can understand history in terms of economic activity, for history is activity. Even sensation is activity: it is the interaction of sense and object. Economic activity progresses according to the Hegelian triad: thesis, antithesis, and synthesis.

It would be really impossible to give an adequate idea of the post-Hegelian movements of thought in the West even if a separate section were devoted to them. Contemporary western thought has developed a great variety of branches. Besides, the lines of thought of each school cross those of some others, and it is difficult to separate any school from the rest. The older ones have not all become extinct, but continue to grow with varying modifications of their doctrines. And there is no unanimity among the followers of any school. But in all the new schools one can notice a growing rejection of the transcendental or at least lack of interest in it, and they approach all problems from the side of man and his experience. One may call this attitude subjectivist or humanistic. However, in some schools matter, though now made transcendental, is not given up; for the ultimate structure of matter is not an object of perception but of inference and is therefore transcendental, and matter ceases to be the hard substance which everyone experiences, but is now found to be pure process, energy, which nuclear physics has discovered. Rigorous attempts are made to explain everything in terms of such matter. Man's inwardness is either left in the background or ignored or rejected. The drive of contemporary philosophy is towards a complete liberation of the outward from the inward. The dream of Descartes is now realized: reason is more at home in extension, outwardness; and though outwardness is no longer conceived as mere extension, but as dynamic energy, process, incessant activity, reason has come to be sure of its powers there.

It would be interesting to trace the vicissitudes of reason in western thought. According to the Greeks in general, it occupied the highest place in man and was akin to the Logos, or the Divine. According to the Pythagoreans, it lifts man to *Theos,* or God. Whether opposed to sense as in Plato or not as in Aristotle, it is the container and custodian of Truth and is the immortal element in man. Not being particular but universal, it is beyond time. Again, reason reveals not only Truth, but also Goodness and Beauty. The Neo-Platonists pulled it down a little and gave it a place next to God. Yet so far as the world goes, the Logos is still the container and custodian of Truth. In medieval philosophy, the Logos was made flesh, a historical person, Jesus Christ, who mediated between God and man like the Logos of the Greeks. But because the Logos was made flesh, the relation between human reason and the Logos was lost sight of, and the former's attempt to understand God was condemned, and faith in the Logos made flesh was extolled. Consequently, by the time of the Renaissance, human reason revolted against the theologians. But this revolt of reason was self-reflective. The faith it had in itself as capable of revealing all truth was found to be overconfidence. The rationalists of the Continent still retained the original faith; but the empiricists of England realized its limits and acknowledged the necessity of experience and patient observation of nature. Kant brought the two lines of thought together. But in the attempt reason lost its constitutive character and became only regulative. The post-Kantians restored its original constitutive character. But the doubt that Kant cast on it got the upper hand and has continuously been raised since. Some treated its concepts as working fictions, scientific conventions, and expedients. Bergson called reason an instrument-making faculty, unable by its very nature to know reality. Contemporary logical positivists treat it as prescriptive, not descriptive; one of their extreme views is that it can tell us nothing about the nature of reality, that all its propositions are mere tautologies. Thus the revolt of reason against faith has ended in its own self-abasement. When reason reflects upon itself, it finds that it can give no information about reality. Not only is the faith of the Greeks that reason can give Goodness and Beauty now doubted, but also that it can give any concrete Truth.

A strong vindication, however, of the reality of reason and of the inward self as constituting the world of experience was made by British idealists, called Neo-Kantians and Neo-Hegelians, the foremost of whom are T. H. Green (1836–82), F. H. Bradley (1846–1924), and B. Bosanquet (1848–1923). They have minor differences. But they all agree on some basic ideas like the reality of the Hegelian Absolute and opposition to the sensationalism of Hume and other empiricists. Green starts his argument with the reality of relations. They are real and yet not objects of experience. They cannot be derived from sense experience; so they must be due to mind. Next, sensations cannot be said to be produced by things in themselves or by some objects lying external to mind; for then we cannot understand how relations can be imposed on some alien material. If sensations are due to mind and also to external objects, we cannot understand how they can derive from both. So sensations also must be due to mind, and the things in themselves do not exist. But this mind cannot be the mind of any finite self, as obviously the finite self cannot produce the sensations and relations experienced in nature. So they must belong to the infinite Absolute Mind.

Bradley starts with rejecting all concepts and entities—substance, quality, activity, relation, even self—as independent realities, because none of them can exist without reference to the others and each taken by itself is riddled with contradictions. For instance, how is relation related to the terms? If it is by other relations, then they have to be related to the terms and the first relation by another set of relations and so on ad infinitum. So none of the categories and none of the entities can be real. Reality is an all-comprehensive whole. Its nature cannot be thought or reason. For reason is relational, but the Absolute is suprarelational. Its nature cannot be even that of self, for self implies nonself and so a relation between the two. It is by nature feeling, which transcends reason. The more any entity falls short of the Absolute, the less real it will be. So there are degrees of reality. In his conception of the Absolute, Bradley goes beyond Hegel, for whom the Absolute is objective reason, the Logos of the Greeks.

Bosanquet, whose name is closely associated with that of Bradley, is more Hegelian than he. The Absolute is a systematic, organic, relational experience, rational by nature. It is the only real individual; Bosanquet calls it the concrete individual. The human self is not a true individual, because, though the feeling nature (formal nature) of each is different from the feeling nature of the others, the contents of all selves are interrelated and form an organic whole, and thus each finite self is transcended and so cannot be a true individual; for individuality implies self-completeness. The content of the Absolute Individual alone is not transcended, and so nothing falls outside it to contradict its self-completeness. Thus while Bradley emphasizes the feeling form of the Absolute, Bosanquet stresses its rational and relational content.

Green appears to be more Kantian in his approach than Bradley or Bosanquet. Though he rejects the things in themselves, he retains the peculiar inwardness of Kant's philosophy in his discussions. Bradley and Bosanquet, in their constructive efforts, make an outward approach and often use the term World-as-a-Whole for the Absolute. Their Absolute thus remains more or less the *natura naturata* of the earlier philosophers, and not the inward Universal Self spontaneously acting through finite individuals.

Mention may be made here of J. M. E. McTaggart (1866–1925), who wanted to be a Hegelian and yet retain the pluralism of Leibniz. The Absolute is not one individual, but a whole of individual selves like a college. Thus the Absolute consists of an infinite number of selves, each being a reflection of the whole. This infinity of selves was defended also by Josiah Royce (1855–1916). But he did not stop with a pluralistic Absolute like McTaggart. The meaning of any experience we have can be found complete only in the Absolute, which knows everything, past, present, and future in an eternal instant and knows also that it knows and that it knows that it knows and so on. Royce is the greatest of the American idealists, and is more Hegelian than Kantian. It is transcendence of the finite individual that leads him to the conception of the Absolute rather than a critical consideration of the inner mechanism of knowledge.

A strong attempt to vindicate the inward from the standpoint of evolution can be noticed in the philosophy of Bergson (1859–1941). According to Herbert Spencer (1820–1903), evolution is the process by which a lower incoherent homogeneity becomes a higher coherent heterogeneity. But, according to Bergson, evolution is creative and starts not with matter, which is outward, but with mind, which is inward. Bergson calls it life, *élan vital.* Time is not one of the forms of intuition as Kant said, but is the very nature of the *élan vital.* Philosophers who start with matter reverse the natural direction of evolution. They start with matter, because matter as extended or spatial is an object of intellect, and they depend upon intellect for their philosophy. But intellect can deal only with space or things spatial, not with time. Time is something that contains at any moment something of both the past and the future; but no spatial part can contain the adjacent parts. So time can be known only by intuition. Time spatialized can indeed be divided into separate parts; but it is not real time. Real time is living time, *durée* is life and mind itself; and in its process it goes on creating ever newer and newer forms without purpose. No teleology is accepted. Teleology is only inverted mechanism, which is a product of the intellect. In this creative process, life leaves many things dead and destroyed, which constitute matter. Intellect is the instrument of life, which utilizes matter. Our physical body is thus an instrument of spatial activity, life's point of contact with the material world.

Bergson's is one of the grandest attempts to vindicate the truth of inwardness; and he has brought out one of the essential differences between time and space. But there are certain aspects of inwardness that are not clearly noticed by him. The distinction between life and mind is not very clear. Retention of the past in the present and a drive into the future are characteristic of time and are found in the habit of life and memory of mind. But if habit of life can be interpreted as akin to memory of mind, why should we not interpret inertia of matter as akin to both? Cannot a materialist say that inertia evolves habit, and habit memory? Correspondingly, cannot we relate mechanism, teleology, and creativity? Then why should space and time, and intellect and intuition, be opposed? If matter is life dead, why should we not say that life is mind unconscious, and mind something else fallen in some other way? Why should mind be the highest and not be the instrument of some agent, just as matter is the instrument of life? If intellect is an instrument of spatial activity, intuition may be an instrument of temporal activity, both being the instruments of some agent. Just as thought does not think, but it is the "I" that thinks, so also intuition does not intuit, but it is the "I" that intuits. Had Bergson probed into these questions, his metaphysics would perhaps have been intensely inward.

It was not, however, for these difficulties that the rival philosophers rejected his theories. Philosophy is an intellectual enterprise, and Bergson condemned intellect. He opposed time to space, but the modern theory of relativity combined them. He spoke of the evolution of the outward from the inward, but all science talks of the evolution of the inward from the outward.

The two greatest attempts made to explain the inward from the outward in terms of evolution are those of Alexander and Lloyd Morgan, both of the present century. Alexander aimed at including not only the concept of evolution but also of relativity. Relativity of knowledge has been familiar to all philosophers right from the time of the Greek Sophists. But relativity of everything with reference to every other thing, relativity within the realm of outwardness, of motion, distance, and the like, is a new idea, which resulted in treating space and time not as two entities, but space-time as one entity. As measurement is fundamental in mathematical understanding, and as it is done with reference to space and time, space-time became the basic category of the physical world. So Alexander started with space-time and said that matter, life, mind, and deity (spirit) are its evolutes. Space-time has a nisus towards deity, which has not yet come into being but will do so in the future. Each higher evolute is a quality of its immediately lower evolute. Thus the agency of creation is taken away from the deity or, we might say, from the most inward and given away to space-time. According to Alexander, God as the creator may be identified with space-time together with the nisus upward.

One need not take much trouble to prove that neither space-time with its nisus nor deity as a future event can be the object of religious consciousness or of inwardness. Further, we cannot understand how life and mind, of which we have at least general knowledge, can be dynamic agents as we find them if they are only qualities of matter. Even accepting that they evolved out of matter, to call them qualities is to use an inappropriate word; for the color of the rose, for instance, is not supposed to act on the material of the rose, whereas life and mind act on matter, appropriate and assimilate it and strive to maintain themselves intact. If Hegel criticized Spinoza for calling God by the name substance, we may as well say that Alexander used an inappropriate word for the higher evolutes. The inwardness that matter attains in becoming life and mind is not the acquisition of a new quality but of a new kind of agency. Alexander's position cannot explain the agency of mind in contributing even the so-called secondary qualities of matter. It is this agency of mind that made the post-Renaissance idealist philosophers and the philosophers before them think of the world as having been evolved, having emanated, or having been created by some agency which is the most inward to man, and which they called God, the Absolute, the One, and so forth. They might have committed excesses and might not have explained many difficulties. But to call life and mind qualities is an excess in the opposite extreme.

For both Alexander and Lloyd Morgan, the higher quality is an emergent out of the lower, not its resultant. A resultant is a product of mechanical activity, but an emergent is something new. Thus creativity, on which Bergson insisted, is accepted by both. Lloyd Morgan, who started as a biologist, modified Alexander's metaphysics by starting with matter instead of space-time and called the nisus itself by the name God. He called his philosophy emergent evolution and, like Alexander, called life and mind qualities that emerge when the lower reality gets into a particular structural pattern. However, though he saved God for religious purposes, he could not defend the agency of life and mind, for they still remain qualities.

The word emergence also has its difficulties. An object is said to emerge, if it is once merged. But Alexander and Lloyd Morgan do not mean such emergence. What emerges is an absolutely new quality, not potentially contained by the lower reality. However, though the word is defective, their meaning is clear. The new quality is the outcome of the creativity of matter, not the resultant of its mechanical activity.

The present age takes seriously not only evolution but also activity. Bergson said that intellect is meant for material activity. Before him Fichte maintained that the Ego posits the world as a field of moral activity. Bentham and Mill asserted that all activity is to be judged by its usefulness. Kant held that one of the conditions of morality is that it should be capable of being realized. That is, nature conforms to moral standards and thus to moral activity. So should not the truths of nature be judged by activity? And how can activity judge such truths except in terms of ends or values towards which activity is directed? If so, the idea of an object will be true if the idea is corroborated by the end for which the object is meant. And this corroboration or verification can be carried out by activity. Then the idea becomes an instrument of that activity, and can be considered true only if useful. Such is the weltanschauung involved in the pragmatism of Charles Peirce (1839–1914), later developed by William James (1842–1910), and John Dewey (1859–1952) in America. Dewey called his theory instrumentalism, as ideas are instruments of action. F. C. S. Schiller developed it into a humanism in England, for this philosophy is based on man's activity and values, and not on the activity of God or some supernatural being. For the reason that this philosophy leaves out of consideration every supernatural agency, Dewey aligned himself with the naturalists also. Peirce indeed had no idea of giving a weltanschauung but only a theory of knowledge. But as every epistemological theory involves a metaphysics, his associates and followers developed a world view also.

Pragmatism is one of the philosophies that have been misunderstood and even ridiculed. But it brought out an essential truth: namely, human activity is an indispensable factor even in epistemology. Man is born not merely to know but also to act. He obtains confidence in his knowledge through his activity. Theoretically, it is easy to be a skeptic, but in practice one has to accept some certainty. Knowledge itself does not contribute to the maturity of man; action brings out more in him. In the world of plurality, man cannot be sure of his knowledge or even of himself without confirmation by action. From the human point of view, this is a great achievement of pragmatism.

Yet pragmatism has not done full justice to the inwardness of man. If we assume a common world—and we have to assume it—should we not also assume a common point at which the inwardness of all men meets? Pragmatism has often been called idealism with the Absolute omitted or struck off. The inward common point is struck off. If we strike it off, then men will be absolutely separated from each other. The tendency of pragmatism is to keep the common point in matter, because natural evolution starts from it. Even then, though men have a common root in matter, the conscious being of each is separate from the conscious being of every other, whatever be the explanation given by the pragmatists for the growth of social consciousness and spiritual life. Without the common inward spirit, spiritual life will be incomplete.

Just as Bacon laid the foundations of empiricism, Auguste Comte (1797–1857) laid the foundations of positivism. He belonged to the age of science, which broke down old beliefs and gave man new intellectual standards and new hopes. He said that scientific thought passed through three stages: the theological, the metaphysical, and the positivistic. In the first stage, phenomena were explained as due to supernatural causes; in the second, as due to hypothetical causes existing behind the observed events; but in the third, mind rejects both kinds of causes and depends only on the observation of phenomena. Science does not confine itself merely to the observation of phenomena but discovers laws in their behavior. It does not, however, treat the laws as causes of phenomena, but only as forms of their behavior. The greatness of science lies in its ability to predict. Comte rejected God and preached love and worship of humanity. Thus, according to Comte, the inwardness of man is to be given up in philosophical exposition.

Fictionalism and conventionalism were more concerned with the philosophy of scientific concepts than with giving a world view or philosophy of life. Kant raised the question: How are mathematics and science possible? His answer was that they are possible because of a priori innate principles used by mind in spontaneously constructing the world. The conception of the a priori and of mind constructing the world was not in accord with the scientific attitude of pure observation and empiricism. The task of science is only patient observation and exact recording. Mach (1838–1916), therefore, said that hypotheses are only temporary expedients or indirect descriptions and that mind and objects are only groups of sensations; the former are, in a sense, shorthand descriptions of the latter and have something pragmatic in them. Knowledge is an instrument of the will, and so all concepts and hypotheses have a practical bearing.

Vaihinger (1852–1933), in his *Philosophy of the "As If,"* propounded a philosophy of combined fictionalism and positivism. The real is really positivistic and empirical. Into this empirical sensory experience mind introduces fictions like substance and causality in science, the acquisitive man in economics, the social contract in politics, and so forth. These fictions can never be verified, and they contradict experience. That is, they can never be experienced. But Vaihinger draws a sharp distinction between fiction and hypothesis. Hypothesis is only generalization, like "All men are mortal," and demands verification; but a fiction does not. The categories of Kant, then, are not hypotheses, but fictions.

Henri Poincaré (1854–1912) went further than Vaihinger and said that all scientific concepts are conventions, definitions formulated for scientific convenience. They are neither a priori nor a posteriori. He distinguishes between two kinds of hypotheses: those that are unverifiable, like Vaihinger's fictions, and those that are inductive generalizations and verifiable, like Vaihinger's hypotheses. Though unverifiable, the former are not arbitrary. They are necessary for scientific purposes. Unlike Vaihinger, Poincaré says that these conventional hypotheses are not contradictory of experience; they are consistent with each other and with facts. Indeed, if science is to reconstruct the world, and if the result of reconstruction is to be consistent with reality, the basic concepts that science assumes by definition have also to form a consistent whole.

The aim of scientific thought thus seems to be to get rid of the absolutely synthetic a priori, which Kant said had to be accepted. Further, science, in order to exclude the personal factor from observation and definition, has to prevent the intrusion of mind into nature. But whether science and scientific thought can ever succeed in enforcing this exclusion is extremely doubtful. If science claims that it has, it claims too much. It can prevent the intrusion of the individual factor; but it cannot prevent the intrusion of the universal factor. If science claims that what is true for any individual normal mind is true for all normal minds, it is assuming that thought in its universal nature is the same for all. This is the claim of the early Greeks also in favor of the Logos, or Universal Reason. It is thought that collates observations, introduces categories, fictions, or conventions—whatever be the name given to them—into sensory experience and builds up experience into a system.

If, with the growth of culture and maturity of the world's thought, our categories are changed, it does not mean that we are not using categories supplied by mind from its inwardness: it only means that mind gradually discovers its own mistakes in formulating its a priori and goes on correcting itself. The necessity of inwardness cannot then be denied; we can only demand that it should be thoroughly objective and universal in order to articulate experience correctly. It may be that human mind uses one set of categories and the mind of some other species some other set. Yet, it is still the human mind that has to interpret the latter set, and neither can the inwardness of the other species be denied. Dogs, for instance, can understand the world in their own way; but all dogs have to understand it in the same way. We have also to say that their inwardness and outwardness meet at common points, and these points again must somehow be related. Scientific thought, however, has mistakenly identified itself with outwardness. But there can be a science of inwardness as well. The significance of the a priori of experience is its inwardness; what exactly the a priori is may be disputed.

The philosophy of analysis also, and of many of those who call themselves logical positivists or empiricists, adopts the attitude of outwardness. It was the belief of the earlier philosophers from Pythagoras onwards that it is through reason, the universal element in man, that he can approach the divinity within, the nature of which also is universal. But because this belief smacks of mysticism and rationalism, the analysts and logical empiricists dissociate mathematics and logic from experience. Nay, even the a priori has little to do with existence, not merely with the inward but also with the outward. The a priori is purely analytic, and the only a priori are tautologies. The existential is purely empirical, a posteriori, positivistic. The philosopher is, then, either to build up a cosmology on the basis of ultimate facts supplied by physics or analyze the philosophical concepts and show which are sense and which are nonsense. The same attitude is taken towards ethics also. The followers of this school—which, like realism and idealism, is not really a school but a tendency—do not maintain the same views. But, on the whole, their thought presents a peculiar combination of empiricism, positivism, mathematical logic, and semantic analysis. Moore, Russell, Witgenstein, Ayer, Schlick, Carnap, and many others have made important contributions to this line of thought. Most of them claim success in ridding philosophy of metaphysics and superstitious nonsense.

One cannot but feel that this school has overshot its mark. If experience is to be analyzed, then only within experience should the distinction between the a priori and the a posteriori be pointed. Of course, logic can be completely formalized, if one wishes. But then one should not forget that one is dealing with an abstraction and that, when reason is turned into abstract logic, the tendency has already appeared to hypostatize reason as abstract logic dealing with tautologies. Then, how are we to deformalize the formalized logic or reason and apply it to existence, if it can have nothing but tautologies for application? Even the distinction between the a priori and a posteriori does not hold then for abstract reason, for it has no concern for the a posteriori, for it all is a schema of abstract tautologies. Existence, as these thinkers admit, does not consist of tautologies. Again, if we are to develop a cosmology either from pure sensation or from the facts supplied by physics, we have to develop it with the help of the a priori. But what guarantee is there that the a priori and its opposite are capable of conformity, and how can the pure tautological a priori develop a cosmology at all? The conformity and applicability are possible, because the a priori is distinguished in, and abstracted from, concrete existence. If this fact is ignored, philosophy, even cosmology, enters a blind alley. The a priori in the outward experience and the inward is to be the same, although we may commit mistakes in determining what exactly it is.

Witgenstein, therefore, is justified in saying that the a priori in both logic and mathematics is merely tautological, a tautological symbolism, because it is completely divorced from existence and experience. Logic cannot have the right even to frame a tautology like "red is red," but only "A is A"; for even "red" is an empirical concept. One will be justified in saying that even the sound "A," and even the letter, is empirical and logic cannot assume what such an entity is. Therefore, the distinction between the a priori and the a posteriori can be meaningful only for and within concrete experience of existence or rather reality, and both again belong to existence and experience. Indeed, there is nothing to prevent us from abstracting either and developing a science out of the abstraction, like logic or mathematics, and out of the pure sense-datum. But the task of philosophy is not exhausted by such work. It is only this abstraction that led to the doctrines that the basic concepts of science are fictions, conventions, mere words, and so forth. But how can such fictions, conventions, or words constitute the being of objects? To say that we could have used one set of categories instead of another is not the same as saying that the categories do not constitute experience. Human experience contains human categories, and the dog's, dog's categories. It is the task of man's philosophy and sciences to determine what human categories are. The dog, if it has its own philosophy and sciences, has also to determine what they are for its own experience.

Again, the tendency that has grown among some thinkers to understand what an object or meaning is by analyzing language looks like putting the cart before the horse. Semantic analysis of language may help us often in clarifying our concepts when they are complex and vague; this is so only because some concepts are vague and complex, not because language was framed first and concepts of objects framed next to suit it. What was language invented for except to express meanings or thoughts about objects? Because language is meant for expressing meanings about objects, its analysis can help us in understanding the latter, but not in determining them. The tendency of this school is thus to carry philosophy into the extreme of abstract outwardness and, consequently, cannot do justice to man and his experience; and naturally with the total separation of the a priori and the a posteriori, it cannot succeed in reconstructing human experience. Indeed, some of the followers of this school do not claim or even care to reconstruct. If so, how can philosophy show a way of life?

A tendency opposite to that of the logical positivists is found in existentialism. Like the followers of the former, the supporters of the latter are not unanimous in their theories. But all of them agree in believing that existence is prior to essence and that essence cannot grasp existence. Sören Kierkegaard (1813–55) is generally regarded as the first existentialist. Indeed, one may call all those philosophers like Plotinus—who maintained that the One, or God, is beyond the Logos, or reason—existentialists; but the peculiarity of existentialism from Kierkegaard onwards lies in this: existence is first grasped in man as an individual. This individualism is the spirit of the time also. Man's existence is grasped by himself through his freedom of choice, which he alone experiences and not others. Just as Descartes said, "I think, therefore I am," these philosophers would say, "I choose, therefore I am." Existence is particular, and therefore cannot be grasped through reason, which uses universals. Because of his feeling of particularity and its limitations, man feels always the presence of an "Other," which is God. Thus Kierkegaard's existentialism is theologically motived.

But why should this "Other" be God? Not agreeing, Heidegger omitted the idea of God in his analysis of existence in his *Sein und Zeit* (1927). The individualistic and antirational approach is common to all existentialists. Man's existence is finite and temporal in that it always feels the inevitability of death and nothingness in tragic anxiety. Thus anxiety and nothingness make human experience peculiar. The individual transcends his existence, not for rapport with God as for Kierkegaard, but with reference to the world, as participating in it, for communion with other individuals, and through anxiety for the future which transcends the present and which is death. Karl Jaspers (born 1883) is less nontheological than Heidegger. Science cannot be self-complete in its elucidation of existence; that is why Kant regarded completeness in the Ideals of reason as regulative. Man's existence is known through his freedom of choice and ethical responsibility. And the One Being of metaphysics, which is the God of religion, cannot be reached through concepts of reason and science, but only through man's existence. But many French existentialists like Sartre understand man's existence in materialistic terms and have introduced a sort of pessimism into the school. Marcel, indeed, remains theological. It seems that, for all, man grips his existence in facing a crisis—a view that reminds us of the Indian doctrine that existence is approached immediately after an intense emotional upheaval.[40]

The philosophy of existence is, on the whole, a philosophy of man's inwardness. By existence all these philosophers mean man's inward existence, not the existence which we generally attribute as a universal predicate to objects, which is called by them *dasein*. But this inwardness does not seem to be investigated in the proper direction and is not carried to the proper limit by some of them. All of them hold that existence is to be found beyond reason, either of man or of the Logos. Their approach is from the side of man and is therefore human and humanistic. And they have rediscovered that existence is not exhausted in concepts or universals. Just as the logical positivists adopted the standpoint of pure outwardness, making even reason outward and emptying it of all existential content, the existentialists tend in the opposite direction of inwardness, making existence inward and divesting it of all rational content. So far as the philosophy of man goes, either extreme is impossible and undesirable. Man as such is an integral unity of existence and reason. He is not completely irrational or nonrational. He reasons, and so the "He" transcends reason; yet when he reasons, he is reason also. And though reason is not the same as existence, it is the clue to existence. It is not meant that all existentialists hold a completely irrationalist view. Jaspers, for instance, admits that reason can be regulative. But what is regulative of existence can offer a clue to existence.

The realistic schools, which started in opposition to Berkeleyan idealism, belong mainly to England and America. In England the realistic reaction started with G. E. Moore (born 1873), who said that Berkeley confused the object of sensation or sense datum and the act of sensing, calling both sensation. Moore maintained that the sense datum is public and exists independently of sensation, even when nobody perceives it. Regarding the physical object, like a coin, he is not so sure. With Mill he would say that it is a "permanent possibility of perception," but has no independent status. Bertrand Russell also belongs to the realistic school; but his views are not the same in all his

[40] See Utpalācārya, *Spandakārikā* ("Vizianagaram Sanscrit Series"), pp. 30–31.

works. In *The Problems of Philosophy* (1911) he maintained that the sense data are not public but private, though different from sensations; and so their *esse* is *percipi*. But the physical object also exists, though our knowledge of it is mediated by sense data. The universals also are real and are intuited by our minds. In *Our Knowledge of the External World,* he changes his position a little, and says that the perceived object does not exist but is a logical construction out of sense data. In his *Analysis of Mind* (1921) he develops this position further. The sense data by themselves are a neutral stuff; and here Russell advocates what he calls neutral monism. The sense data are common to both mind and the object perceived. Thus, from the side of the object, the sense datum belongs to it; but from the side of mind, it is part of mind's biography. In *An Inquiry into the Meaning of Truth* (1940) he seems to revert to his original position of the physical object causing our perception and producing sense data. Through sense data, we infer the physical objects. But this inference gives only probability. When we perceive a cat, there is *probably* a physical cat.

S. Alexander also is a realist, but for him epistemology is secondary to metaphysics. The perceiving mind and the perceiving object are equally real objects, brought together by knowledge relation, which is only a form of spatio-temporal relation.

The school of New Realism belongs mainly to America. E. B. Holt, R. B. Perry, and W. P. Montague belong to it. The chief characteristic of this school is the definite enunciation of presentative perception. The physical object is directly perceived, not mediated by sense datum or essence. As distinct from New Realism, the followers of Critical Realism, which also belongs to America and to which G. Santayana and A. O. Lovejoy belong, maintain representative perception. Our knowledge of the physical object is mediated by ideas, called essences. Both the physical object and the essences are real.

The common effort of all the realistic schools is to defend the independence of outwardness from inwardness; or rather to turn the inward into an outward and treat mind and object as two objects. For this purpose each school developed views of its own. Mind, furthermore, is not a privileged object, as, for instance, it is in Spinoza's philosophy. The reality of the inward and the spiritual is granted only as a sort of concession. Indeed, all have not treated it so; for there are religiously minded among them, like J. B. Pratt. But epistemology seems to be deprived of religious bearings and implications. It is not possible to go into the religious writings of these philosophers. But if the problem of the knowledge of God is not an essential part of epistemology, of what other important discipline can it be an essential part? How is the inward approach to God to be justified? Should God remain outside man and the world? Many of these realists do not care to build up a system of metaphysics and offer world views. Santayana resorted to poetical expression, Alexander became a sort of materialist or space-timist, explaining everything in terms of space-time, and Russell would care little for inwardness and even say that to do so would lead to obscurantism. Yes, the inward is more obscure than the outward reaches; but that is no reason for philosophy's ignoring one of the essential aspects of the being of man and carrying its search into the farthest limits. Corresponding to the farthest limits of the outward, there are farthest limits of the inward.

Giving up the transcendental object and the transcendental subject, phenomenology "brackets" or "eliminates" the factuality (or the existential aspect) of experience and forces attention on the ideal or the essential aspect. Meinong (1855–1921) included in his theory of objects everything intended or thought of. Even mathematical entities are objects. An "objective" is a special kind of object, that which is before mind in judgment or supposition. Husserl (1859–1938) developed this theory further. Phenomenology is a description of subjective processes, not in causal or genetic terms as in psychology, but in terms of ideal meanings and universal relations that the ego confronts in its experience. Yet these ideal objects are not Platonic universals, but are what are intentionally referred to by the subject. Phenomenology thus retains the essential relationship of mind to its object but refuses to carry the outwardness and inwardness to their possible extreme. It is one kind of philosophical tendency to restrict everything to what falls within the conscious experience of man as man.

A similar tendency is found in the neo-idealism of Italy, to which Croce (1866–1952) and Gentile (1875–1944) belonged. The Absolute is not the Hegelian Idea transcending all experience, but the integration of all human motives and interests, which, as a unity, is immanent in every individual mind and acts on it. What thus acts on, and presses forward through, human minds is the historical process or history. The Absolute, therefore, is history. It has four moments—beauty, truth, goodness, and utility—with which the four disciplines—aesthetics, logic, ethics, and economics—are concerned. History progresses not through contradictions, as Hegel thought, but through distinctions. Gentile's views are not the same as those of Croce, though he retains the idea that the Absolute is history. While Croce's philosophy is called historical idealism, Gentile's is called actual idealism, or idealism of the mind as pure act. The moments of history or the four forms of activity are to be deduced from the act itself as mind or history. History preserves its past as a fact, which is nature, and carries it forward again into the future. Thus nature is part and parcel of history, which, as the movement of reflective spirit, is the history of philosophy itself.

Though the immanental idealism of Croce and Gentile makes man more sure of his experience than the transcendental idealism of Hegel does, it fails to recognize the reality of the transcendence of man by both the inward and the outward. History on the one side and nature on the other are certainly more than any individual, and transcend him. But the historical process attains reflectiveness only in the individual's mind and the totality of universal history is never present in it; and as such the totality cannot be said to have attained reflectiveness. So most of it must have been left spread out in outwardness, and it would be unjustifiable to call this whole, only part of which could attain reflectiveness by the name Absolute Spirit, and equally unreasonable to call nature part of spirit, when the major part of spirit is spread out as unreflective nature only. It is difficult to understand and appreciate this essential point of Italian neo-idealism. If it is said that only that part of the universal process that has attained reflectiveness is history and, therefore, spirit; then instead of deriving nature from spirit, we shall be deriving spirit from nature. Then if history itself is the Absolute, we shall have to regard every historical event as justified and good, which is difficult for humanity to do. That nature is the past act of history, which it negates, transcends, and carries forward, has a great romantic appeal and is reminiscent of Fichte's ego positing the nonego as its ethical field and transforming it into the ego through moral activity. But nature shows often much indifference to moral activity, and it is difficult not to doubt this principle. The inwardness of man transcends man inwardly, not as history spread out as nature and become reflective in the minds of a few leaders. It transcends even historical process and time. Time is comprehended by it; it is not comprehended by time. It looks through history and passes judgment on history; but history does not look through it and pass judgment on it.

Understood in this light, neo-idealism cannot do justice to either the inwardness or outwardness of man. The extremes are not within his absolute control, a fact that neo-idealism tends to ignore, supporting a kind of human aggressiveness. Man has to be obedient on the one side to nature and on the other to the Supreme Universal Spirit, which controls history and readjusts it, but does not equate itself to the historical process.

Neo-idealism grew out of Hegel's philosophy by bringing down the Absolute and identifying it with history. The philosophy of Marx (1818–83) also grew out of Hegel's philosophy by inverting it, that is, by starting with matter as economic activity instead of the Absolute Spirit. Marx claims to have set Hegel on his feet. The Marxists contend that the older materialism regarded sensation as passive. But sensation and perception are processes of interaction between subject and object. The bare object is thus transformed into becoming a known object. The truth of perception and thought lies in practice. At this point, Marx is an instrumentalist; and he is an activist through and through. The basic activity in terms of which everything is to be interpreted is economic activity. The subject and the object are in a constant process of interaction, and the process develops according to the Hegelian dialectic of contradictories—thesis and antithesis.

Marx's philosophy has no spiritual interest in the accepted sense, and its ethics also is based on dialectical materialism and economic determinism. Spirit is the outcome of matter, in whatever sense the term is understood, and not matter of spirit. Such a philosophical basis cannot do justice to man. If man cannot succeed in rationally deriving matter from spirit, he fails equally in deriving spirit out of matter. For man as such, the inward is as true as the outward, and whenever he rejects the truth of either, he has to cease being man. Inwardness is as much experienced as outwardness; spiritual activity like devotion and obedience to the Universal Spirit, and self-discipline oriented towards it, is as necessary as obedience to economic laws and self-discipline oriented towards nature. Neglect of either process brings down tragic consequences and produces a sense of aimlessness and failure in life. It is through obedience to both the inward and the outward limits that man transcends his petty self and becomes one with the Universal Spirit, which is the identity of matter and mind, sensation and reason, subject and object, intellect and intuition, and so forth. In the majority of judgments that man makes in his life, he is right. It is the observation of this truth that produces in man the presupposition that ultimately he is somehow partaking in the process of the Universal Spirit, which, Kant said, must be both intellectual and intuitive and which, Spinoza said before him, has mind and matter as attributes. Experience shows that, though man partakes of the knowledge and activities of the Universal Spirit, he has also his own privacy, independence, and individuality, which, being finite, lead to mistakes in perception, thought, and action. And as philosophy is philosophy of human reason and starts with it, man has to treat the two directions of his being, inwardness and outwardness, as real, and act accordingly.

A. N. Whitehead (1861–1947) is so far the latest of the great metaphysicians in Anglo-American thought. He approached philosophy from mathematics and relativity; but his philosophy has affinities with almost every school that went before him. With the idealists he makes feelings the stuff of the universe and says that the whole of western philosophy may be considered as a series of footnotes to Plato. With the realists he refuses to give mind or subject any privileged position and treats both the subject and the object as two objects. All objects, whether mental or physical, have peculiar relations with each other, which he calls prehensions, and perception is a special kind of developed prehension. In fact, all prehensions, of even material objects, are small, unconscious perceptions—which reminds us of the doctrine of unconscious perception advocated by Leibniz. So even material objects have a mental pole. Actually every object, whether we call it physical or mental, has both mental and physical poles, and is a society of prehensions. With the New Realists, Whitehead decried bifurcation of nature into the so-called sense data and the physical objects. But with the Critical Realists, he accepted both, calling sense data essences and making them eternal like Plato's Ideas. Unlike Plato's Ideas, however, they do not constitute the world of actuality. Actuality is a pure process of events of space-time, which theory he developed out of the physical theory of relativity. Again, with the evolutionists like Alexander and Lloyd Morgan, he accepted the evolution of higher and higher realities like life and mind out of the original spatio-temporal stuff of events, and made use of the biological concept of organism in explaining the development. Even material atoms are organisms of events. God supplies the nisus upwards or rather the lure from above for feeling, the eternal desire for integration. As the lure for feeling, God's nature is primordial and conceptual; but as the actuality of the universe, it is consequent and intellectual. As primordial, God has only deficient actuality, which means bare conceptual possibility. As the lure for upward integration, Whitehead's God, like Aristotle's, is the first unmoved mover.

Obviously much of the inwardness of God to man is lost in Whitehead's philosophy. God, in His primordial nature, is the mover of the world towards greater and greater integration. But then He remains outside the world and is not inward to it. He supplies the nisus upward, but how we do not understand. In His consequent nature, He becomes one with it, and, we may say, remains inward. Then, how are the two natures to be unified? If the distinction between the two natures is due to our philosophical approach and is arbitrarily made, it means that this distinction is necessary from the point of view of the reason of man, who is finite. The distinction between possibility and actuality exists for man. Then, if man is actual, God, who is luring man up, must also be actual. Man can think of bare possibilities and also of the sum total of actualities. But when he is to explain actualities, the explanation can be found in an actuality that transcends the experienced actualities but still has to be an actuality. And this actuality, if it is to operate as a lure within man, has to be inward to man. Of course, if the material objects also have a mental pole, they also must have this lure, and then God has to be inward to them also.

If we admit inwardness, then because the lure is felt through this inwardness, we have to say that inwardness is higher than outwardness. Then the mental pole must be higher than the physical pole of everything; and the subject gets a privileged position denied to the object. And then interpretation of the subject as consciousness of this lure or as having the lure for feeling has to be acknowledged to be more important than interpreting it as a nexus of prehensions. It is something that "prehends" rather than a mere nexus of prehensions. The former is the explanation in terms of inwardness and the latter in terms of outwardness. The reduction of the former to the latter may accord with the general outward attitude, but does violence to the ethical and spiritual experiences of man. Yet both explanations are necessary as checks on each other. The former does justice to the ethical and spiritual experiences of man and the latter to physical experiences. We cannot ignore either, if we are to understand their relation at all.

Whitehead's philosophy attempts to do justice to so many currents of thought that it looks unfair to pass remarks on it in a summary fashion. But more cannot be done here; and this criticism is given from the perspective that this book adopts.

Taking Whitehead as the last of the great metaphysicians of western thought and as a clue to understanding its drive, we may say that the general tendency of western philosophy is to disentangle outwardness from inwardness, ignoring or even rejecting inwardness, at least for philosophical purposes. God's place as a cosmological principle, even if what Whitehead gives it is true, is not enough unless it is also shown clearly how He works through human mind as the subject of experience. And when we speak of God, we need not think of a supernatural principle; we may understand Him as the Universal Spirit or spiritual principle working through all men; and such a principle is necessary for philosophy if it is to explain the common elements of man's ethical and spiritual experiences throughout the world. To explain them as due to the commonness of the material world is not enough; that can explain only the sameness or similarity of man's physical experiences; the upward nisus is spiritual, ethical, and rational, and is the same for all men; and it must be as much a fact or actuality as the spatio-temporal events that it guides and patterns. It is inward to all objects, and at the level of man its inwardness is vaguely but consciously felt by him.

Summary of General Characteristics

We may now attempt to give a brief summary of the general characteristics of western philosophy. It is a very rich tradition with pronounced variation. To think of any general characteristic as applying to the whole history of western thought will be a mistake. But we may summarize the general trends and their changes:

1. Greek philosophy started as a kind of naturalism, called hylozoism by Max Müller as the distinction between mind and matter was not clearly recognized at the time, but now called materialism by some philosophers with a scientific bias, who think that its great merit lies in its being the first attempt to formulate a scientific materialism. But

we should note that a naturalism that does not draw the distinction between mind and matter may develop into materialism or spiritualism equally.

2. The Greek gods were natural gods. Cornford says that even the Water of Thales was God. Heraclitus also said that reality is change, or becoming, and identified it with fire, which he treated as God.

3. Because of the naturalistic attitude, a naturalistic approach was encouraged towards even the problems of religion.

4. But a naturalistic approach can be both inwards and outwards. The Apollonian strand of Greek religion was outward-looking, but the Orphic form was inward-looking. The former found its gods among natural forces, and the latter in the spiritual and mental factors. But inwardness did not go much further than reason in man. Hence Pythagoras glorified mathematics. If for the Ionians the creative principle of the universe was water, air, and so on, for Pythagoras it was reason, taking man inwards from sense perception.

5. In Plato, the two strands of thought are blended, and human reason becomes the judge not only of what is true but also of what is good and what is beautiful. But reason still retained some aloofness and inwardness from sense perception. Aristotle made reason more outward, and could preserve inwardness mainly in God, in whom reason became a pale thought of thought. It was still the inwardness approached from man, not inwardness descending into outwardness. The problem of creation was tackled by both Plato and Aristotle; but the solution was mythological in Plato and arbitrary in Aristotle, who was content with calling God the first mover. The ascent from man was not again viewed as descent into man and through him into physical nature.

6. This step was taken by Plotinus, who interpreted the world as an overflowing of the being of Spirit, the One. Plato and Plotinus influenced Augustine, and Aristotle influenced St. Thomas. But the extreme inwardness of medieval philosophy, when combined with faith demanded by Christianity, depressed reason, and man lost confidence in himself and his reason. Reaction against this outlook started from the sixteenth century.

7. As the Greek philosophical approach was made from man and society, the Greeks were able to lay the foundations of systematic social thought.

8. The same reason made the Greeks attach great importance to

the achievements of man, and made them history-minded. History may not have been given divine significance and destiny, yet it was real and important.

9. So far as the Jewish factor of western thought goes, the first feature that strikes an eastern thinker as a peculiarity is the extreme transcendence of the Jewish God. Aristotle's God may be called transcendent, as, after introducing motion into the world, He keeps aloof. Yet, He is to be approached by man through his own reason, but not in the sense of rationally and conceptually thinking about Him; for the being of God by nature is akin to human reason, the immortal element in man, and can be understood in its terms. But the Jewish God is not to be so approached. He is beyond reason and imagination. His nature cannot be understood except as that of a person who gives commandments to be obeyed without question. The similarity between God and man can only be moral. Man is made in the image of God; but man's reason is not an image of God's reason, and we do not know anything about God's reason.

10. Hence we cannot understand whether in Jewish thought God's nature is rational. God does not reason. He is infinite Will. In this respect, the Jewish God is at the opposite pole from the Greek God.

11. So far as Jewish ethics goes, God's Will is good, because it is His Will, and the human will is good, because it obeys God's commands. The nature of the good is not first determined by man and then attributed to God. To judge the goodness of God from the goodness of His commandments is a wrong approach. Here also the Jewish and the Greek conceptions are at variance. But one thinks that, underlying the Jewish conception, the idea is present that communion with God is possible through will or morality, just as it is possible through reason according to Greek thought. But unlike the Greeks, who said that the rational part of man's soul is immortal, the Jews have not explicitly said that the will part of man's soul is immortal. This was said, however, by later philosophers who preached that the ethically perfect soul will live eternally in heaven with God. From the philosophical point of view we may say that will is as important to the Jews as reason is to the Greeks.

12. Love of God and brotherhood of man were established by Jewish thought not upon a study of the nature of man and society as in Greek thought, but only as the dictates of God.

13. The Jewish God, as the ruler of the universe, is not a philosopher like the God of Plato or of Aristotle, but only a creator. He is a will-er, but not a reason-er. So faith, but not reason, is encouraged by Jewish philosophy. Unquestioning faith in God is to be accepted. He reveals Himself only to a few.

14. The Jews took no interest in nature, but in man, to whom nature was subservient. The Greeks were interested in man as part of nature. But the Jews were interested in man as a creature of God and in nature as a servant or object of enjoyment which God gave man. So the Jews gave little thought to nature. Yet, it is curious that the Jews contributed to the world some of the greatest scientists and philosophers.

15. To the Jews time and history are eminently real. Their captivity, freedom, and discovery of a homeland were so strongly impressed on their consciousness that their history became the basis of their ethics and education. The lessons of their own history constituted for them their philosophy of history, the goal of which was final deliverance through faith. History for the Greeks could generally have only a human destiny, but for the Jews a divine destiny. These two destinies were mixed in varying proportion by later philosophers of history in the West.

16. Because of the overwhelming insistence on faith, Jewish thought could not supply as rational a social philosophy as the Greeks did. In this respect, though for different reasons, the Jews and the Indians are alike. The Jews did not care what human nature is but only for faith in God's commandments; the Indians did not care much what happens to man on earth but what would enable man to reach the innermost spirit.

17. The Jewish God was at first a tribal God accepted on faith, not a God of nature.The Jews were His chosen people. This exclusiveness and particularity have not completely disappeared in Christianity and Islam also, which do not generally consider a man saved unless he gets converted. Indeed, religion was universalized by the two, but a kind of communal exclusiveness has been retained. The Jews also later universalized their God; yet they remained Yahweh's chosen tribe, into which, after proselytization was abandoned, no one was admitted. The attitudes of all the three prevented a rational philosophy of Spirit. It should not be thought that there has been no philosophy of Spirit or religious experience explained in universal terms; but that was the

gift of the Greeks to Islam and, through Islam, to Christianity. So far as Islam goes, such a philosophy was heretical in general; to Christianity it was pagan at first, although later on incorporated and made orthodox in some way.

18. But when human reason actually freed itself from servitude to faith after the Renaissance, it was even then unable to develop a rational, existential, and naturalistic philosophy of Spirit, because Spirit remained an object of faith for religion. Hence philosophies of religion, which human reason began to build up, could think of God only as a concept, rationally outward but not existentially inward to man. Those who accepted this inwardness were dubbed mystics, and the main philosophical tradition avoided them. So western philosophy failed in explicating inwardness. It mistook the extravagances of Neo-Platonism as the essentials of inwardness and missed its truth. Here, again, it should not be thought that the West did not produce any great mystic philosopher, who was deeply aware of the inwardness in man; but the very fact that he was called a mystic was itself an insinuation.

19. Later, reason, to which self-confidence was restored by the Renaissance, could not find scope for its freedom even in the limited inwardness generally known to man and turned completely outward towards matter, which it could divide and combine in all ways of which it was capable. Slowly it tended to ignore mind and then deny its reality, the reality of the very entity of which it is a function and without which its own reality becomes doubtful. It ceased even to recognize inwardness, without which the life of man, of whom reason is often a servant, becomes shallow. Further, it forfeited its claim to being the container of the Good and the Beautiful, and began to interpret man's life and mind as if they were misty and evanescent appearances on a conglomeration of atoms. Still later it gave up its claim to being the custodian of the True also, and retained ownership of validity, coming to the conclusion that it can say nothing about what reality is. It turned man into a purely subjective being, disconnected him from the objective world, and made him totally alien to his environment. Such are the achievements of logical positivism and the philosophies of sense-datum, which the exponents, of course, are trying to modify. The gravity of the original mistakes that have led up to these results has not yet been fully realized. Even existentialism has tended to alienate man

from his environment by treating him as an object among objects and ignoring the basic spiritual unity of all men.

20. One saving feature of western philosophy is its boldness and readiness to give up a tradition, if found faulty. No philosopher thinks it necessary to wait for the results of the other approaches, but starts with whatever he thinks to be hard facts and fundamental principles. This boldness saves the various aspects of man's being from being overlooked, though we have to say that today man's inwardness is pushed to the background and sometimes even denied. At the most it is consigned to religion. But on the whole, human and humanistic disciplines and physical sciences have progressed remarkably well. For instance, the social philosopher does not wait to commence his work until the epistemologist shows how other minds can be cognized, but starts with the assumption that society is a group of persons communicating with each other. There may be a conflict between the two sciences; but it is ignored and each works its own way. Similarly, the biologist does not wait until it is shown how life evolves out of matter. But all this is a characteristic of modern western thought; the ancient could have a unified outlook, because the outlook was not varied; the medieval also could have it, but only by checking reason's freedom and boldness.

21. Explanations in terms of reason, imagination, action, will, objects of reason, sensation, and then again in terms of forms of activity like economic activity, spiritual (life) activity, activity of the object (evolution), social activity, activity of speech, etc., etc., have all been tried in western philosophy, because of the freedom of inquiry unshackled by any tradition considered sacred. The main aim of western philosophy, as found in the important trends of contemporary thought, is to liberate the outward from the inwardness of man, to treat the outward as having its own life, nature, and growth, to discover methods for understanding and interpreting them, and then to apply the methods to the inward also. It seems to me that the mistake lies in this application. For it is a problem as to what extent we are justified in completely separating the outward from the inward; and if there is a limit to this separation, the more important spiritual and ethical question arises as to whether the methods applicable to an arbitrarily separated object are applicable to an arbitrarily separated subject: this is the danger in treating subject and object as two ob-

jects. Man's inwardness is to be as real as his outwardness, and has to be as carefully studied with methods of its own.

The foregoing summary of the characteristics of western philosophy may look like a history. But such a summary is inevitable, as the tradition has had a varied development and no single characteristic or set of characteristics is applicable to western philosophy throughout its history. We cannot say that western philosophy is throughout rational, scientific, ethical, humanistic, or mystical. But if we take the dominant trends and latest achievements into consideration, we find that its accomplishment lies in liberating the object, or outwardness, from its entanglement with the subject, or inwardness. Of the two directions of man's being, inwardness and outwardness, the latter has received the greater attention in western philosophy. In truth, the subject and the object are not two objects; they are two directions of one and the same being.

2. CHINESE PHILOSOPHY *and* Human Mindfulness

Introduction

In no other tradition is the idea that philosophy is for man as such, man as a social being, for the guidance of his life in the state and society, so dominant as in the Chinese. For this reason, Chinese philosophy is often spoken of as nothing but humanism, political and social thought, at best a social ethics, or, when it became critical of culture and civilization built up by man, naturalistic romanticism like that of Rousseau. This characterization grasps an important truth, but not the whole truth. Chinese philosophy has its metaphysical background and theories of the ultimate origin and essence of man. But in trying to understand the essence of man, it does not lose sight of actual man. On the contrary, its interest in human relationships is so overwhelming that it treats the essence of man as subservient to actual man and constantly turns from the theory of his essence to explanations of man's concrete relations to man.

In no other philosophical tradition are state and society so conspicuously in the forefront as in the Chinese. It is natural for a student new to Chinese philosophy to get the impression that the history of Chinese philosophy is a history of political and social theory with elaborate discussions on manners, etiquette, and customs; and a hasty conclusion may even be reached that it is nothing but an account of human relationships. The constant refrain of all schools is: This philosophy alone is the best guide to good government. The practical question as to how to lead the best political and social life on earth is considered by every philosopher, be he a political leader, moralist, or ascetic. Whereas John Dewey said that every philosophy is to be tested by its theory of education, a Chinese philosopher would say that it is to be tested by its concept of good government. Man and society are the preoccupation of every Chinese philosopher.

Again, in no other philosophy are history and philosophy so closely connected as in the Chinese. Indian philosophy can be studied without knowing anything about Indian history. Even European philosophy can, in a way, be appreciated without knowing European history.

Plato wrote his *Republic* to explain the best form of state and society; but Thales did not start his speculation with the same purpose. Chinese philosophy, however, started with the avowed purpose of understanding and explaining the ideal form of state and society. State and society are, after all, human relationships; and for human relationships man is primary. So the center of interest for Chinese philosophy is man, not merely what is noumenal in man, but the whole man, both the noumenal and phenomenal. Fung Yu-lan says: "The purpose of the study of philosophy is to enable a man, *as a man,* to be a man, not some particular kind of man." [1] How to be a complete man is the question for Chinese wisdom. The ideal man is one "with sageliness within and kingliness without." [2] He is what Plato called the philosopher-king. Even here there is a difference: Plato's philosopher becomes a ruler unwillingly; but the Chinese sage willingly becomes a king. It is his duty to become a king and set state and society right; the king ought to aspire to being a sage, and the sage ought to aspire to being a king. The sage ought not to avoid worldly duties.

Because of the deep interest taken in man as essentially a member of society and because of the basic value attached to the individual, China was the first country to formulate the idea of egalitarianism. Few of us know that Macaulay and Brunetière laid the blame for the French Revolution upon some distorted notions of China's political institutions.[3] Man is the same everywhere, provided he is ethically perfect and complete. The basis of political and social structure should be equality of all men. Confucius enunciated the principle during the sixth century B.C., and the Chinese people struggled hard to abide by it. No philosophy could be popular in China, if it rejected this principle. But many who preached and defended it were scholars and sages. Hence we read that, when sometimes a king or emperor found the idea inimical to his throne and policies, he persecuted scholars and philosophers and had their books burnt. Emperor Shih Huang Ti of

[1] Fung Yu-lan, *A Short History of Chinese Philosophy,* Eng. tr. by Derk Bodde (New York: Macmillan, 1950), p. 11. Fung has now accepted the Marx-Lenin form of communist philosophy and given up his early views.

[2] *Ibid.,* p. 8. Wing-tsit Chan says that the Confucian doctrine of *chung shu* must not be translated as "sageliness within," but as "consciousness and altruism," and that Fung is reading his Taoist inclinations into Confucianism. See *Philosophy: East and West,* January, 1954, p. 343.

[3] H. G. Creel, *Chinese Thought* (London: Eyre and Spottiswood, 1954), pp. 21–22.

the third century B.C., under the influence of his minister Li Ssu, ordered that all the books of the scholars should be burnt.[4] But all could not be burnt; some went underground and came out again when the political atmosphere changed.

If the sage is to be the king, all administrators should be philosophers. The philosopher is the wise man, and wisdom is obtained by the study of books and training according to their teachings. Hence, there is the famous examination system of China, of which the Civil Service of England is a copy. Opponents of the examination system for the Civil Service condemned it in the Parliament as a Chinese device, which is a tribute to China. The principle behind it is high and well-conceived, though it may degenerate into bookishness: the administrator should be trained in sageliness.

One can therefore understand and appreciate why Chinese philosophy is called a humanism: the reason is the constant anxiety of the Chinese philosophers not to lose touch with the human situation. Abstract metaphysics may be expounded; but it is only for explaining and helping the human situation. This anxiety prevented the philosophers from being metaphysically profound; and they would not carry out an argument or inquiry to its extreme when they thought that the human situation did not demand such labor. That is the reason why Chinese philosophy looks pragmatistic.[5] True theory must work, and it must work in politics and society, and in education—in short, in this life. The Chinese love of life and man's world is well known; and the philosopher always fixes one eye on them and tries to see heaven with the other. He does not lose himself, therefore, in abstract metaphysics. He wants heaven for man and not man for heaven.

Nature! To a foreign student of Chinese philosophy, this word "nature" seems to have a magical significance for the Chinese. Does it have an otherworldly or this-worldly significance? It seems to have as wide, deep, and vague a meaning as *dharma* has in Buddhism. Life according to nature is accepted by many Taoists. But nature for them does not mean the physical world. It is something deep within man. The Tao often has a humanistic ring. Living according to the Tao is not necessarily asceticism, but according to pure human nature. It shows itself in drawing water from the well and chopping wood for the

[4] K. S. Latourette, *The Chinese: Their History and Culture* (New York: Macmillan, 1951), p. 92.

[5] Y. P. Mei, *Motse* (London: A. Probsthain, 1934), pp. 23–25.

kitchen, and so in the usual pursuits of life.[6] The Tao is here in this life itself. Therefore, many scholars call Taoism a kind of romanticism and naturalism, which again shows the importance that the Chinese attach to this world. How can we make this life pleasant, happy, and useful in itself? Wisdom lies in furnishing an adequate answer to this question. Courtesies, manners, etiquette, and mutual relations of man to man and to the state are part of this store of wisdom and are for the philosophers as important as questions about ultimate reality. The motive force behind Chinese thought for centuries was the urge to have this wisdom; and it conferred upon Chinese philosophy its peculiarity.

If we take Chinese philosophy as a whole, we find that, like Indian philosophy, it did not preach control of nature for making it conform to man's needs, but control of man by himself in order to make him conform to nature, understanding nature in an ethical sense. Nature for the Chinese is the essence of man; and so man does not control it, but lives according to it. A philosophy of pure outwardness first attempts to explain the material world and then in its terms to explain the inward. When we understand something, the tendency will then appear, as the next step, to manipulate that something, control it, and make it work for our needs. Knowledge is not virtue but power, power over the object of knowledge. A philosophy of outwardness, therefore, emphasizes control of nature first and then man's effort by self-control to conform to nature. But a philosophy of inwardness attempts to explain the inward first and then in its terms the outward. It would therefore emphasize the control of the inward first and next the control of the outward. The latest tendencies in western philosophy and the tendencies of the classical Indian philosophy are on the whole examples of the two extremes. But Chinese philosophy, though humanistic and outward-looking, emphasized man's self-control more than control of nature. This peculiarity has an important lesson for us.

Chinese thought emphasized man's self-control with reference to state and society, and not with reference so much to the Divine within or physical nature outside. Society, other persons, and state are hard facts for Chinese philosophers, not to be explained away in terms of material particles or Divine Unity. The fact that a great philosophical tradition was guided by this idea shows that man's environment consists not merely of the Divine world, not merely of the material

[6] Fung Yu-lan, *op. cit.*, p. 264.

world, but also of the human world, the world of persons; and his life must have bearings to each of the three. The great traditions must have overemphasized one or the other of the three environments; but for a student of comparative philosophy, all the three must be important if an adequate philosophy of man is to be obtained. The value of the Chinese philosophical tradition lies in the importance it attached to the human environment of man.

The anxiety not to lose touch with the human situation shows itself in the comparative absence of logical development in ancient and classical China. Fung Yu-lan writes that even during his student days there was no one to teach logic in Shanghai.[7] Along with metaphysical profundity, logical subtlety is not a characteristic of Chinese thought. Creel writes: "Hindu metaphysics is so sophisticated that it makes one dizzy; it would seem to have explored every possible position, from pantheism to complete atheism and materialism." [8] Chinese philosophy also has pantheism, atheism, and materialism, but without the metaphysical depth and logical subtlety of the Indian. The need for the development of logic and epistemology was not so keenly felt by the Chinese as by the Indians, because the former did not have to prove the reality of abstract or transcendent realities like the Absolute, Brahman, God, or Prakṛti, but had only to offer a plan for the reorganization of state and society, which were immediate hard facts, the reality of which did not have to be proved. The question, How do we know other persons? would have had no point for a Chinese philosopher, but is important for contemporary western philosophy.

Fung thinks that the absence of scientific development in ancient China was due to the fact that Chinese thought started to find out a plan to know and control mind, whereas western thought started in search of a plan to know and control nature.[9] The obvious lack of mathematics and logic also are due to the same reason. But ancient India offers a contrary example. Indian philosophy is inward and is even more deeply interested in the control of mind than is ancient China. But logic and the syllogism were systematized by Gautama, the author of the *Nyāyasūtras,* as early as about 400 B.C. The concepts of negation and of the negation of mutual negation were earlier than

[7] *Ibid.,* p. 328.

[8] *Op. cit.,* p. 200.

[9] "Why China Has No Science," *The International Journal of Ethics,* April, 1922, p. 258.

Buddha (600 B.C.). The zero was discovered by that time. So we cannot lay down as a rule that science and logic are necessarily due to an outward orientation; they may be due to some inward motive or interest. In spite of the great developments in logic, in ancient India science and technology did not develop so well as in Europe. In India logic and epistemology reached about the greatest heights they could, so far as clarification of inwardness was concerned. But because of lack of outward motive and interest, they were not applied to outward nature. In China, on the contrary, even inwardness did not reach the greatest depths it could. One will not, therefore, be wrong in calling the Chinese attitude pragmatic immediacy. The Chinese philosophers did not care to reach depths and heights beyond the concrete human level, either in inwardness or outwardness.

China is not lacking completely, however, in subtleties of logic and dialectic. It has a separate school of philosophers called the dialecticians, though one cannot but feel that even they did not bring out the systematic implications of their thought. Every school, again, used some method to expound its philosophy and refute its rivals. But even during the two great epochs of Chinese philosophy, the Sung (960–1277) and the Ming (1368–1644), investigation of things (*Ko-wu*) meant chiefly investigation of human affairs, and science meant science of human affairs, which constituted the immediate hard facts of state and society.[10] The desire to press logic to the extreme, to prove invisible ultimates, was not strong. Hence logical method suffered. Even the dialecticians were satisfied with some verbal sophistry that could obtain immediate practical results. Systematic development of the logical and metaphysical implications of a theory seems to be foreign to the Chinese mind, which was on the whole averse to abstract thinking. Even Buddhism, as we shall see, was humanized in China, which accepted and developed its positive teachings.

[10] Hu Shih, *The Development of Logical Method in Ancient China* (Shanghai: The Oriental Book Co., 1928), p. 4.

Growth of Chinese Philosophy

Like that of India and unlike that of the West, the history of Chinese philosophy does not show one school or system growing out of another. Almost all the classical schools started and grew simultaneously, criticizing and influencing each other. In India also all schools—Vedic, Vedantic, and independent—started and grew together, motivated by the same idea of the search for the ultimate ideal of life, an existence without misery, whether it could be found in this world or in another. In China also all schools were motivated by the search for an ideal; but the ideal was the model man, state, and society. The Chinese speak of a legendary hundred schools, but their number was reduced to six by Ssu-ma T'an (*c.* 200 B.C.), who gave the first account of them. They are the Yin-Yang school (the cosmologists), the Ju school (the literati), the Mo school (the Mohists), the Ming school (the school of names), the Fa school (the legalists), and the Tao-Te school (the Taoists). There were other reductions and classifications, but these six schools are now finally accepted as important.[11]

According to Liu Hsin of the first century B.C., during the period of the early Chou dynasty (1200–300 B.C.), there was no separation between officers and teachers. But during the later period of the dynasty, when its power was declining, many of the officers lost their former positions and scattered throughout the country as teachers. The officers thus scattered belonged to different departments of the government, and their teachings reflected the different interests of the state they were serving. Fung finally concludes that the Ju school, to which Confucius belonged, had as its teachers members of the Ministry of Education, who were the literati; the Taoist school was started by the official historians, who became hermits after observing the rise and fall of dynasties and of the fortunes of the people, and learned to hold onto what was essential in man; the Yin-Yang school originated among official astronomers, who observed the heavens and seasons and

[11] Fung Yu-lan, *op. cit.*, pp. 30, 31 ff.

became cosmologists; the legalists sprang out of the Ministry of Justice and emphasized strictness in rewarding and punishing; the School of Names started with the Ministry of Ceremonies, which had to do with titles and positions and the corresponding honors accorded to them; and last, the Mohist school had its origin among the Guardians of the Temple, who preached universal love.

One can easily appreciate now the humanism of the Chinese philosophy and the deep interest it took in man, state, and society. Since the interest of every department is to make the state strong, man and society happy and stable, and the ruler an ideal one, the Chinese schools analyzed human nature for this common end. If they studied cosmology, again they did it for the same purpose. As the state could not function without any of the departments, all philosophies were needed for a comprehensive philosophy of social man, state, and society. But when the Chou dynasty disintegrated and the departments dissolved, the thinkers who originated from each claimed that only their thought contained the true philosophy of the healthy man, state, and society. And so we see the tendency that, when one dynasty fell, the advisers and ministers of the next dynasty would attribute the fall to the falsity and inadequacy of the philosophy of the advisers and ministers of the former. In no other country was there so intimate a connection between philosophy and institutional life as in China.

With the motive of studying the ideal man, state, and society, and in the circumstances mentioned, it was natural for all schools to grow together and cross each other. Even after Buddhism entered China (*c.* the 1st century A.D.), there were crossings between Buddhism, Confucianism, and Taoism. These three ultimately became the three important schools of China, each connected with a religious tradition. Confucius (Kung Fu-tzu) was born in 551 B.C., and was a contemporary of Buddha. Mencius, who belonged to the same Ju school, lived between 372 and 289 B.C. Mo Tzu, who opposed Confucius' doctrines, lived between 479 and 381 B.C. He was the founder of Mohism. Han Fei Tzu, the protagonist of the Legalist school, belonged to the third century B.C. Hsün Tzu, who belonged to the realistic wing of Confucianism, lived during the same period. Mencius belonged to the idealistic wing. Hui Shih and Kung-sun Lung, the great protagonists of the School of Names, lived during the third century B.C. Tsou Yen, the major figure of the Yin-Yang school, belonged to the same time. It is generally thought that Lao Tze was an older contemporary of Confucius. But Fung Yu-lan thinks that he was a legendary figure, who was mistakenly identified by Ssu-ma T'an with Li Erh of the third century B.C.[12] Elsewhere he says that Lao Tzu, the person, may be earlier, and *Lao Tzu,* the book, later.[13] Wing-tsit Chan says that the date is uncertain and assigns him to any time between 600 and 200 B.C.[14] Creel thinks that it is impossible to settle this question but that the book could not have been written earlier than 400 B.C.[15] Yang Chu is assigned to the fifth century B.C., and is regarded by Fung as a forerunner of Lao Tzu's Taoism. But Hu Shih thinks that he must have been later than Lao Tzu.[16] Whatever be the exact dates, the six schools diverged and defined their ideas by the second century B.C.

There are other schools also, like the school of Agriculturists, who claim that, if the emperor becomes an agriculturist, the state and society will become perfect and prosperous; the school of Eclectics, who draw a little from each of the other schools and maintain that a good state and government needs all; and the school of Diplomats, who emphasize the importance of carrying out the orders of the government. But these schools made comparatively little specific contribution to philosophy.

The period from 200 B.C. to 1000 A.D. marks the crossings and blendings of the indigenous schools with each other and with Buddhism. And from 1000 to 1900 the indigenous schools tried to dominate. Confucianism, with all the material it incorporated from Buddhism and the other schools, became the dominant philosophy. Confucius and Lao Tzu did not start what we call a religion, but gave philosophies of practical life. But after Buddhism entered China with its worship of Buddha and temples and monasteries, Confucianism and Taoism—in imitation of Buddhism—became some kind of religions as well. They were indeed identified with some religious rites even before. During the modern period Taoism does not seem to be as strong as Confucianism. Chan says: "Chinese philosophy in the modern period is tantamount to Neo-Confucianism." [17]

[12] Fung Yu-lan, *A History of Chinese Philosophy,* Eng. tr. by Derk Bodde (London: George Allen & Unwin Ltd., 1952), I, 171.

[13] *A Short History of Chinese Philosophy,* p. 93.

[14] *Philosophy: East and West,* July, 1954, p. 347.

[15] *Op. cit.,* p. 110.

[16] *Philosophy: East and West,* July, 1954, p. 347.

[17] *Ibid.,* p. 353.

The contemporary period, since 1900, is strongly influenced by the West. It is difficult to say what exactly it will become. China has now become communist, and Mao Tse-tung advocates Marxism as interpreted by Lenin and Stalin. Chan says that "Chinese philosophy, old and new, is now dormant," and so also is Neo-Confucianism.[18] Creel thinks that it may have a future. He writes:

> What is to happen to Confucius is not yet clear. Many Chinese of this century, and many Communists, have damned him as the chief foe of progress. Others, however, have felt differently. A book that is interesting in this connection was written in 1945 by Kuo Mo-jo, later a vice-premier of the Peiping government. In this work Kuo depicted Confucius not only as a champion of the rights of the common people but also as a fomenter of armed rebellion. Kuo's views concerning Confucius were quoted in a volume of the *Large Soviet Encyclopaedia* published in Moscow in 1935. Thus it is by no means impossible that the idol of old China may come to be hailed as a forerunner, in the revolutionary tradition, of Marx, Lenin, Stalin, and Mao Tse-tung, a hero of the new China.[19]

Reference to Ideal Man as Authority

Consistently with the humanistic tradition and the strong historical sense, it is not in logic, science, and metaphysics that the ancient Chinese philosophers find their authority, but in some ideal man, a sage-king or emperor of old; and as the known kings and emperors had some weakness, defect, or imperfection, the ideal man was associated with some remote prehistoric time. Only one of such models was historical, Chou Kung, the Duke of Chou (1200 B.C.), who acted with exemplary wisdom and morality as the regent of the boy-emperor Ch'eng Wang, whom he could easily have murdered. Confucius was fond of referring to him. This appeal to authority became a fashion

[18] *Ibid.*, p. 357.
[19] *Op. cit.*, pp. 268–69.

with the Chinese philosophers, and the remoter the reference the more authoritative it came to be supposed. Scholars think that many of these ideal emperors are mythical and legendary. Confucian *Analects* mention the names of Yao, Shun, and Yu; of these Yu seems to have some historicity.[20] It is said that Yao did not give his throne to his incompetent son, but appointed Shun as the next emperor, because of his skill. Shun also acted similarly and selected Yu to succeed him. But Yu founded the first dynasty, the Hsia. These legends might have been woven in order to teach that one could become an emperor not only by birth but also through ability. The Chinese were anxious that their emperors should be competent and benevolent. The exemplar of the philosophers was the ideal emperor.

Chinese civilization seems to have taken its rise about 3000 B.C. Because of the close connection between philosophers and ideal emperors, philosophers are as important as emperors for appreciating at least early Chinese thought. Huang Ti, also called the Yellow Emperor, is said to have ruled about 2697 B.C. Yao became emperor in 2357 B.C., and Shun in 2255 B.C. Yu, who was appointed by Shun in 2205 B.C., founded the Hsia dynasty, which ruled up to 1766 B.C. Then the Shang, or Yin, dynasty came to power, and ruled up to 1128 B.C. The earliest Chinese records belong to the Shang period and were unearthed in the mounds of Yin in the town of Anyang in Honan Province. The people were worshiping some god called Ti. The Shang dynasty was replaced by the Chou dynasty, to which the Duke of Chou belonged. Confucius was born during the decadent period of the dynastic rule of Chou.

The four books which every Chinese student reads are (1) *The Confucian Analects,* (2) *The Book of Mencius,* (3) *The Great Learning,* and (4) *The Doctrine of the Mean.* Of the Chinese philosophers Confucius is regarded not only as the first teacher but also as representing the typical Chinese outlook on life. It is said that he himself did not compose the six classics (*Liu Yi*), but collected them. They existed even before Confucius and were a legacy of the past. They are (1) *Yi,* or *The Book of Changes,* (2) *Shih,* or *The Book of Odes,* (3) *Shu,* or *The Book of History,* (4) *Li,* or *Rituals,* (5) *Yueh,* or *Music,* and (6) *Chun Chiu,* or *Spring and Autumn Annals.* The Chinese did not start with any scripture corresponding to the Vedas; and

[20] K. S. Latourette, *op. cit.,* pp. 38–39.

whenever they wanted an authority in support of their views, they referred to some legendary emperor and attributed their views to him. If Confucius referred to Yu, Mo Tzu would refer to Shun and Yao. Indeed, some later philosophers ridiculed and criticized this practice of making a view truer by referring it to a more ancient emperor.

Much of original Chinese philosophy is unfortunately not available in English and other western translations; and the language is one of the most difficult for a foreigner to study. But a few histories, translations, and expositions, like Fung's works, have appeared in English, and western scholars have begun to give more attention to the subject.

Early Philosophers

Confucius.—In the teachings of Confucius, one need hardly expect religion, metaphysics, or even an appreciable logical method. Confucius was avowedly a traditionalist who felt that the chaos and the consequent misery in China of his time were due to the fact that the people, from the emperor downwards, were not following the venerable traditions. He wanted, therefore, to reform society and state, to educate people in what he considered to be right traditions. He found that neither the rulers nor the subjects were performing their duties, and felt that every man should perform the duties pertaining to his position. He was a rebel, but a rebel in the name of tradition. The ideal, he thought, could be achieved by the rectification of names (*cheng ming*). What the ruler ought to do is determined by the meaning of the word ruler, and what the minister ought to do by the meaning of the word minister. Confucius said: "Let the ruler be ruler, the minister minister, the father father, and the son son": and that is the principle of good government, which has to see that every person discharges the duties of his station. But this principle has far-reaching implications. For, if the ruler, though supposed to rule by the Decree of Heaven, ceases to be a ruler by not deserving the name and failing in his duties, he can be deposed. Revolutions, therefore, are justified.

Confucius took for granted that there should be emperors, kings, nobles, and subjects, because to have those distinctions was the tradition. But the greatness of Confucius lay in articulating a philosophical justification for rectification. He developed a contempt for an aristocracy which considered itself composed of "superior men" and was not performing its duties. He said: "It is difficult to expect anything from men who stuff themselves with food the whole day, while never using their minds in any way at all. Even gamblers do something, and to that degree are better than idlers." [21] Any man can be a "superior man" if he is noble, unselfish, just, and kind.

Confucius understood duties in terms of customary rites (*li*), sacrifices, manners, and etiquette. The Chinese word *Li* originally meant sacrifice. Its meaning was then extended to cover the ritual used in sacrifice, and then to every sort of ceremony and courtesy that characterized the conduct of courtiers. Confucius endowed it with moral significance; it represented the right ethos of the people. To observe *li* became a duty. It is like the Sanscrit word *dharma*.

Confucius, indeed, had no method of probing into the meaning of "names" or obtaining definitions of concepts like Socrates; had he had one, he would have started real epistemology, philology, and semantics. The meanings he gave to words or names were the meanings given by tradition, but he idealized the traditions, for he explained that the meaning of a name is what the person with that name *ought to do* according to the norms sanctioned by tradition. He confronted actual conditions with normative traditions. One may find humanism and pragmatism in this doctrine.

Regarding the virtue of the individual, Confucius emphasized righteousness (*yi*) and human-heartedness (*jen*). Righteousness is opposed to profit making. The Chinese word for righteousness also is pronounced *li,* but is different from the *li* meaning ritual. It is difficult to translate the word *jen;* it is what makes man truly human. It means goodness, love, true man-ness, human-heartedness, and benevolence.[22] It comprises what is lovable, loving, and ethical in man. One cannot fail to notice the absence of "rational." Perhaps reason in man did not interest Confucius.

The practice of *jen* consists in regard for others. Its positive aspect

[21] Quoted by Creel, *op. cit.*, p. 219.

[22] See W. T. Chan, "The Evolution of the Confucian Concept Jen," *Philosophy: East and West,* January, 1955.

consists in *chung,* doing to others what one wishes to be done to him by them; its negative aspect is *shu,* which is not doing to others what one does not wish them to do to him. *Chung* and *shu* were later interpreted as the doctrine of the golden mean and harmony. "Neither too much nor too little" does not mean merely the negative avoidance of extremes but harmonizing them. The mean is what keeps things in their proper positions. It is the sense of proportion that Confucius emphasized.

Confucius recognized the importance of knowledge; for without knowledge of things one cannot be a superior man. "He who does not know *Ming* cannot be a superior man"; and *ming* means the total existent conditions and forces of the universe. Still, the Chinese did not make a scientific study of the universe; for their interest lay only in human relationships. It is said in *The Great Learning:*

> Those who anciently wished to exemplify illustrious virtue to the whole world, first ordered well their own states. Wishing to order well their states, they first regulated their families. Wishing to regulate their families, they first cultivated their characters. Wishing to cultivate their characters, they first made their thoughts sincere. Wishing to make their thoughts sincere, they first extended their knowledge to the utmost. Their extending their knowledge to the utmost lay in the investigation of things.

These eight steps were later called the eight wires, and we may call the whole chain the Confucian causal chain, like the causal chain of Buddhism (*pratītyasamutpāda*). However, "things" meant only human relationships, and the ideal was virtue in state and society. Thus the Chinese were content with the observation of human relationships. Chinese philosophy is full of the study of man; but what man is with reference to the material and biological world on the one side and the Supreme Universal Spirit on the other was not carefully studied.

Confucius made use of the idea of Heaven. But it did not have for him the connotation of life after death. He silenced one of his disciples who asked him about it by saying how could he know about death when he did not know life. Heaven vaguely meant for him a sort of moral force in the universe. His ethics was more or less completely divorced from metaphysics and religion, and was based only upon his observation of men. Wisdom, he said, was to know man; and virtue lay in loving men. He was more concerned with *li* (ritual, code of morals, and etiquette), which was also the basis of educational theory, than with ultimate problems. Both intellect and emotions were to be trained. So music was part of education. He preached the essential equality of all men. The question that rent Confucianism later, namely, whether human nature is essentially good or bad, did not trouble him, since he put the emphasis on the "cultivation" of man's inner unity, harmony, or equilibrium.

Confucius wanted not only to educate people but also to advise rulers. But few kings wanted to take him as an adviser or minister. He wanted those trained by him to become administrators. In this respect, he was like the Sophists of Greece, giving instruction for payment of certain fees, though charging poor students very little. His political philosophy lay in keeping everyone strictly to his position and duties.

One interesting similarity between the thought of Confucius and the Indian Brahmanism is that between the connotations of *li* and *dharma*. *Li* originally meant sacrifice and was later given the meanings of ritual, propriety, and moral and political duties. *Dharma* also was originally associated with sacrifice. What the Vedas ordained, the performance of sacrifices and other acts, was *dharma*. What is thus ordained was a duty. *Dharma* therefore came to mean duty. Man's *dharma* is that which sustains him and the world. *Li* is what sustains man, state, and society. We are told that even now *li* means sacrifice.[23]

The idea of *Tao* is common to all philosophies in China, though each school interprets it in its own way. For Confucius, the *Tao* has nothing mystical about it. It is not an entity, not a substantial thing. It is only a way of conduct, leading to the happiness of all mankind, and changing according to circumstances. It is not a rigid path. It is the way that the individual has to choose in his conduct with reference to state and society and the circumstance in which they exist.

Mo Tzu.—The first philosophical opponent of the Confucian doctrine was Mo Tzu, who lived between 479 and 381 B.C. He is the founder of the school called Mohism after him. He is famous for his doctrine of universal love and altruism. He criticizes Confucius for not believing in the existence of God (Heaven) and spirits; for his insistence on elaborate funeral ceremonies; for his stress on the place of music in education; and for believing in a predetermining fate. He

[23] Creel, *op. cit.*, pp. 43–44.

criticizes him also for not believing in universal love. Confucius preached gradations of love; for one loves one's father more than the father of another. Like Confucius, Mo Tzu was opposed to hereditary rulers, and insisted that the rulers should be experienced in the art of the Tao. Like Confucius again, he refers to the sage-kings of old, Yao, Shun, and Yu. Mo Tzu, though himself a soldier, was opposed to war, as it was beneficial to neither party. The world would be conquered not by war but by virtue and justice.

Jen (human-heartedness) and *Yi* (righteousness) are combined in all-embracing universal love. One should love every person in the same way, whether related to them or not. It is the duty of the ruler to exhort people to practice universal love, which is both good and useful. It alone can lead to the best form of state and government. Mo Tzu speaks of five goods: enriching the country, increasing the population, establishment of good order, disappearance of war, and the good will of spirits. He does not condemn war in self-defense. The state should be properly organized and strictly disciplined. For this purpose, Mo Tzu formulated what he called the principle of identification with the superior: the ruler should identify his will with that of Heaven, his minister with his, the subordinate officials with that of the ministers, and so on. This produces iron discipline and rigid organization. Of course, it leads to authoritarianism and totalitarianism. But the Mohists were opposed to all oppression. We read that in the revolt against the oppressive totalitarianism of the Chin dynasty in 209 B.C., the Mohists joined the Confucianists. The Mohists formed a military organization with strict discipline and, when necessity arose, fought to the last and died with the leader. They preached frugality and simple and austere life, and said that education was necessary for training in universal love. Though Mo Tzu preached the doctrine of universal love, he did not believe that man is originally endowed with the nature to love everyone. It appears that Mo Tzu did not think that man is originally good or bad, but that he can be made so through education and discipline. Man's nature is like pure silk which can be given any color by dyeing.[24]

It is often said that Mo Tzu's ethics is hedonism and utilitarianism. But it is difficult to say whether this characterization amounts to condemnation or praise. If it begins from self-interest in practice, it is

[24] Fung Yu-lan, *A History of Chinese Philosophy*, I, 96.

certainly low ethics; but if it begins from interest in others and ends in benefit to oneself, it is certainly to be praised. In fact, every ethics that is based on the idea of the good, as distinct from the idea of the right, and every religion that preaches communion with God as the highest happiness are hedonistic and utilitarian. If the act is right because it is good, it is utilitarian. In this sense, both the Chinese and the Indian philosophies seem to be utilitarian. Why should one realize the Brahman? Because the realization leads to the highest happiness. Why should one practice universal love? Because it is the highest good and is the best form of state and society. And further, Mo Tzu might have advised kings to practice and make people practice universal love, only because the kings were not doing it. He might then have shown them the benefits accompanying the practice. In fact, universal love can be practiced only in an ideal state and society. But that is no reason for the philosophers' not advocating universal love and pointing out the advantages of the practice. As Mei points out, Mo Tzu presented his doctrine too directly and without consideration for details.[25] But this defect does not detract from the sublimity of the doctrine.

Mo Tzu's opposition to music can be appreciated. He wanted absolute discipline and austerity. Music softens man's nature; but Mo Tzu wanted it to be hard. In this respect, he is less humanistic than Confucius; for Mo Tzu did not appreciate the influence of music on the formation of human character. He seems to have little regard for the emotional nature of man.

Mo Tzu's principle of identification with the superior is based on a one-sided conception of the origin of the state. Like Hobbes, he thought that society was originally in a state of disorder and people selected the most virtuous and able man as their ruler. The authority of the ruler, however, comes from two sources, the will of the people and the will of God (Heaven). The ruler has to govern for the good of the people; and this good is achieved through universal love. Because the leader is supposed to be an ideal man, people should identify themselves with him. However, the principle can be abused and turned into oppressive totalitarianism and authoritarianism. Ruler and society are at no time so perfect as to exemplify the principle.

[25] *Motse, The Neglected Rival of Confucius* (London: A. Probsthain, 1934), pp. 188, 192.

Confucius's teaching was more sober and less one-sided and more practicable than Mo Tzu's.

Yang Chu.—It may be said that what the Vedic tradition is for India and the Socratic for Europe, the Confucian is for China. Fung says that at the time of Confucius no definitely formed philosophical groups existed, but there were some recluses who were dissatisfied with the conditions of the world and sought happiness in withdrawal from it.[26] They do not seem to have been monks, as the order of monks could not have existed at that time. Whatever philosophy they had might have been a philosophy of this life, telling man to seek happiness in this life itself by avoiding its turmoil. Confucius is reported to have visited some of them. It is with them that Taoism as a philosophy started. The first preacher of this school of whom we know is Yang Chu. Fung believes that he was earlier than Lao Tzu; but some others say that he was later.[27] However, his teachings are simpler than Lao Tzu's. Some scholars now disbelieve that Confucius met Lao Tzu.

The recluses were all individualists, trying to be away from society and to find happiness in purity and simplicity of life. Our social world, according to Yang Chu, has two sources, Heaven and man. Part of it is Heaven-made, and part man-made. That which is made by man is artificial, and we call it civilization. This has to be shunned, and man should live according to pure nature created by Heaven. Such is the central idea of the recluses. It is not clear that the recluses were aiming at the realization of some transcendental spiritual essence in man. Very likely, they were not; for their aim was to live a life of purity in this world itself. The social consciousness of the recluses was consequently weak.

Yang Chu is assigned to some time between 440 and 360 B.C. Tradition assigns Lao Tzu to 570 B.C. Yang Chu's basic doctrines are that each man is for himself, that life should be valued, and that things of the world should be despised. He is generally interpreted as a hedonist; but this hedonism is of a peculiar kind. For Yang Chu did not advise people to seek momentary pleasures even within limits prescribed by nature, but to shun them. He says that if one prizes life one should shun material things.[28] Rich meats and strong wine harm the stomach,

[26] *A History of Chinese Philosophy,* I, 141.

[27] W. T. Chan in *Philosophy: East and West,* July, 1954, p. 347.

[28] Fung Yu-lan, *A History of Chinese Philosophy,* I, 141.

and the tender teeth and beautiful cheeks of women are "axes that destroy our nature."

What Yang Chu wants is affirmation and completeness of life, realization of its completeness, which is found in purity and simplicity. If this is hedonism and utilitarianism, then, as I have said, all religion will be so. For every religion, in placing God-realization before man, depicts also the advantages of following the ideal and the disadvantages of not following it. Yang Chu indeed did not give a clear conception of God and did not call the highest ideal of life God-realization. The general bent of the Chinese mind, and even of the Indian, is towards a kind of naturalism; for spirit is not conceived in supernatural terms. It is continuous with what we call material and mental nature. Its relation with other natures is also natural and so according to some laws. Even the so-called grace of God (Heaven) is natural, not arbitrary. Of course, the relation between level and level differs in each case; but these differences are natural and can be discovered. Yang Chu in this sense is a naturalist. Instead of calling the pure happy nature of man by the name spirit or *atman,* he calls it nature. To call it nature is in line with the general Chinese tradition, which was interested more in things human than in things material. Nature therefore means human nature. Yang Chu felt that it could be discovered only by avoiding the things of the world. This is asceticism; and one wonders whether it will help clarity of thought to associate hedonism with asceticism. Or it may be called hedonistic asceticism. To call it pure hedonism will be somewhat misleading.

Whereas Confucius was interested in finding happiness in life as lived in state and society, and Mo Tzu in the search for universal peace and order, Yang Chu aimed at individual happiness, which, he thought, would be found in a life of purity and avoidance of material pleasures.

Mencius.—The name of Mencius (372–289 B.C.), one of the greatest of the followers of Confucius, is associated with the famous idealistic doctrine that all things are completely within mind. But knowing the Chinese interest to be mainly humanistic and ethical, one gets the impression that Mencius meant by things moral principles and foundations. If investigation of things meant investigation into human relationships for all Chinese philosophers in general, then Mencius might have thought that all moral principles were embodied in the human mind and that they could be discovered by searching mind. Probably he did not mean that the laws of the material world could be discovered by studying man's mind, though some of his utterances may give this meaning and some of his followers may have drawn that conclusion. However, Mencius may be interpreted as a mystic. "All things are complete within us." "He who completely knows his nature, knows Heaven." Man thus becomes a microcosm, and the macrocosm can be understood by understanding the microcosm. The universe is a moral universe. The moral principles of men are also the principles of the cosmos. But the principles of the microcosm can be understood by looking within. Thus Mencius introduced meditation, which is absent in the teachings of Confucius.[29]

There is a peculiar similarity here between the doctrine of Mencius and the doctrine of the Mīmāmsā. The world is governed by the law of human action (*karma*) as prescribed by the Vedas. Injunctions of the Vedas constitute the duties of men. These duties include sacrifices to gods and duties to family and society. For Mencius also man's duties include duties to spirits, family, state, and society. These can be discovered within man. For the Mīmāmsā, they are once for all given in the Vedas; but the actions of man originate from man, and they are the clue to understanding the universe, which is governed by the law of action (*karma*). Again, the duties of man, the *li*, the *dharma*, had associations with sacrifice both for the Confucians and the Mīmāmsā.

One is tempted to think that originally in the history of human thought moral duties and sacrifices must have been very intimately connected. Sacrifices to gods and spirits and sacrifices to ancestors must have been as important as those based on social relationships. The give and take between gods and men was conceived as similar to the give and take between men and men. All must have been equally advocated for the sustenance of the world, which included both gods or Heaven and men. All must have been equally duties, *li*, *dharmas*.

Another doctrine for which Mencius is famous is that human nature is essentially good. This must have been a corollary of the doctrine that mind contains everything, and that by studying mind moral principles of the universe can be discovered. For if human nature is not essentially good, moral principles cannot be discovered in it. Men-

[29] Creel, *op. cit.*, p. 105.

cius, like Confucius, had a strong social sense, and was more realistic than Mo Tzu in his grasp of the differences between individuals. He differed, therefore, from both Yang Chu and Mo Tzu. Yang Chu's principle of "each for himself" does not recognize the authority of the ruler; and Mo Tzu's universal love does not acknowledge the special affection due to one's father. Love always should be graded. Mencius said: "If Yang Chu could have benefited the whole world by merely plucking out one of his hairs, he would not have done it; . . . Mo Tzu, on the other hand, would have rubbed his entire body smooth from head to heel, if in that way he could have helped the world."

Mencius was opposed to the utilitarianism of Mo Tzu, and also to his rigorism and opposition to music. Virtue should not be made subservient to utility and profit. Yet Mencius also used arguments of utility and enlightened self-interest. But, as I have said, the utilitarianism of these thinkers has to be interpreted carefully. For Mencius, as for Confucius, everything is good that is consistent with the essential human nature and makes man a complete man. Indeed, for Mencius, human nature is essentially good; the differences between men are due to environment.

In political philosophy, Mencius is opposed to the agriculturalists, who preached that the king ought to be a cultivator, because, if the ruler is to till and cook, he will have no time to rule. Mencius distinguishes between the nobility of Heaven and the nobility of men. The latter consists in being a superior man, a duke, a minister, or officer. But the former consists in being benevolent, just, and principled and in finding joy in being good. The scholar is above the ruler, because he understands Heaven. This elevation of scholars by Mencius led to frequent struggle for power between scholars and autocrats.

One may say that the whole of Chinese philosophy aims at depicting the "superior man." Chinese society was class-ridden, though not caste-ridden. The aristocracy considered itself to be "superior men," the rest to be "inferior men." This distinction came to be acquired by birth, whether the aristocrat was an idiot or a moral wretch or murderer. Confucius wanted to supply a philosophy for the distinction, not in defense and justification of the existing conditions, but in criticism. He said that anyone could be a superior man, provided he was noble, virtuous, and skilful. In India, in like manner, the word Aryan was given a philosophical meaning. It had at first a racial meaning, as opposed to the word non-Aryan. But later, particularly by the time of Buddha, it acquired the philosophical meaning of one who was noble-hearted. The Vedic religion called itself the Arya Dharma; for Buddha, the Aryan would be one who followed the noble eightfold Aryan Path; and similarly for Mahāvīra, the Aryan would be one who followed the path prescribed by him and observed *ahimsā* (noninjury) and vegetarianism. The "superior man" for Confucius is not one having wealth and armies, but one who follows *jen* and *yi*. Likewise, for the ancient Indians, the Aryan is not one who conquered the non-Aryans and ruled them, but one who follows the noble spiritual path laid down by ancient religions.

Like Confucius, Mencius is opposed to the principle of heredity. None should be a ruler if he is not virtuous and skilful. Mencius is not opposed to feudalism as such, provided the ruling hierarchy is virtuous and capable. Otherwise, revolution is justified. If a ruler fails to bring about the welfare of the people, he should be deposed. The ruler should be a moral leader of mankind. Mencius, therefore, prefers government by a king (*wang*) to government by a war lord (*pa*), because the war lord governs only by force. The basic postulate of political philosophy is that virtue brings success. Delight in mere strategy and war is criminal. Good will of the people is absolutely necessary for the ruler. Man is a political animal; and so the state is a natural entity. Mencius disagrees with Mo Tzu, who said that the state is a necessity for establishing moral order and peace. For Mencius, as for Confucius, the state is the natural embodiment of moral order, not a necessary evil chosen by the people, but a concrete manifestation of their moral nature. In this respect, the doctrine of Mencius resembles that of some of the idealistic theories of the state in the West.

If man's nature is essentially good, then his emotions also are good. They should not be repressed, as Mo Tzu would wish them to be. "The feeling of commiseration is the beginning of human-heartedness. The feeling of shame and dislike is the beginning of righteousness. The feeling of modesty and yielding is the beginning of propriety. The sense of right and wrong is the beginning of wisdom. Man has these four beginnings." [30] Human-heartedness is natural to man; it is not imposed

[30] Quoted from Mencius in Fung Yu-lan, *A Short History of Chinese Philosophy*, p. 70.

on man. But the universal love of the Mohists is imposed on man from outside. Thus the ethics of Mencius does not derive its sanctions from an external supernatural and superethical agency, but is based on human nature itself. And because human nature contains the four beginnings of virtue, it is essentially good.

The idealism of Mencius is a kind of ethical idealism. If western idealism derives its principles from man's rational nature, we may say that the idealism of Mencius derives its principles from man's emotional nature. Hume wanted to base morality on sympathy; and critics said that it would lead to subjectivism. But really if sympathy is as objective and universal as reason, it also can be a good foundation for ethics. This, in my opinion, is the specific contribution that Mencius makes to ethical thought. And yet he propounds an idealism entirely grounded on human nature, without recourse to a transcendental Absolute. This may have its shortcomings, because emotions are not always equally intense and well-guided and so are not always reliable. They need objective guidance, which reason only can give. Yet, there is a boldness and freshness in the thought of Mencius, which has a lesson for us. Reason is not always a motive force in moral activity; if emotions do not follow reason, it is helpless. So they need training and strengthening along proper directions.

Mencius, of course, could not give us a method for discovering the directions. But the boldness with which he enunciated the doctrine of the four beginnings and proclaimed that human nature is essentially good should make us think whether for ethical perfection strengthening of ethical emotions also is not as necessary as the training of reason. Man is ethical not merely because he is rational, but also because he has the four beginnings. If Mencius' theory is inadequate because it is based only on the four beginnings, other doctrines are defective because they are based only on man's reason. Emotional nature is as heavenly as rational nature. Any ethical idealism based only on either will be one-sided.

If emotions are important, then music also is necessary for training them. Education is moral cultivation, training emotions to flow through proper channels. Commiseration, the feelings of shame, modesty, and right and wrong are all important. Even the practice of the kingly way is the outcome of the feeling of commiseration. The king should know that the desires and needs of his people are the same as his. He should extend the scope of his activity so as to include others. This is true *jen,* which includes *chung* and *shu.*[31]

The School of Names.—The protagonists of the school of Names, or dialecticians, are Hui Shih (350–260 B.C.) and Kung-sun Lung (284–259 B.C.).[32] Their views are complementary to each other. Hui Shih emphasized the relativity of the actual world, and Kung-sun Lung stressed the absoluteness of concepts and names. Both were dissatisfied with the affairs of the world and the existing state of things. Both thought that those could be improved by the rectification of names, which Confucius had taught. This could be achieved by a study of the relation between names and actualities. Confucius was content with inquiring whether a person occupying a particular position designated by a name was or was not carrying out the duties and obligations pertinent to that position. But Hui Shih and Kung-sun carried the inquiry further. What is the nature of names and what is their relation to actualities? The aim of Hui Shih and Kung-sun in making this investigation was, like that of Confucius, ethical and humanistic. Like the Mohists, both of them were pacifists and preached universal love. But they thought that they could establish the truth of universal love by a dialectical rectification of names. Hui Shih would say: All things, the whole multiplicity, is relative; so all things are essentially one; therefore love all and hate none. Kung-sun Lung would say: The smallest can be proved to be the greatest; the similar is dissimilar; the moving is at rest; therefore, the truth is beyond shapes and features and is one; therefore, practice universal love and hate none.

The dialecticians existed even before Hui Shih and Kung-sun, but these two are the first famous philosophers of that school. They are criticized by the rival schools for introducing ethical confusion by proving right to be wrong and wrong to be right. For like Hegel, the Chinese dialecticians noticed some identity of the opposites. However, whatever use might have been made by lesser men of their dialectical training, the aim of these two philosophers was high and noble.

[31] Mencius was interested in economics also, preached equal distribution of land, and advocated the famous well-field system. A piece of land about one-third of a mile square is to be divided into nine equal squares. The central square is to be a public field and the other eight are to be given to eight families. The sketch thus obtained resembles the Chinese character meaning a "well," and so the system is called the well-field system.

[32] Dr. Hu Shih regards Hui Shih as a follower of the Mohist school.

Hui Shih and Kung-sun seem to have taken great delight in discovering and presenting paradoxes and less delight in offering constructive solutions. Hui Shih's final paradox is: "Love all things equally; the universe is one." "If we see things from the point of view of their difference, even lever and gall are as far from each other as the states of Chu and Yueh. If we see things from the point of view of their similarity, all things are one." [33] It is this oneness that Hui Shih wants to bring to the forefront; but he does not explain where the plurality comes from. "The smallest is that which has no form and the greatest is that which cannot be enclosed." Both are formless and therefore one. The idea is that of the identity of infinitesimal and the infinite. "That which has no thickness cannot be increased [in thickness], and yet it is so great that it may cover one thousand miles." The greatest thickness cannot be measured, nor can the smallest thickness, and so both must be one. Great and small, thick and thin, have meaning only relatively, not absolutely. In their absoluteness, they are all one and not different from each other.

Kung-sun Lung is famous for his discourse on the white horse. When once he was crossing a frontier into another city, the guards told him that horses were not allowed to pass. Thereupon Kung-sun replied that his horse was white and a white horse was not a horse, and entered. Perhaps the guards were so bewildered by the argument that they were unable to use force to prevent him from crossing.

Kung-sun's idea seems to be that any object called a "white horse" is an integrated unity of white and horse, which are two universals with two names. It must, therefore, differ from any object called only horse or called only white. So he said that a white horse was not a horse. The name horse and the concept horse have no specific reference to white, and so a white horse does not correspond either to the name or the concept of horse. Names refer to universals without reference to differentia; and so names do not refer to actualities, nor universals to particulars. Every horse, for instance, must have some color and shape; but the universal horse or the name horse has no reference to these specific particulars. In this way, Kung-sun would say that there is nothing in the actual world corresponding to names with an absolute sense. This goes against the teaching of Confucius that the world can be improved by the rectification of names. However, what

[33] Fung Yu-lan, *A History of Chinese Philosophy*, I, 200.

can answer to names must be universals, which alone then must be true and must be beyond shapes and features. This line of thought could easily be taken over by the Taoists to show that the Tao was beyond shapes and features. In fact, the Taoists were opposed to the dialecticians, but made the best use of their enemy's dialectic.

It is interesting to note that one of the paradoxes of the dialecticians is about the flying arrow. "There are times when the flying arrow is neither at motion nor at rest." One can see that the paradox is not exactly the same as Zeno's. Zeno said that the flying arrow is always at rest. He wanted to prove the reality of being and the unreality of becoming, the reality of rest and the unreality of motion. But the Chinese dialecticians wanted to disprove the reality of both the opposites, rest and motion; rest and motion belong to the realm of shapes and features; but the truth is one and is beyond shapes and features. Fung explains the paradox in three ways: (1) the form of the arrow is at rest; its tendency is in movement; (2) the particular flying arrow has moments of rest and motion, but the universal has neither; and (3) if the arrow is at two points of space at the same instant of time, it moves, and if it is at one point of space at two instants of time, it is at rest.[34] These explanations are comments. But the idea behind the paradox seems to be that, if we take the arrow, rest, and motion in their absolute sense, then the arrow can neither move nor be at rest. None of the three in its absolute sense can be a concrete thing of the world.

The idea of negating both the opposites seems to be more common to Indian and Chinese thought than to the western. Indeed, this principle of the negation of both the opposites was developed more systematically in Indian thought than even in the Chinese. In India it was first formulated by some pre-Buddhistic skeptics like Sañjaya, then taken over by the Buddhists, and then by the Advaitins. It developed into a negation of four alternatives, the negations of both the opposites, then of their combination, and then of their exclusion, and is expressed in the form: *S* is neither *P,* nor not-*P,* nor both, nor neither. This four-cornered negation meant that the thing referred to was beyond all description or, as the Chinese express it, beyond shapes and features. When Buddhism entered China, it took with it the principle of four-cornered negation.

Hui Shih calls the actualities by the name *shih* and the names of

[34] *Ibid.,* pp. 218–19.

actualities by the name *ming*. For Kung-sun Lung the names mean concepts or universals, which he calls *chih;* he calls the particulars by the name *wu*. The *chih* alone are real, according to Kung-sun, who thus accepts the Platonic theory of universals. Hui Shih says little about universals.

Lao Tzu.—It has already been pointed out that the date of Lao Tzu is uncertain, though he is the most famous of the Taoists. Yang Chu, the forerunner of the Taoists, preached simplicity and individual purity by avoiding the artificialities of civilization. Lao Tzu developed this doctrine further. According to Lin T'ung-chi, "Taoism is the natural and necessary counterpart to the complacent gregariousness of Confucianism." [35] While Yang Chu was content with advocating the realization of the original pure human nature, Lao Tzu placed nature far above everything including Heaven and *jen* and exhorted man to realize it. This realization is possible by leading a simple and pure life, taking everything as it comes without high ambitions and aspirations. The *Tao* is the "unscathed block"; it is simplicity itself and so can be attained through simplicity of life. The achievement of human-heartedness (*jen*) is not the highest ideal. *Tao, te,* human-heartedness, righteousness (*yi*), and rituals (*li*) are the five ideals in the descending order of importance. A society that insists on the last is already degenerate.

Tao is spontaneous; it is beyond good and evil. It is nature, naturalness itself. Taoism is a kind of nature mysticism, understanding nature in the sense of human nature or some ultimate natural principle in human nature, not physical nature. It is something like the ultimate Dharma of the Buddhists, their *tathatā, dharmadhātu,* or even the neutral Brahman of the Upaniṣads. Taoist mysticism is not a theistic mysticism. The Tao is impersonal. But because of the personalistic associations of the Upaniṣadic conception of the Brahman, and because of the humanistic associations of the idea of the Tao, the Tao and the Brahman appear to be different. For the Taoists, on the whole, life according to the Tao is to be here itself, in the family, state, and society. Even family, state, and society should follow the way (Tao). But in Hinduism or Buddhism, we do not find so much emphasis on life in this world as in Taoism. Naturalism in the wider sense than of physical nature is more pronounced in Taoism than in Hinduism or Buddhism, though all are inherently naturalistic.

[35] Creel, *op. cit.,* p. 106.

The Taoist school took over several elements from the other schools: the orderly sequence of events from the Yin-Yang school, the transcendence by ultimate reality of shapes and features from the school of Names, and some good points from the Confucians and the Mohists. The Han scholars called the doctrines of Lao Tzu and Chuang Tzu by the name Taoism.

The Tao is the Absolute of the Taoists. It is the Way in man. It was made a thing and given metaphysical significance. It is spontaneity itself. It has no purpose and motive. It is both Being and Non-Being; both issue from the Tao. *Te* is the power inherent in a thing and constitutes its nature and law and is derived from the Tao. *Te* constitutes the invariable general principles of the universe. The Tao is imperishable and eternal. It is an undivided unity and, though empty, can be drawn upon endlessly. In fact, everything comes out of the Tao.

If the Tao is of such nature, what should one do in order to live according to it? Do nothing (*wu wei*). The Taoists seem to mean that, in order to live according to the Tao, one has to be naturally spontaneous. To perform an act is to will something, to have a purpose, to accomplish something, and to prevent its opposite. So human activity cannot be entirely spontaneous. If the Tao is spontaneously accomplishing everything, then man has only to identify himself with the Tao and allow it to work through him. He himself should not act (*wu wei*). So by doing nothing the sage accomplishes everything.

The Taoists have another principle based on the principle of the reversal of the Tao. It is the nature of the Tao to jump from one extreme to its opposite. Being becomes Non-Being and Non-Being becomes Being. The sage, therefore, if he wishes to accomplish something, should begin with its opposite.

To live a spontaneous natural life, all artificialities of civilization, everything man-made, should be given up. One should take to primitive life. Feed the belly, and empty the brain: desires have to be reduced to a few. Wisdom has to be banished; for true wisdom is like ignorance.

The Taoists also vied with the other schools in giving advice to the rulers. According to them, the king even has to be a sage. They, too, in the true Chinese spirit, propounded a political philosophy. Political and social institutions produce results diametrically opposite to those intended. The king, therefore, should not try to establish any. He should not try to do anything, but allow nature to take care of all; otherwise, opposite results will be produced through the principle of reversal. The Tao itself will work spontaneously. The king should annul all sources of disorder; so he should annul all laws and traditional virtues of *jen* and *yi*. He should act through nonacting (*wu wei*), rule through nonruling. Thus he can do everything and rule everything. The sage and, therefore, the king should be like a child, ignorant and innocent. For, after all, great knowledge is like ignorance. The ideal society should be like the primitive. It is said that Emperor Wu Ti (*c.* 140 B.C.) of the Han dynasty followed the Taoist precepts and avoided war with the Huns, appeasing them with presents. This policy became a temptation to the Huns, who increased the number of raids on the empire, so much so that the emperor saw the futility of his policy, gave it up, marched against the enemy, carried destruction right into their own territory, and put an end to their raids.[36]

Taoism, in spite of its great laissez faire teachings, was made the basis of totalitarian philosophies in China. The Tao is the Absolute; it is the totality of all that is. The Taoist sage is, again, above all emotions. On the one side, Taoist political philosophy is anarchist, because the ruler rules by not ruling and allowing all his subjects to act according to their nature. On the other, it is totalitarian, because the Tao is one and absolute and works through every person, and every person should allow it to work through him. The Legalists, who preached rigorous application of law, claimed Taoism as their philosophical background.

Chuang Tzu.—Chuang Tzu (*c.* 369–286 B.C.) developed Taoism further. It is said that he refused to become the prime minister of King Wei of Chu, because, if he accepted the offer, he would not be able to follow his inclinations (nature, *Te*). *Tao* and *Te* are substantially the same. *Tao* is universal nature; *Te* is individual nature. *Te* is derived from *Tao*. In this view of *Tao* and *Te,* Lao Tzu and Chuang Tzu are one. One should follow one's *Te* in order to become one with *Tao*. To follow one's *Te* is to be spontaneous; and everyone obtains his *Te* from the *Tao*.

[36] Tsui Chi, *A Short History of Chinese Civilization* (London: Victor Gollancz, 1947), pp. 92 ff.

Happiness is both relative and absolute. If one follows one's *Te,* one attains relative happiness: this is lower understanding.[37] Absolute happiness is possible through higher understanding, which is following *Tao.* The crane may have long legs and may look ugly; but if its legs are cut, it becomes miserable: it is natural for the crane to have long legs. Again, what is natural is internal; so the Tao is internal to man also. But what is not natural and is created by man is external to him. The implication is that the artificialities of civilization are to be given up, and man should live according to his inner nature. Human nature, in its truth, can be discovered only within man, not outside him. The external world must be forgotten, completely effaced. This principle of effacement has three stages: first, the forgetting of each of the worldly things; next of the world as a whole; and then of one's own existence, when one becomes completely one with the Tao, experiences the unity of all things through sudden enlightenment.[38] The idea of sudden enlightenment is stressed by many schools of Chinese philosophy, whether the experience is ethical or mystical.

The sage becomes one with the Tao and immortal. The Tao is not only the principle of the ultimate unitary source of everything, but also knowledge of it. One is reminded of the Upaniṣadic view that knowledge of the Brahman is the Brahman itself. For one who becomes identical with the Tao, his body will be nothing but so much dirt; and death and life will have no more significance than the succession of day and night.[39] Immortality consists in not being lost from the universe, though one dies. This statement sounds like materialistic immortality. But perhaps the Taoists mean more; for nature, with which man becomes one when he becomes one with the Tao, is not materialistic nature, but something within man. The conception is not clear and concrete in Chinese philosophy.

One who has complete understanding of the nature of things will have no emotions. It is not meant that the sage lacks emotions, but that he is not disturbed by them. He has no fear of death and does not experience sorrow when his friends or relatives die.

The highest knowledge is no-knowledge. This means that the highest knowledge is without the distinctions of the "I" and the "Thou," happiness and misery, good and evil. But the Chinese are fond of

[37] Fung Yu-lan, *A Short History of Chinese Philosophy,* p. 104.

[38] Fung Yu-lan, *A History of Chinese Philosophy,* I, 239.

[39] Creel, *op. cit.,* p. 112.

paradoxes and say that true knowledge is no-knowledge and is ignorance. From the highest point of view, there is no evil and everything is good. These distinctions apply only for the finite point of view. In pure experience, in the experience of the Tao, one obtains absolute freedom. "The fast of mind" and "sitting in forgetfulness" are other names for the pure experience. This philosophy obviously cannot be materialistic naturalism, but a kind of humanistic or metahumanistic naturalism. It is at the same time experientialism or idealism; for the ultimate Tao is to be man's experience.

Chuang Tzu believed that everything in the natural world is good; there is nothing in the world that is not good, no point of view that is not right. Here Taoism differs from Buddhism, which says that everything in the world is evil. The Taoists differ from Kung-sun Lung also by saying that everything in the world, including meanings, is relative; the Tao alone is absolute.[40] For Kung-sun Lung the meaning of every word is absolute, for Chuang Tzu it is relative. This view is like Hui Shih's. But Kung-sun Lung also aimed at proving that ultimately everything is one.

Political and social institutions are an evil; they impose suffering on man by preventing him from acting according to his own nature. The best form of government is no government, because it allows everyone to act according to his own nature, and because everything in the world and every point of view is good and right. In political and social philosophy, while Lao Tzu emphasizes the principle that "reversing is the movement of the Tao," Chuang Tzu emphasizes the distinction between what is of nature and what is of man, and advocates the former. On the whole, both hold the same views.

Mencius among the Confucians is a mystic; but the mysticism of the Taoists differs from his. He said that everything is in the mind of man, and man could know everything by knowing his own nature. But man's nature was conceived by Mencius as essentially ethical and good; and besides, it was the ultimate. Man should put forth efforts with vigorous altruism in order to know the *jen* within. But, according to the Taoists, nature in man is beyond ethics. It is transcendental; the Tao is beyond the Te.

Lao Tzu and Chuang Tzu went further than Yang Chu, whose philosophy was rather self-centered. The former two also, in practice,

[40] Fung Yu-lan, *A History of Chinese Philosophy*, I, 230, 232.

may appear self-centered; but self-centeredness went beyond man and reached the Tao, which is universal and transcendent.

Later Mohists.—Like Confucius and Lao Tzu, Mo Tzu had a number of followers, who developed and defended his doctrines and attacked those of the rivals. The rival schools criticized the doctrine of universal love on the ground that (1) infinity is injurious to universality and (2) to kill a robber is to kill a man. If one does not know whom he is to love, how can he love him? If one is to love all men, as the robber also is a man, one has to love him also. The Mohists tried to answer such objections. Even though we do not know which man is to be loved, we know that he is to be included in the totality of men to be loved. And to hate a robber is not to hate humanity; and to wish that there were no robbers on earth is not to wish that there should be no men.[41] Thus the controversies were continued.

The Mohists further developed the hedonism and utilitarianism of Mo Tzu. Utility is valued, they contended, because it brings more pleasure. Intellect is useful, because it can foresee the results of action and evaluate them. Likewise, they explained desire, aversion, righteousness, loyalty, and so forth, in terms of pleasure. Righteousness, for instance, is loving the world for the benefit of the world, and such benefit, being useful, is a pleasure. Similarly, they analyzed action, knowledge, and cause, and attacked reverence for past sages, the idea of *jen,* and the theory of cyclical succession of elements. Action is a combination of will, knowledge of purpose, plan, desire, and movement. Knowing is the ability to know or faculty of knowing, not the actual possession of knowledge. It is like the eye's capacity for seeing objects; this ability for seeing is not the same as actually seeing objects. Causes are of two kinds, the major and the minor. "A minor cause is one with which something may not necessarily be so, but without which it will never be so. For example, a point on a line. A major cause is one with which something will of necessity be so, and without which it will never be so, as in the case of the act of seeing which results in sight." [42] The distinction is between the necessary condition and the sufficient condition.

Of what use is it to refer to ancient sages like Yeo and Shun? They were living in some remote past, when conditions were different. If they were to live and adopt the same methods now, they would be

[41] *Ibid.,* p. 251.
[42] *Ibid.,* p. 258.

incapable of good government. Again, the capacity to love is internal; and the objects of love and benefit are external. Hence, to say that *jen* is internal and *yi* is external is wrong; in both there is something internal and external.

Chinese philosophy accepts five elements: metal, water, earth, fire, and wood. Tsou Yen, a Yin-Yang philosopher, held that there is a cyclic succession of elements, because each element can destroy the others. Fire can reduce metal to liquid, and water can reduce fire to cinders. Wood can scatter water, and water can spoil earth. The Mohists held that the succession need not be cyclical.

These controversies show that the Chinese mind, by the time of these Mohists, was trying to get deeper and deeper into metaphysics, though the philosophical interest was not very systematic.

The Yin-Yang School.—It is the Yin-Yang school that supplied cosmology to Chinese philosophy. Tsou Yen (300 B.C.) was the important philosopher of this school. But the ideas of Yin and Yang seem to be still older and were perhaps derived from the conception of the Mother Goddess and Father God, or concepts akin to them. Yin stands for the female passive principle of the universe and Yang for the male active principle. Whatever be the origin, in later developments they were conceived as impersonal principles, and even thought of as the constituents of the Tao.[43]

The *Yi,* on which this philosophy was originally based, was a book of divination and occult arts, and was the only book not prohibited during the burning of books in 213 B.C. To this school really belongs the doctrine of *Wu Hsing,* or five elements. They are water, fire, wood, metal, and earth (soil). It is curious that wood and metal are regarded as original elements, whereas the Indians have air and ether instead and the Greeks have only four in all, omitting ether, unless we consider Anaximander's Indefinite as ether. The explanation given is that the Chinese were an agricultural people, and for the agriculturist the Chinese five are important. He needs metal for plows, axes, and cutters, and wood for several purposes. Thus man was not only a political animal, but also an agricultural animal. For the Greeks, of course, he was a political and rational animal and in addition a trading animal; and for the Indians, he was a rational and spiritual animal. The five elements combine and produce man and his environment. The elements produce one another in succession. Heaven has

[43] *Ibid.*, p. 384.

four seasons, five elements, nine divisions, and three hundred and sixty days. Man also has four limbs, five viscera, nine orifices, and three hundred and sixty joints.[44] These divisions, of course, do not tally with those of modern knowledge. Life in China was agricultural; and from the agricultural point of view, these divisions worked. Since man was considered to be the microcosmos corresponding to the macrocosmos, he was also supposed to have the same number of divisions. Human life was regarded as the clue for understanding the universe.

There is constant interaction between man and nature. Some of the followers of the school said that wrong conduct of the sovereign infuriated Heaven, which was nature. Others thought that it automatically caused natural calamities like storms, floods, and conflagrations. "The solemnity of the sovereign will be followed by seasonable rain; his regularity, by seasonable sunshine; his intelligence by seasonable heat; his deliberation, by seasonable cold; his wisdom, by seasonable wind."[45] If the ruler has opposite characters, opposite results will follow.

Tsou Yen had a philosophy of history also based on the five elements. At the time of the Yellow Emperor, soil was ascendant, and he took yellow as his color. At the time of Yu (Hsia dynasty), wood was in the ascendancy, and he adopted green as his color. When Tang (Shang dynasty) became emperor, metal was in the ascendancy, and the color of his reign was white. At the time of Wen (Chou dynasty), fire was ascendant, and red was his color. Water would follow next, and its color would be black. When the cycle is complete, soil will again come up. It is said that some emperors tried to follow this theory in choosing their colors, and controversies raged, particularly when the nature of the dynastic succession was in question. For instance, when the Han dynasty came to power after destroying the Ch'in, which was short-lived, it was doubted whether the Han succeeded the Ch'in or the Chou. Hence, disputes arose about the color of the Han.[46]

An interesting doctrine of the school is the mixing up of the elements with numbers in deriving the world. There seems to be some kind of Pythagorean insight in this doctrine. But China developed very little of mathematics. Again, certain trigrams were drawn to represent

[44] *Ibid.*, p. 399.
[45] Fung Yu-lan, *A Short History of Chinese Philosophy*, p. 132.
[46] *Ibid.*, pp. 136–38.

what may have been the basic objects like Heaven, earth, thunder, wood, wind, water, fire, the sun, mountain, and marsh. They were again combined into certain hexagrams.[47] These were used for some divinations, and are not of much scientific and philosophical interest. They show only that there was an attempt to explain the cosmos in terms of certain basic elements, and that cosmological interest was present in Chinese thought. Moreover, for this school also, man is the center of the universe and is the clue to its understanding.

Hsün Tzu.—Hsün Tzu (*c.* 298–238 B.C.) was a follower of Confucius, but belonged to the wing opposite to that of Mencius.[48] While Mencius advocated individual freedom on the one hand and supersocial values on the other, Hsün Tzu stressed social control on the one hand and preached a realistic naturalism on the other. The ethical mysticism of Mencius is absent in Hsün Tzu. It is said that, if Confucius is the Socrates of China, then Mencius will be its Plato and Hsün Tzu its Aristotle. As in Aristotle, there is more of realism and less of idealism in Hsün Tzu.

While Mencius maintained that human nature by itself is good, Hsün Tzu said that by itself it is evil. Hsün Tzu's argument may be summarized thus: (1) The customs of peoples in different parts of the world differ; so men are not born with a single pattern of good conduct; (2) every man is born with love of gain; (3) from birth he shows envy and hatred of others; (4) he is born with desires of the eye and the ear, and is sensuous; if he is allowed to follow his inborn inclinations without restraint, every man will be at every other man's throat and there will be disorder in society. Hence education and social control are absolutely necessary. Goodness is acquired only by training. It is possible for every man to become good. So Hsün Tzu emphasizes the importance of *li,* which is understood by him mainly in the sense of rules of conduct. The function of *li* is to regulate conduct for the satisfaction of man's desires. In the sense of ceremonies and rituals, the *li* produce refinement and purification of emotions. Hsün Tzu does not preach the repression and suppression of emotions, but their refinement and purification. Social organization is important for men and differentiates them from animals. The latter do not have standards of justice and social respect as between son and father,

[47] *Ibid.*, pp. 141–42.

[48] H. H. Dubs produced two important books, *Hsün Tze* and *Hsün Tze: Works* (London: A. Probsthain, 1927 and 1928).

subject and king. Social organization is needed, first, for better living and, second, for conquering other nations. Social institutions embodying ethical principles preserve peoples. Hsün Tzu's is a utilitarian conception of state and society. Men by nature are evil; but they know that it is good to have social institutions. To prevent the strong from oppressing the weak, the superior, or sage-king, is necessary. Hsün Tzu accepts the principle of "agreement with the superior." The sage-king must have absolute power. He alone is the true king. Hsün Tzu prefers the government of the king (*wang*) to that of the war-lord (*pa*).

Heaven for Hsün Tzu is mainly naturalistic. On this point he was greatly influenced by Chuang Tzu. For Confucius, it was mainly a ruling power, somewhat personal. For Mencius, it was slightly personal and at times fatalistic, and at times ethical. For Hsün Tzu, "Heaven is a constant regularity of activity. It did not exist for the sake of Yao nor cease to exist for the sake of Chieh. Respond to it with good government, and success will result. Respond to it with misgovernment, and calamity will result. . . . Hence to understand the distinction between Heaven and man: this is to be a great man." [49]

As all men are born equally evil, all need strict training and education. Even the earliest sages needed a teacher. So the teacher is above all the rest. As a naturalist, Hsün Tzu was opposed to superstitious practices. Sacrifices do not bring rain. The times in the past and in the present are the same: all depends on what we do. The Golden Age does not belong to some remote past. Unlike Confucius, and even Mencius, Hsün Tzu refers to rulers of the recent past and not to those of remote periods, because the circumstances of later times are more akin to ours than those of the earlier.

"Names," says Hsün Tzu, "were made in order to denote actualities, on the one hand so as to make evident the distinction between the superior and the inferior [in society], and on the other hand to distinguish similarities and differences." [50] The true king must not only adopt ancient names but also coin new ones. Such coining of new names and fixing their meanings is the duty of the ruler and his government. We can appreciate this advice only when we remember that things mean for the Chinese philosophers mainly social relationships. Otherwise, this function should be left to the scientists and scholars. When the social relationships are fixed and are named and enforced,

[49] Fung Yu-lan, *A History of Chinese Philosophy,* I, 284, 285.
[50] Fung Yu-lan, *A Short History of Chinese Philosophy,* p. 151.

they will stabilize society and unify people. Hsün Tzu wants the task of analyzing names and their meanings to be left to the king and the government, and taken away from unauthorized sophists, who make right wrong and wrong right through verbal jugglery. All the fallacies of the schools were due to the fact that no sage-kings existed, who could curb the activities of verbal jugglers, stop litigation, and unify the minds of the people by fixing the meanings of words or names connoting social relationships.

Hsün Tzu was neither a complete totalitarian nor a legalist, but a disciplinarian. He admired the ideals later adopted by the Ch'in emperors for this reason. But his two disciples, Li Ssu and Han Fei Tzu, were associated with the hated Ch'in dynasty; and so Hsün Tzu too was held in low esteem by the Confucian democratic circles. Certainly his doctrine that human nature is essentially evil and that all men are born equally evil could not have endeared him to the people.

Han Fei Tzu.—Han Fei Tzu (died 233 B.C.) is the most important of the legalists. He and Li Ssu were students of Hsün Tzu. Li Ssu, who was an official under the Ch'in dynasty, grew jealous of his fellow student and contrived to get him into prison, where he died. Yet Li Ssu considered himself not an equal of Han Fei Tzu.

Most of the legalists came from the ruling class. The problem before them was whether to rule by law or rule by nature. As experienced rulers, they realized that law was more important than nature. They wanted to counteract the influence of the prevailing theories that government exists for the people and not for the rulers. Hsün Tzu's ideas formed the link between Confucianism and legalism. Although Hsün Tzu was opposed to legalism, his doctrine that human nature is essentially evil and requires an authority to make it good was very convenient for the legalists to adopt. Han Fei Tzu blamed scholars as useless, who did not till the soil or do any other useful work, and yet became wealthy and received honors from the rulers. The practice not only ruined the economy of the state but also degraded rulers to a lower class than that of the scholars, though the latter were of plebeian birth. In the state of an intelligent sovereign there should be no books except laws.

Mo Tzu and even the Confucians decried war; but Han Fei Tzu glorified it. The Confucians said that the state should be controlled by virtue; but the legalists maintained that the idea was foolish. A country can be conquered only by arms. For this purpose, one's own state must be made rich and strictly disciplined, and all its people must be trained as soldiers.

Before Han Fei Tzu, Shen Tao, a legalist who was a contemporary of Mencius, held that *shih* (power, authority) is the principle of government; Shen Pu-hai (died 337 B.C.) maintained that it is *fa* (law over regulation); and Shang Yang (also called Lord Shang, died 338 B.C.) thought that it is *shu* (the method of conducting affairs and handling men). Han Fei Tzu said that all the three are necessary.

The legalists also had their chain of conditioned causes and effects. Like the Buddhist *pratītyasamutpāda* (chain of causation), which explained the process of bondage and final deliverance from it, the Confucianists had theirs, which explained how to exemplify illustrious virtue, and the legalists theirs, which explained how to manifest the Tao. They took Taoism as their philosophical background, adopting whatever was useful and rejecting whatever did not agree with their own theories. Fung quotes this summary:

> Those of old who made manifest the great *Tao,* first made manifest Heaven, and *Tao* and *Te* came next. *Tao* and *Te* being manifested, the virtues of human-heartedness and righteousness came next. These being manifested, the division of offices came next. These being manifested, actualities and names came next. These being manifested, employment without interference came next. This being manifested, examinations and discriminations came next. These being manifested, judgement of right and wrong came next. This being manifested, rewards and punishments came next. With the manifestation of rewards and punishments, the foolish and the wise assumed their proper positions, the noble and the humble occupied their proper places, and the virtuous and the worthless were employed according to their nature. . . . This is perfect peace, the acme of good government.[51]

Han Fei Tzu did not accept the Confucian contention that the *li* are universally applicable to every man. The *li* are the unwritten code of honor, etiquette, ceremonies, and ritual, which belong only to *chun tzu* (sons of princes); whereas *hsing,* which consists of rewards and punishments, governs the conduct of *shu jen* (common men) and of *hsiao jen* (small men). The *li* does not go down to the common people, and the *hsing* does not go up to the ministers.

[51] *Ibid.,* pp. 163–64.

The legalists did not deny the existence of ancient ideal emperors, but were opposed to taking them as examples for the present. Confucius often referred to King Wen and the Duke of Chou; Mo Tzu to Yu; Mencius to Yao and Shun; and the Taoists to still earlier kings, Fu Hsi and Shen Nung. But they all lived in primitive times. They lived in thatched huts, used skins and coarse cloth as dress, and tilled the land. So when they selected a new emperor who was not their descendant, but a common man, they passed on to him nothing of value except that of a gatekeeper's duty. Hence succession by heredity was not highly regarded. But now even an ordinary official is richer than any of those emperors, and does not like to give up his small post. Times have changed, and we cannot ignore heredity as a principle of succession.

It is a folly to think that the ruler is like a father and has affection for his people. He rules by rewards and punishments, not by *li* and virtue. Confucius particularly emphasized government by men; human nature should rule human nature in accordance with its own precepts; human-heartedness is primary. But the legalists emphasized law; human nature by itself is selfish and evil. Law is not meant for the protection of the common man from the stronger or against the exactions of the ruler, but for the benefit of the ruler in controlling men. Like the Taoists, the legalists hold that the ruler should rule by nonruling (*wu wei*) ; but they meant only that the ruler governs only through his ministers and subordinate officials, not directly. In political matters, there can be no reliance on gratitude or loyalty; for men are born selfish, and force alone can keep masses in subjection. Education does not necessarily make men virtuous. In economics Han Fei Tzu advocated free competition; for men act only in self-interest, and so free competition increases the prosperity of the state. The Confucian program of equal division of land is inadmissible. The legalists maintained that the ruler should make the actual individuals holding government offices correspond in their activities to the "names" or titles of the offices they held.

Han Fei Tzu was not only an authoritarian but also a totalitarian. Though held responsible for his misfortune, Li Ssu put his doctrines into practice, and advised his emperor, Ch'in Shih Huang-ti, to destroy all books and be rid of scholars. The Ch'in Empire was the strongest and gave its name to China; but its strength was achieved by oppressive totalitarian methods and a thoroughgoing rigorous discipline, which people could not stand. The dynasty could not therefore last for longer than half a century and was quickly succeeded by the Han dynasty. Tsui Chi writes: "The Han dynasty which followed was one of the brilliant periods in Chinese history, and one which left an imperishable mark upon her institutions. It foreshadowed so many of the permanent elements in Chinese life that the Chinese sometimes call themselves 'Sons of Han.'"[52] With the rise of the Han, the books of scholars, which went underground when the order for the burning was given, reappeared, but in a somewhat distorted form. And with the books came Confucianism and Taoism. But in this revival, they became confused with each other and with the books of the Yin-Yang.

Han Philosophies

From the fall of the Ch'in (3rd century B.C.) to the introduction of Buddhism (1st century A.D.), the philosophies of China show peculiar uneasiness, irresolution, uncertainty, and eclecticism. Taoism seems to be strong, but was mixed up with Confucianism and the Yin-Yang. The Tao is mentioned often by every philosophy, but there is an attempt to weave the Yin-Yang concepts into it. The greatest name of the time was that of Tung Chung-shu (179–104 B.C.). Eclecticism must have been due—after the burning of the books—to the loss of constant touch with, and discussion of, the concepts of Confucius and Lao Tzu. The ideas that were revived got mixed up with the Yin-Yang concepts, for the Yin-Yang books were not prohibited by the order, which made an exception. And when the books of Taoism and Confucianism were brought out, scholars may not have been able to distinguish very clearly the Taoist from the Confucian.

The most important metaphysical idea in the "Appendices" of the *Book of Changes* (*Yi Ching*) is that of the Tao; but this Tao is different from that of the Taoists. It is nameable. It is a plurality, not a unity. There are many *taos,* one for the sovereign, one for the minister,

[52] *Op. cit.,* p. 79.

one for father, one for son, and so on; each *tao* is what each individual ought to be. As each has a name, there is to be a rectification of names also. The Yin and the Yang together constitute the Tao. Everything is a Yin and a Yang. For instance, a man is a Yin with reference to his father and a Yang with reference to his son. And there seem to be two kinds of Tao, the Tao that is universal and the *tao* that belongs to each individual.

In spite of Tao's eternal perfection, each individual thing undergoes transformation. If this transformation is to reach perfection, and perfection is to be stable, then its operation is to take place in the right way, at the right time, and in the right place. The right way is to follow *chung* (the mean) and *ho* (harmony). *Ho* is *chung* suffused with emotion, and is the high way of the world.

In perfecting oneself, one should see that others also are perfected; for perfection is possible only in human relationships. For this purpose, one should follow the trinity of *chung* (the mean), *shu* (altruism), and *jen* (human-heartedness). Such are the Confucian ethics and metaphysics mixed up with elements of the Yin-Yang.

Though people did not want the totalitarianism of the Ch'in, they wanted China to be unified and under one emperor, so that wars between the states would disappear and peace could reign. Mencius said that there could be peace only if there was unity. For this purpose the Confucians developed the doctrines of the three cords and the eight wires. The three cords are (1) to manifest one's illustrious virtue, (2) to love the people, and (3) to rest in the highest good. The eight wires are what I called the eight links of the Confucian causal chain. According to later Confucianists, the three cords are one and the eight wires also are one.

Even Hsün Tzu was a kind of eclectic, though a Confucian. He wanted to blend the Confucian Tao with the Taoist Tao. Ssu-ma T'an, a Taoist, maintained that there were several paths to the Tao, though it was one. Liu Hsun, a Confucianist, said that the goal for all was the same, though the standpoints of the philosophies were different.

> All these statements reflect the strong desire for unity in the world of thought. The people of the third century B.C., discouraged by centuries of inter-state warfare, longed for a political unification; their philosophics, consequently, also tried to bring about a

unification in thought. Eclecticism was the first attempt. Eclecticism in itself, however, cannot build a unified system. The eclectics believed in the whole truth, and hoped, by selecting from the various schools their strong points, to attain to this Truth or Tao. What they called the Tao, however, was, it is to be feared, simply a patchwork of many disparate elements, unconnected by any underlying organic principle, and hence unworthy of the high title they attached to it.[53]

Tung Chung-shu was mainly responsible for making Confucianism the orthodox belief of the Han emperors, and he worked for laying an institutional basis for Confucian orthodoxy. The Chinese system of examinations, which elevated the commoner to high status and position, originated during his time.

T'ien meant for Tung Heaven and Nature indifferently, as it did for most of the Chinese. Tung took over the idea of the correlation between man and Heaven, and combined it with Confucian political and social philosophy. Man is a part of Heaven, and so the justification of his conduct must be found in the behavior of Heaven. The universe has ten constituents: Heaven; earth; the Yin and the Yang; the five elements, wood, fire, soil, metal, and water; and finally man. The Yin and the Yang are invisible ethereal principles. The four elements (excluding soil) preside over the four seasons and the four directions, and soil presides over the center. Man is the replica of Heaven and, accordingly, superior to all other creatures. Heaven gives all things their birth, earth their nourishment, and man their perfection. Man perfects everything through *li* (ritual) and *yüeh* (music). That is, man contributes culture and civilization to the order of nature; and so without man, the world cannot be complete and perfect. Hence the importance of man and the Chinese love of everything human. Heaven contains the Yin and the Yang. The Yang constitutes *hsing* (man's nature); and the Yin constitutes *ch'ing* (emotions and feelings). The implication is that Heaven is realized when *hsing* and *ch'ing* are combined.

The five major relationships are those of (1) sovereign and subject, (2) father and son, (3) husband and wife, (4) older and younger brother, and (5) friend and friend. The first three are called

[53] *Ibid.*, p. 187.

kang (major cord). The five constant virtues (*ch'ang*) are *jen, yi, li, chih* (wisdom), and *hsin* (good faith). The *kang* are the ethics of society, and the *ch'ang* are the virtues of the individual.

Men should aim at ethical perfection, which contains the essentials of culture and civilization. But all cannot attain the ideal by themselves. Indeed, all have the basic stuff of goodness, but by themselves cannot be good. For making them good Heaven gave them the king.

Tung's desire to relate Heaven and man led him to introduce many fanciful correlations between the two. The four seasons of Heaven correspond to the four ways of government—beneficence, rewards, punishments, and executions—and to the four grades of the Chinese official hierarchy of the time. And because of the correlation, Heaven is displeased and angry whenever something is wrong in the human government.

Political history repeats itself in cycles, not according to the four elements as Tsou Yen said, but according to three colors, black, white, and red. The Hsia dynasty (2205–1766 B.C.) represented the Black Reign; the Shang dynasty (1766–1122 B.C.) the White Reign; and the Chou dynasty (1122–255 B.C.) the Red Reign. The ruler exercises power through the Mandate from Heaven; and whenever a new dynasty starts, in order to show that it received a fresh Mandate, it changes its color, its capital, and so forth.

Tung believed that Confucius received the Mandate to succeed the Chou dynasty, and that he was king *de jure,* though not *de facto.* According to Ho Hsiu (129–182 A.D.), who discoursed on a commentary on *Ch'un Ch'iu* (*Spring and Autumn Annals*), there are three ages of social progress: (1) the Age of Decay and Disorder, of which Confucius heard through transmitted records, (2) the Age of Approaching Peace, of which Confucius heard through testimony, that is, the age in which Confucius brought peace to the Middle Kingdom through his own efforts, and (3) the Age of Universal Peace, the age which Confucius personally witnessed, and in which the whole world was unified and was in peace. Of course for Ho, the world meant the whole of China. All this was a wish, a hope, a dream of the Chinese of the time.

Tung is the greatest exponent of what is called the New Text School, which continued the idealistic wing of the Confucian tradition started by Mencius. Opposed to it is the Old Text School, which traced itself to Hsün Tzu, who was realistic.[54] The Old Text School took a naturalistic attitude to the universe like Hsün Tzu and the Taoists and paved the way for the revival of Taoism. Wang Ch'ung (*c.* 27–100 A.D.) is the greatest philosopher of the Old Text School. He was a realist and an iconoclast. He argued against superstition and, as a pure naturalist, against all interrelationship, theological or mechanical, between man and the universe. For instance, it was believed that the king's anger produced cold and his joy warmth. But cold and warmth are not responses to acts of government; for the Way of Heaven, by which Wang meant nature, is spontaneous. "Man holds a place in the universe like that of a flea or louse under a jacket or robe. . . . Can the flea or louse, by conducting themselves either properly or improperly, affect the changes or movements in the ether under the jacket?" [55] Wang was not in favor of referring to the past and the ancient sages. The present is better than the past. People like to exalt and idealize antiquity. Regarding human nature, Wang tried to reconcile Mencius and Hsün Tzu.[56] The former, in holding that human nature is essentially good, had in mind men above the average; and the latter, in saying that human nature is essentially evil, had in mind men below the average. Even evildoers can be made moral by ethical training. Wang believed in Fate. It is because of Fate that good and bad conduct do not necessarily result in happiness and misery.

For about seventeen centuries the New Text School suffered an

[54] When Prince Kung of Lu (2nd century B.C.) was dismantling the ancestral house of the descendants of Confucius, he found in the walls hidden tablets on *The Classic of History, The Spring and Autumn Annals, The Analects,* and *The Classic of Filial Piety,* written in the archaic characters of the time of Confucius. The prince sent them to K'ung An-Kao, who rewrote them in the Han script and presented them to Emperor Wu. These texts, considered to be more authentic, formed the basis of the Old Text School. The New Text School, which is Confucianism as revived by the Han dynasty, incorporated into itself many ideas of the Yin-Yang School that the Old Text School rejected. The New Text School regarded Confucius as an unthroned King and Saviour of the world, whereas the Old Text School regarded him as only a sage-scholar. Yang Hsi'ung (58 B.C.–18 A.D.), who belonged to the latter school, further thought that man is neither essentially good, as Mencius taught, nor essentially evil, as Hsün Tzu taught, but a mixture of both. Liu Wu-Chi, *A Short History of Confucian Philosophy* (Baltimore: The Penguin Books Inc., 1955), pp. 128–31.

[55] Fung Yu-lan, *A Short History of Chinese Philosophy,* pp. 210–17.

[56] Fung Yu-lan, *A History of Chinese Philosophy,* II, 158–59, 162.

eclipse and rose again during the time of the Ch'ing dynasty (1644–1911), which came from Manchuria.

The Revival of Taoism

Li Ssu as Prime Minister advised the Ch'in Emperor, Ch'in Shih Huang-ti, to destroy all books of scholars who, through their private teachings, discredited laws and institutions; and the burning of books was ordered. Li Ssu was a legalist, and along with the Ch'in dynasty, the legalists went down. On the recommendation of Tung Chung-shu, Confucianism was revived, and *Liu Yi,* the six classics of the school, were selected by the Han Emperor, Wu (146–87 B.C.), for official state teaching. In fact, Taoism also was revived by the Han. Legalism was opposed to Taoism, in that the former preached rigorous control by law and institutions and the latter taught life according to one's own nature. When the laws of the Ch'in, except some of the criminal laws, were abolished, the Han also had to have some laws and institutions in a concrete form, which Taoism could not supply, but Confucianism did.

From the end of the Han dynasty in 220 A.D. to 589 A.D., when the Sui dynasty succeeded in reunifying China, there was a period of disunity and constant wars among the Six Dynasties which split up the country. It was during this period of confusion and misery that Buddhism made great progress and offered a peculiar escapist appeal to the Chinese, but Taoism also had a similar appeal and was, therefore, revived. It is sometimes called Neo-Taoism. Neo-Taoism was also called the Dark Learning (*hsüan hsüeh*), because the Tao which it preached was the mystery of all mysteries (*hsüan* of the *hsüan*). The revived Taoism or Neo-Taoism was divided into two subschools, the Rationalists and the Sentimentalists. For both, life has to be lived according to internal nature; but according to the former, this internal nature is reason, and according to the latter, it is a kind of impulse.[57] The rationalists were interested in the discussion about names

[57] Fung Yu-lan, *A Short History of Chinese Philosophy,* p. 233.

and their meanings and connected their *hsüan hsüeh* with the *ming-li* (terms and principles). Their implications seems to be that just as *chih* (universal) cannot reach the thing, the Tao cannot reach the world. If it does, it cannot be above the world.

Peculiarly enough, the Neo-Taoists regarded Confucius as the greatest sage. He was greater than Lao Tzu.[58] For Confucius (1) forgot that he forgot, (2) had no desire to be without desire, and (3) did not speak of *wu* (nonbeing), as he identified himself with it, while Lao Tzu only spoke of *Wu*. Hsiang Hsiu (221–300) and Kuo Hsiang (died 312) were the important philosophers of the rationalist wing, and in their teachings Taoism became more pronouncedly naturalistic. The Tao is to be found everywhere, and it is *Wu*. Everything causes itself, and nothing is produced by another. It is spontaneous. If at all, it is produced by the general state of the universe. In a sense, we may say that the universe as a whole is the cause of everything, including social phenomena. And everything is in constant flux; flux is the nature of the world. To allow things to follow their nature is to allow them to undergo change; and to do so is *wu-wei* (nonaction), and to do the opposite is *yu-wei* (action). With the change of time, therefore, it is natural for political and social institutions and for morals to change. One should not, therefore, imitate ancient sages; for they belong to times when things were different.

Here we have a new interpretation of *wu-wei*. *Wu-wei* now means allowing one's abilities free exercise; and *yu-wei* means forcing them into artificial channels. Knowledge is condemned by this school. For it is imitation. Knowledge is activity which tries to achieve what is beyond one's nature; it is, therefore, imitation of something which is not oneself. We should not confuse this imitation with the imitation of which Plato speaks, when he explains perceptual knowledge. Plato's interest is epistemological, while the Taoist interest is in human action.

All things in the world, good and evil, right and wrong, are equal from a higher point of view, by reaching which man attains freedom and happiness. The independent man "chariots on the normality of the universe, rides upon the transformation of the six elements, and makes excursion into the infinite." [59]

The sentimentalists also emphasize living according to one's nature,

[58] *Ibid.*, p. 218.

[59] Quoted from *Chuang Tzu* in *ibid.*, p. 229.

and not according to another's nature; but this nature is impulse, not reason. Rank, riches, reputation, and so forth, are artificialities, which bring no peace. This school does not seem to have very great names. It is highly sentimental in allowing every natural impulse (*feng liu*) to work itself out. It is not sentimental about particular pleasures and gains, but about the general nature of things. For instance, Chih-tun (314–66), a Buddhist monk, was fond of cranes, and clipped the wings of two young ones presented to him. Later, he realized that it was the nature of cranes to fly, and so, when the feathers grew again, he let the cranes off. As regards the following of one's impulse, it is said that Wang Hui-chih (died *c.* 388) went all the way in a boat to see a friend but, when he reached the latter's house, he turned and went home without seeing the friend, saying that the impulse to see the friend ended at that moment.[60]

Though these philosophers were sentimental and not opposed to having emotions, they preached that emotions should be calmed by reason. None should allow himself to be exalted or depressed. These Taoists were highly sentimental about the beauty of women; but their sentiments were aesthetic rather than sensuous. Of course, this teaching could easily deteriorate into winebibbing and momentary impulsive pleasure-seeking.

Buddhism

We have already indicated that some practices of the Buddhists—like refraining from clipping the wings of cranes—were being referred to with appreciation by the Taoists. As a philosophy, Taoism has much in common with Buddhism; but as religions, they were opposed in China. Buddhism entered China by about the first century A.D. via Central Asia. In 121 B.C., a general of the Emperor Wu Ti of the Han dynasty came upon a huge ten-foot-high golden image worshiped in Turkestan and took it to his sovereign as booty. Wu worshiped it. In 65 A.D., Emperor Ming Ti dreamt of a golden man,

[60] *Ibid.*, pp. 235–36.

who was identified by his ministers with Buddha. The Han was followed by the Epoch of Three Kingdoms (220–80), that by the Ch'in (265–420), and that by the Period of the Six Dynasties (420–589).

The first and the third particularly were periods of disunity, wars, and uncertainty, during which Buddhism made great strides. During the first period itself, it became an authorized religion. Emperor Fei of the Kingdom of Wei (one of the three kingdoms) was visited by a Buddhist monk, bringing Chinese translations of Buddhist law; and by the Emperor's edict all the Chinese monks were ordered to conform to it. During the period of the Six Dynasties, the doctrine of the Pure Land developed and promised happiness in another world to the misery-stricken people. The importance of happiness on earth and in this body was diminished. Kuan Yin, the Goddess of Mercy, became the object of popular worship. Buddhism suffered great persecution through the jealousy of the Taoists and the Confucians. It was, after all, a foreign religion. Under the influence of a Taoist minister, Emperor Tai Wu (424–51) of the Wei dynasty (North China) ordered all gods of the foreign land to be wiped out, all their texts to be burnt, and all men who dared to follow them to be put to death with their families.[61] But the popularity of Buddhism can be estimated by the fact that, when the order was revoked, every third house in the capital of Loyang was turned into a Buddhist temple.[62] We read also of the political and military advantage taken of the emperors conforming to the religion of compassion during the dynastic rivalries. Emperor Wu (502–49) of Liang (South China) was a great Buddhist devotee who did not touch meat or garlic, did not hang criminals, and prohibited the embroidering of human figures and life on silks and brocades. Naturally, he could not conscientiously make military preparations. A general of a northern emperor suggested to his sovereign that he kidnap Wu, make him an abbot of the Buddhist Temple of Peace, and annex Liang. The general attacked Liang, feigned surrender, and, when pardoned by the merciful Wu, took over the capital by surprise and carried away Wu, who died brokenhearted in captivity before being canonized.

[61] Tsui Chi, *op. cit.*, p. 115.

[62] Another persecution in 845 was by Emperor Wu Tsung of the Tang dynasty, under whom 40,000 Buddhist temples were demolished, 260,000 monks and nuns were secularized, their slaves set free and lands confiscated. See Creel, *Chinese Thought,* p. 206.

All this shows the great and profound influence Buddhism had over Chinese life and politics. Confucianism was not very sublime; Taoism was not very logical; and Buddhism, being both sublime and logical, became a complement of both. Besides, neither Confucianism nor Taoism was originally and primarily a religion as such; but Buddhism was a highly developed religion and catered to the religious needs of the Chinese. In addition, Buddhism was not a revealed religion, but a religion based on a philosophy of human nature; and the Chinese, being naturalistic by temperament, could find in Buddhism something not completely alien to their ways of thought. China assimilated Buddhism most readily through its Taoist concepts. It was easy to equate the Tao with Tathatā, understanding both as nature and way. And nature meant for the Chinese the essence of human nature. This method of assimilation and translation was called *ko yi* in Chinese, which is interpretation by analogy. Tathatā would be interpreted as the Tao, Nirvāṇa (nonmovement) as *wu wei* (nonaction). The Buddhist middle path (*mādhyamika*) would be the golden mean of Confucius. Mou Tzu (*c.* 200), a Confucian, called the Confucian classics the flowers and Buddhism their fruit.[63] And there was a tradition in China, according to which Buddha was a disciple of Lao Tzu, the implication being that Buddhism was not really foreign to China, but that it was a foreign variant of Taoism.

Thus Buddhism in China became different from that of India, though the texts were the same. It was assimilated by China through the characteristic Chinese mind with its pragmatic humanism and immediatism. Similarly, Japanese Buddhism also is not exactly the same as the Indian. Buddhism had been born in India when the Aryans were at the zenith of their power and Aryanism meant for the Indians a life of peace, compassion, and nobility. This ideal of life was indeed taken over by China, but at a time when the country was disunited and life was precarious, because it offered her, in more decisive terms than Taoism, a justification for escape from turmoil and worldly misery. Fung distinguishes between Chinese Buddhism and Buddhism in China. Whereas the former generally became indigenous Chinese thought and developed in conjunction with it, there were a few groups which maintained the philosophical tradition of India as mostly a scholastic system. Hsüang Tsang, after his return from his

[63] *Ibid.*, p. 203.

pilgrimage to India, belonged to such a group, but such Indian Buddhism in China proved to be of short duration.

Besides the Chinese scholars and thinkers, two great Indian Buddhists contributed much to Buddhism. They are Kumārajīva (344–413), an Indian born in Turkestan, and Bodhidharma (486–536), who was a South Indian. Kumārajīva does not seem to have founded a distinct school; but Ch'an Buddhism (Japanese Zen) is attributed to Bodhidharma. The great Chinese names associated with Buddhism are those of Mou Tzu (170–225) and Seng-chao (5th century), neither of whom founded particular schools; Hui-yüan (5th century), who founded the Pure Land School; Tao-sheng (5th century), who belonged to the Dhyāna (Ch'an) School; Chi-k'ai (born 531), who founded the T'ien-t'ai School; Hsüan-tsang (596–664), from whom the Yogacāra (Vijñānavāda) and the Kiu-she (Kośa) Schools originated; and Tao-hsüan (5th century), who started the Lü (Vinaya) School. Vajrabodhi and his disciple Amoghavajra (8th century) were Indians who introduced Vajrayāna or *tantric* Buddhism, called in China Chen-yen (True-Word) School.

It is not necessary to present here the basic ideas of Buddhism, since that is done in the section on Indian philosophy. But the important deviations and transformations that Buddhism underwent in China may be noted. The Taoist doctrine of *wu wei* was identified with the Nirvāṇa of the Buddhists; Buddha was called a disciple of Lao Tzu; and a certain *bodhisattva* (one who has not yet attained, but is about to attain Buddhahood) was reported to be an incarnation of Confucius. It is also said that at one time there was a Buddhist temple to Confucius.[64] Besides, Mencius' doctrine that everything is within mind accords well with the Buddhist doctrine that every object is *vijñāna,* mind only.

Thus, when assimilating Buddhism, the Chinese made it a system built up of Taoist and Confucian elements. The Chinese did not have ideas of rebirth, and the doctrine was foreign to them. Yet they gave special emphasis to the Buddhist idea that Nirvāṇa is the world and the world is Nirvāṇa. And if Nirvāṇa is the Tao, then it is the essential nature of the universe, according to which man has to live, but not give up life. The techniques of meditation can be used, not to attain Buddhahood necessarily, but sageliness. The sage need not give up the world and become a monk, but could participate in the family and

[64] *Ibid.,* p. 210.

government. The nature of the mysterious Tao could be realized in chopping wood and drawing water, that is, the performance of the usual and normal duties; and if Nirvāṇa is the world, then to follow Nirvāṇa is to follow the universal principles of the world without effort and with absolute spontaneity.

That is how the Chinese mind, with its Taoist and Confucian background, reacted to Buddhism. In fact, some of the Confucians went further: If the mysterious Tao can be found in chopping wood and drawing water, why should it not be found also in taking part in social and political activity? The Neo-Confucians of the Ching era raised even this question. After all, man is a social and political animal; it is natural for him to lead a social and political life; therefore, it will be according to nature, the Tao, Nirvāṇa, to lead such a life. It is not meant that there were no Buddhist monks in China; there were thousands of them. But the Chinese reaction, in general, was to humanize, naturalize, and socialize Buddhism.

Mou Tzu was a Confucian, but did much to propagate Buddhism. Seng-chao was a disciple of Kumārajīva and advocated the doctrine of the immutability of things. All things are immutable, because nothing exists continuously for two distinct moments, and, since being is momentary, there can be no change. He further propounded that *prajña* (highest knowledge) is no-knowledge, because it is objectless. It is like a mirror, which, though vacant, reflects everything. It is the Tao. And like Nāgārjuna, he proved that all things are neither existent, nor nonexistent, but empty (*śūnya*). Mou Tzu and Seng-chao did not follow any particular school of Buddhism. On the whole, it was Mahāyāna, and particularly those schools of Mahāyāna which are more positive than negative in their attitude to the world, that attracted the Chinese. The Hīnayāna and the negative forms of the Mahāyāna were not popular. The Tathatā school was naturally more acceptable than the rest.

It is difficult to differentiate the Chinese schools of Buddhism from each other. They did not differ uniformly in doctrine. They got their names sometimes from the texts followed, sometimes from the doctrines, and other times merely from the localities where the schools were founded. Fung says that, according to the Chinese tradition, there were at first "Six Houses" and "Seven Schools" of Buddhism. But the information about them is obscure. The Six Houses seem to be split up into the Seven Schools.

> The first . . . is the School of Original Non-being, the second is the variant School of Original Non-being, the third is the School of Matter as such, the fourth is the School of Non-being of Mind, the fifth is the School of Stored Impressions, the sixth is the School of Phenomenal Illusion, and the seventh is the School of Causal Combination. What are now called the six houses consist of these seven schools, minus the Variant School of Original Non-being.[65]

Taking these schools, we may say that *śūnyatā* (voidness) was understood as Non-Being by the first and the second. The third, a Hīnayāna school, must have thought that Nirvāṇa lies in analyzing away the material aggregates composing the *pudgala* (human personality). The fourth must be the opposite of Vijñānavāda, which held that ultimate reality is mind only. But this school must have maintained that it is the nonbeing of mind. The fifth preached the Ālayavijñāna doctrine, that there is a storehouse of consciousness out of which everything issues. The sixth must have taught that the world is Māyā. The seventh must have made the doctrine of the causal chain as its basis. This shows that each school took some aspect of Buddhism as the most important.

Chinese Buddhism was later divided into ten schools. In any case, the more permanent, important schools were these: (1) *Ch'eng-shih,* or True Success School, was based on *Satyasiddhiśāstra* of Harivarman, who belonged to the transition period from Hīnayāna to Mahāyāna, and was a mixture of Sautrāntika and Mādhyamika. (2) *San-lun,* or Three Śāstra School, was Mādhyamika and was based upon three works, two of Nāgārjuna and one of Āryadeva. These two schools are not popular in China. (3) *Ch'an,* or Meditation School (Zen in Japan), was first propagated by Tao-sheng and then by Bodhidharma. Tao-sheng is supposed to have taught that even those who were opposed to Buddhism could attain Buddhahood. According to this school, reasoning and scriptures are not necessary for enlightenment; one must meditate on *śūnyatā* (emptiness) and sudden enlightenment results. Buddha had, besides scriptures, an esoteric teaching, which he transmitted to Bodhidharma. He taught that the first principle of the universe is inexpressible. The method of cultivation is practically no-cultivation. The enlightened one does what he used to do before enlightenment; only the mind is changed. The wonderful

[65] *A History of Chinese Philosophy,* II, 243–44.

Tao lies in drawing water and chopping wood. (4) *T'ien-tai,* or Good Law School, was founded by Chi-k'ai, who, though emphasizing meditation, was opposed to the extreme forms of Ch'anism. He founded a monastery at a place called T'ien-t'ai, whence the name of the school.[66] Chi-k'ai regarded the *Avatamsakasūtra* as the most important. He wanted to reconcile all the schools of Buddhism and maintained that Buddha taught all the doctrines but at different stages of life. The doctrine of the first period is to be found in the *Avatamsaka,* when, immediately after enlightenment, he preached the doctrine to gods and not men. During the second period, he taught men as a popular religious teacher, and these teachings are found in the *Sūtrapītaka.* During the third period, he refuted the doctrines of the rival schools, and his teachings are found in the *Vaipulyasūtras.* During the fourth period, he revealed to his disciples the deeper truths of his philosophy; the *Prajñāpāramitās* belong to this period. The fifth period is marked by the culmination of his teachings, as found in *Saddharmapuṇḍarīka,* etc., in which the *bodhisattva* doctrine is propagated. The ideas of the *bodhisattva* and the Tathāgatagarbha are prominent in this school. The Ch'an and the T'ien-t'ai schools became very popular with the Chinese, because the Chinese mind was attracted by contradictions, puzzles, and shock methods and also because it was very tolerant. Buddha is further supposed to be an expert in teaching according to the intellectual maturity of the disciples—which reminds us of the *adhikāri* doctrine of orthodox Indian philosophy, according to which the philosophy should suit the intellectual level of the listeners, who should be able to obtain salvation by grasping the truth in their own terms. The five stages of teaching can also be for the five kinds of *adhikāris,* listeners of five stages of intellectual maturity. (5) *Lien-hua,* or the Lotus School, also called the Pure Land School, was very popular too. It satisfied the Chinese demand for a positive paradise through faith in Amitābha. It was founded by Hui Yüan, a disciple of Kumārajīva. Its text is *Sukhāvativyūha.* The school received its name from a lotus pond, near which Hui Yüan's monastery was situated. (6) *Fa-hsiang,* or the Dharma Lakṣaṇa School, was the Yogācāra school founded by Hsüan-tsang the Pilgrim. This was very close to Mencius' doctrine of the universal mind. (7) But Hsüan-tsang taught Vaśubandhu's *Abhidharmakośa* also,

[66] Sometimes called the Lotus School, as it was based on the *Lotus Sutra,* or *Saddharmapuṇḍarīka.* See *ibid.,* p. 360.

which is a Hīnayānist work. Vaśubandhu was also the author of the Yogācāra work, *Vijaptimātratāsiddhi.* It is said that Vaśubandhu was originally a Hīnayānist and wrote the former work; but later he was converted to Yogācāra (also called Vijñānavāda) by his brother Asaṅga and wrote the other work. *Chu-she,* or the Kośa School, was founded on *Abhidharmakośa.* (8) *Hua-yen,* or Avatamsaka School, was based on *Avatamsakasūtra* and emphasized the unity of opposites and preached monism. (9) *Lü,* or Vinaya School, was started by Tao-hsüan, who approached Buddhism from the side of Confucianism. *Li* of Confucius prescribed rules of conduct; similarly, the *Vinayapiṭaka* of the Buddhists prescribed rules for the monks. Instead of following one's inclinations, Tao-hsüan said, the monks should have definite rules of conduct. Within Buddhism, one may say, this is Confucianism as opposed to Taoism. (10) *Chen-yen,* or the True Word School (Shingon in Japan), was *tantric* Buddhism introduced into China by Vajrabodhi. The primordial principle of the universe is Mahavairocana, who is identical with the Bhūtatathatā. The Chinese themselves had quite a number of magical rites and ceremonies; and so this school did not attract much attention.

Almost all schools preached that everyone could attain Buddhahood.[67] The highest *adhikāri* for the Chinese is the sage, interested in the world of human affairs, not the Buddhist monk with the ideal of Nirvāṇa, though Nirvāṇa is identified with the Tao. So later the tendency became strong to reduce Buddhahood to sagehood, since the central concern was for the Way rather than for Absolute Being or Reality. The Tao, Tathatā, and the Brahman: these are three ultimates for the original Chinese philosophy, Buddhism, and the Indian Vedānta. The Tao is the Way of the processes of the world, and so also is Tathatā; but the Brahman is Being and so is not an attribute of the activity of the world. Therefore, the Vedānta could not so easily be taken over by the Chinese as Buddhism. The Chinese wished to follow a way of life that is in harmony with the ultimate way of the universe, but they did not conceive of static being, however ultimate in its essence. Way implies the process of the wayfarer, and so the Chinese could easily

[67] W. T. Chan says that Chinese Buddhism may be said to consist of four schools and that it is T'ien-tai and Hua Yen in doctrines and Meditation, and Pure Land in practice (*Religious Trends in Modern China* [New York: Columbia University Press, 1953], p. 63). But to an Indian even this distinction is not clear, since theory and practice go together.

adopt the Buddhist doctrine of flux: both physical nature and social institutions are in a process of continual change; and Tao or Tathatā is the way of change. Living according to this Tao is conforming to ultimate nature. And so to live the normal life of man, spontaneously and without effort, is to live according to nature. How is the life of the monk according to nature? Celibacy and renunciation are not natural for man. The Tao is essentially present in all men and in everything; to make a special effort towards realizing it is to treat it as external to us. To live according to our nature is to live according to the Tao. Then, further, if man is a social and political animal by nature, should he not take part in political and social activities? This question was raised for both Buddhism and Taoism by the Confucian revival.

Neo-Confucianism

Pre-Buddhistic Chinese philosophy was ethical rather than metaphysical. Whatever metaphysics there was, was only a handmaid to ethics. Neither the original Chinese religion nor its metaphysics was theoretically profound. When Buddhism entered as both an organized religion and also a profound metaphysics, China was impressed. Both Taoism and Confucianism adapted themselves to the newcomer and began reconciling themselves to it. But the Chinese traditions were so strongly humanistic and naturalistic that, instead of being absorbed by Buddhism, they began to absorb it. Buddhism became either a Confucianist Buddhism or a Taoist Buddhism. In fact, each of the subsequent schools was an amalgam of the three, whatever be the name it adopted. They differed from each other in the emphasis they gave to the Confucianist ideal, the Taoist ideal, or the Buddhist ideal, and in their interpretations of the ultimate. For some time, Confucianism remained an undercurrent. But during the eighth century, in the T'ang dynasty, it came up to the surface in a form that showed enrichment through contact with Buddhism and Taoism. The revival of Taoism and the introduction of Buddhism stimulated interest in metaphysical problems of the nature and destiny of man. Confucianism in its old classic form did not satisfy the new interests of the people. A more systematic cosmology was needed. Confucianism had to show that it could incorporate the essentials of Buddhism and Taoism. It had to offer a cosmology which could compare favorably with the Buddhist and which would serve as the metaphysical foundations of its ethics, and the justification and vindication of social and political activity. It had to affirm that supreme happiness could be found in the pursuits of normal social life. In addition it had to offer a religion, which, like Buddhism, would be more intellectual than the popular cults into which Taoism had fallen.

The earliest leaders of Neo-Confucianism are Han Yü (768–824) and Li Ao (died *c.* 844), who reinterpreted the Confucian classics, *Chung Yung* (*Doctrine of the Mean*) and *Ta Hsüeh* (*Great Learning*) according to the needs of the time. Their doctrine was really a continuation of the mystic teaching of Mencius, which could be developed through the Yogācāra Buddhism and Taoism. Chou Tun-yi, also called Lien-hsi (1017–73), then constructed a cosmology by combining this with the Taoist and Yin-Yang ideas. The Tao is ultimateless (*wu chi*) and yet it is the ultimate (*T'ai chi*). Through movement, it produces Yang. But when the movement reaches its limit, quiescence follows. Through quiescence, it produces Yin. By transformation of Yang and union with Yin, the five elements are produced. Then the two ethers (forces), Yin and Yang, through interaction and transformation, produce all things, which in turn produce and reproduce without end. Man is the highest of all such productions. He continues the creative process by spiritual cultivation; the sage is regulated by the golden mean, correctness, human-heartedness, and righteousness. He takes quiescence to be essential. Neo-Confucianism deprecates the otherworldliness of original Buddhism. There is to be no escapism. Ch'an Buddhism preached *wu hsin* (having no mind) and Taoism *wu-wei* (no-action). Both were reinterpreted as included in *wu yu* (effortless action), which means action according to one's nature. The T'ang had been a powerful dynasty, reunifying China and establishing an effective social and political organization. Zest for social and political activity was the need of the time; so Confucianism came up and was patronized, and gave rise to Neo-Confucianism.

Shao Yung (1011–77) developed the original hexagrams of the Yin-Yang school into a doctrine which united the principles of cosmology with the norms of social morality. Chang Tsai, also called

Heng-ch'ai (1020–77), then developed a cosmology that is more modern and naturalistic and even materialistic.[68] According to him the original principle is *Yi,* which is the same as *Ch'i,* a gaseous ethereal matter. "Great harmony" is another name for it. It is also the same as *śūnya* (void). But it is not *wu* (nonbeing). Chang Tsai was opposed to the Buddhist and the Taoist conception of the ultimate. The natural, material *Ch'i* is one, and so all things, including men, are parts of one great body. The *Ch'i,* which is originally ethereal, produces all things and forms through condensation and diversification.

Neo-Confucianism, after Chang Tsai, divided into two schools founded by two brothers, Ch'eng Yi, also called Ch'eng Yi-ch'uan (1033–1108), and Ch'eng Hao, also called Ch'eng Ming-tao (1032–85). The former is called the *Li hsüeh* (School of Laws or Principles) and was developed by one of the most famous of Chinese philosophers, Chu Hsi (1130–1200); the latter was called *Hsin hsüeh* (School of Mind) and was developed by Lu Chiu-yuan (1139–93). The two schools entered into keen controversy over the problem of whether the laws of nature originate from mind or not. One is reminded of Kant, according to whom their source is mind.

Ch'eng Hao, the elder of the two brothers, reinterpreted the Confucian concept of *jen* in a metaphysical way. All things are one and, as Mencius had said, they are complete within us. Hence the practice of *jen* lies in realizing the oneness of oneself with everything else. What Mencius called the "feeling of commiseration" is an expression of the interconnectedness of things. Ch'eng Yi developed a new category, *Li,* the source of the laws of the universe. Everything is constituted by *Li* and *ch'i.* Chang Tsai said that everything is a condensation of *ch'i,* the ethereal primeval matter. Ch'eng Yi added *Li* to it, because everything has both matter and varied forms or Laws. *Ch'i* is the same for all, but the *Li* is diversified. Every particular thing is what it is because of its particular *Li;* otherwise, it is the same *ch'i. Li* is timeless, but *ch'i* is the power of continuous change. This is in accordance with Buddhism, for which also the *samskāras* are lasting but the material is in a state of constant flux. Every object has its own *Li;* but the ultimate *Li* is the same as the Tao. While Ch'eng Yi accepted the reality of both *Li* and *ch'i,* Ch'eng Hao accepted the reality of *Li* only. Spiritual cultivation consists of substituting attentiveness for quiescence. This is a remarkable departure from Ch'an Buddhism.

[68] Fung Yu-lan, *A Short History of Chinese Philosophy,* pp. 278–79.

The sage does not enjoy the Tao, because it is not external to him; he enjoys what he himself is, which is the Tao. The Tao is not empty, but full of *Li*. It is neither moving nor quiescent. It is ultimately the same in all. To the question how, the answer is given with the help of the example used by the Buddhists. As the moon is reflected in thousands of streams, the Tao is reflected in the infinite number of individuals.

Chu Hsi developed the ideas of Ch'eng Yi further. He is considered to be the greatest synthesizer in Chinese thought.[69] He adopted Chou Tun-yi's cosmology and derived the Yin and the Yang from the Tao, and the five elements from the Yin and the Yang. The supreme ultimate is the highest of the *Li,* and is found in each individual as the universal is found in each particular. It is not destroyed with the particulars. The supreme is the all-inclusive Tao, called by Chu Hsi by the name *T'ai Chi*. Everything contains not only its own *Li* but also *T'ai Chi*. The *T'ai Chi* is not divided among the things, but is reflected as a whole in each. The *Li* is prior to the *ch'i;* but the priority is only logical, not chronological. Things are created by condensation and fermentation of *ch'i* according to *Li*. The *ch'i* is the same in all, in matter and mind, in the saint and the sinner; but it is clear and pure in the sage, turbid and opaque in the foolish. Mencius in effect took only *Li* into consideration when he said that man's nature is good; but man contains *ch'i* also. *Li* in its universal form constitutes the nature of Heaven and earth; nature is nothing but *Li*. The *Li* in man is human-heartedness, righteousness, propriety, and wisdom. Spiritual cultivation lies in following one's *Li* and the Tao. There can be no sudden enlightenment without attentiveness. Chu Hsi attaches great importance to the "extension of knowledge" and "investigation of things" as the method for spiritual cultivation. Investigation of things leads to the extension of knowledge up to the ultimate *Li*. We cannot start with the investigation of the many *Li* in particular things, because they are not concrete, their being is empty. Chu Hsi is not only a Platonic realist but also an empirical realist. In order to understand the nature of the universal, one must observe the particulars. The Chinese were not interested in the "investigation of things" of nature according to the method advocated by Chu Hsi; otherwise, they might have developed systematic natural science. To them "things" were still primarily human relationships. Chu Hsi re-

[69] Fung Yu-lan, *A History of Chinese Philosophy*, II, 533.

minds us also of Kant by saying that the universals without the particulars are empty.

Chu Hsi held that, though every object contains the supreme Tao, the Tao remains concealed in different degrees. Hence arise natural differences. The Tao is perfect and wholly good; but when it becomes actualized in Yin and Yang, it loses its perfection and evil appears. The Tao itself is not conscious. Consciousness is a different principle and belongs to mind, which distinguishes between subject and object. Human nature consists of four virtues—human-heartedness, righteousness, propriety, and wisdom; in addition, it contains the Tao. The Tao is not concrete and is wholly good. Feelings belong to the concrete world, and not to nature. Chu Hsi complains that the Buddhists wrongly identified mind with nature. Chu Hsi's realistic and constructive philosophy was not further developed by the Chinese.

According to Chu Hsi, the *Li* of government are the same both in the past and in the present. It is therefore necessary for the ruler to understand the *Li* and then apply them. Blind application leads to bad government. The ancient sages could understand them and so used the golden mean properly. But the modern heroes do not undergo spiritual cultivation; and some of them who are talented can come only into some seeming agreement with the *Li*. Chu Hsi, like Mencius, maintained that government by *wang* (king) is superior to that by *pa* (war lord), but said that government from the Han and Tang onwards was by *pa* and not by *wang*.

Just as Chu Hsi developed the ideas of Ch'eng Yi, Lu Chiu-yüan, also called Lu Hsiang-shan, developed the ideas of Ch'eng Hao. The former two were realistic, the latter idealistic. Lu accepted Mencius' principle, "the universe is my mind." Chu Hsi said that nature is different from mind; but Lu held that it is the same as mind, as both nature and mind consist of the *Li* only. But according to Chu Hsi, mind consists of both *Li* and *ch'i*. Lu rejects the reality of *ch'i*. Everything in the universe is composed of *Li* alone. And because mind is nature and nature is *Li*, the *Li* can be grasped by studying mind. It is an unnecessary waste of energy to study things, which can be understood when the *Li* are understood. Chu Hsi advises investigation of things through both *Li* and *ch'i;* but Lu through *Li* only. The *Li* are to be grasped intuitively, not by observation of external things. Chu Hsi is a dualist in accepting both *Li* and *ch'i;* but Lu is a monist in accepting only *Li*.

Wang Shou-jen, also called Wang Yang-ming (1473–1528), is the greatest exponent of the Confucian school of mind. He was in his youth a follower of Chu Hsi and, wishing to know the *Li* of the bamboo, began concentrating his mind upon it intensively, day and night, for seven days. In the end he achieved nothing and gave up the attempt. Years afterwards, exiled through some political intrigue, he experienced one night a sudden enlightenment, and he realized that nothing is external to mind. "The substance of the mind is the nature and the nature is *Li*." "My own nature is quite sufficient. I was wrong in looking for *Li* in external objects." He reinterpreted the cords of the *Great Learning*, "to manifest the illustrious virtue, love people, and rest in the highest good." "To manifest the illustrious virtue is to establish the nature of the unity of Heaven, Earth, and all things; to love people is to exercise the function of that unity." To rest in the highest good is to exercise the function of that unity.

> The highest good is the highest standard for the manifesting of the illustrious virtue and loving people. Our original nature is purely good. What cannot be observed in it is the manifestation of the highest good and of the nature of the illustrious virtue, and is also what I call intuitive knowledge. When things come to it, right is right, wrong is wrong, important is important, and inferior is inferior. It responds to things and changes with circumstances, yet it always attains the natural mean. This is the highest standard for the actions of man and of things, to which nothing can be added, and from which nothing can be reduced. If there is any addition or reduction, that is selfishness and a petty kind of rationalization, and is not the highest good.[70]

Wang accepted the so-called eight wires for the rectification of affairs, and says that attentiveness of mind is possible only when we know what we have to attend to. As it is the *Li*, it has to be known by intuition in one's own mind. Learning and discipline are not of much use. In this respect, this school was greatly influenced by Ch'an Buddhism and accepted the idea of sudden enlightenment. Yet the Buddhist idea of emptiness was not accepted. The Tao is full of *Li*, not empty. Wang says:

[70] Fung Yu-lan, *A Short History of Chinese Philosophy*, p. 311.

> The claim of the Buddhists that they have no attachment to phenomena shows that they do have attachment to them. And the fact that we Confucianists do not claim to have no attachment to phenomena, shows that we do not have attachment to them. . . . The Buddhists are afraid of the troubles involved in human relationships, and therefore escape from them. They are forced to escape because they are already attached to them. But we Confucianists are different. There being the relationship between father and son, we respond to it with love. There being the relationship between sovereign and subject, we respond to it with righteousness. And there being the relationship between husband and wife, we respond to it with mutual respect. We have no attachment to phenomena.[71]

Fung says that in all this the Neo-Confucianists are more Taoistic than the Taoists and more Buddhistic than the Buddhists.[72]

Ch'ing Neo-Confucianism

Confucian doctrines went through further modifications in the development of Neo-Confucianism. So far Neo-Confucianism was greatly influenced by Buddhism. But with the advent of the Ch'ing dynasty (1644–1911), the Confucianists tried to weed out the Buddhist elements completely from their philosophy, and for the purpose advocated going back to the pure teachings of the Han times. Juan Yüan (1764–1849) said that the Han learning was closer to the times of the ancient sages and for that reason was purer. Other great names of this period are those of the earlier Yen Yüan (1635–1704) and Li Kung (1659–1746). The school founded by these two was called the Yen-Li school after them. The identification of the Tao with the Buddhist Nirvāṇa as the highest principle was to be given up. The highest principle is the ether itself comprising the Yin and the Yang. The principle of nature is not above the ether, but is the ether itself. Yen Yüan of

[71] *Ibid.*, pp. 317–18.
[72] *Ibid.*, p. 318.

course calls this the Way of Heaven; but there is nothing religious in this terminology. Fung says that the concept of God is superfluous in Yen Yüan's cosmology. Creation begins with the interaction of the Yin and the Yang, which produces the four powers, *yüan* (originating growth), *heng* (prosperous development), *li* (advantageous gain), and *cheng* (correct firmness). The Yin and the Yang are themselves ethers, but together they form one ether, *ch'i*. Though Yen Yüan speaks of Principle also, Ether is still the primary principle in his cosmology. Ether's state of contraction is Non-Being, and its state of expansion is Being.[73]

Wang Fu-chih (1619–93) held that the universe contains only Principle (*Li*) and Ether (*ch'i*). The latter is the vehicle or instrument of the former, through which the universe is orderly. Heaven is another name for the Yin, the Yang, and the five elements. There is nothing above them. Heaven's principle is another name for Ether (*ch'i*). There is no difference between man's moral and physical nature, because there is no difference between Principle (*Li*) and Ether (*ch'i*), neither of which is prior or external to the other. Huang Tsung-hsi, a contemporary of Wang, however, gave primacy to Ether (*ch'i*). Tai Chen, also called Tai Tung-yüan (1723–77), equates the Tao to Ether (*ch'i*). The Ether of the Yin and the Yang and of the five elements is devoid of shapes and is therefore called Tao, above shapes.[74] Tai Chen posits one principle for Heaven, one for earth, one for men, and one each for things, events, and activities. The actuality of things is their nature; their necessity, their oughtness, is their principle. The nature of a thing is its potentiality, its capacity actualizes its potentiality. The Principle (*Li*) is objective and universal, and opinion is subjective and private. As it is for all Chinese philosophy, the Principle (*Li*), though not subjective, is understood with reference to human nature. Evil arises from certain defects and failings in feelings, desires, and knowledge. Fung summarizes the difference between Tai Chen and the earlier Confucian rationalists:

> He, like them, acknowledges that there is an objective principle. Unlike them, however, he denies that this Principle can at the same time be present within man's own nature. Human nature, for him, consists simply of man's blood, breath, and mental faculty; in

[73] *A History of Chinese Philosophy,* II, 638, 639–40.
[74] *Ibid.,* p. 654.

other words, it is what the Sung Confucianists would call physical nature. This physical nature does not itself actually contain the multitudinous Principles of all things. Nevertheless, Tai says, it can, because of its faculty of knowledge, come to comprehend them. This explains why man, starting from what is purely natural to him, can elevate himself to what is morally necessary.[75]

Tai complains that the Sung Confucianists treated the Principles like things, which become embodied in mind. In spite of this criticism, the implications of which do not seem to have been developed by Tai, he says that the Principles are only right feelings, which neither go too far nor fall too short. The doctrine of the golden mean helps in discovering them. For the discovery of Principles which do not fall within human affairs, Tai recommends the method of analysis. He went further than Hsün Tzu in that the latter thought of the Principles as pertaining only to human affairs, rites, standards of justice, and morality, while the former regarded them as objective and universal also. The word things now included what lies beyond human affairs also.

Philosophically, Neo-Confucianism is richer than the earlier schools, wider in outlook, and more comprehensive in its results. The stimulus for the change has to be attributed to Buddhism. The first reaction of China to Buddhism was passive reception and admiration. This was followed by its assimilation to Confucianism and Taoism, giving the latter more content and wider outlook. Buddhism itself was not inactive; it tried, from its own side, to assimilate and absorb the two. But it was easier for naturalistic and humanistic philosophies to add the otherworldly forms of Buddhism to themselves than for the definitely formed monastic Buddhism to assimilate and absorb the this-worldly philosophies. A similar thing happened in India. Buddhism was absorbed by the Vedānta, and the closer it came to the Vedānta the less justification it had for separate existence. The philosophy of monastic Buddhism concerned only the theory of meditation for attaining Nirvāṇa; and when the Vedāntic monasticism was formed, the Buddhist forms went into it.

But what Buddhism did not have a distinct philosophy for was this life, the life of the householder in society and politics. This the Vedānta had, however, in its Pūrva Mīmāmsā (Prior Mīmāmsā). That

[75] *Ibid.*, p. 663.

is why the Vedānta is called the Posterior Mīmāmsā. And the two Mīmāmsās covered the whole life of man, the life of the active householder and the life of the meditating monk. So also when the Buddhist ideas were assimilated to the Taoist and Confucian ideas, the Chinese mind reduced the former to the latter, and, through criticism and reconstruction, transformed all into its own philosophy of life. Practically, we may say that the conflict between Buddhism on the one side and Confucianism on the other corresponds to the conflict between the activism (*karma mārga*) of the Pūrva (Prior) Mīmāmsā and the life of renunciation and gnosis (*jñāna mārga*) of the Uttara (Posterior) Mīmāmsā. I feel that the Buddhists were the first to use the word *jñānamārga* with a definite connotation in Indian philosophy.[76]

The second stage, at which Chinese thought absorbed Buddhism, would naturally be eclectic. The third stage, represented by the earlier forms of Neo-Confucianism, is a reconstruction of elements borrowed from Taoism and Buddhism. The fourth stage, as represented by the later forms of Neo-Confucianism, is one of criticism of the reconstructed philosophies in order to bring them up to the level of original Confucianism; it is richer, deeper, and more articulated. It has become completely naturalistic (understanding nature as the Chinese do), humanistic, and sometimes even materialistic.

The New Text School of the Ch'ing Dynasty and the Advent of the West

During the later part of the Ch'ing dynasty (1644–1911), the New Text School made greater strides and felt more that Neo-Confucianism was not pure Confucianism, but was polluted by Buddhism and Taoism. The followers said: "Chu Hsi was a Taoist monk, and Lu

[76] See the author's contribution, "Buddhism and the Vedānta," to the Buddha Jayanti Symposium, held in New Delhi, November, 1956.

Chiu-yüan was a Buddhist monk." As the Han scholars were nearer Confucius than the Neo-Confucians, *Han hsüeh* (Han learning) was to be preferred to *Sung hsüeh* (Sung learning). The Ch'ing Confucians added very little philosophically to the existing thought, but they were important as reformers. Before that time the Jesuit missionaries had introduced mathematics and astronomy into China, by which the Chinese were greatly impressed. As the Christians began conversions, the Chinese wanted to revive and strengthen their own religion and culture. Mathematics and other subjects could be studied; but Confucianism in its purity should be revived, not only as a philosophy of life but also as a religion. Buddhism could only be a spiritual movement and could easily be absorbed; but Christianity was an institutionalized religion, with a definite creed and dogma and even a social code, and could not be assimilated. Confucius was therefore regarded not only as a social and political reformer but also as a religious leader; his doctrines alone could check the spread of Christianity.

K'ang Yu-wei (1858–1927) was the most important political and social reformer of the period. He reinterpreted the Three Ages of Tung Chung-shu, saying that the age of Confucius himself was the Age of Disunity and Disorder. The age of impact of the West on China is the Age of Approaching Peace, which will be followed by the Age of Great Peace, when the whole world is united. But K'ang had to flee for life, and his followers were executed for his new teachings.

T'an Ssu-t'ung (1865–98), a pupil of K'ang, was another reformer, who, like his teacher, was also a leading spirit in the "Hundred Days of Reform." K'ang placed his ideas before the well-meaning Emperor Kuang Hsü, who issued so many edicts during one hundred days that the Dowager Empress Tz'u Hsi and the conservative party were frightened. Tz'u Hsi imprisoned the Emperor and countermanded most of the edicts. Some of the leaders of the reform movement were executed; K'ang fled, but T'an was caught.

According to T'an, *jen* is only the functioning of the ether *(ch'i)*. Both K'ang and T'an seem to have been acquainted with some western ideas. K'ang thought that the spiritual energy in Heaven and man is electricity possessed of consciousness. T'an advocated the study of Ch'an and Vijñānavāda doctrines and the New Testament for understanding *jen*.[77] He said that *jen* was ether *(ch'i)* itself manifest in

[77] Fung Yu-lan, *A History of Chinese Philosophy*, II, 692.

action. The same was referred to by Buddha as Buddha-nature, compassion and mercy, and by Jesus as spirit and love of neighbors as oneself. The scientists refer to it as attraction.

The tendency of the New Text School of the period seems to have been to reduce the Supreme Ultimate to a more concretely naturalistic principle, which they called by the neutral name Ether (*ch'i,* Power), and then to derive social and political virtues from it. The Ultimate is naturalistic, humanistic, and ethereal at one and the same time. It has also some materialistic coloring, in spite of the fact that it is called Heaven.

Chinese philosophers so far had had little or no knowledge of western philosophy. K'ang Yu-wei and T'an Ssu-tung knew a little about western science, mathematics, and Christianity brought into China by the missionaries. They knew also of the superiority of western technology, which they witnessed in the machines, guns, and warships. But they still thought that their own philosophy and culture were superior to those of the West. The first person to introduce western philosophy into China was Yen Fu (1853–1920), who was sent to England to study naval science, but read works like Huxley's *Evolution and Ethics,* Adam Smith's *An Enquiry into the Nature and Causes of the Wealth of Nations,* Spencer's *Sociology,* Mill's *Liberty* and *Logic,* Jenks's *History of Politics,* and Jevons' *Lessons in Logic,* and translated them into Chinese. Another Chinese scholar who studied western philosophy was Wang Kuo-wei (1877–1927). But logic was something almost new to the Chinese. Fung tells us that, when he was a student at Shanghai, there was no one to teach him logic. Jevons' *Lessons in Logic* was taught just like a textbook on English language. When Fung attempted to do the exercises, there was no one to help him; even the missionary stopped teaching logic when Fung approached him with his exercises. John Dewey and Bertrand Russell were invited to lecture at the University of Peiping in 1919. Their lectures gave an impetus to the study of western philosophy. Fung says that the permanent contribution of western philosophy to Chinese philosophy is its method of logical analysis. "Buddhism and Taoism both use the negative method. The analytic method is just the opposite of this, and hence may be called the positive method. The negative method attempts to eliminate distinctions and to tell what its object is not, whereas the positive method attempts to make distinctions and tell what its object *is*."[78] The classical Chinese wanted to learn how to live, not how to think; and hence the lack of logic.

Whatever may have been the philosophical views held by Fung previously, he has now become a Marxist. It is said that he is reinterpreting Chinese thought; but his older works will remain the authentic interpretations of Chinese thought as it was, presenting the ideals of life, aims, and aspirations of the Chinese people as the ideals appeared to those people themselves, and not as they would appear to a Marxist.

Contemporary Thought

China has become communist, and though we do not hear about persecutions of ancient ideas, Marxism as interpreted by Lenin and Stalin has become the official philosophy of the nation. Mao Tse-tung has rendered it to the Chinese. But Confucianism does not seem to be completely given up and condemned. Some, of course, condemn it as reactionary and unprogressive, because of Confucius' insistence on the authority of the ancient sages and tradition. On the other hand, Confucius was opposed to dogmatism, meaningless tradition, and so on. The communists identify his "universal *li* (principle)" with the "universal truth of Marxism-Leninism." Mao hates Confucianism. But Liu Shao-ch'i, a vice-chairman of the Peiping government, refers to Confucius, Mencius, and others in support of communism whenever he finds it convenient to do so. Kuo Mo-jo, a vice-premier of the Peiping government, regards Confucius as not only an advocate of the rights of the common people, but also of armed revolution. Creel concludes: "It is by no means impossible that the idol of old China may come to be hailed as a forerunner, in the revolutionary tradition, of Marx, Lenin, Stalin, Mao Tse-tung, a hero of the new China."[79] China may develop its own communism, a Confucian communism.

[78] *A Short History of Chinese Philosophy*, p. 330.
[79] *Op. cit.*, pp. 265, 269.

The new philosophy that Mao Tse-tung preaches is a philosophy of action, an activism along the lines of Marxism, which appealed to him as a philosophy of dynamic life, the aim of which is to change the world, a rationalistic activism in which life of knowledge and life of action cannot be separated. "Marxism is not a dogma but a guide to action." Pre-Marxian materialism committed the mistake of separating the problem of knowledge from social practice. There is no reality without social practice. Success in practice depends on the correspondence of our ideas to the objective world, so practice is the criterion of truth.[80] Lenin said, "Practice is higher than [theoretical] knowledge because it has not only the virtue of universality, but also the virtue of immediate reality." Marxism has two characteristics: one is its class nature, and the other is the emphasis on the dependence of theory on practice. The criterion of truth is social action only. Perception belongs to the lower stage of knowledge, and reason to the higher; but both are united in practice. The saying that "a scholar does not step outside his gate, and yet knows all the happenings under the sun" is mere empty talk. Empiricism committed the mistake of thinking that knowledge stops with perception. Life is one and contains perception, reason, and action.

Life is meant for changing the world, and unless knowledge leads to activity, it would be incomplete. Knowledge is not meant merely for understanding the world, but for changing it. Mere theory without performance is insignificant. Stalin said: "Theory becomes aimless if it is not connected with revolutionary practice, just as practice gropes in the dark if its path is not illumined by revolutionary theory." [81] The aim of communist philosophy is the concrete and historical unity of the subjective and the objective, of theory and practice. In practice man is in contact with reality. The world is in continual process, the process is dialectical, a unity or synthesis of opposites, not an increase or decrease of some ultimate metaphysical principle. The development of everything, through the synthesis of opposites, is inherent to it and necessary.

The this-worldliness of Marxism, its activism and pragmatism, and its sociological orientation, agree well with the naturalistic, humanistic, and pragmatic tendencies of the general Chinese tradition. The

[80] *Selected Works of Mao Tse-tung* (London: Lawrence & Wishart Ltd., 1954), I, 293.

[81] *Ibid.*

traditional Chinese principle of government by the elite and agreement with the superior support communist authoritarianism and totalitarianism.[82] If Confucianism could become Taoist and then Buddhist, it can easily become communist also. We have already seen the materialistic tendencies in some of the later forms of Confucianism. These may easily be transformed into the Marxian type of materialism. The Taoist reversal of the Tao can be reinterpreted as the Marxian dialectical process. It will be no wonder, therefore, if a Confucian variety of communist philosophy should appear in China at some future time. It can meet the philosophical needs of the Chinese people perhaps more adequately than the communism of Marx, Lenin, and Stalin in its western robes. With the change of political forms, China is changing its social forms also. The traditional Confucian *li* as expressed in the relationships between son and father, wife and husband, brother and brother, subject and sovereign, will no longer be accepted. But there will be new *li;* some of the Confucians accepted the idea that social and political forms would alter with the change of times. The reference to ancient sages was ridiculed by some of the tough-minded among the Confucians themselves. So Confucius may remain a hero even in the future. Chinese philosophy has been keenly mindful of man all along. Marxism also is a form of humanism; though, instead of the general definition of man as a social animal, it would accept the narrower view that he is a class animal, and would say that the broader definition might apply when a classless society was established everywhere in the world. The Confucian idea that man is a social and political animal and that everyone can become a "superior man" through training and education can still be an ideal for the Chinese communists.

[82] Creel, *op. cit.*, p. 265.

Summary of General Characteristics

We may now review the prominent general characteristics of Chinese thought: [83]

1. The first impression that any foreign student of Chinese philosophy gets is that it is neither extremely inward nor extremely outward. It always keeps a balance between the two, a sort of golden mean, and is more at home with man in society than with ultimate problems. Generally no problem is pushed to the extreme; no argument is pressed to its logical conclusions. Chinese thought affirms man first, and never forgets this commitment. Confucianism affirms man in society, and Taoism man by himself; but in either case, it is man who is more or less affirmed, although Taoism was inclined to belittle his material existence. On the whole, Chinese philosophy is outward-looking, if Confucianism is considered typically Chinese.

2. Indeed, a few questions about the ultimate nature of the Tao are raised; but the inquiry is not very thorough and is every time brought down to human nature. Mencius said that the universe is within mind; but none probed into mind systematically, and what was found within mind were good human feelings, sentiments, emotions, etc., which contribute to happy social life. They could as well have been found in society and read into the individual's mind. Hence arises the somewhat superficial and unsystematic nature of Chinese philosophy.

3. Looked at with the background of Indian and western philosophies, there is a distinct contribution that Chinese thought makes to world philosophy. It persistently tries to build ethics and even metaphysics on the emotional nature of man, and not on his rational nature. If there is an ethical idealism based on human reason, there can be an ethical idealism based on man's emotions and sentiments also—

[83] In summarizing these characteristics, the author makes use of W. T. Chan's article in *Essays in East-West Philosophy*. Dr. Chan himself gives most of these characteristics.

on the four beginnings, as Mencius said. The former ignores the driving forces in man in his ethical activity. One should not miss this peculiarly Chinese contribution.

4. Chinese philosophy shows great anxiety for the immediate life of man. A peculiar pragmatism characterizes its doctrines. If a doctrine works in building up a good state and society, it is accepted; when it does not, it is rejected.

5. Chinese philosophy is more concerned with the Good than with the Beautiful, and less with the True than with the Beautiful. Again, it finds the Good in normal (normative) human life, not in communion with God but with other men, not in controlling and manipulating physical nature, but in controlling oneself with reference to others.

6. There is some mysticism; but it is a kind of nature mysticism, nature understood only as human nature. Mysticism, as we understand it—the life of contemplation and absorption in the most inward—is almost absent. Taoism has elements of it; and Buddhism deepened China's mystical trends; but it was again and again brought back to the human level in the history of Chinese thought.

7. China also does not have a well-developed materialistic philosophy. It was human nature that was elevated to the Tao of the early Taoists or to the material Tao of the later Confucians. We may say that matter or spirit was of interest to the Chinese because of human nature. There is pronounced interest in human nature, but not in material or spiritual nature. Because of its strong humanism, China showed very little concern for extreme forms of mysticism or materialism. This Chinese attitude has a lesson for us: it is, after all, man's being that is to be elevated to spirit or reduced to matter. Neither has significance without man's being.

8. Because nature meant human nature, China did not feel the need for developing a method or technique for understanding nature. Human nature, as expressed in good life, was immediately available for inspection and study. China, accordingly, did not develop systems of logic and epistemology. The need for both is felt only when the objects to be studied are remote. The nature of outward matter is as baffling as the nature of the inward spirit; and so methods for their study have to be developed with precision. But neither extreme interested the Chinese.

9. For the same reason, there is very little categorization of reality. There is some categorization of human virtues, of which human-heart-

edness is the highest, and in terms of which other virtues are explained; some categorization in terms of the Tao, which is idealized human nature—whatever be the heights of the idealization—just as the God of Hegel is idealized human reason, the God of Aristotle idealized human thought, and the God of Plato idealized human good; and some categorization in terms of the elements of the Yin-Yang. For the Chinese, reality, we may say, is human nature; so there is some categorization of human nature, based upon, and developed from, human nature. But as the categorization is not carried out methodically and systematically, we find very little of rational importance attached to categories; even the categories of the Yin-Yang are not very logically discussed.

10. For the reason that the Chinese philosophers were not interested in ultimate questions of inwardness or outwardness, we do not find any grand metaphysical system.

11. Because of the keen interest in human affairs and achievements, China had a strong sense of history, and constructed some philosophies of history, besides a few doctrines of evolution. Whether they are profound or not is a different question. Any philosophy that is deficient in both logic and metaphysics will not be profound. What interests us is that China did not regard history as unreal and insignificant. The aim of the Chinese mind is universal peace, and it interpreted human events and achievements as progressing towards universal peace.

12. Man is the highest object in creation, not because he alone can obtain salvation among the creatures of the earth as the Indian philosophers thought, but because he alone can build up culture and civilization. Other animals, however gregarious, have no culture and civilization, and culture and civilization are therefore not to be undervalued. As a check to this attitude, Taoism preached avoiding them and living a primitive life. But Confucianism gave them the highest value possible.

13. Because of the deep interest in man, culture, and civilization, China could develop good social and political thought and also good life-affirming ethics. The ideal of democracy really started with Confucius, and the French Revolution seems to have been influenced by his ideas, whether directly or indirectly. Even semantics must have been first discovered by the Chinese school of Names. China again was the first to invent paper, printing, and gunpowder, but could develop

none of these for want of systematic methodology. She had therefore to be content with only so much credit for her inventions as Egypt received for the discovery of geometry. But because of her humanistic interest, China pushed her inquiries in social and political thought farther than in her inventions.

14. In spite of deep interest in man and human nature, one feels that pre-communist Chinese thought viewed man as an emotional and social animal, but not as a rational animal. The Platonic and Aristotelian view that the rational part of the human soul is immortal would be foreign to the Chinese mind. It has not given proper recognition to the importance of reason in man. This feature also explains the lack of the development of logic and epistemology in Chinese thought.

15. Another striking feature is the absence of a definite conception of spirit, soul, or self (*ātman*) in Chinese thought. The question of the immortality of the soul did not engage the Chinese thinkers very much. They were referring to spirits of the ancestors, spirits of the water, mountains, and so on, but not so much to the spirit within man. Even when some philosophers said that every man has his Tao besides the universal Tao, they do not seem to have been thinking so much of the spirit within man as of some ultimate human "ought," which is nature in man in the Chinese sense.

3. INDIAN PHILOSOPHY *and* Explication of Inwardness

Introduction

The Indian philosophical tradition has a less varied development than the western. As in the Chinese tradition, almost all systems of thought were born simultaneously and grew alongside one another. All of them are quests for the ideal of life. But the approach to the objective was made from several points of view: the Cārvākas made it from the materialist point of view; the Nyāya and the Vaiśeṣika from the outward point of view, as beholders of all existence, treating the spectator and God as objects of outward consciousness; the Sāṅkhya and the Yoga from the inward point of view, but regarding the world not as the manifestation of the most inward, not as a telescoping outwards of the inward reality, but as something separate in which the inward got entangled, and telescoped outwards; the Pūrva Mīmāmsā from the standpoint of man as the agent of action, building up his destiny in this and the other worlds, which were separate from him, but conforming to the requirements of his action; and the Uttara Mīmāmsā, or the Vedāntic systems, from the purely inward point of view, explaining the world as the telescoping outwards of something inward to man.

The two heterodox schools of Jainism and Buddhism broke off from the orthodox Vedic ones in religion and adopted peculiar viewpoints of their own: philosophically, Jainism adopted the attitude of outwardness to the world, and Buddhism a combination of both outwardness and inwardness, becoming inward more and more as its metaphysics developed; but in deciding the questions of the ultimate ideal of life, they were extremely inward. Buddhism passed through so many stages of metaphysical development that it is difficult to characterize the whole with the help of any single adjective; but taking the final stage of its development as a clue, we may say that it was a philosophy of inwardness like the Vedānta. Furthermore, we have to say that some of these schools did not grow quite consistently as philosophies of inwardness or outwardness, but adopted either attitude towards different problems. On the whole, the great philosophies of the

Vedānta and Buddhism are overwhelmingly philosophies of inwardness; and we can say that the classical Indian philosophy is more inward than outward, for the Vedānta enjoys the greatest prestige among the orthodox schools and Buddhism among the heterodox.

The history of Indian philosophy is not marked by the development of one school or system out of another, but by the growth of systems—almost simultaneously born—into greater and greater clarification, articulation, and synthesis of their ideas. Like western philosophy, Indian philosophy grew out of religion; but it has not divorced itself from religion. In this respect, Indian religion is more like Greek religion—the religion of the philosopher—than like Christianity, Judaism, or Islam. Revelation it had, but not the revelation of any one individual, rather that of many pooled together, compared, criticized, and integrated. Hence philosophy is not divorced from religion and religion from philosophy. The advantage is that, like Greek religion, Indian religion is tolerant, rational, and considerate. It is an advantage for religion to be philosophical and experiential, for it will then have fewer chances of being discarded than when based upon some one individual's revelation, giving the prerogative of revelation to him alone and only faith to others; for no man will give up religion so long as he is convinced, through reason and experience, of its truth. This association of religion and philosophy has an advantage for philosophy also, which can treat religious experience and truth as part of man's natural experience, continuous with his perceptual and rational experience, and find solution of some ultimate problems in religious experience. But it has disadvantage for philosophy in that philosophy gets associated with religious sectarianism and cannot break through the limitations on reason in order to extend over scientific and humanistic experience. There is no real justification for this limitation; but the tendency to place limitations on philosophy has become so deep-rooted in religious loyalty that man becomes a little averse to working through the mazes of science and humanities, the discovery of the truths of which requires great patience and perseverance, without impatiently jumping back to take a restful refuge in the truths of religion, saying that the value of everything else is secondary and relative. Not only does sectarian loyalty lead to apologetic research, but also those who are interested in the pursuit of science and humanities tend to ignore religion as an obstacle and those interested in religious studies tend to dismiss scientific and humanistic truths and studies as impediments.

By Indian philosophy is meant all philosophy born in India. Just as it is said by Whitehead that western philosophy is a series of footnotes to Plato, it may be said that Indian philosophy is a series of footnotes to the Vedas and the Upaniṣads. The Veda has four parts: the *Samhitās,* or hymns; the *Brāhmaṇas* dealing with sacrificial rituals; the *Araṇyakas,* or forest treatises, containing the reflections of those who retired to the forest; and the Upaniṣads, also called the Vedānta, containing philosophical ideas. The Upaniṣads are actually parts of the Veda, though it has been usual to speak of "the Vedas and the Upaniṣads." The Vedas are four in number, Ṛk, Yajus, Sāma, and Atharva; and each has the four parts. The first two parts of the Veda contain material dealing with life and action in this world; and this material is systematized by Jaimini in his *Dharmasūtras,* also called *Mīmāmsāsūtras.* The material of the Upaniṣads is systematized by Bādarāyaṇa in his *Brahmasūtras,* also called *Vedāntasūtras.* The third part of the Veda, namely, the *Araṇyakas,* contains much of the Upaniṣadic material and has no separate systematization. I feel that Jaimini's *Dharmasūtras* and Bādarāyaṇa's *Brahmasūtras* have a real inherent relationship, as together constituting the philosophy of life of the time: this view is held by some teachers like Rāmānuja, though Śaṅkara minimizes the importance of the former. Commentaries upon commentaries were written upon both the *Sūtras,* not only explaining the aphorisms and original passages of the Vedas, the performance of rituals, the nature of sacrifice, but also interpreting them, giving them different shapes, and introducing new conceptual links for the purpose.

The heterodox systems fall within the Upaniṣadic tradition, for they rejected the Vedic rituals, sacrifices, and rules of conduct based upon the Brahmanic ethical philosophy of Jaimini. Also, they did not accept the wording of the Upaniṣads, since they formed part of the Vedas. But if we can say that Descartes, Leibniz, Locke, Berkeley, Kant, Hegel, and others belong to the Platonic or Aristotelian tradition, we have greater justification for saying that Jainism and Buddhism belong to the Upaniṣadic tradition. They not only grew within the Upaniṣadic atmosphere, but also seem to have influenced some of the later Upaniṣads and the systems that grew out of the Upaniṣads. The Nyāya, the Vaiśeṣika, the Sāṅkhya, and the Yoga grew less dependently on the

Upaniṣads than the Vedāntic systems, but acknowledged the Upaniṣads as an authority, and Vijñānabhikṣu even wrote a commentary on the *Brahmasūtras* from the side of the Sāṅkhya.

Though one may call the western by the name Platonic tradition and the Indian by the name Upaniṣadic or Vedic tradition, one finds within each tradition so many "isms" that it is difficult to brand either as any one "ism." Materialism, of course, cannot be either Platonic or Upaniṣadic. But in both traditions we have activism and quietism; realism and idealism; monism, dualism, and pluralism; spiritualism; and so on. The main and most important difference that offers a tough problem for comparative philosophy is the one between the great progress that western philosophy has made since the Renaissance, incorporating scientific thought, and the comparatively stagnant condition of Indian philosophy from about the sixteenth century, so that the difference between the two traditions now seems to be vast and comparison becomes unfavorable to Indian philosophy. But if we compare the western and the Indian traditions up to the sixteenth century only, the result may be the opposite.

The predominant interest of all the Indian systems, except the Cārvāka and the early Mīmāmsā Brahmanism, lies in the most inward reality of man. It is a human interest, but not humanistic, the latter understood in the sense of making the life of man as man here and hereafter as good as it can be. The interest of the *Dharmasūtras* of Jaimini is essentially humanistic and activistic, but as a philosophy it has come to occupy a place next to those systems that are primarily concerned with the most inward. Jaimini was not primarily concerned with the innermost reality, but with the duties and conduct of man, and with reality, both here and hereafter, in which those duties and actions were to be performed. He cared very little for the problem of God, as though he were averse to shifting the responsibility for the condition of man on to God. He placed implicit faith in the potency of human action to produce the results man wanted. His aim, like that of every other philosopher in India, was to show the way to the highest happiness, here and hereafter; and he believed that it could be attained only by performing one's duties as prescribed by the Vedas. The Cārvāka philosophy, as often represented by the orthodox, believed neither in ethics nor in inward reality and was materialistic and Epicurean.

The Cārvākas supplied a philosophy that was absolutely materialistic and this-worldly, and, because of the strongly spiritual atmosphere of India, became less popular than any of the other schools. The Nyāya and the Vaiśeṣika maintained a strongly logical, realistic, and pluralistic outlook. The Sāṅkhya and the Yoga retained realism and maintained a peculiar unity or oneness of the material world and a qualitative dualism in which the primeval matter is one but the spirits are many. The Mīmāmsā maintained a completely realistic and pluralistic attitude to the world, but endeavored to explain it in terms of human action and as conforming to human action. The Vedānta, on the whole, became idealistic, found the highest goal of man in the reality innermost to him, and explained the world as the outward manifestation of the inward reality. Jainism was realistic and pluralistic like the Nyāya and the Vaiśeṣika and, like them, pointed to the spirit within man as the reality of the highest value; but unlike the Mīmāmsā, it denounced human action. Buddhism, in the final phases of its growth, became idealistic like the Vedānta, and found ultimate reality in the most inward reaches of man. In its earlier phases, it was realistic and pluralistic.

Usually, the schools of Indian philosophy are given as the Cārvāka, Jainism, Buddhism, Nyāya and Vaiśeṣika, Sāṅkhya and Yoga, Mīmāmsā (also called Pūrva, or Prior, Mīmāmsā), and Vedānta (also called Uttara, or Posterior, Mīmāmsā). There are others, but these nine schools are the most prominent. Buddhism has two branches, Hīnayāna and Mahāyāna, and in India itself about eighteen schools are mentioned under Hīnayāna and three under Mahāyāna. In China and Japan, the Mahāyāna has more branches. Under Vedānta, or Uttara Mīmāmsā, there are eleven schools of which we know. Besides these schools, we have sectarian schools like the Pāśupata and the Pāñcarātra, both of which entered the Vedānta. Some of the schools, both orthodox and heterodox, incorporated elements from one another. Buddhist schools also crossed one another and gave birth to some hybrids. Mādhavācārya in his *Sarvadarśanasaṁgraha* mentions a few other schools, which are philosophically not very important.

Looking at Indian philosophy as a development of Indian religion, one may find six tendencies. The first is the religion of the *Brāhmaṇas* with its cult of Vedic ritual, sacrifices, and duties, culminating in the philosophy of Jaimini's Mīmāmsā, which, so far as life in this world goes, is held in the highest esteem by all orthodox schools. The second is that of the Vedānta, of the schools of which Śaṅkara's is regarded as the most orthodox (*smārtha*), because he relies mainly on the Vedas and not upon the sectarian Āgamas. The Āgamas are sectarian and are of three kinds, the Pāñcarātra, the Pāśupata, and the Śākta. Śaṅkara rejects them as authorities in his commentary on the *Brahmasūtras*. Now, the Pāñcarātra and the Pāśupata traditions produced Vedāntins, who commented not only on the *Brahmasūtras* but also on the Upaniṣads. No Śākta commentary on the *Brahmasūtras* has yet been available. Besides, the Śākta tradition has a peculiar position, in that it can attach itself to all the other traditions—whether they like it or not—and accept their philosophies. Even Jainism and Buddhism could not avoid it, although the orthodox among them would denounce it. Thus the third tendency may be regarded as that of the Pāñcarātra and the fourth as that of the Pāśupata, although both acknowledge the Vedas as an authority. Some, indeed, of the followers of the Pāśupata regard the Vedas as next in importance to their own scriptures and a very few even reject them. The fifth will be that of Jainism and Buddhism, which reject the religion and philosophy of life of the Brāhmaṇas. Thus, while all the orthodox schools hold Jaimini's Mīmāmsā in high esteem so far as this life is concerned, Jainism and Buddhism will have nothing to do with it. We may add the Cārvāka as the sixth tendency, which accepted neither the ethics nor the spirituality of the Vedas. Jainism and Buddhism, though they reject the teachings of the Brāhmaṇas, will accept, like the Upaniṣads, a spiritual reality, but not so the Cārvākas. It is, therefore, difficult to call the Cārvāka by the name religion.

The philosophies of the above religions appropriated elements from the Nyāya, Vaiśeṣika, Sāṅkhya, and Yoga. The followers of the Nyāya and Vaiśeṣika are on the whole Śaivas, following the Pāśupata; the followers of the Sāṅkhya and Yoga are on the whole Vaiṣṇavas, following the Pāñcarātra. The followers of these two traditions introduced their ideas into the Vedānta also in a constructive effort.

Growth of Indian Religion

It will not be of much use to give a history of Indian philosophy, as it is to give a history of western philosophy. The history of any system of Indian philosophy, particularly of the orthodox schools, can serve as a guide to the nature of the history of Indian philosophy as a whole, because all systems developed together out of inchoate beginnings in nearly the same way.

Since even at present philosophy and religion are not separated in India, it will be interesting and useful to point out the stages of development of the Indian religion, before treating the evolution of Indian philosophy. To say that Indian religion has had no history is as wrong as to say that at every stage it became completely different from what it was before. The Universal Eternal Spirit, which is in every man, may not change; but man's experience and understanding of it and his attitude towards it alter; and the change, when we take a long stretch of time, is often for the better, although in some unfortunate circumstances, it may be for the worse. The primitive man, whether he felt the divine presence within himself or outside himself, saw everything as a person like himself. It took several centuries for the mind of immature humanity to depersonify the physical and distinguish between the physical and the psychical. When once this distinction was made, man took some object outside him or within him as the highest divine. He then passed from one object to another, higher and higher outside and deeper and deeper within, in his search for the Supreme, sometimes giving up one for another, sometimes accepting several, and other times relating and identifying them. The quest for the Supreme Ultimate thus became both a scientific and a religious quest. Man must have made the greatest discovery with the greatest wonder, when, in the Upaniṣads, he realized that the deepest reality within him was also the highest reality outside.

Religion in India is now traced back to the time of the Mohenjo-Daro civilization, which existed about 4000 B.C., according to some scholars, and somewhat later according to others. What exactly the religion of the people was, investigators are not yet able to say. But it is surmised that some kind of Śakti worship or religion of the Mother Goddess and meditative Yogic practice may have been current. That is, some religion of inwardness, which tries to seek the Supreme within man, must have been practiced. Written religious records begin with the Ṛgvedic Hymns, which are generally assigned to about 2000 B.C. They are on the whole addressed to gods of nature like the sun, wind, and sky, and the religion seems to be a religion of outwardness, indicating that the mind of the early Aryans was turned outwards (*bahirmukha*) and not inwards (*antarmukha*). There are certain passages like the *nāsadīya* hymn containing abstract speculations about Being and Non-Being and hymns addressed to female deities. But on the whole, the hymns are more indicative of outwardness than of inwardness, and the mind of the early Aryans must have been more full of ideas of concrete objects than of abstract entities and psychic forces.

The first stage in the development of Indian religion may be regarded as that of the Ṛgvedic Hymns, and is nature worship and, hence, of outwardness. The Mohenjo-Daro civilization is considered to be pre-Aryan. It is difficult to say whether the early Aryans, whom the Ṛgvedic Hymns show to be predominantly outward-looking, came across the meditative inward religion after they entered India or whether they brought elements of it along with them into India. We cannot maintain that meditative religion was peculiar to pre-Aryan India only. Greece had the Orphic religion, which can be traced back to earlier times. It is natural for man, whether in India or elsewhere, to look both inwards and outwards. The presence of both inward and outward realities must have struck man everywhere. But the importance of inwardness as a definite factor in religion might have been impressed on the Aryan mind by the extensive presence of the meditative cults present in India of the time, which might have produced the inwardness that is a predominant feature of the religion of the Upaniṣads. One wonders why the same Aryan mind strengthened in Greece a way of thinking that resulted in scientific and social philosophies and was mainly outward-looking, but produced in India philosophies of the inner Spirit by looking inwards. But whether outward-looking or inward-looking, the Aryans in both the East and the West were rational thinkers, philosophers, and metaphysicians. Science and philosophy seem to have been in the Aryan blood of the time. However, from about 2000 B.C.—or the beginnings of the Ṛgveda—to about 900 B.C.—or the time of the *Bṛhadāraṇyaka Upaniṣad*—a slow but sure blending of the two religions, the religion of outwardness and that of inwardness, seems to have taken place, after which the emphasis was shifted from the outward to the inward. This period of blending may be treated as the second stage in the development of Indian religion.

This second stage is significant for both philosophy and religion. In religion it gave importance to the realization of the Ātman and relegated sacrifices to a lower level; in philosophy it gave primary importance to explanations in terms of the Ātman and only a secondary place to explanations in terms of natural processes and activities of gods. During this period, five ways of explaining the world seem to have been accepted: *adhilokam, adhijyotiṣam, adhividyam, adhiprajam,* and *adhyātmam:* that is, as physical processes, as due to gods or deities, as due to sacrificial acts or incantations, as results of cosmic sex contacts, and as processes of the Ātman. Of these, the last was considered to be the highest explanation. To this period could belong the composition of the third and the fourth parts of the Veda, namely, the Araṇyakas and the Upaniṣads. The greatest achievement was the discovery that *sa yaśca ayam puruṣe yaśca asau aditye sa ekah* (he who is in man and that which is in the sun are one),[1] and that the *satyabrahman* (the True Brahman) is the *ahah* (light) in the sun and the *aham* (I) in man's eye.[2]

The religion of the pre-Aryans in India consisted not only of meditative but also of various barbarous cults of a crude and primitive type. The conquering Aryans did not destroy all of them. The Aryans interpreted most of the idols worshiped and the forms of worship as symbols of spiritual stages and processes. The symbols were to be discarded when their truth was realized. Thus Hinduism conquered without destroying, but did this by interpreting and conferring upon all cults the inwardness that it had itself attained. This is the *modus operandi* of Hinduism for absorbing and assimilating a great variety of social groups and forms of worship. This is the third stage in the development of Indian religion, the stage during which it spread by attaching its own inwardness to local cults and absorbing them.

Chronologically, it is difficult to fix the limits of the third stage. The number of local cults must have been very large. The first reac-

[1] *Taittirīya,* III, 10, 4.

[2] *Bṛhadāraṇyaka,* V, 3–4.

tion of the more civilized Aryans to the religious practices of the conquered tribes may have been repulsion, disgust, and contempt. This does not mean that the early Aryans were all saints. They show the greed of the conqueror for the wealth of the vanquished. But they were not even idol worshipers but worshipers of natural forces. They do not seem even to have had temples. Their first reaction to the local forms must have been hostile. But as they got more and more accustomed to seeing them, the Aryans proscribed only some of the most objectionable forms, and gave a spiritual symbolic interpretation to the rest. As rulers, they must have found it necessary to patronize them by taking part in them, just as even now, before the Harijan's entry into temples, Brahmins visit and make offerings in temples of some goddesses, the priests of which have traditionally been Harijans. This process of participation, assimilation, and absorption and interpretation may have been started right from the time the Aryans themselves realized the truth of inwardness and must have lasted throughout the period of the epics, and it is still a feature of most of the religious bodies.

If inwardness is the truth of the world, why should one retain outwardness even as a symbol? The religion of outwardness, like that of the Brahmanic sacrifices and the barbarous cults, has forms that are not only meaningless by themselves but also repulsive, involving the shedding of blood of innocent animals. So inwardness should be caught and retained in its purity, and outwardness discarded. This is the essence of the teaching of Jainism and Buddhism, which appeared during the sixth century B.C. as reform movements within Hinduism, which was called at that time, not by the name Hinduism, but by the name Arya Dharma, the Aryan Path, the religion of the Aryans. It had nothing to do with the meaning that Hitler gave to the word Aryan. It meant noble, sublime. Both Jainism and Buddhism were Arya Dharmas. They would not call themselves Vedic Dharmas, but only Arya Dharmas, though each would claim to be the true Arya Dharma. The word Hindu is not to be found in any of the Sanscrit lexicons, being a corrupted form of the word Sindhu (Indus) used by aliens like the Persians and the Greeks. For them, the Hindus were all the people living on and beyond the river Indus.

The intensification of inwardness is the fourth stage in the development of the Indian religion. Inwardness is found in the second stage also in the philosophy of the Upaniṣads. But it was balanced by outwardness, to which it became complementary. Life in this world was not despised by the Upaniṣadic philosophers. The principle of the *āśramas,* or stages of life, made *sannyāsa,* or renunciation, come towards the end of life. The first three *āśramas—brahmacarya,* or that of the student; *gārhasthya,* or that of the householder; and *vānaprasthya,* or that of the forest-dweller—could be the life of this world, and were punctuated and controlled by the Brahmanic view of life and rules. Jainism and Buddhism, however, repudiated all that was Brahmanic and rejected the Vedas, but offered nothing definite in their place. One could take to the fourth *āśrama,* namely, *sannyāsa* (renunciation), the moment one felt the urge for inwardness, disregarding one's duties to family and society. The highest aim of life is the realization of the Ātman or Nirvāṇa, not heaven and the achievement of worldly values; it is *mokṣa* (salvation), not *artha* (wealth), *kāma* (love), and *dharma* (duty). Then why should one, it was argued, waste one's time and energy in following the last three? Even Śaṅkara was influenced by this argument.

The intensification of inwardness and its one-sidedness had far-reaching effects not only on the life of India but also on its philosophy. The whole of the Mīmāmsā philosophy, which covered practically the first three values of life, and particularly the third, was given not merely a secondary place but an unimportant place; for the first three values were not regarded as necessary steps to the fourth, but only as expedients for some immature minds (*adhikārins*). An inherent necessary relation between the four stages was not accepted. The epic philosophy, which tried to cover every aspect and part of the life of man, was given a still lower place, except for a few *gītās,* like the *Bhagavadgītā* and *Aṇugītā,* which could as well be utilized as philosophies of the fourth value. The Nyāya logic and the Vaiśeṣika metaphysics were either discarded or, whenever suitable, pressed into the service of the philosophy of inwardness; and both the schools had to accept salvation or the realization of the Brahman as the highest aim of life.

Philosophy became the philosophy of inwardness, not a philosophy of the whole life of man. It is not enough to say that this life has only secondary importance and must lead to the realization of the Ātman, which is of primary importance; philosophy has also to say what exactly this life is and how it is to lead to the realization of the Ātman. But none of the classical philosophers cared to tell us much about this life and looked at the Mīmāmsā and the epics with condescension. This is the reason for the western criticism that Indian philosophy has no ethics, a criticism which is not correct if the Mīmāmsā and the epics are taken into consideration, but correct if they are not. The epics have no one definite system of philosophy; but they offer several elaborate philosophies of life. We shall be disappointed if we study epics to discover any rigorous system of metaphysics. In fact, they give brief presentations of many schools, but discuss more the *mārgas,* or ways of life.

The fifth stage in the development of Indian religion is the orthodox reaction against the one-sided inwardness brought about by Jainism and Buddhism in life and thought. The intense inwardness, which became popular after the two schools spread in India, and the extreme forms of asceticism which both preached and popularized, could not indeed be attacked by the orthodoxy, as it itself had some forms of both in the Upaniṣadic philosophy. But the social life of India was disturbed and enervated. Magadha, the seat of many imperial dynasties, became Bihar, the land of monasteries (*vihāras*). There was nothing in the two new religions to emphasize the importance of life in this world and its values. The best men became monks, whose numbers swelled throughout India. The order of nuns was introduced, and their numbers also grew. The best of them could certainly have been the best and the ablest among householders and housewives, the flower of society. And also the worst of society found a comfortable place in the orders of monks and nuns.

The economic and political life of the country suffered immensely, and it became an easy prey to the foreign invader. Besides, the admission of women into monasteries led to corruption; and monasteries lost the respect they had commanded from the laity, who were supporting them. Buddhism was particularly confined to the monasteries, as it lacked a moral code corresponding to the orthodox *dharmasūtras* (ethical codes). So when monasteries disappeared for lack of support, Buddhism disappeared. Jainism was saved only by tacitly allowing its members to become part of the main Hindu fold by adopting the rules of conduct of the third caste, namely, Vaisyas, or traders. Even today in Rajasthan, the Jainas employ Brahmin priests to perform their ceremonies, and some of them are Vaiṣṇavas, worshipers of Viṣṇu. In the same family, some may be Vaiṣṇavas and the others Jainas.

If one views religion as a human and sociological phenomenon, one finds three main causes for the downfall of Buddhism in India. The first and the main cause was the neglect by the monks of this life and its values. It is not meant that the Buddhist teachers did not realize that many men and women were not fit for monastic life; it is meant that, if this life is also part of the life of man, it should be given as much attention and thought as the life of the monk. Human life is not merely a life of inwardness, but also a life of outwardness; and both aspects need careful examination, study, guidance, and control. It is not enough to say that the householder's life is to be a steppingstone to the monk's. Why and how it is so, and what relation it bears to realities, have to be explained. Instead, Buddhist philosophers began to teach that this life was nothing but a vale of tears and misery. Some forms of the Vedānta also tended towards the same teaching; but the strong Mīmāmsā attitude towards life and the teachings of the epics saved Hinduism from the fate that overtook Buddhism in India. Many great Indians were highly susceptible to spiritual teachings and followed them to the letter; but unless there were some codes extolling the values of the world, the Indians tended to becoming one-sidedly otherworldly.

The second important cause was the admission of women into monasteries and the more or less indiscriminate conversion of men and women into monks and nuns. The Buddhists themselves seem to have regretted this mistake later. When true renunciation and celibacy are lauded, people would like to see them well practiced. When people supported with their toil the numerous monks and nuns, they did not do so to keep them in luxury and enjoyment of the very values they condemned. At that time, if monks and nuns had followed the rules they taught, people would have received the fall of empires, destruction of kingdoms, and loss of liberty with equanimity, and would still have supported the monasteries with hard labor.

The third cause was the deterioration of the economic and political life of the country. Monasteries were supported not only by the common people but also by kings and emperors. But when a dynasty fell, the next dynasty might not give the same support. Their thoughtful members might realize that the fall of the previous dynasty was due to the loss of the best men, fighters, and leaders, who had become monks.

These causes lent support to the orthodox revolt, which was however bloodless, in the eighth century A.D. The revolt was staged from two sides, the Brahmanic and the Upaniṣadic. Kumārila was the leader of the former and Śaṅkara of the latter. Kumārila is said to have been hostile to *sannyāsa* and asceticism and would regard any Vedic ceremony performed in the presence of a monk as polluted. We do not know whether Jaimini, whom Kumārila followed, was similarly opposed to *sannyāsa;* but the latter was strongly opposed to it. Whether he was right or wrong—Śaṅkara thought that he was wrong—he succeeded in reviving a strong affirmative attitude towards the world and its values and all that could be called human and activistic. Śaṅkara, from his side, showed that everything that was good in Buddhism was already to be found in the Upaniṣads. In fact, Gauḍapāda, the grand-teacher of Śaṅkara, unified the current *spanda* (vibration) doctrine of Śaivism, the *vijñāna* (mind) doctrine of the Buddhists, and the Ātman doctrine of the Upaniṣads in his *Māṇḍūkyakārikās,* and made the way easy for Śaṅkara to assimilate and absorb Buddhism. Thus Buddhism found no justification for separate existence in India; it had no social ethics and consequently no hold on society; and it could not exist even as a spiritual discipline, for its discipline was shown to be a part of the Upaniṣadic. Even as a philosophy, it was shown that its teachings were contained in the Upaniṣads. Buddhism slowly died out, lingering up to about the fifteenth century. Its recent revival by Ambedkar is more for social purposes, as a protest against some caste superiority, not as a spiritual discipline.

The later stages in the religious development of India do not have much philosophical importance; they have mainly social significance. The sixth stage begins with the advent of Islam with fanatical militant zeal and iconoclasm. With a definite social structure, religious dogma, and theology, Islam refused to be assimilated by Hinduism, but attacked it, mainly physically. It also encouraged opinion against the caste system. The result was the appearance of Vīraśaivism (militant Śaivism) in the south, the Sthānakavāsi Sect among the Jainas in western India, and Sikhism in the north. All the three gave up idol worship and the caste system. But even Sikhism is only a reform movement within Hinduism, like Jainism and Buddhism, though demanding distinct recognition. Indeed, Sikhism wanted to synthesize Hinduism and Islam; but Islam refused to recognize the objective and wanted to destroy it. Sikhism had to defend herself with the sword from the attacks of Islam and lean towards Hinduism.

The seventh stage starts with the introduction of Christianity. Christianity, like Islam, is a revealed religion, and its inwardness is encased in dogma and creed. But it entered India along with science and humanism. Though Christianity was itself opposed to science and rationalistic humanism in many ways in Europe, it criticized Islam and Hinduism from these two points of view, i.e., of science and humanism; and in this it did good service. So far as philosophies of Spirit go, the Christian teachers in India were no match for Hindu philosophers; but the latter had to be apologetic concerning Hindu social customs like the caste system, position of women, and untouchability. The courageous among the Hindu leaders started reform movements like the Brahmosamaj, the Aryasamaj, and others. These movements were partly revivalistic and looked back to the Vedas for inspiration; and whatever new they contained concerned social practices. Even such practices were traced back by the leaders to the Vedas. In independent India, of course, no new religious movements are necessary for introducing social reforms, which are enacted by legislation. Regarding spiritual discipline, there has been nothing new that the ancient spiritual leaders did not teach. One may, however, find new interpretations and explanations of ancient texts in the light of new developments in science and philosophy.

Stages of Philosophical Development

The history of the development of Indian philosophy also may be divided roughly into seven stages. Because of the very close association of religion and philosophy in India, the first two periods in the development of religion are also the first two periods in the development of philosophy. There are very few philosophical speculations in the Samhitās and the Brāhamaṇas; they belong to the Araṇyakas and particularly to the Upaniṣads. The central principle of philosophical inquiry was the Ātman. The Upaniṣads contain clear enunciations of inward reality; outward reality is finally given a secondary place. Performance of sacrifices and the duties of the householder are still preached; yet the realization of the Ātman is extolled. Life in this world is not despised but, on the whole, taken as a necessary stepping-stone to the realization of the Ātman. We have yet to remark that the first three stages (*āśramas*) are not explicitly regarded as requisite steps: it is not said that man cannot and should not take the fourth *āśrama* without passing through each of the first three, although, also, it is not said in the early Upaniṣads like the *Bṛahadāraṇyaka* that one may take to the fourth stage without passing through the other three. People of the time living in the atmosphere of the Brahmanic religion naturally inclined to the first two stages, and it was not necessary at that time for the Upaniṣads to exhort men to take to them. Only after Jainism and Buddhism made *sannyāsa* (renunciation) popular did the orthodox feel it necessary to condemn the fourth. Rāmānuja, for instance, felt that inquiry into the nature of the Brahman (*brahmajijñāsā*) should begin after inquiry into the nature of duty (*dharmajijñāsā*). Kumārila, we have already said, condemned *sannyāsa* outright.

Philosophically, we find a clearly noticeable difference between the religion of nature and the propitiation of the gods of nature through prayers and sacrifices, on the one hand, and the meditative inward religion of the Upaniṣads, on the other. But they got blended. The historical development could not have been sudden; it must have been slow. An intervening stage may therefore be accepted, roughly corresponding to the ideas of the Araṇyakas and the stage of the *vānaprasthya* (forest-dweller's), in which an attempt was made to blend and coordinate the ideas of outwardness and inwardness. The duty of the *vānaprasthi* (forest-dweller) is to evaluate the experiences and values of this world and discover their bearings to the inwardness of life. If the intervening stage is regarded as the second, the Upaniṣadic stage may be regarded as the third.

It has been mentioned that the Jainas and the Buddhists did not accept the Vedas as scriptural authority and rejected the Vedic tradition. The early Upaniṣadic period must have lasted from about 900 B.C., to about 400 B.C., during which time philosophy, though not very systematic, must have struck a fair balance between inwardness and outwardness. But after the rise of Buddhism and Jainism, the scales were turned in favor of inwardness, for these two religious movements would have nothing to do with the outwardness of the Vedic tradition and had little of their own to substitute for it. For a student of comparative philosophy with a historical perspective, Jainism and Buddhism should be interpreted as the intensification of the inwardness reached by the Upaniṣads. We should not forget that neither was Jainism called Jainism, nor Buddhism, Buddhism, when the movements started; they were only forms of Arya Dharma or Arya Mata. That Mahāvīra and Buddha, the founders of the two movements, were more concerned with the discipline of inwardness shows that the people of the time already recognized inwardness as the truth of religion and as the highest aim of life, and saints and philosophers naturally took upon themselves the clarification and teaching of inwardness as their main task. Philosophy became the philosophy of inwardness, and the philosophy of outwardness was either relegated to a secondary place, as it was by the orthodox, or ignored, as it was by the heterodox, who did not think it worth while to give much thought to life in this world. Philosophical interest began to grow one-sidedly, and became concerned only with one value, namely, the realization of the Ātman or Nirvāṇa. This is the fourth stage in the development of Indian philosophy.

It was during this fourth stage that philosophical systematization began. The Upaniṣads are not systematic presentations of Vedāntic philosophy. The orthodox had to argue with the heterodox in defense of their positions. But when their own ideas were not systematic, they could not do so. The heterodox also had to do the same; but as they had no scriptures to rely upon, they had to depend only on logic and experience. As the teachings of Buddha and his immediate disciples were elaborate and could not easily be remembered, they had to be codified. This was generally done in the form of *sūtras,* or aphorisms. The orthodox had already done the same. Thus started the *sūtra* literature. The *sūtras* of the Buddhists, however, are not pithy utterances like those of the orthodox schools. But the word *sūtra* must have had a special appeal to the philosophical schools, and so was used for the early literatures of all. It is difficult to fix the dates of the different *sūtra* works; but the literature must have started from about the fourth century B.C. The *Prajñāpāramitās,* which formed the basis of the Mahāyāna schools of Buddhism, are generally assigned to the period between 100 B.C. and 100 A.D. The *Vaiśeṣikasūtras* of Kaṇāda, the *Nyāyasūtras* of Gautama, the *Mīmāmsāsūtras* of Jaimini, the *Vedāntasūtras* of Bādarāyaṇa and the *Yogasūtras* of Patañjali belong to the period between 400 B.C. and 400 A.D. The *Sāṅkhyasūtras* of

Kapila may have belonged to the beginning of this period; but they are lost. What is now available as the *Sāṅkhyasūtras,* scholars think, was composed by Vijñānabhikṣu during the fifteenth century A.D. The *Jainasūtras* of Umāswāti, also called *Tattvārthādhigamasūtras,* are assigned to the third century A.D. Roughly the period from 400 B.C. to 400 A.D. may be treated as the main *sūtra* period, the period of the first systematization of the philosophical ideas.

Most of the *sūtras,* being very pithy sayings, needed further elaboration and interconnection, and so commentaries began to be written on them. This is the fifth stage of philosophical activity. By about the seventh century A.D., commentaries were written on almost all the important *sūtras,* though no commentary on the *Vedāntasūtras* before Śaṅkara (8th century) is now available. The practice of writing commentaries on the *sūtras* continued right up to the sixteenth century, and even now the practice has not been given up.

The sixth stage is marked by the development of polemical literature. The school of Neo-Nyāya, which specialized in the framing of exact definitions of concepts, set the fashion for exactness in thinking, and all the other schools adopted the method for use in their dialectics. This activity started from about the thirteenth century and lasted until the sixteenth. To this period also belong independent treatises presenting the different systems, and they are not mere commentaries.

From about the sixteenth century up to the advent of the British, the history of Indian philosophy is on the whole a blank, after which the seventh period, characterized by researches adopting western methods, began. If one likes, one may call the blank period the seventh and the next the eighth. The contemporary period may be called the ninth; but no strikingly new system of philosophy has yet emerged; it is still reinterpretation, reshuffling of old ideas with some admixture of western ideas. On the whole, the Indians know more of western philosophy than the western philosophers of the Indian. And if in India a new standpoint is to emerge, it will be through comparative philosophy.

There is one point to be emphasized here. The periods delineated cannot be fixed chronologically. They may, therefore, be treated as stages through which the development of every school passed. Any kind of activity, once started, tends to continue indefinitely even when a new kind of activity supervenes on it. The religious schools and the philosophical schools have continued to be the same till today.

Vedic and Non-Vedic Strands

Although, when one speaks of Indian philosophy, the Vedānta comes at once to mind, and then, too, the Advaita of Śaṅkara, it is wrong to think that even all the orthodox schools developed as elaborations of the Vedas or the Upaniṣads. Obviously, Jainism and Buddhism are not such elaborations. The Mīmāmsā of Jaimini is a systematization of all the duties and acts, sacrificial and otherwise, of the Brahmanic religion, and an elaboration of the philosophy of action underlying those duties. Jaimini would not recognize the importance of the Upaniṣads as primary for philosophy. His philosophy represents the vigor and zest for life of the Aryans, their faith in man and in his action (*karma*) as capable of making or marring his destiny. In fact, for Jaimini there is no life without action either in this world or in the next. Without the Mīmāmsā leaven in the life of India, Hinduism would have met the same fate as Buddhism. It may be that faith in sacrifice is false and outmoded, and it may be that Brahmanism was the faith of the primitive Aryans, who peopled nature with gods or presiding deities, personifying the natural forces or conceiving them as being presided over by some spirits. But the philosophy of action and duty, which was mixed up with, and made a basis of, the sacrificial religion, is full of ethical interest and is one of the best activisms in the world. Even in India, it is the basis of *karmayoga,* the yoga of action or the life of action leading to salvation, and also of the legal and moral codes. The other orthodox schools may question the ultimate validity of the philosophy of Mīmāmsā, but they would consider it a sacrilege to doubt its injunctions, so far as life in this world is concerned.

Leaving out the Mīmāmsā and the Vedānta, which are systematizations of the Vedic ideas, the orthodox schools that accept the Vedas, including the Upaniṣads, as an authority are the Nyāya, the Vaiśeṣika, the Sāṅkhya, and the Yoga. The Vaiśeṣika does not accept them as a distinct authority, *pramāṇa,* or source of knowledge; but it regards them as giving truth. The schools accept the pre-Upaniṣadic parts of the Vedas as containing the truth about this life and the Upaniṣads as containing the truth about salvation. But this acceptance is only general; otherwise, all the schools would have become Vedāntic or Mīmāmsic. Acknowledging the Vedas as a scriptural authority conferred prestige on the schools and obtained recognition among the orthodox. But the non-Vedāntic orthodox schools could not go beyond this general acknowledgment: this is especially the case with the Nyāya and the Vaiśeṣika. They could not interpret the Upaniṣads as supporting their own philosophy. The *Vedāntasūtras* were accepted as systematizing the ideas of the Upaniṣads. But the Nyāya and the Vaiśeṣika could not furnish any commentary on them. And even from the side of the Sāṅkhya and the Yoga, a commentary was written by Vijñānabhikṣu only during the fifteenth century. This shows that the orthodoxy of these four schools—the Nyāya, the Vaiśeṣika, the Sāṅkhya, and the Yoga—went only so far as the acceptance of the Brahmanic portion of the Vedas. They did not, indeed, accept the Mīmāmsā philosophy, but only its schedule of life and duties in this life. They do make reference to the Upaniṣads, but only at random to a few passages which support a view or two of theirs. There is a striking similarity between the metaphysics of the Nyāya and the Vaiśeṣika, on the one hand, and the Mīmāmsā, on the other. All the three are realistic and pluralistic; but while the Mīmāmsā is activistic in the extreme and does not even think of God as a necessary concept of philosophy, saying that human action itself is the controller of everything, the Nyāya and the Vaiśeṣika accept God as the creator of the universe, controller of human action, and originator of grace.

Then, in what respects are the four schools, the Nyāya, the Vaiśeṣika, the Sāṅkhya, and the Yoga, orthodox? One is inclined to believe that they are orthodox, not because they ever cared very much—except in the case of Vijñānabhikṣu—to accept the philosophy of the Upaniṣads or even of the Mīmāmsā, but because they accepted the Brahmanic cult, the Mīmāmsā schedule of life, and the ethical codes (*smṛtis*), so far as life on earth was concerned. The philosophical speculations of the schools progressed independently of the Upaniṣads, but in an atmosphere permeated by the Upaniṣadic ideas. We have evidence of philosophers independent of the Upaniṣadic tradition even before Buddha's time.[3] Even during the Brahmanic times, there were dissenters.[4] So there must have been thinkers reflecting on life and its ideals independently of the Upaniṣadic tradition; some of them like Gautama, Kanāda, Kapila, and Patañjali may have been following, or have accepted for all practical purposes, the Brahmanical cults and social codes; others like Ajita Kesakambali, Sañjaya, Mahavira, and Buddha may not have accepted them and may have rejected the Vedas on which the cults were based. But the philosophical theories of both the groups must have been independent, based only on experience and logic. We are therefore justified in thinking that not only Jainism, Buddhism, and the Cārvāka, but also the Nyāya, the Vaiśeṣika, the Sāṅkhya, and the Yoga started and developed independently of the Upaniṣadic tradition, insofar as the Upaniṣads are a controlling authority. Some of them like the Mahāyāna Buddhism in its later developments and the Sāṅkhya-Yoga in the hands of Vijñānabhikṣu may have come nearer the Upaniṣadic conception of ultimate reality in their own ways. But in the formulation and development of their theories, they were untrammeled by the Upaniṣadic authority and would not at first have worried about the agreement of their theories with those of the Upaniṣads.

There is another noteworthy feature in the development of Indian thought. There were sectarian traditions like the Vaiṣṇava, Śaiva, and Śākta, of which we get good accounts in the epics, but which had their own scriptural authority, the Āgamas, which are distinct from the Vedas and the Upaniṣads. Of the Vedāntic commentators, all except Śaṅkara and Bhāskara own allegiance to both the Vedas and the Āgamas. The rest interpret the *Vedāntasūtras* in accordance with their respective Āgamas, thereby not breaking off with their Āgamas and yet at the same time showing that their views are Vedāntic. Such attempts are condemned by Śaṅkara as *avaidic,* or un-Vedic. The Āgamas, however, are monistic, monotheistic, dualistic, pluralistic, realistic, and so forth, and are on the whole more cosmological and constructive than the Upaniṣads themselves, which are more interested in proving the reality and oneness of the Brahman than in expounding the positive nature of the world. The commentators who approached

[3] E. J. Thomas, *The Life of Buddha* (London: Kegan Paul, 1931), pp. 124 ff. and R. L. Mehta, *Pre-Buddhist India* (Bombay: Examiner Press, 1939), pp. 332 ff.

[4] H. G. Narahari, *Ātman* (Madras: Adyar Library, 1944).

the Vedānta from the side of the Āgamas made, therefore, a more constructive effort than Śaṅkara.

Now, for any constructive philosophy, the Nyāya logic, the Vaiśeṣika pluralistic metaphysics, the Sāṅkhya oneness of physical nature and plurality of selves, and the Yoga theory of the psychological technique for attaining inwardness are very handy. The sectarian Vedāntins used them systematically. With necessary modifications and each in his own way, they derived the Sāṅkhya-Yoga realism of matter, dualism of matter and spirit, and pluralism of spirits out of the oneness of the Brahman; and out of the Sāṅkhya-Yoga dualism again, some of them derived a pluralism like that of the Nyāya-Vaiśeṣika. There are indeed differences of views; but the general trend is clear: and all this is to be found in agreement with the Āgamas. Because a constructive effort needs and implies an affirmative and realistic attitude towards nature, all these Vedāntins are realistic, not only in epistemology but also in metaphysics. Hence the furious controversy over the nature of Māyā between them and the advaitins (non-dualists). The point of interest for us, however, is that the Nyāya-Vaiśeṣika and the Sāṅkhya-Yoga got incorporated into the Vedānta by some of the Vedāntins. The advaitins would regard these philosophies as true only for the lower levels of intellectual maturity; but the other Vedāntins would regard them as essential elements in any true philosophy of even the Brahman. It has, however, to be added that the cosmological efforts did not result in intensive cosmological inquiries but were content with incorporating and weaving the Nyāya-Vaiśeṣika and the Sāṅkhya-Yoga into their own philosophies. It must also be added that perhaps nothing more could have been done then, if we take into consideration the stage of development of scientific and humanistic thought of the time, both in the East and in the West.

The nature of any philosophical development is influenced by religious, metaphysical, humanistic, and scientific viewpoints. These standpoints may be taken simultaneously or in succession; and they may be either coordinating or conflicting. In primitive thought, religion and metaphysics cannot be separated, and they cannot be separated even now. The thought of the primitive man tends to personify principles and even natural forces, both physical and psychological. But as it becomes clearer and clearer to itself, it depersonifies some of them and systematizes its own methods of procedure, thereby developing logic. Logical methods gain in clarity as they become more highly scientific. The purification and clarification of metaphysical speculations of any philosophical tradition are determined by the nature of the empirical knowledge that the thinkers of the time possess. If it is limited only to their knowledge of human nature, then their logic is determined by the known principles of human nature. But knowledge of human nature cannot be complete without adequate knowledge of physical nature also. Extravagances in religious thought can be checked only by an adequate knowledge of human and physical nature. Indeed, excesses may be committed in interrelating religious thought with the humanistic and the scientific, as we find it now and then in the scientific philosophies of the West, which tend to ignore, if not reject, the validity of religious experiences and even of the human, thereby producing the tendency opposite to the extreme claims of intuition and revelation.

It is also wrong to think that metaphysical thought replaces, or ought to replace, the religious; the humanistic, the metaphysical; and the scientific, the humanistic. Each latter trend of thought only clarifies and purifies the former and checks its excesses. Scientifically viewed, man is a combination of material particles; it is wrong for any humanistic thinker to overlook this fact. But it is equally mistaken to think that man is nothing more than a material complex. It is erroneous to say that man is not an animal, a biological entity; but it is equally wrong to think that he is nothing more than an animal. If religion asserts that man is nothing but a divine spark and has nothing to do with matter, it will be one-sided in its affirmation; but this one-sidedness does not necessarily mean that man has no divine spark in him. If religious experience reveals it, it has to be accepted. Thus religion, metaphysics, human experience, and science are complementary to one another, though religion is the oldest and science the youngest.

Science and scientific thought, however, did not begin to influence even the West till about the sixteenth century, at which time the development of Indian thought practically ended. Medieval philosophy, which was Christian, was opposed to paganism; but in philosophy it did nothing but more or less incorporate the pagan philosophies of Plato and Aristotle. The clarification of the Christian philosophical concepts, the very articulation and development of Christian thought, was made possible by the adaptation of Plato and Aristotle and by the application of their logical methods. The philosophies of Plato and

Aristotle were metaphysical and humanistic—and logical and scientific only to the degree to which their methods could be developed at that time. Moreover, the scientific thought of the Greeks went only so far as analysis of human and social phenomena. But even that was a great achievement, which the Christian philosophers could appropriate.

In India also there were analyses of man and society. The analysis of man was guided and motivated by the ideal of the realization of the Ātman and was free, each school being at liberty to formulate its own theories, based upon the experience of its founders and followers, and guided by the logic they were capable of formulating, which was motivated again by the ideal of salvation. But the analysis of society was not free; it was limited by the idea of the caste system, the foundations of which the orthodox would not question but always took for granted. Plato and Aristotle also had some divisions of society; but the divisions were classes, not castes. Indian writers, too, tried to furnish reasons, resembling Plato's, for caste divisions; but the castes became too rigid and far from fluid, and it looks as though the reasons were invented because of the existence of castes rather than that the castes came into being because of the reasons.

India's social and ethical thought, therefore, could not be as rational as that of the Greeks. The logic of social and ethical thought could not form a check upon religious thought. The latter was not developed out of the former as in Greece, though it supplied a goal. So in spite of intensive development of logic in India, its reference to ethical and social phenomena is very slight, and its reference to nature, as one would expect, much less. But too many harmful extravagances and excesses in religious thought were prevented by the absolute freedom it enjoyed from its very beginnings. Religious truths, though intuited and revealed, were not the monopoly of anyone, and were considered to be natural. The check on religious thought was made at first by the logic of religious experience. But later, when the schools were crystallized into sects, their followers used the available logic in defense of their doctrines. And their logic was naturally based on the knowledge and experience of the time.

Thus, even in the orthodox tradition, many of the schools grew independently of the Vedic and the Vedāntic scriptural authority, though making a formal acknowledgment. Such schools did not defend their doctrines with the help of the scriptures, but with the help of logic and experience. And along with the heterodox schools, they contributed much to the growth of the Vedāntic tradition. As a result, there has been more independent thinking in India than what a superficial observation may reveal.

Epics as Full Philosophies of Life

So far as the philosophy of the whole life of man is concerned, it is naturally not to be found in the philosophies of salvation, but in the epics, the ethical codes, and the Mīmāmsā. Though the Mīmāmsā is regarded as one of the orthodox philosophies of India and is a system, the epics and the ethical codes are not systems. The Mīmāmsā did not at first care to give a philosophy of salvation, but only of human action, although later the idea of salvation entered its philosophy. Man's life is a life of action; action produces various kinds of results, good and evil. The Mīmāmsā endeavors to show which actions are conducive to the greatest happiness of man, here and hereafter. But the epics from the beginning try to give, in a popular way, an integrated view of life, including the highest ideal, salvation (*mokṣa*). If the Mīmāmsā is a philosophy of this life and of action, then the Vedānta is a philosophy of the other life and of the renunciation of action (*karma-sannyāsa*). If the Mīmāmsā furnishes a philosophy for the first two stages of life (*āśramas*), then the Vedānta furnishes a philosophy for the other two. But the epics try to furnish a philosophy of both action and renunciation of action, and for the four stages of life. They may be regarded as furnishing a philosophy for the whole life of man. Again, if the Mīmāmsā is a philosophy of the Samhitās and the Brāhmaṇas, and the Vedānta is a philosophy of the Araṇyakas and the Upaniṣads, then the epics contain a philosophy of all the four parts of the Veda. That is the reason for calling the *Mahābhārata,* for instance, the fifth Veda; for it is supposed to teach everything contained in the Veda, through examples, stories, and histories.

We need not go into the origin and growth of the epic literature. It is regarded more as a part of letters than of philosophy. Its aim is to be a popular exposition of the whole Vedic philosophy of life; it will be a worthwhile attempt to understand the philosophy of life of the times through the epics; but it will be a futile attempt to discover any particular system of philosophy in them. If the Vedānta contains several systems, and if the Mīmāmsā differs from all of them, then one should not attempt to find in the epics a system that will agree with all the systems. Besides, the epics try to expound the non-Vedāntic systems also, like the Sāṅkhya and the Yoga. Though people follow different systems of salvation philosophies, their lives should follow certain principles in this world of action; and it is these that the epics present. On the whole, the epics extol life of action (*karmamārga*) as leading to salvation; they do not overemphasize renunciation, or *sannyāsa*.

It is said that the epics were written for the people who were not allowed to read the Vedas and perform sacrifices and other rites enjoined by the Vedas. The Aryans had already settled down socially into castes, and politically into some states. They identified their Arya Dharma (way of life) with Vedic Dharma, which consisted of the four castes, the four *āśramas* for the three higher castes, the cult of sacrifice for the householder, and the meditative religion of the Araṇyakas and the Upaniṣads for the third and the fourth *āśramas*. The whole life of man was geared to the highest ideal, the realization of the Ātman, and so to renunciation, and it was generally presumed at the same time that one should not take to the fourth *āśrama* without going through the first three. Educational institutions also were started for the same purpose. But this plan could not effectively cover the fourth caste and also the untouchables, who were outside the fold of an established society divided into four castes.

Besides, new hordes, many of whom were Aryan in blood, were pouring into the country. As the Aryan religion was equated to the Vedic religion, which some of the new invaders did not follow, they were not regarded as following the Aryan Way. For all those who did not follow the Vedas and perform sacrifices and who were not allowed to read the Vedas in the original, the essence of the Vedic religion had to be taught without actually expounding the texts. Among those who did not care to follow the Vedic way of life, it had to be popularized by appealing to their imagination and emotions. Furthermore, there were numerous local gods and goddesses and their cults; they all had to be Aryanized, which meant that they should be related to the Vedas. These gods and goddesses had to be reinterpreted and identified with the Vedic gods and goddesses, and the task was accomplished through associations discovered between forms, functions, or both. When the cults were inward, it was easy for the Vedic Aryans to point it out; but when they were outward, outwardness was interpreted as symbolic of inwardness. Through this process pre-Aryan Indian religions became Aryanized; and the Aryan religion became Indianized.

When the Vedic religion had to be taught without actually employing the Vedic texts, new texts had to be written, and they were the epics. The epics had to include all gods and goddesses, both the Vedic and non-Vedic. Then the chief god of each had to be exalted in order to meet the needs of the particular cult; hence the large number of epics (*purāṇas, itihāsas,* etc.), the chief god of each of which was finally identified with the Brahman of the Upaniṣads, by treating him as its manifestation or incarnation. If the chief deity was a goddess, she became the consort, an inseparable part of the chief Vedic Deity. Since the epics were meant for people who were not philosophically trained, the Vedic way of life had to be taught by example. And so even the non-Vedic heroes and leaders of men were identified with the Vedic, their lives celebrated as examples of the essence of the Vedic way of life, and their histories included in the epics. Hence the large number of histories, stories, anecdotes, and episodes contained in the epics.

Thus, for a fuller view of the classical Indian conception of human life, one should study the epics, and not merely the six orthodox schools, the two heterodox ones, and the Cārvāka. But because social and ethical thought was not as rigorously and rationally systematized as the philosophies of salvation, it has been common to think of Indian philosophy as consisting of these schools only. Rigorous thought was devoted mainly to philosophies of salvation. If salvation (*mokṣa*) is the ultimate aim of human life, reality itself must have meant that man should realize it. The possibility of salvation has, therefore, to be shown to be in accordance with reality. The other values of life must be subservient and secondary to salvation. If subservient and secondary, and also relative to circumstances, why should philosophers worry about them? This was the attitude of the schools to any philosophy of this life, which is through and through permeated by relativity and compromise. There can be no theoretical absoluteness about such a philosophy.

The peculiar contribution that the epics seem to have made to Indian philosophy of life is their bringing together the three ways to salvation: namely, *karmamārga,* or the way of action; *jñānamārga,* or the way of knowledge or gnosis; and *bhaktimārga,* or the way of devotion. The Brahmanic philosophy emphasized action, and regarded man himself as the ultimate agent of his destiny. Man and none else is responsible for his future, here and hereafter. The Upaniṣadic philosophy also made man responsible for his salvation. The Vedic tradition, including the Brāhmaṇas and the Upaniṣads, may therefore be said to have asked man to be entirely self-reliant and have faith and confidence in his own endeavors. The Upaniṣadic tradition, however, preached that the essence of man, the spirit within him, is either partly or wholly identical with the Supreme Spirit, the Lord of the universe. So ultimate surrender of one's individuality, whatever be the nature of that surrender, is the essence of salvation. But the same surrender may be made through love and devotion to the Supreme Spirit.

So if the Brahmanic tradition preached the importance of action (*karma*), and the Vedāntic tradition the importance of knowledge, then both could be included in devotion: one may perform all acts and regard oneself as only an instrument in the hands of the Supreme Spirit and not as the agent of the actions; and one may surrender oneself in devotion to the Lord. Thus the path of devotion also can lead to the same results. Though there can be excesses in the path of devotion, as in the other paths, the idea behind it is sound, with this difference that self-reliance is weakened. But self-reliance, too, has its own risks. If the path of self-surrender breeds resignation, self-reliance may breed conceit and lead the finite imperfect man to committing mistakes.

It is not our aim here to evaluate the three paths; but the epics elevated each in turn and tried to keep a sort of balance. Our contention is that a full picture of the classical Indian view of life cannot be found in the systems alone. But the systems became the philosophies of

India with respect to the question of the ultimate aim of life, whether it was the Epicurean life of the Cārvāka, the happiness here and hereafter of the Mīmāmsā, the Ātman of the orthodox schools, or the Nirvāṇa of the heterodox.

Development of Vedic Thought from Polytheistic Outwardness to Monistic Inwardness

The religion and philosophy of the Vedas is a good illustration of the growth of a philosophical monistic religion out of polytheism. It is at the same time a fine example of the gradual transformation of the polytheistic religion of outwardness into a philosophical monistic religion of inwardness. Take, for instance, the absolutistic spiritual monism of western philosophy, and raise the question: How does the Absolute Spirit or God work in creating the world? What is its or His *modus operandi?* The external logical approach adopted by Plato, Spinoza, and Hegel does not help us very much in answering this question. The attempt to establish a logical relation between God and the world is justifiable but not adequate. That is the reason for saying that the interest of Indian philosophy begins when that of the West ends.[5] The Supreme Spirit cannot be known by man if he looks outwards towards material nature. If he looks outwards, he sees only matter; hence he has to look inwards. The Supreme Spirit is the Spirit of all spirits: this is the central doctrine of the Upaniṣads and the *Brahmasūtras*.[6] The cosmological and epistemological theories must accord with this central theory.

[5] See P. T. Raju, "The Development of Indian Thought," *The Journal of the History of Ideas,* October, 1952, p. 528.

[6] *Brahmasūtras,* IV, I, 3.

The Neo-Platonic and other mystic schools of the West enunciated the same truth; but they were discarded by most of the philosophers and religious leaders of the West and not given the consideration they deserved. Further, the truth did not obtain that amount of articulation and rational development which similar thought obtained in India. We do not find so much logical explanation of the situation in metaphysics and so much development of psychological technique for bringing the situation within experience as in India. Judaism cared little for such a philosophy and for psychological technique; Christianity depended too much upon faith and grace to encourage the development of such philosophy; and the few attempts that were made in that direction were regarded as either unphilosophical or oriental. To call them oriental was enough to discourage and even condemn them. But if this aspect of spiritual experience is ignored, how can we explain the statement that God created all things simultaneously? Scientists speak of the evolution of the universe, evolution of the earth, and evolution of man, which took billions of years. The Church at first treated the doctrine as an enemy and then reconciled herself to it. This was due, however, to the Church's understanding God's simultaneous creation with an outward attitude.

But take man suddenly waking up from deep sleep in which everything is nothing. His first experience is that of himself and the objects he experiences all around at the moment, all simultaneously coming into being. This is the explanation of the simultaneous creation from the standpoint of inwardness. This is the explanation of only one meaning of creation; but it seems to be the only justifiable elucidation of the idea of simultaneous creation, for other explanations come into conflict with the scientific doctrine of evolution. The suggestion may look strange to the western thinker, but not to the Indian thinker.

A systematic detailed development of the philosophy of inwardness is therefore the greatest contribution that Indian philosophy has made to world thought, however one-sided it became in the process. The early Ṛgvedic religion, according to scholars, is outward-looking nature-worship. There seems to be little idol worship, as the natural forces were worshiped directly, not through symbols. In the earliest stages, it must have been rank polytheism, each natural force being worshiped as a distinct god. Just as man feels himself to be an animated being, the primitive man must have seen nature at first as an animated being and the natural forces also as animated beings, each with a will of its own, and man must have worshiped them. This is the stage of animatism. But when man was able to distinguish between his body and self, either as a double of his physical body or as some living entity that moves about in dreams and leaves the body at death, he must have thought that the natural forces also must have been inhabited by some presiding spirits, which, in the Vedas, are called *adhidevatās*. If, in the earlier stage, man thought of worshiping the sun itself, in the later stage he thought of worshiping the deity presiding over the fiery disc. Similar change must have taken place in the mind of man in his worship of the wind, fire, water, earth, rivers, sky, and mountains. The second stage may be called animism.

The third stage in the development of the Vedic thought would be what Max Müller called henotheism, in which each god, when worshiped, was thought of as the Supreme God. During this stage, great developments must have taken place in the religious thought of the early Aryans. When worshiping natural forces separately, they must have also noticed some order and regularity in their movements. The sun rose and set regularly; the moon waxed and waned at regular intervals; the winds, the rains, and the fires of the forests came at fixed periods. If the natural forces were ordered and interrelated, their presiding deities also must be receiving certain orders. But who was that great God whose orders they were obeying? The Vedas indicate that at one time the early Aryans spoke of Him as the sun in the name of Viṣṇu; at other times as Varuṇa, enveloping the whole universe; at a third time as Prajāpati,the lord of all living beings; at a fourth time as Viśvakarman, the architect of the universe; at a fifth time as Brahmaṇaspati, the lord of sacrifices and sacrificial incantations, who could move the whole universe towards the fulfilment of the sacrificer's wishes; and another time as Indra, the wielder of the thunderbolt and the destroyer of the non-Aryans. These gods were enthroned as supreme one after another and dethroned also, until at last the Brahman of the Upaniṣads was accepted as the only Supreme Deity.

Henotheism is an indication of mind's wavering between polytheism and monotheism. It belongs to the period of transition from one to the other. It is due to the fact that monotheism was not forcibly imposed on the mind of the Aryans, who were therefore allowed to formulate their religious ideas slowly and steadily by themselves, using their reason and experience. But as man was allowed to use his reason and experience, he did not stop with monotheism, for which God is a personal being. If He is a personal being, does He have hands and feet, eyes and ears, like human beings? Does He act with a motive like us? Does He have likes and dislikes? It was difficult for the Upaniṣadic thinkers to think of God necessarily as a person like man. God was therefore often depersonified, and a monistic religion was the result. The Supreme Brahman of the Upaniṣads is an It, not a He or She.

But neither monotheism nor monism retained the outwardness of the earlier forms. The development of inwardness also was a gradual process; and by the time the Vedic religion became monotheistic, it seems to have become inward also. The Vedic thinkers noticed a peculiar correlation between the experiencing man and the experienced world. When the eye is healthy, the forms and colors of objects are seen; when there is no eye, nothing is seen. Similarly, when there is light, the forms and colors are seen, but not in the absence of light. Hence there must be some inherent correlation between the eye and light. This correlation, the ancients thought, can be explained only as two aspects or poles of the same entity. This entity, according to them, was fire, the giver of light. Sometimes it was the sun. Now, fire was one of the five elements—earth, water, fire, air, and ether. The argument led the ancients to think of earth as dividing itself into the sense of smell and the smells, water as dividing itself into the sense of taste and the tastes, air into the sense of touch and the touches, and ether into the sense of hearing and sounds. And because each presiding element was presided over by a deity, the deity was conceived as presiding over the sense also. Sometimes we find the names of the elements and deities slightly varying; but the principle underlying the thought is the same.

There is an interesting narrative in the beginning of the *Aitereya Upaniṣad*. At first the Ātman existed alone and wanted to create the worlds. It then created the worlds above the heavens, the heavens, the earth, and the worlds beneath the earth. Then it wanted to create the rulers of the worlds. So it brought the worlds together and formed them into one substance, which is the egg of the universe (*brahmāṇḍa*). Then it fixed its mind on the egg. The face of the egg burst, and through the hole speech came out, and out of speech fire. Its nostrils burst, and out came the sense of smell, and out of it came wind. Its eyes opened, and out came the sense of sight, and out of it the sun. Its ears burst, and through them came the sense of hearing, and out of it the deity of space.[7] Its skin burst, and there came the sense of touch and through it the deity of air. Its heart burst, and then came mind, and through it the moon. Its anus opened, and out came *apāna,*[8] and through it the god of death. Its penis opened, and out came semen, and through it the god Prajāpati. These deities found themselves in an unbounded expanse, and, overtaken by hunger and thirst, wanted a habitat. The Ātman then showed them a cow and then a horse. But they said that the animals were not enough. The Ātman then showed them man. They were pleased, and said that he was a proper habitat. Then fire became speech and entered the mouth of man; wind became the sense of smell and entered the nostrils; and the other deities also became the respective senses and organs. And in man they began to satisfy their thirst and hunger.

The above account of deities, senses, and their objects is very significant, being indicative of the way in which the gods of nature were made inward to man by the Upaniṣadic thinkers. The gods of external nature as experienced by man have now become the presiding deities of the sense organs, mind, and the organs of action.[9] The external Supreme God has now become the Supreme Ātman or the Brahman. The impossible situation of directly contacting the external God is now changed; the external God becomes the Spirit of all spirits. The gods of polytheism are now placed in control of the elements that constitute man's mind, senses, and organs of action and their respective objects, all of which are again under the control of the Ātman. The Ātman now creates the world through man's mind and senses and organs of action; or to be more exact, the Ātman creates man and the world together, senses and their objects together. When the *Muṇḍaka Upaniṣad* compares the Ātman creating the world out of itself to the spider producing the web out of itself, we have to understand the example in this way. Man is the medium of this creation; he is the arena in which all the cosmic forces and deities act; and he is the clue to the understanding of creation and of the relation of the Supreme Ātman and the outward plurality of the world.

Only one more step is needed to turn this religion of inwardness into a philosophy of inwardness, namely, omitting the personified

[7] At other places, it is *ākāśa,* or ether. Similarly, in other places the deity and the element concerned with smell is earth.

[8] One of the vital principles.

[9] The accounts of presiding deities are very elaborately given in Śākta literature.

deities presiding over the elements or natural forces, and calling them only subtle elements. This was done in the Sāṅkhya-Yoga and the Vedāntic schools. Though they did not repudiate the conception of the presiding deities, they did not care to mention them often in their discussions. The subtle elements (*tanmātras* or *sūkṣmabhūtas*) are the subtle forms of gross elements we perceive around us, and constitute the stuff of the objects of our dream. Modern psychology would say that the objects of our dream are only impressions left in our mind by objects of our waking consciousness. But the question that the Upaniṣadic thinkers will ask is: Why should the eye perceive colors and forms, the ear sounds, and so on? And what are the elements of which the dream objects are made? Only when we know that the eye perceives colors can we give the fact as an explanation for the eye's leaving their impressions on our mind; but the hypothesis of subtle elements, though at first derived from a kind of mythological conception of the presiding deities and their origin, is the Upaniṣadic explanation of why the eye perceives colors. In this again, we find the general trend of the Sāṅkhya explanation of the evolution of the world. Substitute the Ātman for the Puruṣa, the cosmic egg for the Unmanifest, man for the ego, and the creation out of the cosmic egg for the contact between the Puruṣa and the Unmanifest and evolution of the latter—and the rest of the Sāṅkhya can be found with a few differences. The process of one category issuing out of another is otherwise understood by the Sāṅkhya and the Vedāntic schools; but the basis of this explanation is to be found in the inwardness of the Upaniṣadic philosophy.

Because of this inwardness, of the peculiar correlation of man and the world, of his mind and senses on the one side and the objects on the other, of the common roots, in short, of the subject and object of experience, the Upaniṣadic philosophy has become essentially idealistic, in spite of all the differences between the Vedāntic schools. If the senses and the objects are two poles of the same element, then each pole is as real as the other, and so realism is a dominant trend of the Vedāntic thought. From this point of view, the quesiton whether the world is Māyā or not is of secondary importance. That it issued out of the Ātman through the creation of the correlated poles of elements is of primary importance. Similarly, that God or the Brahman is the Spirit of all spirits is of primary importance; that there is difference between the Brahman and the Ātman or that there is identity is of secondary importance. That the reality is absolutely inward and that the world is due to turning this inwardness outwards is the central doctrine of the Upaniṣads, which all Vedāntins had to accept. Differences of view arose in the elaboration of this idea.

Central Ideas of the Upaniṣads

The Upaniṣadic philosophy is a philosophy of the inwardness of the Absolute Reality. It is a culmination and consummation of all the Vedic trends of thought that started from the early Ṛgvedic times. The Supreme Universal Spirit, which is the Absolute Reality, is inward; and when stretched out and turned outwards, the world of nature appears. Reality is like a telescope; when its parts are pushed inwards the Absolute is seen, but when they are pushed outwards the physical world is seen. Man is the central lever of this mechanism; and his reason (*buddhi*), mind (*manas*), and senses (*indriyas*) are the parts, which can be pushed inwards and also drawn outwards. The *Kaṭha Upaniṣad* says that the Lord created the senses outwards and so the objects are seen as separate from, and external to, man; but the wise man closes his eyes and sees the innermost Ātman.[10] The same Upaniṣad says that the objects (elements) are deeper than the senses, mind (*manas*) deeper than the objects, reason (*buddhi*) deeper than mind, *mahat* (the Great or Cosmic Reason) deeper than reason, the Unmanifest deeper than the *mahat,* and Puruṣa (Ātman) deeper than the Unmanifest.[11] There is nothing beyond Puruṣa.[12] Thus each succeeding category is deeper and more inward than the preceding one. Man therefore has to push in or merge each outward category in the inward in order to reach the Ātman.[13]

[10] II, 1, 1.

[11] *Manas* in Upaniṣadic psychology is not the same as mind in western psychology; for *buddhi,* or reason, is a higher entity than *manas* for the former, but reason is only a function of mind for the latter.

[12] I, 3, 10–11.

[13] I, 3, 13.

The Yoga philosophy calls the process of pushing inwards *pratyāhāra,* or withdrawing, which is withdrawing the world into the Ātman. This explanation of the world is not merely psychological, but also metaphysical. If man's conscious being is a correlate of the physical world, metaphysics can be developed from either of the correlates, that is, both from the side of psychology and from that of physics; metapsychology and metaphysics can lead to the same point, and are explanations of the same reality. In a different language, the former will be the metaphysics of inwardness and the latter the metaphysics of outwardness.

The Upaniṣadic conception of the Ātman must have been arrived at, gradually and by steps, after serious inquiries, probings, and self-reflection. The *Taittirīya Upanisad* gives an idea of these steps. The word *ātman* is used in the pre-Upaniṣadic Vedic literature also, but not always in the metaphysical sense that it acquired in the Upaniṣads.[14] There it is a sort of double of the physical self of man, and leaves the body after death for the enjoyment of the fruits of sacrifices in heaven. But this naive conception must have been purified and deepened as the Vedic religion became more and more philosophical and inward. The *Taittirīya Upaniṣad* says that *ākāśa* (ether or space) issued out of the Ātman, air out of *ākāśa,* fire out of air, water out of fire, and earth out of water. Thus the five cosmic elements are created. Then plants are born out of earth, food out of plants, semen out of food, and man out of semen. Man is the essence of food and is the physical body, which is not the *ātman,* or self, of anything. Of this body the vital principle (*prāṇa*) is the *ātman;* of *prāṇa* mind (*manas*); of the *manas* reason (*buddhi,* or *vijñāna*); of *vijñāna* bliss (*ānanda*); and of *ānanda* the pure Ātman.[15] This lesson was taught by Varuṇa to his son Bhṛgu. The son wanted to know the Brahman. Varuṇa told him to know that principle from which all things were born and into which they entered. Bhṛgu did penance for the purpose—which means that he meditated on the problem deeply—and discovered that the principle was food or matter. But

[14] Narahari, *op. cit.*

[15] Rāmānuja says that *ānanda* is the same as the *ātman*. It has to be noted that the Brahman also is called the Ātman. So when the word is used in the sense of the universal Spirit, the word is written as Ātman, and when used in the sense of the individual spirit, as *ātman*. According to some, they are one and the same.

not satisfied with the discovery, he approached his father again, and was asked to do further penance. Bhṛgu discovered that the principle was the vital principle, mind, reason, bliss, and finally the Ātman.

What happened in the life of Bhṛgu must have happened in the life of humanity also. The most ordinary tendency is to identify our self with the material body. Next, to the primitive man, the "I," which disappears at death, must have been a shade, a double of the physical body; and because one does not breathe at death, the "I" must have been identified with breath or air, which is also the etymological meaning of the word spirit. We now know that the spontaneous synthetic processes of the human body like breathing and assimilation of food are due to the vital principle. The search for the root of the "I" did not end with the discovery of the vital principle. Man breathes in sleep, but does not answer when called. We say that he is alive then, but that his mind is absent. It is the next step then to identify the self (*ātman*) with mind; and mind is inward to the vital principle. This inward probing was further carried on by the Upaniṣadic thinkers. One, though awake but not in his reason (wits), may deny his own "I." He may say: "I am not alive." So the real "I" is reason. But in deep sleep, one's reason is not active; yet when one wakes up, one says, "I slept well." So the "I" must be that deep unconscious state, which the Upaniṣads call bliss. But the nature of the "I" is consciousness; and so the unconscious of deep sleep must be a shroud. Hence consciousness within the bliss state is the *ātman* in its purity.

The bliss state in deep sleep is also called the causal body by the advaitins. In it the whole content of human personality is said to be latent. In the reverse direction, the bliss state of deep sleep is the body of the pure *ātman;* reason of the bliss state; mind of reason; the vital principle of mind; finally the physical body of the vital principle. The pure *ātman* is not the body of anything; and the physical body is not the *ātman* of anything.

When it was realized that ultimate reality could be reached at the most inward point of man's conscious being, the Upaniṣadic thinkers devoted all their thought to understanding its inwardness. The *Māṇḍūkya Upaniṣad* explains it in a different way. It is interested, not in the levels of the "I," but in the states through which the "I" passes and in the ultimate ground of the "I" consciousness. This ground is the Ātman.[16] If we are to find it in its purity, we have to disentangle it from the three states. It is called *vaiśvānara* (mundane person) in the waking state.

The function of its reason (*buddhi*) is concerned with outward objects. It has seven parts or organs: head, eyes, life, middle part of the body, pelvis, feet, and face.[17] It has nineteen openings for reaching its objects: the five senses,[18] the five organs of action,[19] the five vital forces (*prāṇas*),[20] and the four internal instruments.[21] It enjoys gross objects.

In dream the self is called *taijasa,* because it is constituted by *tejas,*[22] the psychic force in which all urges and impressions lie latent. In this state also, it has seven parts and nineteen openings. It enjoys the subtle forms of objects, that is, objects made up of subtle elements.

In deep sleep the self is called *prajña,* because it is solid, intense, and integrated consciousness. Here all the senses, mind, etc., are completely unified (*ekībhūta*) and, with their distinctions lost, are merged in the unconscious state of deep sleep. This state is filled with *ānanda* (bliss). The idea that in deep sleep the *ātman* is full of consciousness and bliss is not easily appreciated. It is differently explained by different Vedāntins. The advaitins argue that there is consciousness in deep sleep, because one who wakes up says that he slept well, and unless one were conscious, one could not have known of one's sound sleep. There is bliss, because the *ātman* has nothing to desire, no object to hanker after, as all the elements that constitute such an object are withdrawn into a unity, which is one's own being. Everything comes out of the Ātman or Brahman, which divides itself into subject and object and pursues the

16 For a discussion of the Indian conception of spirit, see P. T. Raju, "The Concept of the Spiritual in Indian Thought," *Philosophy: East and West,* October, 1954. A few paragraphs are taken from that article.

17 The presiding deities of these parts are also referred to.

18 Sight, hearing, smell, touch, and taste.

19 Feet, hands, mouth, penis, and anus.

20 *Prāṇa, apāna, udāna, samāna, vyāna.* These are the synthetic vital forces responsible for the sympathetic and involuntary processes within the body.

21 *Manas* (mind), *ahaṁkāra* (ego), *buddhi* (reason), and *citta* (apperception).

22 This word should not be translated as fire or light.

> object. When both subject and object are withdrawn into a unity, there can be nothing outside to pursue, and every desire becomes realized. But in deep sleep, the *ātman* is overwhelmed and stupefied by some mysterious dark force, the Unmanifest, and so it does not realize its true nature. Therefore, this shroud has to be removed, and then the fourth stage of the pure Ātman is revealed. This is the real spirit within us. If one could enter into deep sleep and at the same time retain one's consciousness, one could realize the fourth state; it is true spiritual realization. Thus deep sleep is understood by the *Māṇḍūkya Upaniṣad* not as mere nullity, but as something similar to the unconscious of modern psychology. It is the unconscious integrality of our whole being.

Bliss is integrality and intensity of being.

One important doctrine, which is not clearly stated in the Upaniṣads but which seems to be developed out of the *Māṇḍūkya Upaniṣad,* is that the three states of the finite person correspond to the three states of the Cosmic Ātman. We have, as described above, four states of the individual, *ātman, prajña, taijasa,* and *vaiśvānara.* Correspondingly, we get four states of the cosmic person, Brahman, Iśvara, Hiraṇyagarbha (also called Sūtrātman), and Virāt. The former are the four states of the *ātmans* separately (*vyaṣṭi*), and the latter of all of them taken together (*samaṣṭi*). The implication of this doctrine is that the *ātmans* are not really separate, but are knit together into a totality. Dream is inward to the waking state, deep sleep inward to dream, and the pure *ātman* inward to deep sleep. Similarly, Hiraṇyagarbha is inward to Virāt, Iśvara to Hiraṇyagarbha, and the Brahman to Iśvara. Virāt is the unity and totality of all the *ātmans* in their waking state; Hiraṇyagarbha of all of them in their dream state; Iśvara of the same in deep sleep; and the Brahman of the same in their pure original state. This doctrine as such is not accepted by all the Vedāntins.

The *Bṛhadāraṇyaka Upaniṣad* gives another clue to the understanding of the *ātman.*[23] King Janaka asks his teacher Yajñavalkya about the light by which man is guided. The first answer is that it is the light of the sun. But when the sun sets, what is that light? It is the light of the moon. When there is no moon? Then it is the light of fire. But in the absence of fire? Then it is the light of speech. But

[23] IV, III, 2 ff.

when there is no speech? In dream, for instance, we are not guided towards dream objects by anybody's speech, and yet we cognize them. The answer is: The light of the *ātman*. So to get at the light of the *ātman,* we have to catch the light with the help of which we see objects in dream. The implication is that this light is as different from dream objects as the physical light is from the objects it illuminates. The clue for the light of the Spirit, therefore, is to be found in the light that illuminates dream objects. And the Upaniṣads affirm the ultimate identity of the light of the *ātman* with the light of the sun. If ultimately the light of the Lord is to be reached, it can be reached inwardly. Such is the central metaphysical doctrine of the Upaniṣadic philosophy and religion.

The Upaniṣads contain other philosophical doctrines also. The doctrine of *karma* enunciated in the Brahmanic literature had come to stay, and by the time of the Upaniṣads had obtained greater elaboration. It found so deep a root in the philosophical thought of the times that even in the Nyāya-Vaiśeṣika it entered its epistemological doctrines. Originally man performed *karma* in the form of sacrifices and other duties in order to obtain his wishes through propitiation of gods and ancestors. But the Vedas developed this idea into *karmas* (actions) themselves being the agents for producing the corresponding results. Man would take appropriate births for enjoying the fruits of action. For philosophies like the Nyāya-Vaiśeṣika, which accept a personal God to supervise the process of *karmas,* God has to create the world according to the *karmas* of the souls. If so, not only the enjoyment, but also the perception, of objects is guided and controlled by *karmas.*

Besides, when the Vedic thinkers accepted the truth of inwardness and began giving philosophical explanations from that point of view, they must have found also that the explanation of the world in terms of the *karmas* of the souls fitted their standpoint fairly well. Fanciful deductions may have been drawn by later thinkers and religious leaders from the doctrine of *karma;* but the idea behind the doctrine and the standpoint that it suited can well be appreciated.

The next important doctrine of the Upaniṣads is the distinction between higher and lower knowledge. Higher knowledge is the knowledge of the inward reality, and lower knowledge that of the outward. The former leads to salvation (*mokṣa*); the latter is that of arts and sciences pertaining to this world. The Upaniṣads distinguish between higher and lower self also, which are the noumenal and empirical selves both within man. The latter enjoys the objects of the world and the fruits of action; but the former only looks on like a disinterested witness.

Though for the Upaniṣads the central doctrine is that of the Ātman, they now and then refer to views which were current at that time and which they reject as not ultimately true. There were speculations in India like those of early Greek philosophers. There were thinkers who traced the origin of the world to water, fire, air, ether, space, Non-Being, Being, Vital force, Time, chance, nature, fate, some cosmic womb, etc., etc. But, except in a few cases in which the names of the thinkers are mentioned, it is difficult to say who they were, nor can we give their dates. The Upaniṣads mention the views only to refute them or give them a lower place. Commentators reinterpret them, taking all the Upaniṣads and all of their statements as being meant to support ultimately the same doctrine of the Ātman, although the Upaniṣads were not composed by the same man or at the same time.

Cārvāka Materialism and Hedonism

The Cārvāka is the only thoroughgoing materialistic system in Indian philosophy. As a system of philosophy, or even as a religion, it does not seem to have had much of a following. Its development also does not equal that of the other important systems. Cārvāka is supposed to be the name of its founder, who may have belonged to the Vedic times. His *sūtras* seem to have been irrecoverably lost, except for those that are referred to by others. Recently scholars tried to collect as many as available. *Tattvopaplavasimha* by Jayarāśi (*c.* 700 to 800 A.D.) is a developed account of Cārvāka philosophy. But it is doubtful whether the author himself was a follower of this school. For he was a Brahmin, and no orthodox Brahmin would accept this philosophy. It is a philosophy justifying the first two values of life, wealth and enjoyment, and ignoring the two other values, duty and salvation. It is therefore thoroughly materialistic and hedonistic. If the Vedānta is a philosophy of salvation, preaching non-action, the Mīmāmsā a philosophy of duty, preaching ethical action, then the Cārvāka is a philosophy of wealth (*artha*) and enjoyment (*kāmā*), denouncing the philosophies of both duty and salvation. It believes in the reality of matter only and so would support the acquisition of wealth also, for without it there can be no enjoyment.

It was the fashion of the orthodox, in expounding their philosophy, to anticipate and elaborate objections from the materialistic point of view, and thus exercise their intellect. It is possible that *Tattvopaplavasimha* was written in such spirit. Or Jayarāśi may have been a forerunner of Śrīharṣa in showing the invalidity of all forms of knowledge. But while Śrīharṣa says that therefore everything in the world is not ultimately true and the intuition of the Brahman alone can give us ultimate reality, Jayarāśi says that therefore we should make the best of the situation and rely on pragmatics. He would justify pragmatics, *lokavyavahāra* (not pragmatism), expediency, and Machiavellism, though he did not show interest in politics.

The Cārvākas preached materialism in metaphysics and, as represented by the other schools, a rank type of hedonism. Everything that could not be perceived had to be rejected. So even ether, which was accepted as one of the five elements by the other schools, was rejected by the Cārvākas. The universe is made up of four elements—earth, water, fire, and air. The Cārvākas could not have accepted the atomic theory of the Nyāya Vaiśeṣika; for only particles could be perceived, not atoms. Man is a peculiar grouping of the four elements. Consciousness is not due to the *ātman,* the existence of which cannot be proved, and has no reality of its own. It is a kind of emergent quality that the elements acquire when grouped by nature in a peculiar pattern. The *ātman* is not real, because it is not perceivable. Inference cannot establish the reality of the *ātman,* because a perfect inference is never possible and the inferences we make are all invalid, their occasional validity being only accidental. The Cārvākas refute the validity of inference from the Humian empirical and sensational standpoint. Any inference is valid only if the major premise, which has to be universal, is true. But who can establish the truth of any universal empirical proposition? So every object and doctrine that is proved with the help of inference is unreal and false. Hence, the *ātman,* life after death, heaven and hell, salvation, gods, and goddesses are all unreal and untrue. The Vedas may ask us to perform sacrifices, but who can have faith in the Vedas, which are inconsistent in their injunctions, sometimes asking us to kill animals in sacrifices and other times preaching against destruction of life? If animals killed in sacrifices are said to go to heaven, then why should not one sacrifice one's parents and send them to heaven? Even Vedic statements are not true unless they accord with our perception.

The ideal of man, therefore, is to make the best of life. The ethical theory of the Cārvākas is hedonistic and Epicurean. It may be that, as also in the original doctrine of Epicurus, rank sensualism was not preached by the Cārvākas; and they were even perhaps vegetarian and eschewed animal food. But in the orthodox literature, they are represented as rank sensualists, antisocial and unethical.

Though the early Cārvākas accepted perception as the only source of knowledge, later Cārvākas rejected even perception, for often it is deceptive and objects are always seen through a medium which may distort their appearances in space and time and in form.

Obviously, the philosophy of the Cārvākas is not a philosophy of inwardness. It tried to be quite thoroughgoing in its empiricism and in its later developments tended towards skepticism. The overwhelming inwardness of the general philosophical and religious outlook prevented further development of the Cārvāka.

Jainism

Jainism is generally considered next after the Cārvāka. But Jainism is spiritual in its motive, believes in the reality of the spirit, accepts the validity of inference, and preaches salvation as the highest ideal of life. Rising in protest against the Vedic religion of sacrifices, it condemned all shedding of blood, preached noninjury to all living beings, and advocated vegetarianism. In preaching noninjury, it went farther than Buddhism; for Buddha taught his disciples to eat all food—both vegetarian and nonvegetarian—if offered to them as alms; but the Jainas would accept only vegetarian food. Besides, the Jainas held that all philosophies and religions contained both truth and untruth, and developed the idea into conditionality of all truth.

Vardhamāna was the original name of the founder of Jainism, and he was given the titles of Mahāvīra (the Great Hero) and Jina (the Conqueror). He was an older contemporary of Buddha and belonged to the sixth century B.C. But Jainism traces its origin to Ṛṣabha, who is a Vedic personality and is the first of the twenty-four *tīrthaṅkaras* (holy men) of Jainism. The Jainas do not accept the reality of God, but worship their holy men and teachers.

There are four ways in philosophy for preserving the unity of the universe, including man and nature (1) by postulating the ultimate unity of all objective nature, (2) by postulating the ultimate unity of all spirits within men, (3) by postulating the ultimate unity of both unities, and (4) by postulating a unitary controller of spirits and nature, both of which may be pluralistic. In Indian philosophy, we find all the four attempts. Philosophical explanation is an inherent drive of reason to discover unity in plurality. Even if the unity is not treated as an entity, it is treated at least as a law, expressed as the similar or coordinated behavior of plurality. The logical consequence of the last attempt would be to posit a unity in terms of activity. For to say that the unity of the universe is due to the similarity or coordinatedness of the activities of the plurality is not enough, because there must be a reason for that similarity or coordinatedness. To say that it is nature is again to posit some unitary entity to be called nature. So it must be the unitary coordinated activity itself.

The orthodox Sāṅkhya, as expounded in the *Sāṅkhya-kārikās,* accepted the unity of the objective world, saying that it is due to the transformation of a unitary entity, Prakṛti. Spirits constitute a plurality independent of each other, coming into contact with each other only when they get enmeshed in the workings of the selfsame Prakṛti. Certain forms of the Vedānta, like the Advaita of Śaṅkara and the Śuddhādvaita of Vallabha, accepted the unity of the spirits of all men, and each in its own way rejected the separate reality of physical nature. Certain other forms of the Vedānta accepted the unitary Prakṛti of the Sāṅkhya, the plurality of the finite spirits, and unified both by postulating the Universal Spirit residing in both the finite spirits and Prakṛti. This was done also by the Yoga of Patañjali and the theistic forms of the Sāṅkhya. The other forms of the Vedānta accepted a plurality of nature and a plurality of spirits and unified both with the help of the Universal Spirit or God. This was done by the Nyāya and the Vaiśeṣika also.

But the original Mīmāmsā and Jainism did not accept either God or the unitary Prakṛti. The conception of the unitary Prakṛti is not really consistent with the conception of independent atoms. If the atoms are independent of each other and eternal, why their activities should conform to each other in creating the common world cannot be explained. Those who accept God can at least say that He is so powerful as to compel them to behave in ways necessary for creating and maintaining the common world. Our reason may not be satisfied with this explanation; but it is some explanation, and our religious feeling at least may be appeased. But a pure pluralism of spirits and nature cannot give even this explanation.

It seems that the unifying principle for both the original Mīmāmsā and Jainism is *karma,* or human activity. Orthodox interpreters of the schools already recognized that the role played by God in theistic systems is played by *karma* (action) in the Mīmāmsā.[24] Accepting for argument's sake the truth of the Mīmāmsā and Jaina metaphysics, if we ask what it is that brings all the atoms of the physical elements and the plurality of the souls together in such a way as to make each soul obtain the proper environment it deserves and constitute a common world, the answer is *karma.* We may leave out for the moment the question how *karma* is understood by the two schools. For Jainism it is *karma* that binds the souls to the material world; and for the Mīmāmsā it is again *karma* that produces the environment and the enjoyment that the souls deserve. So what makes the universe a coördinated unity is, for the two schools, human action. It may be pointed out that all the Indian schools, except the Cārvāka, accept the doctrine that *karma* binds down the souls to the material world. But for the theistic schools, the workings of *karma* are supervised by God or the Brahman; and the realization of the Brahman frees the souls from material bonds. Further, God makes the atoms come together

[24] Cf. the oft-quoted verse:

Yam śaivāh samupāsate śiva iti brahmaiti vedāntinah
bauddhāh buddha iti pramāṇasacivāh kartaiti naiyāyikāh
arhannityatha jainaśaśanaratāh karmaiti mīmāmsakāh
soyam vai vidadhātu vāñcitaphalam trailokyanātho harih.

according to the *karmas* of the souls. But for the Mīmāmsā and Jainism, there is no God; and so the ethico-religious *karma* itself must be the unifying force.

The Sāṅkhya does not have to explain how the atoms come together only because it does not accept eternal and separate atoms as the stuff of the world. On the contrary, the physical world of plurality is due to the transformation of the unitary Prakṛti (nature), which evolves the physical world for the enjoyment of the souls according to their *karmas*. Of course, no philosophy has a satisfactory answer to the question how before any *karma* was performed the world evolved, whether from the plurality of the atoms to the unity of nature or from the unity of nature to the plurality of the physical world, if the world is to be in accordance with the *karmas* of future souls. The Upaniṣads in a semimythological and philosophical way, as mentioned earlier, say that the physical world and man were created out of the Cosmic Egg (*brahāṇḍa*) for the enjoyment of the deities of the elements, which also came out of the Cosmic Egg. If we leave out the deities for philosophical purposes, it is the elements that enjoy themselves by splitting themselves into the subjects and their objects. In this explanation also, plurality comes out of an original unity through creative desire on the part of the Ātman. But the original plurality was not created according to anybody's *karma*. *Karma* gets its significance only after man is created. The significance of the Upaniṣadic doctrine is that the Cosmic Egg contains rudimentary urges or instincts corresponding to our senses, organs of action, and mind, and man everywhere has the same senses, organs of action, and mind.

The Jaina metaphysics is pluralistic and qualitatively dualistic. The two main categories are *jīva* and *ajīva*, the animate and the inanimate; and both are substances. Time also is a substance. All substances are extended except time. The inanimate consists of motion, rest, space, and matter. Matter consists of atoms. The *jīva* (soul) is bound to matter by its own *karma;* but when *karma* is renounced, the soul is freed from bondage. *Karma* is like dust, consisting of small particles, found everywhere, and ready to work like a glue binding the soul to matter.

In epistemology, the Jainas take a very liberal view. Every doctrine contains both truth and untruth. If so, the rival schools ask, is the Jaina doctrine also both true and untrue? The Jainas, however, say that every judgment is enunciated from a standpoint (*naya*). From that standpoint, it is true; but from the opposite standpoint, it is false. Every judgment is thus conditioned. The doctrine of conditioned predication is called *syādvāda* by the Jainas.

Jaina philosophy is therefore outward-looking, though its religion is inward-looking. For all schools except the Cārvāka, religion is spiritual inwardness and is inward realization. For Jainism also it is inward realization of the original perfection of the soul. The Jainas prefer the word *jīva* to *ātman,* and say that there is no difference between the two. The *jīva* in its original purity is the same as the *ātman.* In that state the *jīva* has some limited infinitude and is omniscient. But when bound by a physical body, it assumes the size of the body.

Buddhism

If the fourfold Aryan truth is an original doctrine of Buddha himself, then a detailed articulation of pessimism and emphasis on it have also to be attributed to him. He is said to have first preached that (1) everything is a misery, (2) everything has a cause, (3) there is a way of stopping misery by stopping its cause, and (4) so there is cessation of misery. As a philosophy of life, Buddhism was made to focus on misery. The original Upaniṣadic distinction between lower and higher happiness is now transformed into the distinction between misery and happiness. And this pessimism later entered all schools of Indian thought, at least as a strain, which in popular renderings became somewhat conspicuous. But we have to add that, if religion is essentially concerned with spiritual realization only and not with social and political forms of human life, then Buddhism is the religion par excellence. The compassionate Buddha took it as the mission of his life to lift human beings out of the misery of the world.

Assuming that life is misery, Buddhist philosophy worked out an explanation for the causation of this life and the method of rising above it. This world, *samsāra,* is a continual flow of birth and rebirth, according to *karma*. But our individuality is due to a chain of causation with twelve links, which is called *pratītyasamutpāda*. The idea of continuous flow was developed by the Buddhists into the doctrine of momentariness. Everything in the world is momentary; it comes into being and disappears the next moment. But it leaves some impressions (*vāsanās, samskāras*), a latent potency of form or urge towards form in the next moment of existence, which again leaves it in the next, and so on. While being is momentary, the impressions are not and correspond to universals, although, again, the Buddhists reject the doctrine of real universals. The aim of life is to get over momentary existence, which, because of the destruction involved at every next instant, is full of pain.

Because everything is momentary and so every cause is momentary, it cannot pass over into the effect. The effect, therefore, is not the cause in a different form, but is something new that comes into being depending on the cause. Everything is not the cause of everything; the laws of causation are fixed with reference to particular causes and particular effects. Only an acorn can produce an oak; but the acorn has to destroy itself before the oak appears. Thus the oak can come into being depending on the acorn. The acorn is a necessary condition of the oak. *Pratītyasamutpāda* is therefore dependent emergence. The word emergence itself is not appropriate, as it suggests the coming up of something that is already there but merged. The doctrine is really a kind of occasionalism: the cause is really an occasion of the effect, but a necessary occasion.

So far as human life is concerned, its causation has twelve links: nescience (*avidyā*), impressions (*samskāras*), initial consciousness (*vijñāna*), body-mind (*nāma-rūpa*), the six fields of experience (*ṣaḍāyatana*),[25] sense-contact (*sparśa*), sense-experience (*vedanā*), thirst (*tṛṣṇā*),[26] clinging (*upādāna*), tendency to be born (*bhāva*), birth (*jāti*), and old age and death (*jarāmaraṇa*).

The twelve links explain the individual and his misery. The first link is ignorance. But whose ignorance is it? The individual is a product of ignorance; therefore, it cannot be his ignorance. Then it must be some cosmic state. But it is difficult to understand how there can be ignorance, if it is not the ignorance of anybody. The answer to the problem is as difficult to get from Buddhism as from the Advaita

[25] Of the five senses and of mind.

[26] That is, desire.

Vedānta. For both schools the problem is the same, as Buddhism identified ignorance with Māyā in the Mahāyāna. Next, out of ignorance come forth impressions (*samskāras*). But again whose impressions are they? There is no individual as yet. They seem to be cosmic, all-pervasive, the creative forces of the universe. They are the latent forces, drives, instincts, tendencies, and together correspond to the causal body of the Advaita. Out of the network of these impressions issues forth *vijñāna,* the initial integrated consciousness, the knot of the individual. One is reminded of the Upaniṣadic conception that *vijñāna* (reason) is the body of bliss (*ānanda*), the unconscious, the causal body, in which all drives, instincts, and impressions lie latent. Out of *vijñāna* comes the psychophysical individual (*nāmarūpa*).

Next appear the six fields of experience: namely, the five senses and their objects, and mind and its objects. Here one can see a general similarity between this view and the Sāṅkhya view that mind, senses, and their objects are born out of *buddhi* (which is also called *vijñāna* by orthodox schools). From here onwards Buddhism gives an ethical derivation. So far it has been metaphysical also. Mind and senses go after objects; and thirst, or desire, for them appears next. Then the psychophysical individual clings to the objects, becomes attached to them. He finally develops a strong tendency to be born in order to enjoy them. The result is birth, which involves old age and death.

The above is an inward account of the explanation of the appearance of man and his world. Buddha was not inclined toward affirming the metaphysical reality of the *ātman,* and so the links of causation did not start with it. But if we take the *Taittirīya* and the *Aitereya* accounts together, we find a significant similarity between them and the Buddhist account. The latter certainly does not make any reference to the Ātman, and is purely rational and metaphysical and ethical. The psychophysical individual, man, is there. How could he have come into being, if we adopt the inward explanation? The twelve links are an answer.

Then what is man to do to get over the world (*samsāra*) of births and rebirths? He has to adopt the eightfold Aryan path: right views (*samyagdṛṣṭi*), right resolve (*samyagsaṅkalpa*), right speech (*samyagvāk*), right conduct (*samyakkarma*), right livelihood (*samyagjīva*), right effort (*samyagvyāyāma*), right mindfulness (*samyagsmṛti*), and right meditation (*samyagsamādhi*). In *samādhi* one attains Nirvāṇa, the highest realization.

The word *nirvāṇa* occurs in the Upaniṣads, but it is interpreted as the realization of the Ātman. But Nirvāṇa especially for the early Buddhists is only a kind of negative state, meaning the unagitated or undisturbed. For the Upaniṣads also it has the same meaning. For if it is like the unperturbed deep sleep, although conscious, it also is unagitated. The essential core of man, according to the orthodox schools and Jainism, is the *ātman*. But *ātman* does not have any single meaning, and so Buddha refused to answer the question whether the *ātman* is real or not. But something that is the essence of man's being has to be realized. This realization is possible by excluding whatever is not the essence. For the purpose, man is asked to analyze himself. The psychophysical person (*pudgala*) is only an aggregate of aggregates. He consists of the aggregate of matter (*rūpaskandha*), aggregate of feelings (*vedanāskandha*), aggregate of sensations (*samjñāskandha*), aggregate of consciousness (*vijñānaskandha*), and aggregate of impressions (*samskāraskandha*). Now when a person analyzes himself away into these aggregates, what will be the residue? Buddha could not say that the residue is a unitary conscious being called *ātman;* and so he refused to answer the question and allowed his disciples to find it out for themselves. If the *ātman* is the "I," and if the "I" is taken to be the psychophysical individual, when the physical and psychical elements are analyzed away, it is difficult to say that any remainder will be left. So many of the followers of Buddha said that nothing would remain. The remainder would be *śūnya* (void); if anything remains—since everything is momentary and subject to change, birth, and destruction—there will be no Nirvāṇa.

According to Mādhavācārya's *Sarvadarśanasaṅgraha,* epistemologically the main Buddhist schools are regarded as four in number: the Vaibhaṣikas, who were presentationists; the Sautrāntikas, who were representationists; the Yogācāras, who were mentalists; and the Mādhyamikas, who were taken by the rival schools to be nihilists. Epistemology, however, is not the driving force in the development of Buddhism, but the philosophical clarification of spiritual experience. Unlike Jainism, Buddhism was not satisfied with a single system of philosophy. Schisms arose within Buddhism time after time, and we read of Buddhist councils—one immediately after Buddha's death, the second a hundred years later, the third during Asoka's time, and the fourth during Kanishka's time—in which attempts were made to fix Buddha's doctrines. The dissenters started their own schools.

As Buddhism entered into keener and keener controversies with the orthodox schools and exchanged views about spiritual experiences, it tended to approach the Upaniṣadic philosophy more and more. In these controversies, the metaphysical ideas of Nescience (Ignorance, Avidyā), Māyā, Śūnya, and Vijñāna became the common property of the Buddhists, the Vedāntins, and the Āgama thinkers—Śaiva, Vaiṣṇava, and Śākta. The basic question for all was not merely whether each of these concepts was true or not, but also which of them was the ultimate truth and, if it was not the ultimate truth, what it was and what truth then the others possessed. It is very easy to see that Māyā, Avidyā, and Vijñāna are Upaniṣadic terms, if not clearly defined ideas, and it is interesting to note that Śūnya was incorporated by the orthodox schools and identified with some form or other of the Avyakta (Unmanifest).[27] Buddhistic thought became Upaniṣadic, although as a religion, Buddhism remained heterodox. Gauḍapāda in his *Māṇḍūkyakārikās* wove up the Śaiva doctrine of *spanda* (that the world is the vibration of Śiva), the Buddhistic doctrine of Vijñāna, and the Upaniṣadic doctrine of the Brahman into one philosophy. The period from the sixth to the eighth century especially was a period of synthesis of the Buddhist and the Vedāntic thought, after which Buddhism slowly declined, having lost its *raison d'être* for separate existence in India.

The doctrine of Māyā, it seems, is the greatest debt that the Vedānta owes to Buddhism.[28] Certainly, Māyā is an Upaniṣadic term. But what it exactly meant in the Upaniṣads is not known. So far as the available literature goes, its connotation—namely, that it is neither existent, nor nonexistent, nor both, nor neither—is found in the *Prajñāpāramitās,* which are generally assigned to the period between the first century B.C. and the first century A.D., but not later

[27] For the Pāñcarātra, see F. O. Schrader, *Introduction to the Pāñcarātra and Ahirrbudhnya Samhitā* (Adyar, Madras: Theosophical Society, 1916), p. 86, and *Ahirbudhnya Samhitā* (Adjar, Madras: Theosophical Society, 1916), pp. 36–39. For Pāśupata, see K. F. Leidecker, *Pratyabhijñāhṛdayam* (Adyar, Madras: Theosophical Society, 1938), pp. 37–42.

[28] See the author's contribution, "Buddhism and the Vedanta," to The Buddhajayanti Symposium, November, 1956, New Delhi.

than the third century A.D. This connotation is given to the word Śūnya as well; and both words also are used later in the *Laṅkāvatārasūtra*. All this literature is certainly earlier than Śaṅkara. Leaving out the question whether Māyā means a real entity or an unreal entity or an entity both real and unreal or an entity neither real nor unreal, it is another name for the Avyakta of the Upaniṣads, the inarticulate and latent state of the plurality of the world.

It was therefore easy for the Vedāntic and the Āgamic thinkers to equate Śūnya, which was another name for Māyā, to the Avyakta, because what is undifferentiated appears empty. Whether the Avyakta issues out of Śiva or Viṣṇu or the Brahman is of secondary importance here. Whether it is real or unreal, and so on, also is of secondary importance when we are taking an overall picture of the Vedāntic, the Āgamic, and Buddhist thought. Māyā and Avidyā (Ignorance) are accepted by all the Vedāntins, though in different meanings; for the Avyakta, or inarticulate state of the world, has to be accepted by all, and with it *avidyā* has to be accepted in addition, because differences cannot be known when there is ignorance. But the question whether Māyā is real or unreal may be left open; and in answering this question, the Vedāntins differed from each other. But we have to admit that Śaṅkara accepted the logical connotation of Māyā just as it was given by the Buddhists. And if we accept that Śaṅkara belonged to the original Vedic (*smārta*) tradition, we also have to accept that Buddhism made a very significant contribution—which has come to stay—to the orthodox tradition.

The history of Buddhist philosophy is, in a very significant sense, a history of philosophy itself, showing how some original ethico-spiritual teachings developed, through various forms of naive realism, into some of the highest forms of spiritual Absolutism. The schools of Buddhism are first divided into two, the Hīnayāna and the Mahāyāna, often translated as the Lower Vehicle and the Higher Vehicle. According to Vasumitra, the Hīnayāna consists of eighteen schools, some of which are philosophically important. Some of them differ from each other on questions of some minor monastic practices like whether the monks should use metal bowls for begging. Of the Mahāyāna schools, three are important, the Vijñānavāda (also called the Yogacāra), the Mādhyamika (also called the Śūnyavāda), and the Bhūtatathatā. There are differences within each of these schools, which to an external observer look like overemphases or underemphases on some ideas; and there are also crossings of schools with one another. Buddhist philosophy had a very complicated development, which must have been due to the great freedom of inquiry enjoyed by the followers. System following system, furnishing a history, if it is to be found at all in Indian thought, can be found only in Buddhism. From this point of view, as an example of free development of spiritual investigation and philosophical systematization, Buddhism has greater interest than any other school.

Buddhism started as an ethico-spiritual inquiry. Its ethics, like most of Indian ethics, is spiritually oriented and is psychological and individualistic. Its aim is how and why man should practice self-control in order to have the highest realization. Except in the Mīmāmsā and the epics, Indian ethics has little social orientation. Buddha's fourfold truth is an analysis of the human situation for immediate application. The urge for salvation is primary, and intellectual curiosity secondary. Out of this ethico-spiritual teaching, subsequent followers of Buddha developed their logical and metaphysical theories. Early Buddhistic philosophy, therefore, is realistic, pluralistic, and analytical. Some Buddhistic schools even accepted the atomistic theory and even tended to give up the doctrine of momentariness.[29] Some even said that something like the *ātman* or *vijñāna* is the residue[30] in Nirvāṇa when the psychophysical individual is analyzed away into the aggregates. Some again treated even Nirvāṇa as a *samskāra* (impression),[31] which, like the instincts of life and death according to Freud, must be latent in man for drawing him towards itself. For all, Nirvāṇa is the residue and is *śūnya* (empty). All these views belong to the Hīnayāna schools.

When once *vijñāna* (consciousness) was accepted as the characteristic of Nirvāṇa and was called Śūnya, the Mahāyāna thought was given its roots. All that was needed was to show that the essence of the world is mental and yet is void, and out of that ultimate reality the world of appearance consisting of the aggregates is to be derived. That everything is Śūnya was shown by Nāgārjuna (2nd century A.D.) in the elaborate dialectic of his *Mādhyamikakārikās,* which later in the twelfth century was adopted by Śrīharṣa in his *Khaṇḍanakhaṇḍkhādya* to prove that everything in the world is Māyā. The adoption

29 The Vaibhāṣikas and the Sautrāntikas.

30 The Andhakas.

31 The Andhakas.

was very easy, because the terms, Śūnya and Māyā, have the same connotation: neither existent, nor nonexistent, nor both, nor neither. For Nāgārjuna, there is nothing beyond the Śūnya; if the Śūnya is the essence of the world, then we realize the essence when we realize the Śūnya. If the Brahman also is the essence of the world, the Buddhists thought, then there will be two essential truths, the Śūnya and the Brahman. But oneness of essential truth is the aim of philosophy and religion. Śrīharṣa, as an advaitin, however, would argue that Śūnya or Māyā is the essence of the world in terms of *sat* (existence). And as existence is not Māyā, it must be different from Māyā. Māyā is the essence of the world; not in the sense of a self-subsistent reality, but in the sense of relative existence; and what is relative cannot be absolute. The Absolute alone is *sat* (existence); it is the Brahman.

A similar difficulty must have been felt within the Mahāyāna fold itself. In the twelve-linked chain of causation, Nescience (ignorance) is placed at the top. The tendency must have grown to identify Nescience with Māyā and Śūnya. But if the highest spiritual ideal is the removal of Nescience and if Nescience is to be overcome, what will be there when the ideal is achieved except some kind of perfect knowledge or consciousness? Hence *vijñāna,* not the lower type of knowledge but the higher type, must be still above the Śūnya. Hence, the Vijñānavādins taught that Vijñāna is the essence of the world, and differed from the Mādhyamikas. Maitreyanātha, who is believed to be earlier than Nāgārjuna, is regarded as the founder of the Vijñānavāda. But both the schools seem to have started together and to have drawn their inspiration from the *Prajñāpāramitās.* However, the two brothers, Asaṅga and Vasubandhu, who belonged to the second century A.D., did much to propagate this school of thought through their works, *Mahāyānasūtrālaṅkāra* and *Vijñaptimātratāsiddhi.* This school of the Mahāyāna must have been greatly influenced by the atmosphere of the Upaniṣadic ideas, and in its turn influenced it greatly. Indeed, the ideas of *śūnya* and Nirvāṇa were not given up by the Vijñānavādins, but were reinterpreted. Vijñāna itself is so transcendent that we cannot attribute either of the opposite predicates, existence and nonexistence, to it. Because it is pure and without impressions, it is unagitated, *nirvāṇa.*

The founder of the Bhūtatathatā school was Aśvaghoṣa, who is said to have lived even before Nāgārjuna. This school takes a more positive attitude to ultimate reality than either of the above-named schools. The concept of *tathatā* is to be found in the *Hīnayānist* school of Uttarāpathakas, but it was turned into the primary metaphysical principle by Aśvaghoṣa in his *Mahāyānaśraddhotpādaśāstra*. *Tathā* means thus or such, and *tathatā* means thusness or suchness. *Bhūtatathatā* means the thusness or suchness of the elements or things. Freely translated, it means the way of the world, which reminds us of the Tao of Lao Tzu.

It would be interesting to trace the inner relation of *tathatā to* the Buddhist concepts of *samskāra* (impression) and *dharma*. Everything is momentary according to Buddhism. Every momentary existence transmits its own *samskāra* to the succeeding momentary existence. *Samskāras* are originally the inherent forces responsible for the continuity of form in any group of momentary existences. Now our human body, within any span of time, appears to be the same. This sameness is due to the transmission of *samskāras* by the physical particles of one moment to the physical particles of the next. Like Whitehead, the Buddhists explain the continuity of any object in terms of the continuity of form that the elements constituting the object at any moment retain and transmit to the events constituting the so-called same object at the next moment. Thus form is continuous, and substance is the continuity of the form of process. But the form of the process is a quality, not of substance, but of activity. The words that characterize verbs, which express activity, are adverbs. Thus the essence of the world becomes the way of the world-process, and is Tathatā or Bhūtatathatā.

The essence of the world is understood in terms of *dharma* also. *Dharma* in Buddhism means anything and everything. As Yamakami Sogen says, it is like a blank check that can be filled by everyone as he likes.[32] *Dharma* etymologically means what holds or sustains. What holds a thing is its nature. What holds any man as man, or what makes him man, is the nature of man; whatever object possesses the nature of man is man. But the nature of man is constituted by the *samskāras* essential for man. The *samskāras,* as explained above, play the role of active dynamic universals in Buddhist philosophy. Any individual object is what it is because of its *dharma*. Because we cannot separate a thing from its nature, both are called *dharmas*. Thus,

[32] *Systems of Buddhistic Thought* (Calcutta: Calcutta University Press), pp. 113–14.

in Buddhism, however strongly it was opposed to the reality of universals, *dharma* obtained the meaning of both the particular and the universal, the thing and its law or way of behavior. Then when the tendency to derive plurality from a single unitary principle—whether it was called Vijñāna, Śūnya, or Tathatā—became strong, Buddhism derived the plurality of *dharmas* from a single Dharma (Law), which it called Dharmadhātu. When Buddha was called Tathāgata, or one who attained Tathatā, and docetism (the doctrine that denied human nature to Buddha, saying that his body was only a semblance) entered the school, the origin of the world was called Tathāgatagarbha, or the origin (womb) of the Tathāgata. It was also called the Dharmakāya of Buddha, the body that was Dharma, to distinguish it from the lower bodies. And Dharmakāya, Dharmadhātu, Bhūtatathatā, Śūnya, Vijñāna, and Nirvāṇa were equated to one another. This whole development could not have been sudden but must have taken some centuries and had several stages and interpretations.

Bhūtatathatā, according to Aśvaghoṣa, is both the essence and the source of the world. Nescience supervenes on it, and the world issues forth. Bhūtatathatā is not to be confused with mere negation (*śūnyatā*), because it contains all perfections and is self-existent. It is devoid of all determinations and distinctions, and is therefore *śūnya* (void). As it is above all predicates, one may even say that it is neither *śūnya* nor *aśūnya,* neither void nor nonvoid, for even *śūnya* and *aśūnya* are predicates. Yet Bhūtatathatā is affirmative truth.

The Buddhists themselves made it easy to develop the Upaniṣadic Advaita out of their three Mahāyāna schools.

Nyāya and Vaiśeṣika Schools

Though all orthodox schools started almost simultaneously, it is usual to present the Nyāya and the Vaiśeṣika first, since they are considered to be the first steppingstones to the Vedānta. The ordinary man thinks that the world is a plurality of independent objects; only when his intellect matures does he think of their unity. Again, mind and the world may be thought of as separate, though the world of physical objects may be considered to form a unity. It requires deeper thinking to think of both as having a unity. So between the pluralism of the Nyāya-Vaiśeṣika and the monism of the Vedānta comes the dualism of the Sāṅkhya-Yoga. Hence, according to the Vedāntic opinion, the Nyāya-Vaiśeṣika occupies the lowest ladder of philosophical systematization, the Sāṅkhya-Yoga the middle, and the Vedānta the highest. Naturally, the so-called lower schools would not accept this gradation.

From the point of view we are taking, namely, that of man and his two dimensions of inwardness and outwardness, the Nyāya and the Vaiśeṣika and also the Mīmāmsā are philosophies of outwardness, and the Vedānta on the whole a philosophy of inwardness. For the outward attitude, the world is a plurality, which can be classified under different categories; and a rigorous system of logic is necessary for understanding its nature. The Nyāya developed logic, and the Vaiśeṣika metaphysics. And as each accepted practically all that the other said, they are generally hyphenated and called Nyāya-Vaiśeṣika. Salvation as the highest aim of life was accepted by both, and both declared that the aim of their philosophy was to show the way to salvation.

The author of the *Nyāyasūtras* was Gautama. When one reads his first *sūtra* (aphorism), one wonders what it has to do with salvation. It says that one attains salvation by understanding the sixteen topics: (1) valid means of cognition (*pramāṇa*), (2) objects of cognition (*prameya*), (3) doubt (*samsaya*), (4) purpose (*prayojana*), (5) example (*dṛṣṭānta*), (6) view or doctrine (*siddhānta*), (7) members of the syllogism (*avayavāh*), (8) indirect proof (*tarka*), (9) ascertainment (*nirṇaya*), (10) discussion (*vāda*), (11) mere wrangling (*jalpa*), (12) criticism without any position of one's own (*vitaṇḍā*), (13) fallacies (*hetvābhāsas*), (14) quibbling (*chala*), (15) shifty argument (*jāti*), and (16) grounds of defeat (*nigrahasthānas*). Except for the second topic, which can include the nature of the world and the *ātman,* all are connected with logic, dialectic, and controversy. There must have been keen philosophical disputes at that time; and the parties of the controversies must have been using all kinds of expedients, including fallacies, psychological appeals, insinuations, and others in order to obtain victory. Hence comes the desire of Gautama to regularize and systematize the methods of controversy.

The objects of knowledge, according to Gautama, are twelve: (1) self (*ātman*), (2) body, (3) senses, (4) objects of senses, (5) cognition (*buddhi*), (6) mind (*manas*), (7) activity (*pravṛtti*), (8) mental defects (*doṣas*), (9) rebirth, (10) enjoyment, (11) suffering, and (12) salvation. These twelve objects are not all metaphysical, but mainly ethico-spiritual. The metaphysical classification is supplied by the Vaiśeṣika system, as expounded by Kanāda in his *Vaiśeṣikasūtras*. Praśastapāda, the commentator on this work, says that one attains salvation by understanding the nature of the seven categories: substance, quality, activity, universal, particular, inherence, and negation. The first six are positive, and the last is negative. Later, the Naiyāyikas found that the Vaiśeṣika categories were more systematic for metaphysics than theirs, and the two schools merged into one. The differences between the two are treated as of minor importance.

Salvation in a pluralistic universe always means dissociation from the plurality of objects. Even for early Buddhism, for which Nirvāṇa meant analyzing away the aggregates (*skandhas*), it entailed dissociating oneself from them and so a kind of retreat from them. Only in the Mahāyāna, in which the world is explained as being due to the transformation of the original Vijñāna, could Nirvāṇa mean the retransformation of the plurality into the original unity; there is no retreat from the world, but only a transformation or, in terms of ethics, a transvaluation. For the Mīmāmsā in its early forms, there is neither retreat from, nor regaining of, the original unity, but only continuous activity in order to impose on the world the necessity to supply the requisite forms. When the idea of salvation entered the school, there was, indeed, a getting away from the world of plurality, but through activity alone. Jainism also became a philosophy of retreat. But ethically there is as much difference between salvation by the way of action and salvation through renunciation of action as between the man who saves himself by driving away the enemy and the man who saves himself by running away from the enemy. The metaphysical implications of the way of action, which does not involve avoidance of the world and yet preaches transcending it, do not accord with the Mīmāmsā philosophy and are not worked out anywhere except in a general way in the *Bhagavadgītā*. For if salvation is transformation and transvaluation of the world through action, and not retreat from the world of physical atoms, then everything in the world must ultimately have issued forth from a unitary principle like the Brahman of the Upaniṣads. But the Nyāya-Vaiśeṣika does not accept such a philosophy: the world of matter, the limit of outwardness, is not the manifestation, through man, of the innermost Spirit.

In the Upaniṣads it is said that the elements in a subtle form issue forth from the Ātman, and combining together produce the world through man and his senses. The *Kaṭha Upaniṣad* declares that the Unmanifest (Avyakta) comes out of the Puruṣa (Ātman), the Cosmic Reason (Mahat) out of the Unmanifest, the individual reason (*buddhi*) out of the Cosmic Reason, mind out of reason, the elements out of mind, and the senses out of the elements. Thus reason is not lost, but is turned into the Cosmic Reason, and that finally into the Ātman. But the Nyāya-Vaiśeṣika account significantly differs from the *Kaṭha* in this connection. By *buddhi* the followers of this school mean cognition, and say that, when mind comes into contact with the *ātman, buddhi* arises and at other times there is no *buddhi*. In salvation there is no contact between mind and the *ātman,* and the latter, like a stone, becomes insensitive to pains and pleasures, since there is no cognition of anything at the time. Thus consciousness is an adventitious quality of the *ātman,* which by nature is unconscious.

Mind ceases to come into contact with the *ātman* when the latter desires that there should be no contact with the external world, which is made up of physical atoms, time, space, ether, mind, universals, particulars, and negation. Salvation is a dissociation from all of them by giving up *karma*. God is only one of the *ātmans,* though the most important of all. In a theological way, He has the power of controlling everything, although everything exists independently of Him. Obviously, the Nyāya-Vaiśeṣika philosophy does not agree with the Upaniṣadic philosophy of inwardness; and so its followers could not write a commentary on the *Brahmasūtras*.

There are two ways of explaining the relation between the *ātman,* mind, life, and matter: one may start with the *ātman* and say that the others successively evolved out of it, and this is the explanation from the inward point of view. Or one may start with matter and say that the others successively evolved out of it, and this is the explanation from the outward point of view. The Cārvāka philosophy, had it been developed further, would have given a systematic philosophy of outwardness. The Nyāya-Vaiśeṣika accepted neither explanation, and gave a pluralistic and realistic philosophy of simultaneously and eternally existing *ātman,* mind, and matter. It gave little thought to the problem of the relation between God and the plurality of the world in this fashion. The Cārvākas could have given one answer by developing their idea that the unifying principles called life and mind are qualities that emerge when material particles enter peculiar combinations.

Sāṅkhya and Yoga

The Sāṅkhya offers a qualitative dualism of spirit and matter. But it is difficult to classify the Yoga, because Patañjali, the author of *Yogasūtras,* accepted the reality of God, though his own explanation of the relationship between God and the world of spirits and matter is not very clear. For metaphysics, the only important difference between the Sāṅkhya and the Yoga is the latter's acceptance of God; otherwise, their metaphysics is the same and, like the Nyāya-Vaiśeṣika, they are written with a hyphen and called the Sāṅkhya-Yoga. We have already noted that in the hands of Vijñānabhikṣu, who wrote a commentary on the *Brahmasūtras,* they became Vedāntic. Patañjali was interested in explaining the yogic technique for the realization of the *ātman,* and the Sāṅkhya supplied the underlying metaphysical theory. We may therefore say that Vijñānabhikṣu developed the Sāṅkhya into a Vedāntic system through the Yoga of Patañjali by equating God to the Brahman.

According to the Sāṅkhya, the plurality of the physical world comes out of a unitary principle, Prakṛti. But the *ātmans* or Puruṣas are many and independent not only of Prakṛti but also of each other. Thus there is unity in the physical world, but no unity among the spirits. The reason given by the Sāṅkhya for the plurality of spirits is that, if all are ultimately one, if one of them attains salvation, all the rest must also attain it. But if, as the Sāṅkhya itself holds, the Puruṣas are eternally pure and it is not they but their reflections that enter the bonds of Prakṛti, one may say, like the Advaita, that the reflections only are many but the Puruṣa is one, and that when one reflection realizes its original nature, the rest may not. However, according to the Sāṅkhya, when Puruṣa comes into contact with Prakṛti, the former throws its reflection into the latter. Prakṛti is originally undisturbed. It has three *guṇas* (attributes)—*sattva* (purity), *rajas* (activity), and *tamas* (passivity)—which lie in a state of equilibrium and rest till the Puruṣa leaves his reflection in Prakṛti.[33] As soon as the reflection is received, Prakṛti loses its equilibrium and begins to create the world for the Puruṣa. It creates the world in the same way for all Puruṣas, and hence the world is the same for all of them. In fact, the plurality of the world is potentially present in Prakṛti. Creation is really manifestation, through which Prakṛti transforms itself into the plurality. Prakṛti has this power also, namely, of remaining unitary and inactive for the liberated, and plural and active for those in bondage.

The first evolute out of Prakṛti is Mahat or *buddhi* (reason). Out of Mahat comes *ahaṁkāra* (ego); out of *ahaṁkāra* come *manas* (mind), the five senses, the five organs of action, and the five subtle elements; and out of the five subtle elements the gross elements, which constitute the objects of the world of waking consciousness.

We see the similarity of this account to that given by the *Kaṭha Upaniṣad*. Prakṛti is the Avyakta (Unmanifest). But while, according to the general Upaniṣadic thought, the Avyakta is to be understood as coming out of the Ātman, the Sāṅkhya treats it as having an eternal and independent existence of its own. According to the *Kaṭha*, Mahat is higher than *buddhi*, and so the two are different; but the Sāṅkhya equates them. The reason is that the Sāṅkhya has no need for the Brahman or God and so no need either for a separate Cosmic Reason or Person (Mahān Ātma). The *Kaṭha* does not mention *ahaṁkāra*, but the Sāṅkhya mentions it as a distinct category. Again, for the *Kaṭha*, the elements come out of *manas*, but for the Sāṅkhya, both *manas* and the elements come out of the ego. In spite of these differences, the similarity is significant in that both the *Kaṭha* and the Sāṅkhya try to explain the world of man and his environment as due to an evolutionary process from the inward.

The Sāṅkhya, in spite of its qualitative dualism, is inherently a philosophy of inwardness, since it took the most important and necessary step to becoming such a philosophy. This step is the explanation of the world through man's inwardness. Right from *buddhi* (reason)

[33] *Guṇa* is sometimes translated as quality, and *sattva, rajas,* and *tamas* as goodness, activity, and inactivity.

downwards, everything is animated matter, a transformation of Prakṛti made conscious by the reflection of Puruṣa. But from the standpoint of man, even the physical world is an evolution of man's inwardness: the world is due to the issuing forth of the subjective and objective correlates out of the ego. *Buddhi* (reason), being cosmic in its function, is above the distinction between the subjective and the objective. If we miss this inwardness, we make nonsense of the Sāṅkhya doctrine of evolution; for it appears to be nonsense to say that the world evolved out of the ego. And this Sāṅkhya doctrine is incorporated, with some modifications, by many of the Vedāntic schools.

The Sāṅkhya doctrine of *guṇas* is not a doctrine of the usual attributes or qualities. For attributes or qualities are only passive forms, whereas the *guṇas* of Prakṛti are active factors or constituents. The reason for the Sāṅkhya use of the term *guṇa* is that they constitute the psychophysical character of human personality and activate it. The doctrine of *guṇas* became so important that the whole psychological ethics of India was based on it. Temperament, character, conduct, in short, the very constitution of the human person, was thought of as having been constituted by the *guṇas*. The predominance of one of the three *guṇas* and the degree of predominance were considered to be determinants of one's character and conduct. If man's personality is a correlate of the environment, then the environment also is constituted by the *guṇas;* for both man and his environment are correlated evolutes out of Prakṛti. The doctrine of *karma* and rebirth is accepted by the Sāṅkhya also; the world is, therefore, for every man what he has made it to be through his *karma*—within the limits, of course, prescribed by the constitution of Prakṛti. Salvation lies in getting above the world of *karma* and being freed from Prakṛti.

The Yoga of Patañjali accepted the Sāṅkhya metaphysics and added God to it. But Patañjali's own work gives the impression that God does not have an inherent necessity, and the acceptance of God is perhaps a concession to popular opinion. How meditation on God leads to *samādhi* (trance), and how He is related to the different categories is not explained. So far as the Yoga technique is concerned, Patañjali follows the Sāṅkhya metaphysical theory. Out of Prakṛti evolved Mahat, *ahaṁkāra, manas,* senses, organs of action, subtle elements, and gross elements. The different steps for *samādhi* follow the reverse order: concentration on gross elements, subtle elements, senses, *manas, ahaṁkāra,* and Mahat. When concentration is purified and perfected at the highest level, the reflection in Prakṛti of Puruṣa realizes that it is only a reflection and that it falsely identified itself with Prakṛti and its evolutes. The moment this realization dawns, Prakṛti ceases to be active, the *guṇas* regain their equilibrium, the reflection disappears, and the apparent bondage of Puruṣa ceases.

Mīmāmsā

Mīmāmsā means inquiry, investigation, discussion. It originally meant inquiry into the meaning of the Vedic statements in order to make them consistent with one another and with what could be understood to be the nature of reality. But as the Vedic Dharma was the law of life according to reality as understood and conceived by the Vedas and began to be distinguished into the religion of the Brāhmaṇas and the religion of the Upaniṣads, two Mīmāmsās arose, the Pūrva Mīmāmsā, or the Prior Mīmāmsā, which explained the religion and the underlying philosophy of the Brahmanic texts, and the Uttara Mīmāmsā, or the Posterior Mīmāmsā, which explained the religion and the underlying philosophy of the Upaniṣads. When no adjective is used before "Mīmāmsā," only the Purva Mīmāmsā is meant. Another name for Uttara Mīmāmsā is Vedānta.

A peculiarity to be noted here is that, though the Brāhmaṇas and the Upaniṣads are parts of the Veda, the metaphysics underlying the Brāhmaṇas as explained by Jaimini and the metaphysics underlying the Upaniṣads as explained by Bādarāyaṇa are different. Life of action needs, as explained earlier, a pluralistic metaphysics like that of the Nyāya-Vaiśeṣika; but life of meditation and renunciation can work with monistic metaphysics. But if the Veda is a unitary whole, how can it preach a pluralistic metaphysics in one of its parts and a monistic metaphysics in another? This becomes a puzzling problem. Certainly both systems of metaphysics cannot be equally true. In commenting on the first of the *Brahmasūtras,* Śaṅkara treated the inquiry into the nature of *dharma* (duty) as unimportant, and said that one could start the inquiry into the nature of the Brahman when one found that he had no attachment to the values of the world. Rāmānuja held the opposite view. But how, if Jaimini's *Dharmasūtras* involve a system of metaphysics different from that of Bādarāyaṇa's *Brahmasūtras,* both can be accepted as true could not be explained by any. And it is difficult to accept that even metaphysics can be different for different minds or *āśramas.* For we have to show how one leads to the other. And this can be done only when the first is necessary for the second. Just as the life of action and the life of renunciation have remained unreconciled, the two systems of metaphysics also have remained unreconciled. Reconciliation is possible only when each is necessary for the other; and in metaphysics this necessity implies the recognition of the reality of the pluralistic metaphysics also.

Though the problem is puzzling for both metaphysics and philosophy of life, the Vedāntins were not troubled by it. It was usual for them to say that a pluralistic metaphysics was meant for the lower immature intellect; since the intellect of the man of action was immature, a metaphysics like that of the Mīmāmsā could be given to him. Few of the Vedāntins would accept *karmayoga* (the way of action) as the highest. For them the highest Yoga is either *jñānayoga* (way of knowledge) or *bhaktiyoga* (way of devotion). Either is subservient to the other, and the way of action is subservient to both. But it is not consistently accepted that the way of action is necessary even as a steppingstone. Then there will be another difficulty in metaphysics; for we cannot say that one system of metaphysics is a steppingstone to another, since each metaphysics deals with ultimate reality, and ultimate realities cannot be steppingstones, which can be discarded one after another. If each is necessary for the others, then each must also be ultimately true. I have not seen a final solution of this difficulty.

One way of reconciling the two, which some Vedāntins followed, is to incorporate the pluralism of the Nyāya-Vaiśeṣika or the Mīmāmsā into the dualism of the Sāṅkhya and that into the monism of the Upaniṣads, and to say that pluralistic philosophies, if half systematized, will be dualistic, and, if fully systematized, monistic, just as the life of action according to *dharma* as prescribed by the Vedas will lead to the life of contemplation and self-realization particularly taught by the Upaniṣads.

As a pluralistic philosophy, the Mīmāmsā is akin to the Nyāya-Vaiśeṣika. It is especially concerned with duty (*dharma*) and action (*karma*), which require a pluralistic philosophy. It should be noted that the primary meaning of *karma* is not Fate, but human action. The idea of salvation should not produce in our mind the impression that we are really giving up the values of the world; the attainment of Brahman-realization should be the attainment of everything; so salvation needs a monistic philosophy. Indeed, monistic philosophy was not invented in order to console people who sought the realization of the Brahman by telling them that they were not going to lose anything: it was first discovered that the Brahman was everything, and then the ideal of salvation was added to the other ideals of life. Wealth is meant for enjoyment; enjoyment should not be disorderly, but according to the injunctions of *dharma* (duty); and the performance of duties should ultimately lead to salvation. Thus, though duty and salvation were related, their two metaphysics could not be related. The incorporation of pluralism into dualism and dualism into monism could not be complete; for pluralism postulated atoms with an independent existence of their own. In fact, atomism could not be accepted by the Sāṅkhya or even the reconciling Vedāntic systems. The Mīmāmsā accepted the atomic theory.

Although both the Mīmāmsā and the Nyāya-Vaiśeṣika are pluralistic, they have very significant differences. The aim of the latter was to show the way to salvation; but that of the former was to expound the path of duty and action. The Mīmāmsā was indifferent to the conception of God and did not accept that the Vedas were composed by God or were His utterances. But the Nyāya-Vaiśeṣika accepted God and said that He was their author. The Mīmāmsā said that the Vedas were eternal. No word is born and destroyed, but is eternal, and so the injunctions of the Vedas have eternal and cosmic validity. The Vedas contain eternal truths, are not prejudiced against anybody in the world, and are interested in the good of everybody; therefore, their words are the most reliable. All this may not stand scrutiny. But the permanent contribution that the Mīmāmsā made to Indian thought was its philosophy of action.

The idea of *karmamārga* or *karmayoga* (path of action) as leading to salvation must have been developed when the idea of God entered the philosophy of the Mīmāmsā. The followers of the school, as a philosophy of action, could not say that action had to be given up in order to obtain salvation; they had to say that action itself could lead to salvation. Hence, they said that, if one performed one's actions only as an instrument in the hands of God and attributed the agency to God Himself, actions would not bind him. This is, of course, the teaching of the *Bhagavadgīta;* for strict *karmayoga* should imply that salvation is not possible without action.

Vedānta

Of all the Vedāntic schools, the Advaita of Śaṅkara is considered to be the most important. Not only is Śaṅkara the earliest commentator on the *Brahmasūtras,* so far as the available literature goes, and so has to be reckoned with by all the subsequent commentators, but also he relies mainly on the Śruti (Vedas) and *smṛtis* (epics) only. The other commentators, except Bhāskara, approach the *Brahmasūtras* from the Vaiṣṇava or Śaiva Āgamas. For this reason, Śaṅkara is called the *smārta* (orthodox) Vedāntin.

Whether the approach is made from the side of the Śruti or *smṛti* or the Āgamas, the central conception of the Vedānta is the inwardness of the Brahman to man, because the *Brahmasūtras,* which are accepted as the basis of all the Vedāntic schools, say in so many words that the Brahman is to be realized by all as the *ātman.*[34] This *sūtra* is interpreted in different ways: that the Brahman is the self-same Ātman of all men; that the *ātmans* of men are different from one another, but the Brahman is the Universal Ātman residing in all the *ātmans;* again, in the second case, that the Universal Ātman is different from the individual *ātmans;* that it is both identical with, and different from, them; that, when it is identical with, and different from, them, it is identical in being but different in form, identical in form but different in being, or both identical and different in both being and form; and that, if both identity and difference are not accepted, it is the Ātman of all individual *ātmans,* which along with the physical world constitute its body. In every case, it is the innermost spirit of man, though these different interpretations are given by the different

[34] IV, 1, 3.

Vedāntins. These interpretations may safely be taken as the summary of the Vedāntic schools.

Then, how are we to understand the creation of the world, if the innermost Universal Spirit is eternally complete? It is due to the Śakti, or energy, of the Brahman. Next, what is the relation between the Brahman and its Śakti? If the world of plurality is due to the Śakti, does the same Śakti produce the plurality of the *ātmans* and also the plurality of the insentient material world? Or are there two or more Śaktis? In answering these questions also the Vedāntins differed from each other. Śaṅkara said that the Brahman alone is real, and the Śakti, which he called Māyā, is not real. To say that the Śakti is real is, Śaṅkara contends, to say that it has a reality separate from that of the Brahman; but the Brahman alone is the reality according to the Upaniṣads. Vallabha (fifteenth century), who was also an Advaitin but belonged to the Vaiṣṇava tradition, said that the Brahman alone is real and transforms itself into the world. There is no Māyā, real or unreal. He calls his system Suddhādvaita, Pure Non-dualism, because it does not need the help of impure Māyā to explain the world of plurality and the oneness of the Brahman. The example taken by the Advaitins to explain this point is that of fire and its energy (*śakti*) to burn. Is this energy or power to burn the same as fire, or different from fire, or both identical with, and different from, fire? And what further can be said about the power of fire? Is it its power that burns objects or is it fire itself? Śaṅkara would say that the power has no existence apart from fire, and yet we cannot say that it is nonexistent. Vallabha would say that it is the same as fire.

Bhāskara (ninth century) said that the Śakti of the Brahman is matter and is real and existent, but not as the individual *ātman*. This Śakti forms a limitation (*upādhi*) of the Brahman and turns it into the individual *ātman*, which is called the *jīva* (soul). Bhāskara's system looks like the Sāṅkhya without the plurality of Puruṣas. Rāmānuja (eleventh century) said that the Śakti is existent and includes both the *ātmans* and matter, and also constitutes the body of the Brahman. It undergoes *pariṇāma* (transformation) in order to create the world. Madhva (thirteenth century) said that the Śakti, though separate, is entirely dependent on the Brahman, and so, though it has separate existence, the Brahman can still be the Lord of the universe. The plurality of the *ātmans* and the plurality of the world constitute the Śakti. Madhva is very adamant about this plurality. At no time does the plurality of the world and the plurality of the *ātmans* become a unity. Each thing is a particular or rather has a particular (*viśeṣa*). There are an infinite number of particulars, each residing in each of the *ātmans* and the material things. It is difficult to understand how so many particulars together constitute the unitary Śakti of the Brahman. Madhva's philosophy has many similarities to the Nyāya-Vaiśeṣika. But the latter does not accept any *śakti* as a category at all.

Some Vedāntins like Nimbārka (a Vaiṣṇava of the thirteenth century) said that the Śakti is both identical with, and different from, the Brahman, in both its forms, as spirits and as matter. Śrīpati (a Śaiva of the sixteenth century) also held the same view. Bhāskara before them upheld the doctrine of both identity and difference; but this double relation held only between the Brahman and the material world, not between the Brahman and the *ātmans*. There is difference between the *ātman* and the Brahman only during bondage, not during salvation, when the two are completely identical. But Nimbārka and Śrīpati maintained that both identity and difference obtain between the Brahman and the *ātman*, even during salvation. Śrīkaṇṭha (thirteenth or fourteenth century) held the same view as Rāmānuja; but Rāmānuja, as a Vaiṣṇava, identified the Brahman with Viṣṇu, while Śrīkaṇṭha, as a Śaiva, identified it with Śiva.

It has already been mentioned that Vijñānabhikṣu (fifteenth century) made a laudable attempt to turn the Sāṅkhya into a Vedāntic system. Already the Yoga of Patañjali accepted God and the metaphysics of the Sāṅkhya. God could be identified with the Brahman of the Upaniṣads, and a relationship established between the Brahman, on the one side, and the Puruṣas and Prakṛti on the other. It was easy to identify both with the Śakti of the Brahman—which Vijñānabhikṣu did, saying that between the Śakti and the Brahman there is no difference. This denial of difference, however, was not literal but metaphorical. Just as there is no difference between son and father for certain purposes, there is no difference between the Brahman and the *ātman*. All that Vijñānabhikṣu meant was that the two were inseparable. Though essentially different, the Śakti is entirely dependent on the Brahman. As a Vedāntin, Vijñānabhikṣu had to give up the atheism of the Sāṅkhya.

Another school of importance is that of Śrī Caitanya, a Vaiṣṇava of the fifteenth century. Baladeva, one of his followers, wrote a commentary on the *Brahmasūtras,* and called his system *acintyabhedābheda,* inconceivable identity and difference. If two objects are different, they cannot be identical, and vice versa. But in the case of the Brahman and its Śakti, both relations are true, though we cannot understand how. The Brahman has three Śaktis, one for constituting the material world, another for constituting the world of *ātmans,* and the third for controlling both.

It is difficult to classify the Vedānta into the two opposing divisions of idealism and realism, though some scholars have attempted to do so. For almost every school of the Vedānta, even including that of Madhva, is generally idealistic; every school has to accept the Upaniṣadic view of the correlativity of sense and object and that the correlativity is due to the same element's dividing itself into the subjective and objective poles. Epistemological subjectivism is not completely absent; but it belongs only to one subschool of the Advaita. Even if not avowedly monistic, every school has a monistic trend, explaining the world in terms of the Brahman, which is the innermost universal spirit in man and is discovered when man's consciousness is directed inwards. The Vedāntic schools may, therefore, be regarded as varieties of the philosophy of inwardness and, accordingly, as more or less idealistic.

Except Śaṅkara, all the Vedāntins maintain that the Brahman is personal. There is one school of Advaita which is not Vedāntic but which was greatly influenced by Śaṅkara. It is the Kasmir School of Śaiva Advaita, of which Vaśugupta (ninth century) and Abhinavagupta (tenth century) are the greatest protagonists. They are not inclined to accept Śaṅkara's meaning of the word Māyā, but say that it is Śakti and is real and identical with the Brahman, which is the same as Śiva. Just as some pictures, when looked at from one side, appear to be elephants and, looked at from another side, appear to be horses, the same reality is seen sometimes as the Brahman and other times as this world.

It has been said already that all the Vedāntins, except Śaṅkara and Bhāskara, drew their inspiration from some Āgama or another, and that the Āgamas tried in different ways to knit together the monism of the Upaniṣads, the dualism of the Sāṅkhya, and the pluralism of the Mīmāṃsā or Vaiśeṣika. It was, of course, difficult to incorporate the Vaiśeṣika and Mīmāṃsā doctrine of eternally existing atoms. But we have said that Madhva took over the Vaiśeṣika concept of the particular (*viśeṣa*). The Śaiva Āgamas start with Śiva and the Vaiṣṇava Āgamas with Viṣṇu and derive plurality through duality. And in this derivation, one sees more influence of the Sāṅkhya than of the Vaiśeṣika or the Mīmāṃsā. There are differences in derivation, but it is difficult to give them all. Only the main trends may be presented here for appreciating the inward evolution accepted by the schools.

In the derivation given in Chart 1, one can easily see the influence of the Sāṅkhya. Time is accepted in both the subtle and gross forms, psychical and physical. Prakṛti and Puruṣa are unified in the subtle form of Aniruddha and are further transmuted through the other stages of pure creation. The relation between Viṣṇu and Śakti, as described above, has been variously explained. In some of the details, again, the Āgamas differ from one another.

In the derivation of Chart 2 also, we see the influence of the Sāṅkhya. The general drive towards inwardness and monism is the same as in the Pāñcarātra.

A corresponding Upaniṣadic derivation may also be presented. But it is difficult to prepare a chart acceptable to all the Vedāntins. For those who approached the Upaniṣads from the side of the Āgamas will naturally try to reduce the Upaniṣadic derivation to that of the Āgamas. The Advaita of Śaṅkara, which did not follow any Āgama, will be somewhat as shown in Chart 3.

It will be useful to give the *Kaṭha* Upaniṣad categories and the Sāṅkhya categories together (Chart 4), in order to understand their relationship easily. The Sāṅkhya, though somewhat independent of the Upaniṣads, has associations with them. But it cannot be in agreement with all the Upaniṣads, because some of them derive the elements one out of the other, for instance, air out of ether, fire out of air, water out of fire, and earth out of water, but the Sāṅkhya regards them as issuing forth simultaneously out of the ego.

Contemporary Indian philosophers like Radhakrishnan, Tagore, Aurobindo Ghose, and Bhagavan Das are more or less Vedāntic, following one or the other of the traditional schools and sometimes incorporating elements from two or more schools. But the inward standpoint has not been given up by any, and everything is traced somehow to the integral unity of the Brahman. But all of them deny that Indian philosophy is negative in outlook, that it is world-and-life negating. They reformulate the Vedāntic philosophy as a philosophy of world-and-life affirmation and show their difference from the classical philosophers. Aurobindo Ghose adopts the second alternative and is known also for his doctrine of the Superman, who is an ego-surrender-

CHART 1

Vaiṣṇava or Pāñcarātra Derivation *

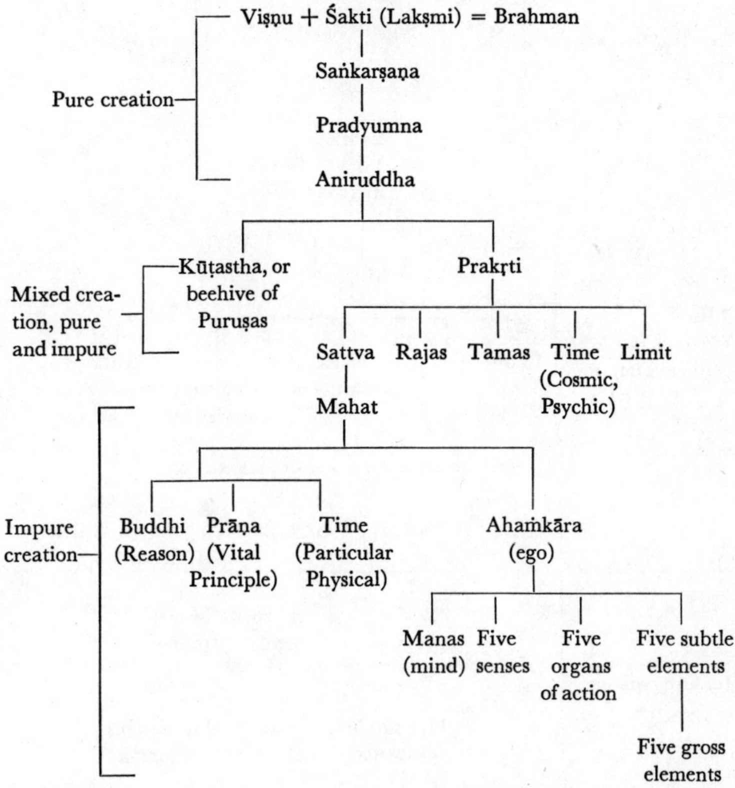

* The terms of mixed creation and impure creation do not need much explanation for a general understanding. But the terms of pure creation, which are more or less proper names for the suprarational stages, need explanation. For a somewhat detailed clarification, the reader may see the author's *Idealistic Thought of India* (London: George Allen and Unwin Ltd., 1953). Viṣṇu is the same as the Brahman. But His great attributes cannot become manifest without His Śakti, which is called Lakṣmi. This Śakti has two aspects, Activity and Becoming. When the Śakti begins to act, the six great attributes of Viṣṇu become manifest: Knowledge, Lordship, Ability, Strength, Virility, and Splendor. Two each of these attributes begin to dominate over the others. First, Knowledge and Strength become dominant, and Viṣṇu becomes Saṅkarṣaṇa; next, Lordship and Virility dominate, and Pradyumna becomes manifest; and then Ability and Splendor dominate, and Aniruddha becomes manifest. This derivation is less epistemological and psychological than that of the Pāśupata.

CHART 2

Śaiva or Pāśupata Derivation *

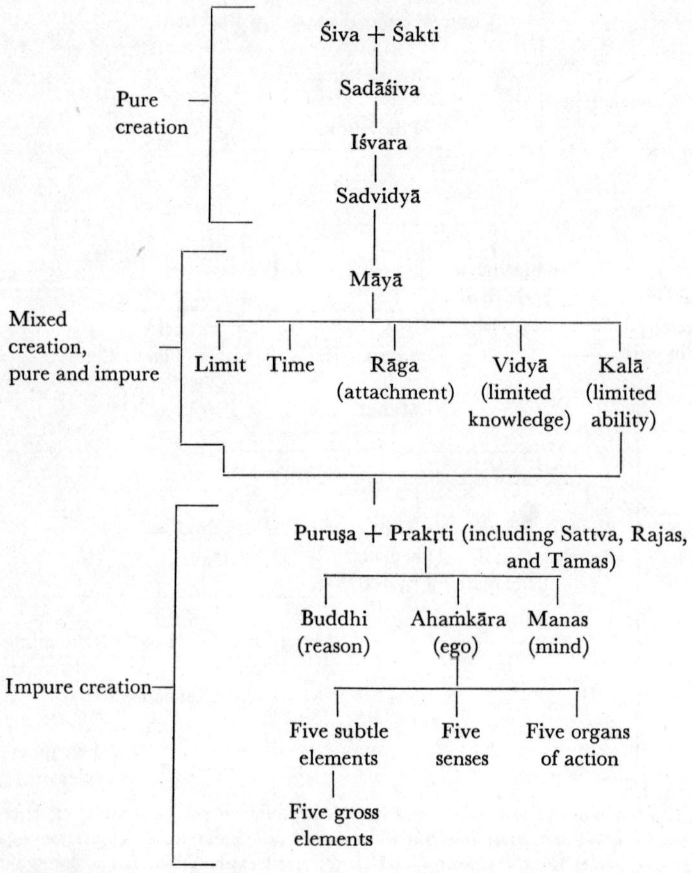

* Here also the terms of pure creation may briefly be explained. Śiva is the Brahman. His nature is the pure "I," not even "I am." He is really pure consciousness without even its self-affirmation. The decision to affirm itself is not yet present. This is supplied by Śiva's Śakti. When the Śakti appears, Śiva becomes "I am." This Śakti has three aspects, Will, Activity, and Knowledge. Each of the three aspects dominates the others in turn. First, Will becomes dominant, and Śiva becomes Sadāśiva. Here the "I am" becomes the "I am this," but in an indistinct way. Then Activity dominates, and Iśvara appears. Here the "This" factor of consciousness becomes clear, but the "I" factor remains indistinct. Then Knowledge becomes dominant, and Sadvidyā appears. At this stage, the "I" factor also becomes clear. These are the descending

CHART 3

Upaniṣadic Derivation according to the *Māṇḍūkya*

Brahman

- Individual
  - Prājña (Māyā in causal unitary deep sleep)
    - Taijasa (Māyā in the pluralistic state of dream and subtle elements)
      - Vaiśvānara (Māyā in the pluralistic state of wakefulness and gross elements)
- Cosmic
  - Iśvara (Māyā in unitary causal state, not overwhelming)
    - Hiraṇyagarbha (Sūtrātman) (Māyā in pluralistic subtle effect state)
      - Virāṭ (Māyā in gross pluralistic effect state)

ing yogi, unlike the aggressive egoist of Nietzsche. But he seems to have ignored the philosophies of the Pāñcarātra and the Pāśupata schools, which do not treat the world as unreal. Indeed, our knowledge of scientific philosophy and of evolution will enrich them, if incorporated. But to condemn the whole of the ancient Indian philosophy, ignoring the importance of these two Vedic-Āgamic traditions, is to be unfair to them. There is a great deal that they said in favor of world-and-life affirmation in terms of inwardness.

All contemporary philosophers, however, say that, in order to realize our oneness with the inward Cosmic Spirit, intellect (reason) has to be transcended; and if the distinction between subject and object is

stages of pure consciousness into the distinctions of the subject and the object. The ascending stages will be in the reverse direction. At the level of Sadvidyā, Māyā does not overwhelm consciousness. At the next stage, it overwhelms consciousness, and binds the individual with its five bonds. In some works, Māyā is added to the five as the sixth, and six bonds or sheaths (*kañcukas*) are mentioned. Māyā is a form of the original Śakti and is not at all unreal, as in the Advaita of Śaṅkara. Indeed, Śaṅkara denied its unreality, too; but in any case, he denied both its reality and its unreality. But the Pāśupata says that it is real.

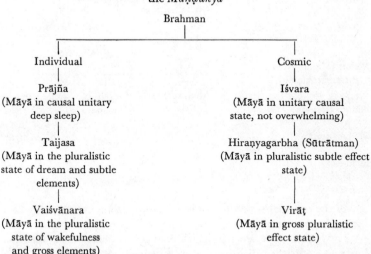

CHART 4

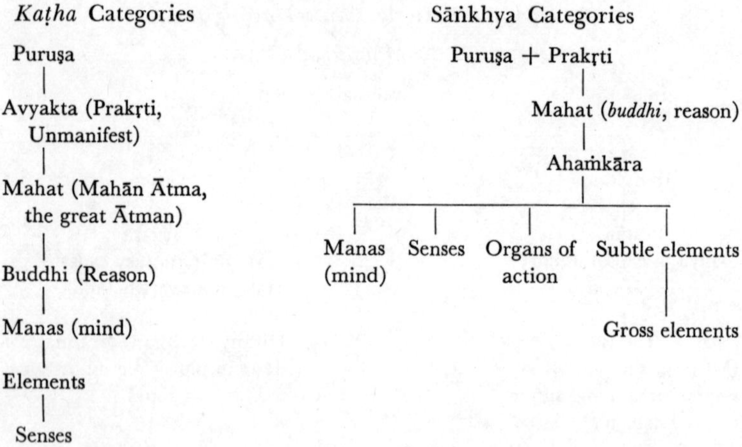

one of the essential conditions of epistemology, then epistemology also has to be transcended.

The highest experience in which man realizes his oneness with the innermost Spirit is called integral experience by Radhakrishnan. It is the final postulate of our phenomenal experience. Creation starts with the self-affirmation of the Absolute. Radhakrishnan modifies Śaṅkara's position that the world is neither existent nor nonexistent into the view that it is both existent and nonexistent. His general approach is epistemological and logical. Aurobindo dispenses with many epistemological subtleties and explains how the original integrality of Spirit is split up at the phenomenal level. At the level of Spirit, knowledge, volition, action, and feeling (delight) are one: to know is to will and feel. But at our level, all of them are different: we may see an object, but it may not be real; we may will, but may not act; we may will and act, but may not succeed and so feel pain and not pleasure. These divisions are overcome at the level of integrality, which is called Saccidānanda (Existence, Consciousness, Delight). Tagore also rejects Śaṅkara's position, takes the Brahman as personal by humanizing it, and gives man greater importance in his philosophy, in which love occupies the place that knowledge occupies in Śaṅkara's philosophy. For love as a relation not only unites the terms but also implies knowledge of each other, thus preserving the individuality of each. Bhagavan Das is better known for his works on social philosophy. Drawing his inspiration from Fichte and rejecting Śaṅkara's view of the Brahman, he says that the Absolute is the Absolute Ego, plus matter, plus the relation of negation between the two. This negation is the creative force of the Absolute Ego. The unity of the three is the Brahman, the Advaita of the Upaniṣads.

Summary of Important Characteristics

We may now give a summary of the prominent general characteristics of Indian philosophy:

1. The first important characteristic is the reflective inwardness of Indian philosophy.

2. The interest that Indian philosophy showed in the ultimate nature of the *ātman* (self) is overwhelming.

3. Another feature is the naturalistic attitude towards all philosophical problems, including the religious. The object of religion, the Brahman, is conceived to be as naturally connected with man as mind is with life, and life with matter.

4. Because of this naturalism, rationalism is encouraged, so much so that foreigners find it difficult to say whether Indian philosophers are discussing philosophy or religion. There is an intensive reflective study of the nature of Spirit.

5. Because of the naturalistic and rationalistic attitude, there are no dogmas in Indian religion.

6. For the same reason, faith in the sense in which it is accepted in Christian and Islamic religious thought is not found in Indian thought. God does not become a conceptual abstraction in India as in the West, but the subject of existential philosophy. For the same reason, Indians do not adore the founders of religion as much as the followers of some other religions do. Buddha is adored because he is said to have told the Truth; what he said was considered true, not because *he* said it, but because it was found to be true on its own merits. Hence, no exclusive revelation to individual persons is generally accepted. Everyone can become a Buddha.

7. Everyone can have the revelation, and it is called intuition. The philosophical importance lies in its being accepted as naturally common to all, whether they do or do not care for it. Intuition is naturally coexistent and continuous with intellect, not opposed to it. The emphasis on intuition is not due to irrationalism, but to the combination of empiricism, naturalism, and rationalism in Indian thought.

8. The highest in man, in his soul or self, is regarded as reason by western thought; but Indian thought declares that it is the *ātman,* and that the *ātman* is above reason. Rational nature is not the highest in man, but lower than the highest. But the West's faith in reason is, on the whole, supreme. The view of Plato and Aristotle that the rational part or aspect of the soul is immortal will not be accepted by Indian philosophy. It may be relatively immortal, but the truly immortal is the *ātman.*

9. As the *ātman* and the Brahman are beyond reason, they are known by suprarational intuition. Reason works only so long as the distinction between subject and object, and between subject and predicate, lasts. The field of epistemology, so far developed, belongs to this distinction and is confined to it, because the distinction is one of the conditions of epistemology. The recent western attempt to make intuition an epistemological method in order to synthesize East and West in philosophy has, therefore, to be cautious, for intuition is said to work without the distinction, but intellect cannot overcome it. But if the distinction is given up, epistemology may have to be thrown overboard, as it is indispensable only for understanding man's outward experience.

10. Classical Indian philosophies, except the Mīmāmsā, showed marked indifference to man as he exists in society. This indifference was due to their overwhelming inward interest. Since the Mīmāmsā philosophy and the epics did not enjoy high philosophical prestige, India has not developed social thought to any appreciable degree.

11. As human events were considered to be insignificant moments in the being of inwardness, history did not raise any philosophical problems for the philosophers, because it consisted of human events. Whatever good was achieved in history was accomplished by men as their steppingstones to inwardness, but the steppingstones were not considered to be necessary and indispensable. The progress of culture and civilization, the achievements of man, did not attract the mind of philosophers.

12. Activism and the reality and importance of human action (*karma*) were emphasized and even overemphasized by the Mīmāmsā and the Brāhmaṇas. The reality of action was so much overemphasized that it became practically equivalent to Fate in popular conceptions. But it is a mistake to equate *karma* to Fate. *Karma,* as understood by the Mīmāmsā, is human action as the controller of the universe. But it was reduced to insignificance and even unreality by the purely inward philosophies, which became dominant.

13. With the dethroning of activism and the enthroning of the philosophies of salvation through realization of what is eternally present inwards, philosophies of knowledge, and along with them epistemology and logic, obtained tremendous development. But the philosophy of activism did not remain quiet; it also developed its logic and epistemology. It is wrong to think that India had no logic and epistemology; but it is right to think that they developed as handmaids to metaphysics, the truths of which were first obtained through some kind of intuition. For the Upaniṣadic truths were not first obtained through logic and epistemology.

14. Because of naturalism and rationalism, there is elaborate deduction of categories even of inwardness.

15. Indian philosophy is concerned equally with the True, the Good, and the Beautiful. It finds all the three and their identity at the extreme end of inwardness, not of outwardness. The three highest attributes to be realized are Existence, Consciousness, and Bliss (*Sat, cit,* and Ānanda). Truth, Goodness, and Beauty have outward significance; but Existence, Consciousness, and Bliss have inward significance. But Existence and Consciousness cover Truth, and Bliss covers Goodness and Beauty. The Brahman or, according to some schools, the *ātman* alone, is ultimately True, Good, and Beautiful; and it is Existence, Consciousness, and Bliss. This is the final view of at least all the Vedāntic schools. And the Vedānta is the dominant philosophy of life in India.

16. The conception of evolution and the derivation of categories are not foreign to Indian thought; but the process is from the inward to the outward. The reverse process is not scientifically studied, except for the purpose of Yogic meditation. For instance, how matter evolves life has not been a problem of serious interest. The Cārvākas said something interesting, but never pursued the problem into any detail.

Appendix

Meanings and Uses of Term Māyā

In order to remove a very common misunderstanding about Māyā, namely, that it means nothing but illusion and unreality, it is useful to give a chart of its meanings and uses as found in the different Vedāntic systems, Mahāyāna Buddhism, and Kāsmir Śaivism. Only one Vedāntin, Vallabha, does not have anything to do with it and gives no place to it in his system.

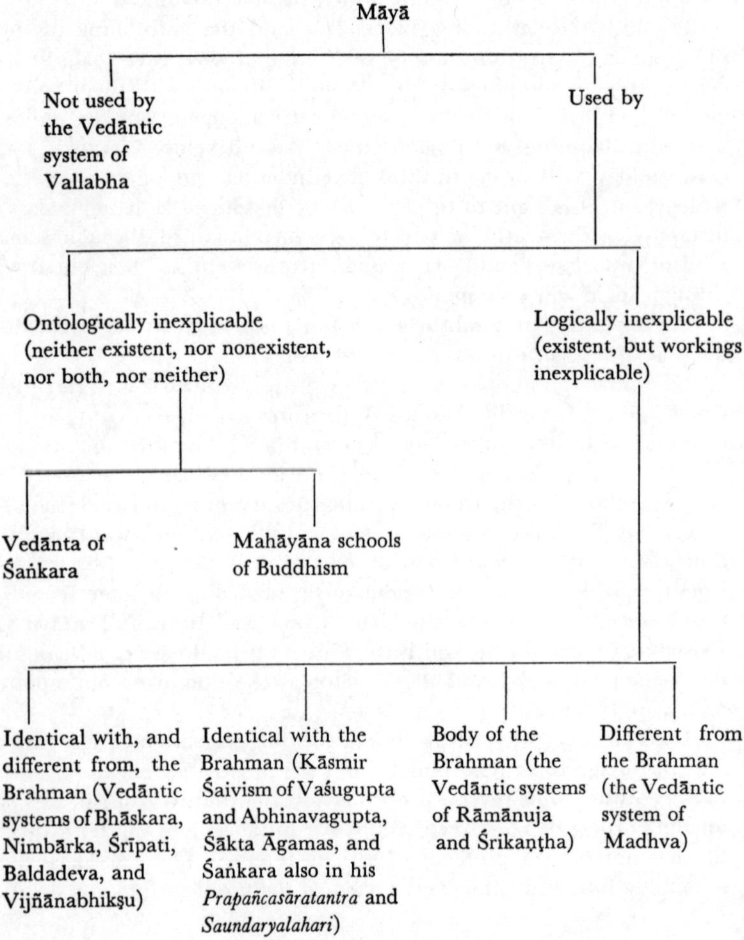

4. COMPARISONS *and* REFLECTIONS

Evaluation of Traditions and Its Principles

At the present stage of the development of comparative philosophy in the world or in the author's own work, it is as yet difficult to present a system of ideas constituting a whole; for comparative philosophy is a very young and recent subject. It is, therefore, safer to start with reflections on the three traditions. We have examined in the preceding sections how philosophy started and developed in the three traditions, the western, the Chinese, and the Indian. Of the three, the western has a more complex development than the other two. In evaluating a tradition, if we want a principle to be applied, we may draw some inspiration from the one laid down by Śaṅkara for interpreting the Upaniṣads, which do not constitute a systematic work and which are not written by a single person or even by a group belonging to a particular place or time, but which are the utterances of several persons belonging to different places and times and which are even conflicting. In interpretation, according to Śaṅkara, the clues are the starting point, the end or result, repetition or constant occurrences, novelty or freshness of a rule or principle, praise or approval, and arguments.[1] Every philosopher has a starting point, wants to establish something as the result, either the nature of reality or of man, repeats something he wants to stress on several occasions, enunciates something new not enunciated by others before, approves of something, either a method or a way of life or some ideal man, and advances some arguments. The same clues can also be found in traditions as wholes. Indeed, in some philosophies of the West we do not find praises (*arthavādas*). But in religious philosophies and philosophies of religion, whether tacitly or overtly accepted, there is some ideal person—a prophet or saviour or one who followed that philosophy of life—extolled and

[1] *Upakramopasamhārau ābhyāso apūrvatā phalam*
Arthavādopapattī ca liṅgam tātparyanirṇaye.

held up as an example. Western theology has Christ in mind. The Jewish tradition has Moses and other prophets. In Greek philosophy, we do not find such praise, though the ideal man is clearly depicted. Likewise, in modern philosophy we do not encounter such practice, because the emphasis is more upon understanding the nature of reality than upon the ends of life, and so a hero does not generally come into the picture. The exceptions are the Nazi, the Fascist, and the communist philosophies. However, approval or disapproval of certain theories and even witty remarks about some philosophers are not absent. In Chinese philosophy, though praise of heroes is not given a definite place, the sage-kings, both mythical and historical, are referred to and extolled quite often, and even made authorities by many philosophers. Confucius was almost deified and made an example for other men; and the acts of the followers of Confucius, of Lao Tzu, and others are cited for the guidance of men.

It is indeed true that any tradition as a body contains many schools and systems, and the philosophers belonging to it do not regard them as equally true and important, whereas all the Upaniṣads and all their statements are considered to be true by the classical philosophers of India. Yet, in spite of this difficulty, Śaṅkara's principle helps us in understanding the spirit behind any tradition. We have already seen how the starting point determines, to a very large extent and for a considerable time, subsequent development of the philosophies of a tradition. Greek philosophy really had two strands or two starting points, the purely cosmological standpoint of the early Ionic philosophers and the humanistic standpoint of the Sophists, both of which were blended in Plato and Aristotle. But because man as such, not as the pure spirit, was the starting point, and because he was a politico-social and arguing animal, Greek philosophy pre-eminently became nation-and-society conscious, rational, and scientific.

To the Greek tradition, Christianity added the Jewish tradition, which is pre-eminently nationalistic, and originally even tribal, and also supernatural. It is difficult for rationalistic philosophy to go with supernaturalism. But after some struggle the two strands again reconciled themselves to each other. The later half of the Middle Ages is marked by this struggle; but after a time the two were somehow made to coexist, till in recent philosophy the Greek scientific and humanistic outlook got the upper hand. And one may add that, of the scientific and the humanistic strands, the scientific got the upper hand. Spirit or soul for the Greek philosophers was a natural entity. Even God was connected with nature in a natural way. On the whole, recent western philosophy has restored to man and nature the primary place that they had in Greek philosophy. The attempt to explain the inward in terms of the most outward, which is matter, is one kind of naturalism, though it cannot be sufficiently humanistic. Even idealistic philosophers explain the world in terms of man, his feeling, his imagination, his action, or his reason.

In Chinese philosophy also we find that the starting point determined the nature of subsequent development. It was to solve the problem of human institutions that Confucius started his thinking. What should be the nature and duties of the rulers, of the subjects, of the family and its members, so that man and society can have a peaceful and prosperous life? The ruler has to be a sage. But what is the nature of a true sage? These questions and their answers are a constant refrain of Chinese philosophy. Even Buddhism, which in India did not care to raise and answer these questions, was obliged to do so after it entered China. Neo-Confucianism, in spite of the strong influence that Taoism and Buddhism had on it, raised these questions as keenly as Confucius himself. The theory of the ruler and social institutions became the test of every philosophy.

In India it was the theory of salvation that became the test. Which philosophy offers the best doctrine of salvation (*mokṣa*)? The materialism of the Cārvākas, which did not offer any theory of salvation, could not prosper. The Mīmāmsā did not have at first a definite theory of salvation; but the idea was so popular and its influence so strong that finally the school had to adopt it; and the Mīmāmsā doctrine of *dharma* as action prescribed by the Vedas became the doctrine of *karmayoga,* or the *yoga* of action leading up to salvation, a doctrine elaborated by the *Bhagavadgīta,* the *dharmaśāstras* (ethical codes), and the epics. The idea of salvation formulated in the Upaniṣads influenced all subsequent philosophies, both orthodox and heterodox, except the Cārvāka, and is still influencing present-day thought.

If we take the end, we find that western philosophy has got back the original humanism and rationalism of the Greeks. The reaction against supernaturalism is quite strong. Almost all the contemporary schools of existentialism are more or less humanistic. Contemporary western man, if he has faith at all, has faith in human reason. Faith in the supernatural is limited to only a few thinkers; and for many religion is a social function. Thus western thought can still be called humanistic and rationalistic. In Chinese philosophy also, the end has not differed from the beginning. China, indeed, has wholeheartedly changed over to communism, Marxism, and Leninism. But communism is humanistic like Confucianism and is concerned with social institutions. Its main stress is on human activity, particularly economic activity. Confucius did not question the necessity of having a king; but communism does. Whether right or wrong in its conclusions, communism goes into the nature and source of human relationships. Confucius wanted to reform and purify the existing human relationships; communism wants to revolutionize them. But man and society are still the center of interest for both.

So far as Indian philosophy is concerned, the aim of philosophy is still salvation. This aim—as the aim of Chinese philosophy is repeated throughout its own history—is repeated by the Indian schools throughout their history. But in western philosophy, the philosophies of the Middle Ages form an exception to the general Greek outlook, which regained its original nature in contemporary thought. Medieval philosophy pushed man and nature into the background, explained everything in terms of God, extolled faith, and made reason subservient to faith. Further, the rise of science and technology and the tremendous progress that they made strengthened man's certainty of matter and faith in reason so much that even humanism is in danger of being pushed into the background. Thus, there have been constant changes in outlook in western philosophy. And though there have been logicians and scientific philosophers who assert that philosophy has to be philosophy of life, life itself has become a subject of secondary interest. In this respect western philosophy offers a contrast to Chinese and Indian philosophies, which kept up a continuity of interest and outlook. Western philosophy has been richer, more detailed and varied. But on the whole, if we take the general knowledge man had during the Greek times and that which he has now, we may say that the general outlook of the present is naturalistic and rational like that of the Greeks.

What is the novelty that each tradition has for the other? Chinese philosophy has a novelty for the Indian and the Indian for the Chinese. Both are essentially and obviously philosophies of life. But if we want a philosophy of manners and etiquette, we do not find so much of it in the Indian as in the Chinese philosophy. Similarly, if we want a political and social philosophy, we find more of it in the Chinese than in the Indian. But if we want a philosophy of the *ātman* (spirit), we find it in the Indian, but little of it in the Chinese. Humanism is common to both the Chinese and western philosophies; but if we want systematic logic and method, we find it in the western, not in the Chinese. We have already noted that to press a problem to its logical extreme is not the Chinese practice. But the Indian mind is not afraid of logical and metaphysical depths and abstractions. It is unfair to compare modern western philosophy with the classical Indian philosophy, for modern western philosophy starts from the sixteenth century, but Indian philosophy has had little development from that time till recently.

Science and scientific thought, the philosophy of mathematics, and all such rigorous disciplines in the West belong to a period much later than the sixteenth century. It will be fair to compare Indian thought with Greek thought and the thought of the Middle Ages. Then Indian logic may not appear to be much inferior to that of the West. Logic was not developed in exactly the same way in India and in Greece; and different branches of logic received attention in the two countries. If the Greeks showed greater analytic skill, the Indians showed greater ability in constructive definition. It is wrong to think that Indian logic is only negative logic. We can say this of Buddhism and the Advaita. But all the other schools gave elaborate definitions to fix the positive nature of entities, and very elaborate proofs to prove their reality. Yet in spite of the common logical interest, Indian philosophy presents a novelty to the western. There is no definite conception of the *ātman* in the West. The *ātman* in its three states of waking, dream, and sleep, and with its five bodies, material, vital, mental, rational, and blissful, is not commonly found in western thought. This reasoned conception of the *ātman* and salvation is the most important central topic of the whole of Indian philosophy, and all the logical interest that was developed was developed for or against proving their nature and truth.

Because of the varied development of western philosophy, it is difficult to say that it differs completely from the Chinese and Indian philosophies in aim. Leaving out Buddhism in China, the idea of salvation seems to be foreign to Chinese thought. It is the best and happiest kind of existence here on earth and to be a complete man that the Chinese want. But the Indians want salvation, which is a different kind of existence even if it can be had on this earth. Many philosophers accepted salvation in this bodily existence (*jīvanmukti*); but it is an absorption in a state of existence different from the ordinary. The Tao lies, according to Chinese thought as it developed later, in chopping wood and drawing water and, according to later Neo-Confucianism, in taking part also in the political and social life of the community. But *jīvanmukti* does not lie in such activities, although a *jīvanmukta* (one who obtains salvation in this body) may be performing them. So far as western philosophy goes, all these ideals are placed before man at one time or other. Though in some of its recent trends western philosophy is in danger of ceasing to be a philosophy of life, western philosophers, on the whole, have stressed that philosophy had to present a way of life; and every way of life presents some ideals and values. Though the western idea of salvation is not always the same as the Indian, now and then western philosophers presented a similar idea. The Neo-Platonic ideal and the ideal of some Christian mystics are similar to the Vedāntic. The Chinese concept of good life on earth is also present in western thought, though the latter tries to fathom the deeper presuppositions of such a life.

By applying all the tests, we may say that, taking the traditions up to the present day, western philosophy is richer, more detailed, and more varied than the Indian and the Chinese. The Indian has tried to keep up a continuous and consistent spiritual tradition with an overwhelming interest in the nature of the ultimate spirit. The Chinese has tried similarly to make its humanistic tradition continuous and consistent, always mindful of man, society, and state.

Beginnings of Philosophy

The starting point of philosophy is sometimes said to be wonder and curiosity. The view that philosophy begins in wonder is generally attributed to Plato. Evidently, Chinese philosophy and Indian philosophy did not begin in mere wonder. It is doubtful that any philosophy of life can really begin in wonder. The problems of life have a seriousness about them that is not always associated with wonder. Confucius was made to reflect by the chaos and confusion that prevailed in China of the time. Such chaos was not a cause of wonder but of pain. The Upaniṣadic thinkers were certainly not impressed by the defects and imperfections of social and political life. Yet they were keenly sensitive to the defects and imperfections of life in general, the conditions of phenomenal existence. Plato wrote his *Republic* because he was dissatisfied with the conditions of society at the time. The urge for writing the *Republic* did not originate in wonder. The earlier Sophists might not have been serious-minded philosophers; but Socrates was serious in his inquiries, and so was his disciple Plato. So neither with the Upaniṣadic thinkers nor with Confucius nor, again, with Socrates and Plato did philosophy start in wonder. With Buddha it started with the idea of suffering: the world is full of suffering, how can man overcome it? So no philosophy that wanted to show a way of life could have begun in mere wonder. It was a desire for some existence higher than the present, whether in the cosmos, society, or the state, and for a perfect life, happier and less defective than the present, that offered the motive force for every philosophy of life.

Whitehead said that thought starts with negation or the negative judgment. In logic the negative may presuppose the affirmative; but in life the first act of reflection starts with the negative. If life runs smooth and unobstructed, there will be no thought and consequently no philosophy. When there is obstruction, either thought must arise or life must become extinct. But life resists extinction and produces thought. Thought seizes upon the obstruction, avoids it, or discovers a way for overcoming it. When the impediment was great and vast and was traced to the conditions of man and society or the phenomenal world, social philosophies and philosophies of the world must have started. It is man's hope that perfection can be attained and life can be made smooth, pleasant, and happy by improving the conditions of the world and making them conform to the nature of man or by making man conform to them or by doing both. Science, technology, and social and political guidance do the first; ethics and religion do the second. And both are necessary for the life of man: if man's ability to control nature has its limits, his ability to control himself also has its limits; each has to be controlled and made to conform to the other.

Without dissatisfaction with the present, there can be no science and no philosophy, because thought then has no stimulus to commence its work. If this observation has truth, then the charge of pessimism against some philosophies and of optimism against others is ill founded. What is sometimes said about religion—that it could not have started without some pessimism—holds true of philosophy also. Curiosity will be present to the extent that man wants more and more and desires to know what more there is. In India, the spiritual quest was called *rājayoga,* or the royal *yoga*. But the original urge to have more must have started with some dissatisfaction.

It is true that some philosophies have overstressed the imperfections and miseries of the world and others have pronounced that all is well with it. It is said of some of the German pessimists and their families that they were the happiest people of the country; and Bradley described optimism as the belief that this world is the best of all the possible worlds and in it everything is an evil. Too much pessimism is as wrong as too much optimism. But some kind or degree of pessimism is essential for all philosophy, which is a search for something more and better. If there is no falsity, there will be no search for truth; if there is no evil, there will be no search for the good; and if there is no ugliness, there will be no search for beauty. Every search, therefore, is motivated by some value. All philosophy, accordingly, is a philosophy of value, whether the object valued is social, political, or cosmological. Even scientific search is a quest for value. If all human activity is purposive, then scientific investigation also is purposive; if the difference between pure science and applied science is slowly diminishing, then the difference between fact and value will atrophy. The only difference between value and value can be that one may be direct and the other indirect; one may be given, the other may have to be built up; one may be artificial, the other may be natural; one may be spiritual, the other may be material; and so on. Of these some must be made to conform to the others. No such activity takes place unless man finds some imperfection in the present and is also hopeful of improvement in the future.

Thus, philosophy involves both pessimism and optimism. But the human situation contains both man and his environment; and for smooth and harmonious living man has to control himself in order to conform to the environment, and he has to control the environment in order to make it conform to him. Thus, human activity is needed for both the purposes. The environment of man consists not only of physical nature but also of society and spirit. Of these, physical nature can be controlled, society can be reformed, but spirit cannot be changed.

Man has to adjust himself completely to the spirit within him. The modern, particularly the contemporary, philosophical outlook is emphasizing and even overemphasizing control of physical nature and reformation of society. Western thinkers themselves, in saying that the ethical progress of mankind has lagged far behind his intellectual progress, are admitting this fact. The reformation of society that the West is attempting is not based on explicit ethical principles, but on the economic, the interest of which is materialistic, for which reason the West is branded by the common man in the East as materialistic, in spite of the fact that the West also has had many ethical and spiritual leaders. Greek philosophy emphasized rational reform of society, and medieval philosophy, that of man with reference to God, treating physical nature and society as evils that could not be improved. Chinese philosophy thought in terms of self-control with reference to state and society and of reform of state and society; and though it is similar to Greek thought in this respect, it did not push its inquiries to their ultimate foundations, material or spiritual. Indian philosophy also emphasized self-control, but in terms of the spirit within man, and differs from Chinese philosophy by pushing its arguments to their ultimate spiritual implications.

Schweitzer's Views and the Three Traditions

In the light of the distinctions mentioned, we may appreciate Albert Schweitzer's observations about the cultures and philosophies of the world. His contention is that western philosophy is life-and-world affirming and that the Indian is life-and-world negating. Radhakrishnan answered this interpretation brilliantly. He says that the real contrast is not between Hinduism and Christianity, but between religion and self-sufficient humanism. All true religion is essentially otherworldly; if it does not say that spiritual life is higher than mundane life, it is not worth the name of religion. Christianity also said it.

> [But] religion and humanism do not exclude each other. If we wrongly identify religion with life and world negation and ethics with humanism and social progress, the two become quite different and require to be pursued on their own separate lines in obedience to their own separate principles. They are, on the contrary, organic to each other. While the chief value of religion lies in its power to raise and enlarge the internal man, its soundness is not complete until it has shaped properly his external existence. For the latter we require a sound political, economic, and social life, a power and an efficiency which will make a people, not only survive but grow towards a collective perfection. If a religion does not secure these ends, there is a defect somewhere, either in its essential principles or in their application. A spiritual view is sustained not only by insight but by a rational philosophy and sound social institutions.[2]

Religion, if it is healthy, must be adequately humanistic; and humanism, if true, must be the embodiment of spiritual life.

Schweitzer made very penetrating observations about the cultures and philosophies of the three traditions. And his criticisms go deeper than the answers given so far. Of the three traditions he shows the highest regard for the Chinese as an ethical culture. He writes: "Nowhere, again, has the problem of world-and-life-affirmation, both in itself and in its relation to ethics, been felt in so elemental and comprehensive a fashion as in Chinese thought."[3] Western philosophy also is world-and-life affirming; but it takes this affirmation as self-evident, and has not raised it to the status of a philosophy that finds a significant meaning in life. "It did not succeed in grounding its world-and-life-affirming world-view convincingly and permanently in thought. . . . Hence our civilization also has remained fragmentary and insecure."[4] Elsewhere he says:

> . . . we cannot feel ourselves completely justified in the face of these strange Eastern theories. They have in them something full of nobility which retains its hold on us, even fascinates us. This tinge

[2] *Eastern Religions and Western Thought* (Oxford University Press, 1940), pp. 64 ff., 75, 76.

[3] *Civilization and Ethics* (London: Adam and Charles Black, 1949), p. xiv.

[4] *Ibid.*, p. x.

> of nobility comes from the fact that these convictions are born of a search for a theory of the universe and for the meaning of life. With us, on the other hand, activist instincts and impulses take the place of a theory of the universe. We have no theory affirming the world and life to oppose to the negative theory of these thinkers, no thought which has found a basis for an optimistic conception of existence to oppose to this other, which has arrived at a pessimistic conception.[5]

The West has no developed ethical philosophy with a world-view, giving a positive meaning to life, though such a view is implicit in the activities of the West. Only the Chinese and the Indians developed an ethical philosophy of life. And, according to Schweitzer, it has become in India world-and-life denying, but in China world-and-life affirming. In China, he says, "life-affirmation made the attempt to come to clear ideas about itself. In Lao-tse and his pupils it is still naively ethical. In Chuang-tse it becomes cheerful resignation; in Lie-tse the will to secret power over things; in Yang-tse it ends in an all-round living of life to the full." [6]

Schweitzer tells us that a sound ethical culture needs three things: a sound theory of the universe, an ethically activistic mental attitude, and reverence for life.[7] For some reason or other, he finds all philosophies from Plato to the present defective as philosophies of life. Christianity is not devoid of pessimism.[8] "Mysticism is not a friend of ethics but a foe." [9] Even materialism is an ally of pessimism, and "has done much more to shake the position of the optimistic world-view than has Schopenhauer." [10] Every philosophy that preaches surrender to an Absolute preaches resignation. Like materialism it undervalues man's life and makes it unimportant. Ethics of social welfare has also its defects: it impoverishes ethics, for the individual is the source of morality, and he is given no value. Personality is submerged in society. Schweitzer's analysis of the basic ideas of western philosophers is very instructive, and his criticisms deserve careful attention.

[5] *The Decay and the Restoration of Civilization* (London: Adam and Charles Black, 1950), p. 99.

[6] *Civilization and Ethics,* p. 177.

[7] *The Decay and Restoration of Civilization,* pp. vii, viii, xi.

[8] *Civilization and Ethics,* p. 66.

[9] *Ibid.,* p. 235.

[10] *Ibid.,* p. 13.

Then on what world-view should we base our ethics? Schweitzer seems to think that we cannot have any.

> I believe I am the first among Western thinkers who has ventured to recognizing this crushing result of knowledge, and the first to be absolutely skeptical about our knowledge of the world without at the same time renouncing belief in world-and-life-affirmation and ethics. Resignation as to knowledge of the world is for me not an irretrievable plunge into a skepticism which leaves us to drift about in life like a derelict vessel. I see in it that effort of honesty which we must venture to make in order to arrive at the serviceable world-view which hovers within sight. Every world-view which fails to start from resignation in regard to knowledge is artificial and a mere fabrication, for it rests upon an inadmissible interpretation of the universe.[11]

One is afraid that Schweitzer is here violating one of his three conditions for a healthy ethical culture, namely, a sound theory of the universe; for we cannot have any theory without knowledge. One can understand why Schweitzer is so much impressed by the Chinese philosophical tradition; for it cared very little for a system of knowledge or for its method, and much less for a theory of the ultimate nature of the universe than for full and healthy life. Its sense of the reality of life was so strong that it tended to treat the four beginnings, sympathy, and so on, as foundations for its belief in the interconnectedness of the universe. In no other philosophical tradition do we find this idea more strongly emphasized than in Chinese thought. The four ethical beginnings—not God, not matter, not even reason—are the basis of our knowledge of the universe. Yet, one has to ask: If we want an ethical philosophy, should we treat life as inclusive of knowledge or as blind? Indeed, reverence for life is one of the highest ideals, if not the highest; it is only a few like Buddha and Mahavīra in the past and Schweitzer and Gandhi in the present who showed and preached this reverence. It is true that Schweitzer's will-to-live is not to be found in Buddhism and Jainism with the emphasis wanted; but the great doctrine of vegetarianism has its roots in the universal respect for life, which both Buddha and Mahavīra preached and the followers of Mahavīra carried to its logical extreme. But why should life be respected? Because spirit is the same for all, according to some philosophers, and

[11] *Ibid.*, p. xv.

similar for all, according to others. Every life is a developing spirit and should be allowed to develop into spirit. But, again, why should it be allowed to develop? One answer at least is that spirit is the same in all. The spirit within me is the same as the one developing in the animal before me, and my own spiritual development requires that I realize this sameness. Unless I am guided by this feeling of oneness in my attitude towards the animal and in my activities with reference to it, I cannot realize the universality of the spirit within me; in short, spiritual realization will be impossible for me. This is the answer given by the Vedānta and later Buddhism. Thus a theory of the universe is supplied by the Indian philosophers for their ethical views. And every concept of the universe developed its own theory of knowledge. One may not find the theories satisfactory in all respects; but each ethical code is followed and supported by a view of the universe and a theory of knowledge. In fact, Buddhist philosophy started as a spiritualistic and psychological ethics and then developed its theories of the universe and epistemology. A simple code of spiritualistic ethics without a metaphysics and theory of knowledge could not be self-supporting.

It is unfortunate that Schweitzer did not know about the importance attached to *karmamārga,* or the way of action, by some of the Indian philosophies. It may be that some of the Vedāntins gave it a secondary or a tertiary place, and the primary place to *jñānamārga* (way of knowledge) or *bhaktimārga* (way of devotion) ; but many of them recognized its importance. Of all the paths to spiritual realization, these three are the most important; of the three one or the other may be placed first. The recognition of the three shows that action, knowledge, and devotion (love) are the three important aspects of life able to lead man to spiritual realization. It is also true that Indian philosophy has taught that, whichever of the three ways is chosen, it leads man beyond the realm of action. Hence the will to action, or rather the will to right action, belongs only to life in the mundane world. But should will to action be justified by treating the Universal Spirit as an Absolute Will to Action? The essential teaching of the Vedānta is that the Absolute is neither action nor inaction, because its action or inaction is not like ours. It is eternally creative and so active; but, as infinite, it adds nothing to itself by creation, since the infinite does not grow by addition or decrease by subtraction. At this point we can understand Schweitzer. No theory of the universe satisfies him. Philosophers have tried to explain morality as action in accordance with some ideal. The *Gitā* explained it as action in accordance with the processes of the Cosmic Person. But "in accordance with" always implies surrender and resignation. Schweitzer, however, probably does not want this implication. If so, morality cannot be explained. He then not only gives up a theory of the universe, but also precludes all possibility of a basis for morality. For if morality is to have a basis, then it has to be based upon a world-view.

The result is due to the skepticism he wishes to accept with regard to epistemology.[12] He has, therefore, to face a dilemma: either build a theory of the universe with the help of epistemology and lay a foundation for morality or renounce epistemology and with it the theory of the universe and be content with morality without a foundation. But the morality of a culture without a philosophical foundation, however activistic, will be unreflective, irrational, blind, and aimless. Even the Chinese had to provide a theory of the universe, however incomplete.

Schweitzer also accepts some Absolute Will-to-Live, to which we belong as finite wills-to-live. He writes:

> When it comes to clearness about itself, the will-to-live knows that it is dependent on itself alone. Its destiny is to attain freedom from the world. Its knowledge of the world can show that its striving to raise to their highest value its own life and every living thing which can be influenced by it must remain problematic when regarded in relation to the universe. This fact will not disturb it. Its world-and-life-affirmation carries its meaning in itself. It follows from an inward necessity, and is sufficient for itself. By its means my existence joins in pursuing the aims of *the mysterious universal will of which I am a manifestation.*[13]

Is this mysterious universal will-to-live a blind force or a conscious force? If it is to sustain its manifestations, are the finite wills-to-live to act according to its processes or according to their whims and momentary impulses? If the former, then there is resignation and surrender, which Schweitzer does not want. It may be said that resignation is not necessary; just as man respects his own life, if he respects that of the others also, he has an adequate criterion to test his morality. But at least two difficulties arise here. First, morality arises and gets meaning only because immorality is present. In all spheres and

[12] *Ibid.*

[13] *Ibid.*, p. 214. Italics are mine.

levels of life, where immorality has no meaning, morality loses its significance. I may respect my life as well as that of the other; I may allow his will-to-live to work as I allow mine. What am I to do if he does not respect my life and allow my will-to-live to work? Morality is felt acutely whenever there is such conflict. If the other wants to cut me down, should I or should I not cut him down? In the second place, I shall have to ask myself: Why should I accept the criterion, "respect life and the will-to-live"? I may be the manifestation of the mysterious will-to-live; but why should I respect another's life? Is it not because the other's life also is the manifestation of the same entity? Even then, why should I respect it unless by not respecting it I should lose my own good? But does not this condition need an explanation in terms of a world-view? If it does, resignation and surrender follow.

So a measure of resignation, surrender, pessimism, is necessary for any ethical philosophy; and it is not absent even from Chinese philosophy. Confucius may not have bothered about a world-view; but he was certainly hopeful of improving the lot of man on earth. But Mencius, Lao Tzu, Chuang Tzu, and others did have some world-view, and they were also hopeful of improving the lot of man on earth and gave advice to both rulers and subjects. Some of them, however, found perfection, not in the artificialities of civilization, but in life according to basic human nature. In the opinion of Lao Tzu, this basic nature transcends man. It is a paradox that the essential human nature transcends man, and man has to live according to it. But life according to it means surrender; even life according to ordinary human nature means some self-control and some surrender. It is true that many forms of Buddhism preached a doctrine that is antagonistic to the will-to-live. It is also true that the Vedānta found the ideal life, not in the everyday functions of life like drawing water and chopping wood, but in a life of identity with the Universal Spirit or its processes or both, and it, too, sharply distinguished this life from ordinary life. But any excess in theory or practice may be abandoned; yet we cannot abandon the very foundation of morality.

Schweitzer writes: "The discoveries in the field of knowledge which the will-to-live encounters when it begins to think, are therefore altogether pessimistic. It is not by accident that all religious world-views, except the Chinese, have a more or less pessimistic tone and bid man expect nothing from his existence here." What then are we to do? Should we allow the will-to-live to work blindly? "The will-to-live which tries to know the world is a shipwrecked castaway; the will-to-live which gets to know itself is a bold mariner." [14] But does not the mariner need to know the directions? How can life know itself adequately without knowing the world in which it exists? Or is it to be exhorted to follow its blind impulse? We cannot think that that is the view of Schweitzer or of any one of his eminence as a philosopher. Otherwise, Schweitzer's criticism of Nietzsche's philosophy, as a philosophy of brutality, would be pointless; there can be no morality, whatever be the degree of progress civilization reaches, unless there is the distinction between the ideal and the actual, a world-view in terms of the ideal, a feeling of necessity to live and act according to the ideal, and, consequently, surrender to the ideal and resignation.[15] Mere respect for life and for the will-to-live is not enough. It should be respect for life in accordance with an ideal.

Certainly respect for life and for the will-to-live is absolutely necessary for any ethics. It is to the great credit of Schweitzer that he brings its importance to the forefront. Explanations of life in terms of Absolute Spirit or of matter, as Schweitzer shows, have often been equally inimical to ethics; for the explanations could easily be abused and misused. Unless the importance of the will-to-live is explicitly recognized, ethics becomes defective, and culture and civilization become meaningless. They may appear to be much ado about nothing, about mere effervescences from the standpoint of materialism, and about momentary bubbles of existence from the standpoint of absolutism. If for a spiritual philosophy human existence is a valueless manifestation of the Universal Spirit, we do not understand why it is manifested at all. Our ethics and civilization need not wait until they get an answer. Similarly, if human life is an emergent quality out of matter for materialism, we do not understand why this emergent should have any value at all. And we need not be disheartened and become pessimistic about the value and future of life. As Schweitzer observes, theories of knowledge and world-views have not so far given us satisfactory answers to the questions.

We need not, therefore, wait for the answers in order to start our ethics. We have got to start it, taking the will-to-live as one of our

[14] *Ibid.*, pp. 210, 212.

[15] Cf. "Nietzsche is a synthesis, appearing in European mentality, of Lie-tse and Yang-tse. It is only Europeans who are capable of producing the philosophy of brutality." *Ibid.*, p. 177.

axioms. This is in accordance with the opinion that an ultimately unified system of knowledge is an unattained goal of philosophy, only because all branches of knowledge are equally incomplete and we have to treat such a system as an ideal and goal and proceed with each of the branches as if it were autonomous. The biological sciences were once upon a time treated as parts of the physical; but now they are given autonomy. Then why should we not give autonomy to ethical sciences also, by accepting the will-to-live as real and fundamental? In this spirit only can Schweitzer's contention be accepted. World-views and epistemology cannot be given up. We may say that they are imperfect; we cannot justify that they are unnecessary. Our ethical philosophy can be perfected when they are perfected and vice versa; each grows in relation to the others.

The Universal Spirit transcends the spirit of man, and so man cannot fully understand the ways of the former. But the principle of surrender to it is absolutely necessary as a foundation of all ethical philosophy. An overemphasis on this surrender, particularly in despair of understanding the ways of the Universal Spirit, may sometimes lead to extreme forms of pessimism, although really, if everything is a manifestation of the Universal Spirit and the ways of the world are its ways, there is no reason for pessimism. Pessimism must be due to ignorance and lack of nerve. Surrender does not mean inactivity, but activity according to another and higher, which is working through us. But how is it working through us, and how are we to make our actions accord with its processes? It is difficult to answer this question. But we think it must be a process that binds creature to creature, and makes them live in harmony. As Mahatma Gandhi said, we do not know why and how it destroys creatures but only that it loves them, and we may say that it promotes the lives of creatures through each other.[16] The processes of promotion of life are love, affection, sympathy, compassion, and harmony. Chinese philosophers, who did not care for a world-view, utilized these qualities of man for founding their ethical philosophy of world-and-life affirmation. Empirical and materialistic philosophers of the West did the same thing, without seeing the contradiction between their ethical philosophies and their empirical and materialistic world-views. Because the metaphysical theories of the Chinese philosophers were not very deep, not logically complete and detailed, and because they did not start with world-views but with

[16] See P. T. Raju, *Idealistic Thought of India,* p. 294.

ethical theories, many contradictions were not felt by them, though some were not unnoticed, as the mutual criticisms of philosophers by one another disclose. The Mohist theory of universal love was criticized by the Confucians; Mencius' doctrine of the essential goodness of man and his idealism were criticized by Hsün Tzu; and similarly, Hsün Tzu's theory that human nature is essentially evil was rejected as false by his rivals.

But all these contradictions were noticed in theories of human nature and in the attempt to perfect human life. If no theory of human nature that fails to perfect human life is true, then also no world-view which fails in that attempt can be true. This is what Radhakrishnan might mean when he says that a spiritual view of the universe must be capable of being sustained by a rational philosophy and sound social institutions. Till we get such an adequate spiritual world-view, social institutions must be built upon qualities like human-heartedness, sympathy, compassion, and love which make men promote each other's lives; and the institutions must be developed and completed with a spiritual world-view in mind, however vague it may be. And it is bound to be vague, until man's knowledge of the world including the human and spiritual realms is complete. This is where Chinese reasonableness and human mindfulness help philosophy.

The Chinese philosophers themselves feel that it is lack of development in epistemology and methodology of knowledge that prevented Chinese civilization from attaining the heights reached by the West. In philosophy, it prevented the development of great systems of metaphysics, comparable to either those of India or the West. Metaphysics did not lead the Chinese philosophers to dizzy speculative heights or mystic spiritual depths. Buddhism spread the ideas of Nirvāṇa, Dharma, and Vijñaptimātratā. But, as we have seen, the Neo-Confucians, who combined the ideas of Buddhism, Taoism, and Yin-Yang, raised the question: How does a man of realization live, and where does the mysterious Tao lie? The answer they gave was: In chopping wood and drawing water, and even in leading a regular political and social life. It lies in life lived according to human nature. By nature itself they understood human nature.[17] The tendency is strong in Chinese philosophy to treat man as the highest manifestation of nature; and if everything can be best understood in its highest development, then nature also can be best understood in its highest

[17] Hu Shih, *The Development of Logical Method in Ancient China,* p. 4.

development, man. Applying the same principle, human nature also can be best understood in its ideal form, the sage, who lives the best social and political life. Thus, whatever mysticism Chinese philosophy contains is a mysticism of nature, which is human nature. How can this be understood? The reply of Chinese philosophers, on the whole, is: By reflecting on human nature itself in its social and political relationships. This is, perhaps, Schweitzer's will-to-live, which, in its human form, tries to know itself, without trying to know the world.

That the being of man transcends social and political relationships was not absolutely unknown to Chinese philosophers. When they drew a difference between things Heaven-made and things man-made and exhorted the people to give up the latter, when Wang, following Mencius, said that Heaven was in the mind of man, and exhorted him to live according to its nature, the philosophers drew a distinction between ideal nature and actual nature and preached resignation and surrender to the ideal. For them reality is human nature; the will-to-live and the will-to-act are natural to man. The natural, again, is finally the ideal. Human nature, except for a few philosophers, is not petty, selfish, unreasonable, and cruel, but large, human-hearted, righteous, reasonable, and sympathetic. The Chinese wanted to have full life; and so they searched for it. They showed only an occasional interest in what lies beyond life and in questions about the ultimate foundations of life. Even retreat and escape from culture and society, wherever advocated, was meant for a fuller human life, for its completion. Yang Tzu would not pluck out one hair from his body to save the world, lest his life would be less by one hair.

Yet, though the idea that man and Heaven (nature) are intimately connected was strong in Chinese thought, it did not occur to the Chinese philosophers that human nature cannot adequately be understood unless man's environment also is adequately comprehended. Man's environment is both internal and external, and his being has two directions, inward and outward. Thus, the foundations of human life are both spiritual and material. It is in understanding these foundations that Chinese thought remained incomplete and imperfect, confining its activities to the field of human relationships. It has not been seen clearly by the Chinese thinkers that human nature extends in both directions. Higher and deeper mysticism found in Indian thought, in spite of its excesses noticed here and there, is a sign that it attempted to reach some ultimate spiritual foundations. The same signs are found in western philosophy also, but only occasionally, not consistently. On the other hand, it has made a dogged attempt, particularly in its recent developments, to base itself on ultimate outward foundations. No philosophy should violate the principle of life; it should not underrate the value of the noble qualities of human nature, which contribute to the full and harmonious life of man and society. But no philosophy can be complete and adequate unless it gives the fullest recognition to both the inward and the outward reaches of man's being. Spiritual life enables man to reach the inward depths of his being, and material life its outward breadth. Only one who has attained both can be considered to have lived the fullest life. No philosophy should be preoccupied either with life after death or with prosperity in this world; but no philosophy should neglect either. Both are facts and necessities that gravely concern man. And as human life is founded on both matter and spirit, it is their integral unity. Man is not a mere compound as the modern scientific mind thinks and the *saṁghātavāda* (doctrine of aggregates) of Buddhism tended to preach. Otherwise, his life or even his noblest qualities will have no reality and value. Again, though he is an integrality, his integrality shows itself in several forms—the rational, the mental, the vital, and the material—which philosophers and scientists have been able to study separately, and which constitute the ingredients of man's being. And the study of man's life both in its integrality and in its constituent forms ought to supply a complete philosophy of man, which I prefer to call critico-integral humanism, and which will not be antimetaphysical like the usual forms of humanism, but will be a system of metaphysics itself.

Similarities and Differences

We may now recount the main similarities and differences of the three traditions in the light of their general features.

1. So far as religious thought is concerned, one gets the impression that the West gives a higher place to its Jewish factor than to its Greek

factor. Greek religion, however it might have originated, became philosophical and rational. But Judaism eschewed all philosophy. It did not repudiate reason, but refused to raise rational questions. It is the nature of reason to interconnect entities thought about, thereby making the supernatural lose its peculiar tinge. Christianity also obstructed the entry of reason into some of the basic problems. Great value is attached to the Renaissance of the sixteenth century; but what was revived was Greek philosophy and literature, not Greek religion. The contradiction between the extreme rationalism of the West and its religion of faith has not been removed. It has been eliminated by communism only by violently rejecting religion altogether and by substituting materialist faith for the religious. The attempt to fathom the relation between the so-called supernatural and the natural, made by post-Aristotelian Greek philosophy, particularly Neo-Platonism was condemned as oriental and discarded, so that it was not felt to be an essential aspect of our life itself, and the possibility of laying a rational foundation for spiritual philosophy was lost. It is not meant that no attempt was made to found a rational spiritual philosophy; but such attempts were branded as mystic and have not been very successful. Had the Renaissance included the renaissance of Greek religion, communism of the antireligious type might not have been born. Greek philosophy was, indeed, utilized by Augustine and Thomas Aquinas before the Renaissance, and by writers on philosophy of religion after the Renaissance. For the former two philosophy was the handmaid of religion and reason of faith, and much irrational use of faith by the interested was made possible. In the hands of the latter, the object of religion either became a pale, bloodless truth, a concept, or, whenever it became an experienceable living entity, tended to deprive philosophy of its philosophical importance.

In Indian philosophy, on the contrary, religious thought, though conceptual, always insisted on the experiential and existential nature of the object of religion, for which reason it is often called mysticism. It is true that God or the Absolute is often spoken of as beyond speech, thought, and mind, but volumes have been written about His nature. To say that God is beyond speech, and so on, is not peculiar to Indian thought alone. Christianity, Judaism, and Islam also hold the same view. But for Indian thought, to say that God is beyond thought is not the same as to say that He is beyond experience. Experience of God may transcend reason; but that it transcends reason is given by reason itself. The higher experience is not sense experience, and not mere reason, and is called intuition. This intuition, however, is not a method of philosophy, but a way of knowing. Intuition thus fills a place in Indian philosophy that is occupied by faith in western religious thought. But faith is neither a way of knowing nor a method of philosophy. Faith does not know objects, but unquestioningly assumes their reality. There is nothing in India corresponding to faith in western religious thought. Faith in the teacher and the scriptures is spoken of. But it is not faith in a religious dogma, and so there is nothing in India corresponding to dogmatics and theology.

In China also we find little dogmatics and theology; there is no insistence on faith, no prevention of reason from entering any field it can.

2. Generally the dogmas of western religion are due to the opinion that one or a few individuals only have the revelation of spiritual truth. As the rest do not have it, mystery grows about religious truth, and its custodians add their own beliefs to it. But where this prerogative is not allowed, as in China and India, and if all men are declared to be equally capable of having the revelation, philosophy—and along with it, reason—tries to light it up so far as it can, and with the growing maturity of mankind religious experience can be shown to be an essential and normal part of human experience. Then the conflict between religion and science will be less keen and marked than it is now in the West. Religion or spiritual experience is an expansion and deepening of ordinary human experience. If so, reason has to be allowed as free an entry into religious experience as into ordinary experience. Whether reason can or cannot articulate every aspect of religious experience is a different question; but if it is prevented from entering any part of experience, it will treat that part first as supernatural and next as unreal.

Naturalism rose in the West mainly as a protest against supernaturalism. But in India and China, spirit is considered to be as natural as matter, life, or mind. And so the conflict between naturalism and supernaturalism does not characterize the Chinese and Indian traditions. The disadvantage of the conflict is that—because spirit is understood to be supernatural—naturalism refuses to recognize its reality and explains it away. Religion for most people in the West even now is an institution organized around a certain set of dogmas; but in India and China, it means mainly spiritual life, life with reference to the inner spirit, whether our understanding of it is profound or superficial. And there are no unquestionable truths about its relation to our outward experience. This is the reason for the comparative inseparability of religion from philosophy and of philosophy from religion in India.

The significance of the Indian attitude is that metaphysics becomes a reflection about the nature of the innermost spirit and its relation to the outermost existence. Its relevance to life is not lost. This peculiarity is at the root of the differentiation that Indian and Chinese philosophies are ways of life and western philosophy is a mode of thought.

3. But one would be unfair to western philosophy if one overlooked the view often expressed by some of the leading thinkers of the West, including the highly analytical-minded Bertrand Russell, that the aim of all philosophy, even of philosophical analysis, is to suggest and inspire a way of life. Western philosophy is quite practical; it is theory meant for guidance and application. If a theory is wanted for social and political practice, almost the whole of the East looks to the West. If there are metaphysical principles, man in the East wants to raise his being to their level in order to experience them; but man in the West treats them as theoretical, brings them down, applies them to the human level, and embodies them in his concrete life. Since the Indian philosophers did not do the latter, they could not develop social and political theories, although they developed profound metaphysics and had a number of ethical, social, and political ideas dispersed in the literature of the Mīmāmsā, the ethical codes, and the epics. The Indians used their metaphysical theories for lifting man to the level of Spirit; the westerners used them for embodying them in mundane life. The Chinese could start many ethical, social, and political theories, like democracy, totalitarianism, and monarchism; but because of the lack of deep metaphysical interest, their systems remained incomplete, though intensely human. For profound metaphysical system-building, the Chinese did not develop the necessary speculative and logical methods.

4. Consistently with the denial of the prerogative of a few to revelation, India developed a technique with elaborate theories of man, mind, matter, and spirit, which is called Yoga. Thus, metaphysics was not meant for mere intellectual satisfaction, but for supporting a theory of the highest reality, which is also the innermost reality in man.

In this respect, both the Chinese and the western traditions, if we take them as wholes, differ from the Indian. The western is occasionally interested in the inner reality; but because the interest is occasional, the attempt to experience the object has not developed into a systematic technique. The Chinese tradition, in general, refused to go deeper than what it considered to be the basic human nature, sometimes deriving it from the Tao as Lao Tzu did, and other times identifying it with the Tao, as Mencius did. Whenever its naturalism became materialistic as in Hsün Tzu, it did not do either.

5. Yoga is meant to develop the power of direct and unmediated knowledge of the highest reality, which cannot be directly experienced through mediated knowledge as in the case of the objects of sense perception and inference. Sense perception is often called immediate knowledge; but really it is not unmediated knowledge, as it is mediated by the senses and reproductive imagination. Sometimes it is called intuition also, as by Kant; but this intuition is, even for Kant, mere sensation, and sensation is not the same as perception. Direct experience of the innermost reality also is called intuition. Yoga constitutes the technique for developing this intuition. It is misleading to say that this intuition constitutes a philosophical method, because there is no philosophy for such immediacy, but only for mediacy, which is reason.

In China also we find some philosophers like Wang Shou-jen emphasizing the importance of intuition for knowing the universals (*Li*). They say that the highest knowledge is no-knowledge. But they did not develop a technique like the Yoga, except what was introduced by Buddhism. In western thought also we do not find a systematic theory for the development of intuition. The extreme transcendence of God incorporated from Jewish thought may have prevented the development of such a theory. An idea underlying the technique is that one who has the intuition of the highest reality becomes one with that reality; but this attainment of oneness with the Supreme will not be acceptable to western religion.

6. One topic that distinguishes Indian philosophy from the Chinese and the western is that of the *ātman*. Almost the whole philosophy of India is *ātman*-centered. Most of the schools of Buddhism denied the reality of the *ātman;* but they substituted Śūnya and Nirvāṇa for it, and their inward interest is beyond dispute. So much inward interest is not to be found in China and the West. The West has ideas

of mind, soul, self, spirit; but the theories of these entities are not as philosophically profound as that of the *ātman*, which is regarded by Indian philosophy as lying beyond the state of deep sleep and by the Advaita as identical with God or the Brahman. In China Mencius started the doctrine that the universe is within mind. But this mind is the ordinary mind of the sage, and does not correspond to the *ātman* of the Upaniṣads, but to what the Indian philosophers call *antahkaraṇa,* or inner sense.

7. The engrossing interest of Indian philosophy in the *ātman* made the tradition inward-looking. When it explained the outward, it generally explained it in terms of the inward. This inwardness is particularly characteristic of the Vedānta and Buddhism, and to a lesser degree of the Sāṅkhya, the Yoga, and to a still lesser degree of the other schools, except the Cārvāka. In comparison, the western and the Chinese philosophies, if we exclude Buddhism, are outward-looking. Their interests lie in the objects of outwardness. Of the two again, the western has become eminently outward. As we have seen, the western has been many times inward, but not continuously and throughout; the scientific and humanistic attitudes were more dominant and have become still more dominant than the spiritual, so much so that the impression is created that the western tradition is losing even the necessary minimum of inwardness. It has become one-sidedly outward, just as the Indian has remained one-sidedly inward. This one-sidedness is inimical to true humanism and tends to undervalue man and his life on earth. Chinese philosophy could avoid the excesses by not caring for them. Thereby it could be eminently humanistic, but only at the sacrifice of depth and breadth. Its outwardness also is practically limited to the recognition of other persons and does not care much to penetrate the material constituents of life. It has not, therefore, developed any great materialistic or spiritualistic philosophy. But confining itself to man and his relationships to other men, it has laid the foundations of a very significant practical ethics.

8. Compared to Indian and western philosophies, the Chinese is less intellectual and analytical. It contains very few of the puzzling logical complexities of western thought; and its logic does not take us to very great metaphysical heights like the Indian. Whether positive as in the Nyāya or negative as in the Advaita and Buddhism, the logic and the dialectic that Indian philosophers used was the most intricate for the time, and, though developed in its own way, it was not less

profound than that of the West. The Chinese, too, had their dialecticians; but because of the dominant pragmatism of the Chinese outlook, they did not care to develop their logic and its principles. Paradoxes like those of Zeno were discovered in China also, but their fuller implications were left undeveloped. If every philosophy is a philosophy of life, as many philosophers all over the world wish it to be, then even western philosophy must have a pragmatic interest. But the tenacity in trying to understand the world thoroughly and then to build our life on that understanding does not seem to characterize Chinese thought. Plato, for instance, would equate the True to the Good, and so also did most of the Indian philosophers. So Truth has as much importance as the Good. But one may say that the Chinese seem to be concerned with the Good mainly, and care less for the True. Chinese philosophy, therefore, contains very few theories of illusion, falsity, error, in short, very little of epistemology, and hence very little of logic also. The significance of this defect, as mentioned above, is being felt now by the Chinese thinkers. So long as a conception of the world and social relationships is taken for granted, the problem of the philosophers will be how to build the Good on them. But when the conception is found to be wrong or unworkable, they become perplexed and puzzled, unless there is a method for finding out the Truth. The question, What is truth? was not raised seriously by the Chinese philosophers. Western philosophers have therefore an advantage over Chinese thinkers.

The Indian philosophers also gave equal importance to the True and the Good. The question, What is ultimately true (*paramārthasatyam*)? is as important as the question, What is the ultimate Good (*śivam*)? *Satyam, śivam, sundaram* (Truth, Goodness, Beauty) and *Sat, cit, ānanda* (Existence, Consciousness, Bliss) are two sets of values regarded as ultimate. But the Indian thinkers searched only man's inward reality for the True. Herein lies the one-sidedness of Indian philosophy; it did not search for the truth embodied in human relationships and in external material nature. Some schools that made the search were relegated to a secondary place, and the endeavor itself was given a secondary or even an unimportant place. India, therefore, did not develop social philosophies and philosophies of nature. In this respect, the West has an advantage over India. But because India was as much interested in the True as in the Good, it developed elaborate doctrines of logic and epistemology.

9. Regarding social and humanistic thinking, India offers a contrast to both China and the West. Indian philosophers analyzed human nature, but not with reference to social relationships. They have profound theories of psychological ethics, trying to discover the principles of ethics in the psychological constitution of man, but only with reference to the innermost reality, not society. Social ethics has, as a result, remained at the level of codes. The philosophers developed elaborate theories of action (*karma*), made detailed logical analysis of the concept, and expanded it into the doctrine of *karmayoga* (way of salvation through action); but the social implications of action were philosophically ignored. All ethics, whether social or individualistic, implies self-control. So even the ethics of spiritual discipline implies self-control, being directed more insistently towards inward reality than towards other men. And so it did not spread outwards. The control of socio-political activity by making it embody the spiritual ideal was not considered to be very important; hence the ancient Indian indifference to history.

Western philosophy, right from the time of the Sophists, came to be deeply interested in man and society. The ethics of the Sophists was individualistic and practically selfish. But when Socrates raised the doctrine of truth to the topmost level of importance, and man, as the locus, medium, and measure of truth, ceased to be the particular individual but became the universal standard and the normative member of a normative society, the foundations for a universal ethics and social thought were laid and Plato's *Republic* was made possible. A world-view was made the basis of humanistic discipline. This turn given to western thought still continues. The three ideas, Truth, Beauty, and Goodness, were thus made to interpenetrate each other without losing reference to man and society. Hence the problem of history was a real one to the West.

In Chinese philosophy, as we have noticed, the idea of the True played very little part. Chinese philosophy, as its historians say, was not started by any individual in search of ultimate Truth or Reality and of the meaning of life in its terms, but by men connected with the practical affairs of state and society. So logic and metaphysics were very little cared for. Even the idea of the Beautiful does not seem to have played an important part, and is less tangible and concrete than the idea of the Good. Just as there is no definite system of logic and epistemology, there seems to be no definite system of aesthetics either.

The importance of music is explicitly recognized, but only for training emotions, thus being in the service of the Good. It is the idea of the Good rather than the idea of the Beautiful that seems to be the *terminus ad quem* and *terminus a quo* of the Chinese philosophers. And for realizing the Good, they did not raise questions about the ultimately true constitution of man and the universe as the Greeks did, or about the ultimate spiritual foundations as the Indians did, but about the ultimately good dispositions in man, which can be developed into full virtues. This is seen in Mencius.

Thus human-heartedness became the highest virtue. But neither the Greeks nor the Indians would have been satisfied with a concept like human-heartedness and would have asked: First, what is it to be human, and next, what is it to be human-hearted? For instance, Plato attempted to explain temperance, courage, wisdom, and justice by analyzing the nature of the soul. Similarly, the Indians explained ethical virtues as leading to spiritual realization through nonegoism. But the Chinese philosophers made neither kind of approach in a systematic way. Their main question was: What human virtues make man and society perfect? Hence their philosophy appears to be eminently human and humanistic. Hence also the strong historical sense of the Chinese. But because of the lack of inward interest and interest in ultimate problems, we do not find problems like the relation of time to eternity in Chinese thought. Indian philosophy was too engrossed in the spiritual foundations of existence to give adequate attention to human and humanistic problems. So, in spite of the naturalism of the spiritual in Indian thought, it appears to be too otherworldly. The problems of spiritual life are not the common problems of man and society. However, the Indians developed the theories of the True, the Good, and the Beautiful, all with reference to the innermost Spirit in man.

10. It is usual to divide East and West on the basis of the difference between intuition and intellect. But Indian philosophy would not have reached the great metaphysical heights it did, had it not been for its intellectualism. Communion with the Supreme Spirit is not possible without intuition; but to recognize this role of intuition is not the same as to develop an epistemology of mere intuition. An epistemology that tries to prove the validity of intuition is so theoretical that it becomes intellectual. Besides, the acceptance of the validity of intuition does not necessarily imply the rejection of the validity of intel-

lect. Intellect proves a theory; intuition confirms it by experience. In addition, there are various forms of intuition: sense-intuition, intellectual intuition, and the higher intuition for which the West seems to have only one term, "mystic intuition." But by the last the Indians mean an experience that is not mediated by anything, sense, mind, or reason. About sense-intuition there is no divergence of opinion; but about intellectual intuition there is. Kant used the term for the experience of God in which to have an idea is also to have a corresponding sensation. But Plato and Aristotle used it with a different meaning, viz., in the sense of intuiting the concepts. The forms are known, according to Plato, not through sense-perception, but by reason. The soul remembers them; but for remembering them it must have known them previously, which means that it must have intuited them.[18] This intuition must therefore have been, not sense-intuition, but intellectual intuition or rational intuition. The idea of remembering sounded mysterious, and so Aristotle maintained that reason intuits the universals in the particulars themselves. In either case, like sense-intuition, there is intellectual intuition, which is not exactly the same as the intellectual intuition of Kant's God.

Thus, if intellect itself contains an intuitive factor and cannot work without it, it will not be a right procedure to separate intellect and intuition and to say that the procedure of western philosophy is based on the former and that of India and China on the latter. Northrop oversimplified the difference between the eastern and the western philosophical traditions when he made such a division, which may hinder true appreciation. The Chinese philosophy is not intellectualistic and its epistemology is not well developed. We cannot for this reason generalize and say that it is intuitive in method. In that case, all undeveloped reason would be intuition. Lu Chiu-yüan and Wang Shou-jen may be called intuitionists. But Chu Hsi is an intellectualist. If the whole of Chinese philosophy is to be characterized, it cannot be characterized as intuitionist, though some of the Chinese philosophers seem to be ready to accept this characterization. Wang, for instance, accepted intuition as the way to know the universals, and this intuition is not the intuition of the object, but the intuition of one's own mind. It is not, therefore, Aristotelian, as the universal is

[18] See Walsh, *Reason and Experience* (Oxford: Clarendon Press, 1947), pp. 57 ff. and *Essays in East-West Philosophy* (Honolulu: University of Hawaii Press, 1951), chap. vii.

not intuited in the object, but Platonic, as it is intuited in the mind.

It is not clear whether the part of mind that intuits is reason or not. And we know nothing more about this function. One may even denominate this undeveloped intellectualism or rationalism. In any case, intuition is not made a method for building up a philosophy, but for knowing either objects or universals. Further, intellect itself contains some intuitions. It starts with intuitions—sensuous, intellectual, or spiritual; interrelates them with several others; and builds up fresh wholes, which also are intuitions. Intellect and intuition are, therefore, not two separable factors of mind, and perhaps Northrop does not mean that they are separable. Neither the West nor the East could have used them separately, but only more or less. Though they are two functions of mind, they interpenetrate each other. In mind's cognitive activity one of the two aspects may be predominant at one time and the other at another time.

There are two trends in Chinese thought regarding extension of knowledge: observation of things and observation of one's own mind. According to the first, the universal in the objects can be known through the observation of things, and according to the second, through the observation of one's own mind. But the two kinds of observation can be both intellectual and intuitive. It may be wrong to think that the universal of many objects can be known by looking into one's own mind; but this wrong explanation of knowing cannot be raised to the status of a philosophical method called intuitive method. Then Plato also must be said to have used the intuitive method. Just as a universal proposition cannot be obtained merely from empirical observation, the universal of any object cannot be derived from the observation of any particular object. But it is obtained by the mind. From where, then, is it secured? Wang thought that it was obtained by the mind from itself. From our modern knowledge of mind's workings, we may interpret Wang as meaning that mind, with the help of imagination and reason, builds up the universal and presents it to itself. But Wang did not realize that the universal of the bamboo could not have been presented by his mind, if his senses had not, at anytime, come into contact with the bamboo tree. Instead of saying that without the mind's activity the universal of the bamboo could not have been presented, he said that the universal belonged to the mind alone and that it had to be intuited in mind. His explanation is not complete, and he ignored one side of the situation, that in the intuitive process is involved a rational process also. Serious observation and understanding of mind is as much an intellectual process as serious observation and understanding of external objects. Observing one's own ideas may be an intuitive process, but interrelating them is an intellectual process. Chinese philosophy appears to be intuitive only so long as we ignore the specific roles played by intuition and intellect at the different levels of our being.

Indian philosophy also is not merely intuitive. Not even the Vedānta is so, and much less are the Nyāya and the Vaiśeṣika. The atoms are not merely intuited but intellectually postulated. Even the existence of God is proved as that of the creator of the world and as that of the author of the Vedas. Although it is said that reason cannot reach the Brahman, it is argued that its reality is the postulate of our conscious existence. All schools accept that the theoretically proved Brahman can be an object of intuitive knowledge also. But none makes intuition the basis of its proof, as we make sense-perception the basis of proof. Of course, in scholastic literature we find that the statements of the scripture are made the basis of proof. But this can be done only if both the parties accept the same scripture. In the discussions with heterodox schools, the orthodox did not and could not insist upon such acceptance.

It is not enough that the God of western religion is transcendent in order to prove that He is only a theoretical concept. The transcendence is a legacy of Judaism to Christianity. But the Jews themselves refute the idea that God is an intellectual being, a philosopher, an infinite thought thinking itself. Of course, the philosopher might develop a theory out of that transcendence, never insist on communion with God, since communion would be a form of intuition, and relate God conceptually with the concepts of the world that can be experientially verified. God then becomes a theoretical concept. But this has been done by all the philosophers of the Brahman also. Most of them did not have the intuition. But they accepted the reality of the Brahman conceptually, and worked out their philosophies. However, we should not forget that in western theology God is accepted on faith and no theory is allowed by the orthodox to touch Him. This implication of faith has not been fully seen by many philosophers and theologians, although many orthodox Jewish theologians pointed it out.

God can be an intellectual concept only if He is an object of reason; and if He becomes a concept, reason will relate it with the concepts of the phenomenal world. Then the absolute transcendence of God will have to be given up. And along with it, both the doctrines of faith and creation out of nothing will be at stake. Transcendence itself does not justify conceptualism. What can be intuited, but is not yet intuited and is only accepted, can also be a concept till it is intuited.

A distinction is drawn between concepts of intuition and concepts of intellect. But there are difficulties in defending this distinction. All concepts, provided it is recognized that they have relations with other concepts and with their own particulars, are intellectual as well. Indeed, there are certain concepts the objects of which cannot be brought into direct experience, for instance, the concept of the center of the earth and the concept of the atom. We may say that they are theoretical and intellectual only. In comparison, the concept of man, and the concept of a new planet only mathematically located but not yet seen with the telescope, can become concepts of intuition also. The latter, till it is seen with the telescope, is only a theoretical concept, but later when seen with the instrument, an intuitive concept. The concepts of man, horse, and so on, are derived from direct experience in the sense that they are rationally intuited in the objects of sense-perception. But if a philosophy uses only such concepts as that of man, we have to say that the logic of that philosophy is not yet well developed, not that it used a distinct kind of method called the intuitive method in order to formulate its concepts. Similarly, if a philosopher uses the concept of God only theoretically, we should say that he did not care for communion with God or does not believe in it, but not that he has a distinct kind of method called the intellectual method. So far as the innermost Spirit goes, Indian philosophy accepted and utilized both intellect and intuition equally.

Compared to Indian philosophy, western philosophy is certainly greatly varied, and it has remained purely theoretical in the hands of many and from the hands of a few only has communion with God received specific recognition. And the interest of philosophers is very diversified. But the interest of the majority of Indian philosophers remained consistently spiritual; and this creates the impression that Indian philosophy is intuitive in its method. But intellect plays as important a role in explaining spiritual life as in explaining mundane life.

It is the realms of major interest that distinguish the three philosophical traditions, western, Indian, and Chinese, not intellect and intuition. Future philosophy has very important lessons to draw from the differences of interest.

Subject Matter of Comparative Philosophy

What is the subject matter of comparative philosophy? "The scope of comparative philosophy," says Masson-Oursel, "is universal history and cosmos." [19] And he declares that true philosophy is comparative philosophy. There is truth in this view. Philosophy has to explain man and his universe; the nature of man is expressed in history; and so the scope of philosophy is universal history and cosmos. Man has expressed himself in several ways in the different races and cultures; and a true and comprehensive philosophy will be one based on a comparative estimate of the many ways of his expression. The scope of comparative philosophy is as wide as the universe.

But what is it that we compare? Is comparative philosophy a mere comparison of the different cultures in general and of the histories of the various countries in general? We may compare Chinese history with Indian history, and we may certainly derive some useful lessons. We may as usefully compare Chinese history with the history of Rome. The results may form useful material for comparative philosophy, but will not be comparative philosophy. Similarly, one may compare the ways of life of the different peoples as did Keyserling in his *Travel Diary of a Philosopher;* his reflections are very significant, and he gives some brief accounts of the philosophical ideas of the countries. But his reflections also do not constitute comparative philosophy, nor have they given rise to the subject, though they can be useful. A work like Schweitzer's *Civilization and Ethics,* if it entered the Chinese and In-

[19] *Philosophy: East and West,* April, 1951.

dian traditions as it did into the western, would be more useful for comparative philosophy than comparisons of cultures and ways of life.

Every great civilization and culture raised itself to the reflective level in its own philosophy. Its own philosophers know more than others about its aims and methods and the values it struggles to uphold. It is true that no culture has had only a single system of philosophy. Oversight of this fact has led to many oversimplifications, false generalizations, and unhelpful comparisons. In China one hundred schools are said to have existed in the beginning. Whether this is true or not, the Confucian, the Mohist, and the Taoist schools presented distinct philosophical attitudes. The West has indeed had quite a large number. In India, even the Vedic tradition split up into the Brahmanic (of Jaimini) and the Vedāntic (of Bādarāyaṇa). Among the orthodox, the Nyāya-Vaiśeṣika and the Sāṅkhya-Yoga made independent approaches. Of the heterodox, Jainism and Buddhism were independent of each other and of the orthodox. And in every tradition the schools more or less crossed and recrossed each other in the process of history. But the Indian and Chinese traditions, in spite of the diversity of schools, present a consistency and continuity of aim for several centuries.

So we expect or hope to find such consistency and continuity in all traditions. We may be mistaken, and are certainly mistaken if we think that the western tradition also presents them. If a tradition does not present them, it is not necessary for us to read them into it. We may be tempted to treat the striking peculiarities of some recent western philosophies as characterizing the whole of the western tradition and to call it naturalism or materialism. But it is not binding on any comparative philosopher to discover such characteristics even if they do not exist. We may now interpret the whole development of western thought as a slow and cautious drive towards naturalism. However, if spiritual philosophies begin again to dominate the West, such an interpretation will be falsified. But a combined humanistic, and rational and epistemological approach seems to be the characteristic of all its great philosophers: the ultimate nature of reality has to be known, but what is the best way of knowing it? The conclusion should not be predetermined or assumed, we can know it only if we have the correct way of knowing it: this attitude, if we leave out the medieval philosophers, is a distinguishing characteristic of western philosophy; and this characteristic is not likely to disappear.

The subject matter of comparative philosophy as a distinct subject is mainly the philosophical traditions. Two traditions may aim at upholding the same values or similar values; but comparative philosophy need not separate the values only because they belong to different traditions. Generally, however, a tradition shows a particularly strong interest in tackling the problems of a particular aspect of life and attaches especial importance to values relevant to that aspect. This is the reason for the general opinion that different philosophies uphold different values. The Chinese philosophy, for instance, upheld the values of man and society in this world. Whether it is the ethico-political humanism of Confucius, the rigorism of Hsün Tzu, the universal love of Mo Tzu, or the naturalistic romanticism of Lao Tzu, the problem is: What kind of human life is the best and the fullest? Indian philosophy fairly consistently upheld the reality of inwardness and its values, whether the system is pluralistic or monistic, realistic or idealistic, activistic or quietistic. In certain aspects, each tradition developed up to the highest level possible; the other aspects are left undeveloped or ill-developed. And observers tend to characterize the whole tradition in terms of those aspects that received the highest development. In western philosophy many aspects received great developments; and so it becomes difficult to characterize it by any one. As we have seen, it is difficult to characterize western thought as inward or outward only. There are periods in which it is inward and periods in which it is outward, although the dominant systems of recent times are essentially outward. The adjective rationalistic does not mark it off from the Indian tradition; nor does the adjective humanistic distinguish it from the Chinese. Similarly, the designation spiritual or religious does not mark off the Indian from the western, though it may discriminate between the dominant schools of contemporary western thought and the dominant schools of the Indian.

Then what is the use of the comparative study of traditions? The comparative philosopher will be benefited by his studies as he can obtain clues to the solutions of various problems of life and philosophy by observing how they are solved when different values are upheld as ultimate. Different traditions adopted different values of life, or the same tradition supported different values of life at various times. Western philosophy obviously upheld different values at different periods of its history. Within limits even the Chinese did it. The classical Chinese schools had a set of values different from the Buddhist, though

Buddhism was later assimilated and turned Chinese. Within limits again, the Taoists differed from the Confucians and both from the Mohists. Even in India, the original Mīmāmsā advanced a set of values different from the Vedānta, although together they constitute the philosophy of the Veda. To suppose that there is a philosophy in the West exactly corresponding to the Mīmāmsā or the Vedānta either in results or in methods should not startle the comparative philosopher.

All philosophies are diggings into the nature of life; they may dig in different directions or in the same, with different tools or with the same. It is the duty of the comparative philosopher to observe and find out the significance of both similarities and differences in results as well as methods. But significance for what? Significance for human life. Life is the same everywhere. As Radhakrishnan observed,

> the fundamentals of human experience, which are the data of philosophical reflection, are the same everywhere. The transitoriness of all things, the play of chance, the emotions of love and hate, fear and jealousy, the continual presence of death, the anxiety to overcome the corruptibility of things, to enjoy the fleeting moment—these have determined for each man his life's meaning and value.[20]

Though human life is and has been the same everywhere, some phases of life have been smooth-going in some countries, but posed problems in others. The phases that raised problems focused man's consciousness on the values which they involved and which man became afraid of losing. And he developed philosophies in terms of those values. The Chinese were afraid, at the time of Confucius, of losing human and social values; and these values dominated the whole of classical Chinese thought. The Indians did not fear the loss of worldly values; and so they were concerned with values that were still higher. One religious man humorously remarked that the Indians were the most materialistic of peoples; and so the Vedānta, Buddhism, and Jainism gave them the most antimaterialistic ideals, which were badly needed as counterpoise. There is truth in the assertion that, at least in the ancient times, when mere intellectual curiosity was at the minimum, people developed philosophies for what they lacked, but not for what they possessed. The extreme inwardness of Buddhism was not escapism during the time of Buddha, though it may have become

[20] *Philosophy: East and West*, April, 1951.

so later. It was a counterpoise to the extreme activism of the Mīmāmsā. One can see the truth in the extremely opposed meanings given to the word *dharma* by the Mīmāmsā and Buddhism: for the Mīmāmsā *dharma* means pure activity according to the injunctions of the Veda, but for Buddhism it means finally the quiet Nirvāṇa.

Thus, if a tradition, throughout its history or through a considerably extended period, devoted itself to upholding a particular set of values, accepting a particular aspect of life as a basic hard fact, the comparative philosopher can observe the problems which that aspect of life can raise and see how they can be solved in terms of the values accepted. Just as the different sciences are given each its autonomy and each is allowed to treat its subject matter as a hard fact without raising questions of its reality, a philosophical tradition may treat some aspect of life as a hard fact without raising questions about its reality. Then what are the problems, and how are they solved? The comparative philosopher will be benefited by getting answers to the question from his study.

Comparative Philosophy and Philosophical Synthesis

It is unnecessary to stress further the advantage of comparative study. The world is becoming smaller and smaller every day. Man is conquering physical time and space, and is now thinking of conquering the planets. Every part of the earth has become a few hours distant from every other part. Many ways of life in several areas of the world are becoming the same, and are bound to become everywhere alike. Political and social ideologies, which control our lives, are spreading fast. It is not meant that differences will be completely annihilated; but they will acquire secondary importance, and similarities will become more numerous. The highest universal ideals will be, and will have to be, the same for all. Values unknown to some cultures will be presented to them; and if they are true values, they will not only be welcomed with enthusiasm but also demanded with vehemence. Then the problems and solutions of one culture will be the problems and solutions of all. While welcoming and demanding some values, the cultures must face the problems those values create and be prepared for the solutions. It is here that comparative philosophy helps.

The opinion is growing strong that every man on earth should be allowed to live the fullest life possible, to realize all the values of life, and to enjoy all the human rights. Then he will have all the problems of life and will have to find out all the solutions. Certainly, every man in every country is not a philosopher. Even within a limited field his problems are generally solved by proxy, by leaders of thought and action. But such leaders must now have a wider perspective than before, which can be supplied by comparative philosophy. This will be the world-perspective and can lead to world-philosophy. It should not be thought that world-philosophy will be someone's system, just as Buddhism is Buddha's religion. It is not something to be imposed by someone upon the rest of mankind. It will be developed by each philosopher and by each culture in his or its own way, but with due recognition of all values of life upheld in different parts of the globe. It is for developing the conception of a fuller life that world-philosophy is needed, not for cultural dominance of the rest by some part of the world.

If human life is essentially the same everywhere, if all values of life are to be made accessible to all men, then every culture will develop philosophies that bear essential similarities in thought, outlook, and aim. The aim of comparative philosophy is such cultural synthesis, which implies not dominance but development, not imposition but assimilation, not narrowing of outlook but its broadening, and not limitation of life but its expansion. As we have seen, if the Chinese philosophers could preserve human values as Schweitzer says, and none of the European philosophers could because of the world-views they developed, in spite of the strong desire to preserve them and the great emphasis laid on them, then it is necessary for western philosophers to do some self-reflection and reflection on the Chinese methods and concepts and reformulate their world-views. Whether Schweitzer's estimate of Indian philosophy is wholly true or not, it is necessary for the Indian thinkers to reflect and reformulate their world-views and basic concepts and methods in the light of the demand for a stronger emphasis on life-affirmation. Similarly, if the shortcomings of the Chinese civilization are due to its lack of depth, inward and outward, and its shirking of intellectual strain, it has to make up its defects by philosophically developing in the directions it has not taken. This activity means growth, assimilation, and expansion, not their opposites.

One feels, therefore, that Santayana did not approach philosophical synthesis in the right way when he said, "it could be reached by blurring or emptying both systems [East and West] in what was clear and distinct in their results." The differences between the problems that life presented to men of different cultures and the various ways in which men sought to solve the problems were not due to the eastern man's being a species of animal distinct from the western man, but arose because the conditions of human life—natural, social, and political—varied, presented different problems in different ways, and suggested different forms of solution, thereby determining the general trend and interest of much of subsequent philosophy. Santayana does not seem to subscribe to the view that the eastern man and the western man are of different kinds. But he seems to take philosophy to be of only literary or aesthetic (intellectually aesthetic, I suppose) interest when he says, "for a literary or humanistic point of view I think that it is the *variety* and *incomparability* of systems, as of kinds of beauty that makes them interesting, not any compromise or fusion that could be made of them." [21]

Philosophical variety is interesting only because the problems of any culture can be problems of all the rest in a more or less pronounced form. If they are less pronounced, imagination knows how to lift them to the level of acuteness and feel their importance. For that very reason, they are comparable, not incomparable. The richness of philosophical variety is not lost if all the real and important problems of life felt everywhere in the world are brought together. Even if the philosopher refuses to do it, actual life does bring them together when cultures meet. If a personal God is necessary for religious consciousness in the West, He is necessary for religious consciousness in India also; and an overwhelming majority of Indians worship a personal God, even when many describe Him as impersonal. If sympathy, human-heartedness, and other such qualities are necessary for a happy social

[21] *Philosophy: East and West,* April, 1951.

life in China and are even the basis of political life there, they are equally necessary for the West and India. If rational analysis is necessary for understanding man, society, and their environment in the West, it is equally necessary for India and China. If humanism is incomplete without spiritual roots in India, it will be equally incomplete in China and the West.

Our fear should not be about cultures becoming alike all the world over, but about ignorance, intolerance, and arrogance preventing any life or culture from developing to its full. Full life everywhere does not mean absolute uniformity in every detail. The ideals of Beauty, Goodness, and Truth are everywhere the same. But the peculiarity of each culture lies in how those are embodied in it, and whether they are embodied fully and properly, and also how its members react to them with their sensations, emotions, affections, and volitions. If man is essentially the same everywhere, life's highest ideals also will be the same. If life is full and complete everywhere, differences assume secondary importance.

John Dewey, therefore, gave expression to the right spirit of comparative philosophy in saying that the objective of the synthesis of East and West "is to help break down the notion that there is such a thing as a 'West' and 'East' that have to be synthesized. . . . The cultural matrix of China, Indonesia, Japan, India, and Asiatic Russia is not a single 'block' affair. Nor is the cultural matrix of the West." "They are all inter-woven in a vast variety of ways in the historico-cultural process." "To adopt a phrase of William James, there are no 'cultural block universes' and the hope of free men everywhere is to prevent any such 'cultural block universes.' "[22] As Professor Sheldon says, the West is more theoretical than the East when we omit India or take India and China as one block and compare modern and contemporary western philosophy with classical Indian philosophy.[23] But if we compare western philosophy up to the sixteenth century with the classical Indian, then both will be equally theoretical. Indian philosophy is neither exactly the same as, nor absolutely different from, European philosophy. This observation holds true in the fields of logic, epistemology, and metaphysics. But it is also true that Chinese philosophy is neither too close to, nor too remote from, western thought in humanistic interest. Hegel noticed a *waltz of ideas* from

22 *Philosophy: East and West,* April, 1951.
23 *Ibid.*

East to West in ancient times; and this waltz has taken the opposite direction from about the sixteenth century.[24] The Absolute as the Ātman in India is turned into the Absolute as the Logos in the West; but Hegel did not know that the same was done in India also. The philosophy of the Brahman as the Word, or Logos, is a distinct school of Indian thought, though not a prominent one.

It is not necessary to seek differences where they do not exist, only because we want to synthesize something and without differences there can be no synthesis. There are indeed differences which we cannot ignore and which are the occasion for the problem of synthesis. But there are also equally significant similarities. The aim of comparative philosophy is to find out which problems of life are solved in which ways by the several traditions, and which aspects of life, when treated as basic hard facts, give rise to which philosophical problems and which kinds of solution. If man is so completely unlike in the East and the West as some suppose, then it is futile to attempt to understand each other. But if we are to understand each other, what is the common denominator for the various philosophical traditions? The same common denominator has to be chosen as the aim of comparative philosophy. If it is full and complete human life, then man becomes the common denominator. How far and in what respects has each tradition helped man in living a full life? This is what has to be known. A certain tradition may have wrestled with problems that only some aspects of human life create, as the Chinese and the Indian, for instance, did. A comparative philosopher has to bring all traditions together and study all problems in their conspicuous forms. Then only will synthesis be fruitful.

Aim of Comparative Philosophy

One may ask whether comparisons can be made between system and system or concept and concept. Indeed, they can be. But they will not be so useful as comparison of traditions. Comparison of traditions

[24] See Hocking's article in *Philosophy: East and West,* July, 1952.

enables us to know which aspects of life and which values are considered to be important by each and how each formulated and solved the problems relevant to those values. Intellectual curiosity is not the ultimate aim of comparative philosophy; as much humility is needed in studying it as in studying nature. Certainly, the same problems may not have been solved in the same way by all schools of the same tradition. So detailed comparison of traditions involves comparison of schools and systems of the same tradition, and of the concepts of one system with those of another within the same tradition. But comparison of mere concepts or mere systems is not an end in itself.

Generally in philosophical and semiphilosophical literature, the term comparative philosophy is used with reference to comparison of cultures. But comparison of cultures and comparison of traditions have so far been vague, and too generalized comparisons will not yield very useful results. Every culture, however, tried to come up to the level of rational consciousness in each of its great systems of philosophy. So systems have to be studied in that light; and they have to be compared not only with each other but also with systems of other traditions. When they are compared with each other, we understand how they seek to understand and uphold the same value; and when they are compared with similar systems of other traditions, we understand how apparently similar systems are made to uphold different values. For instance, Mencius' doctrine that the universe is within my mind looks like the Buddhist doctrine that the objects are mere ideas of mind; but Mencius wanted to maintain that the essential moral principles are deep-rooted in human mind and a study of mind reveals them; whereas the Buddhists wanted to show that, because no object has external reality, it has no value outside mind. Mencius' doctrine, again, may be compared to Berkeley's earlier doctrine of subjective idealism. Even then Berkeley's interest lay in demolishing materialism; but Mencius aimed at establishing the supremacy, dignity, and goodness of human nature. Besides, Mencius' doctrine tended towards a subjectivistic but ethical idealism of the universe, whereas Berkeley's tended towards a subjectivistic but epistemological idealism of reality. But there has been no great subjectivistic ethical idealism in western thought. Again, the Absolute of Hegel may be compared with that of Rāmānuja, interpreting Rāmānuja's Absolute as an identity in difference, which some have done; but Hegel's Absolute is embodied in the political state, whereas Rāmānuja thought of it as the Universal Soul to which inward devotion was due from us.[25] Thus both differences and similarities are of value to the comparative philosopher if he aims at building up a philosophy that is to do full justice to the whole life of man.

It will not be very useful, therefore, if we only analyze the traditions into classifications like realism, idealism, monism, pluralism, mechanism, vitalism, spiritualism, naturalism, rationalism, empiricism, intellectualism, intuitionism, logicalism. Such analysis and classification will certainly be helpful, but cannot be the final aim of comparative philosophy. S. C. Pepper, for instance, classified the systems of western philosophy, and his classification may be applied to the systems of the other traditions also.[26] W. H. Sheldon showed how philosophy polarizes itself, and the same polarization can be found in different ways in the different traditions.[27] Such studies will be of immense use and will contribute to the development of world-perspectives.

Any world-perspective has to be given with reference to human life and for human life. It should enable us to understand and present human life in as complete and comprehensive a manner as possible. The comparative philosopher will therefore endorse Giuseppe Tucci's opinion that both the East and the West "should cooperate towards reintegration of man, simply of man, whether Western or Eastern." [28] But granting the need for reintegration implies the admission that the integration attempted so far by the East alone or by the West alone is not adequate. An inadequate endeavor requires further integration of whatever has been achieved in both the East and the West. They may have achieved similar results and also dissimilar ones. To similar results, if they are true, have to be added the dissimilar, if they are true. What is true and good for man in the West is true and good for man in the East and vice versa. It is, therefore, difficult to subscribe to Tucci's opinion that a synthesis of East and West and of their different philosophies is not possible. If man has to

[25] Rāmānuja explicitly rejects the concept of identity in difference, and accepts the soul-body relationship between the Brahman and the world. But there are others like Nimbārka and Śrīpati who accept identity in difference. They call it identity-cum-difference.

[26] *World Hypotheses* (Berkeley: University of California Press, 1948).

[27] *Process and Polarity* (New York: Columbia University Press, 1948) and *God and Polarity* (New Haven: Yale University Press, 1954).

[28] *Philosophy: East and West,* April, 1952.

be integrated, outlooks and philosophies must also be. If differences have their truth, and yet man and his universe are essentially the same, the differences ought to be, and can be, integrated.

Perhaps Tucci was asking himself whether the theism of western Europe can be integrated with the atheism of eastern Europe. In face of the question, any thought about the synthesis of East and West may be suspected of having political implications. Catholicism and communism are now great enemies. Then where can the two meet if they are to meet in friendship? Only at the human and humanistic level. Whether God exists or not is now a less important question than whether man should exist or not. In this context, one can understand the importance of Tucci's placing the problem of the reintegration of man before comparative philosophy. In this context again, Schweitzer's contention that respect for life and the will-to-live are more important than any world-view assumes great importance. As we have seen, he even condemns all past world-views, because they have not been able to secure respect for human life, and made it a "shipwrecked mariner." His view boils down to this: Whether we have some world-view or not, and whatever be the world-view, the basic and minimum requirement of all philosophies of life, if they are to be true, is that they should secure respect for life and the will-to-live, without which there can be no life and hence no ethics. What Schweitzer says of world-views holds equally true of ideologies. It is difficult to prove the existence of God and His ways, even if He exists; but the problems of human life are too urgent to wait till God's existence is once for all established or disproved. So let life start its ethics with reverence for life. Buddhism in many of its forms denied God, and yet developed sublime ethics, although it is not as life-affirming as Schweitzer would wish. Philosophers like Confucius and Mencius gave no thought to the problem of God or to the ultimate material constitution of man, but were still able to develop vigorously life-affirming ethics.

So whatever be our ideological, philosophical, and religious differences, can we not develop a universal ethics in which respect for life plays the decisive role? The fate of humanity depends on whether we can or cannot develop such ethics. Communist ideology is based on dialectical materialism; the ideology of the western democracies may be based on personalistic spiritualism; and some other ideologies may be based upon some other world-view or social philosophy.

But none of them can be worth much for man if it does not support respect for human life and the will-to-live. It is here that they should meet; and it is from here that they may be allowed to march off from each other so long as the foundations of human life, both spiritual and material, are not understood with certainty. So long as this ignorance lasts, we may differ from each other philosophically, ideologically; but we can ill afford to differ from each other so far as respect for human life and the dignity of man goes. Man is the common denominator in terms of whose life different philosophies and ideologies are and will be tested. Hence, for comparative philosophy also, man, the concept of man, of human life, is the common platform, or what the Indian logicians would call *sarvatantrasiddhānta* (proposition accepted by all schools). About every other doctrine there can be differences of view; but that man exists, that his life is to be respected, and that all philosophy is a theory for furnishing him with a plan for full life cannot be and should not be disputed by any philosophy.

Does the affirmation of human life necessarily mean that we should not have a world-view, because every world-view, when based upon ultimate foundations, inward or outward, lessens the value of human life by making it an instrument of the higher Spirit or by treating it as an effervescence or attribute of the lower matter? It is here that Schweitzer's ethics of life-affirmation will be incomplete. It is right that we should not undervalue human life in any way. But man cannot find the whole significance of his life by knowing it alone. The will-to-live which gets to know itself may be a bold mariner; but a mariner, if he is to be successful, has to know his bearings; and so human life, if it is to be successful, must know its bearings to the environment, both spiritual and material.[29] Such knowledge necessarily leads to a world-view. Schweitzer has to accept that "ethics must originate in mysticism. Mysticism, for its own part, must never be thought to exist for its own sake. It is not a flower, but only the calyx of a flower. Mysticism which exists for itself alone is the salt which has lost its savour." [30] One's will-to-live is a part of the mysterious universal Will-to-Live. "Then with humility and courage it can make its way through the endless chaos of enigmas, fulfilling its mysterious destiny by making a reality of its union with the infinite Will-to-Live." [31] What

[29] Schweitzer, *Civilization and Ethics,* p. 212.
[30] *Ibid.,* p. 236.
[31] *Ibid.,* pp. 214, 216.

Schweitzer wants, then, is an ethical mysticism of the Will-to-Live, but a mysticism that starts with the affirmation of the reality of human life—however vague the understanding of it may be at first—aiming at expanding and deepening it. But this is not possible without developing a world-view. If so, Schweitzer's condemnation of theory of knowledge needs modification.[32]

Because man's knowledge of life is, at the start, vague and indefinite, his theory of knowledge is equally vague and indefinite; therefore, if he attempts to derive his philosophy of life from his imperfect theory of knowledge, he fails and gets only a perverse philosophy of life. But if he makes his theory of knowledge subservient to life, then he can at least be safe so far as his life is concerned, even when his theory of knowledge is imperfect. The attitude behind this approach is the same as the one that wishes to treat the sciences as subservient to humanities, as so many humanities. "Knowledge for knowledge sake" is good because unbiased knowledge alone can discover truth, which is a human value, but not because knowledge has higher value than life. Even Bacon's "knowledge is power" is good because knowledge adds to the power of man for controlling brute nature and for making it subservient to his life. If life is true, then every truth must be made compatible with, and conducive to, life. It is not meant that man cannot utilize his discoveries for destroying himself, but that he can and should utilize them for promoting life. Only when his world-view enables him to do so, can it be a healthy and true guide to life.

Thus, a philosophy that gives excessive emphasis to outwardness or inwardness tends to underemphasize the importance of human life; but again, a philosophy that ignores the depths of inwardness or the expanse of outwardness fails to be an adequate guide to life. Contemporary western philosophy and classical Indian philosophy committed the former mistake; and classical Chinese philosophy committed the latter mistake. Philosophy, if it is to serve its purpose fully and wholeheartedly, has to start with the reality of man and his life as a basic hard fact, not with matter or spirit, which, when discovered, can form its guideposts. All early philosophy, which Schweitzer calls elemental, is generally of this type. But as philosophical inquiry progressed, and disciplines became compartmentalized, man's original integrality of outlook was lost; one or the other disciplines, dealing separately with one of the many aspects of life, whether inward or

[32] *Ibid.*, p. 220.

outward, first assumed exceptional importance, and then began treating its own subject matter as the basic reality from which everything else was to be derived. The aberrations of this tendency are being increasingly recognized, not only by philosophers but also by educators. What comparative philosophy can do is to revive the original integral outlook, but in a richer and more articulated form, which will then become what we call the world-perspective in philosophy. If comparative philosophy cannot do this, then it will fail its purpose and will only satisfy the curiosity of intellectuals and dilettantes.

Approaches to Comparative Philosophy

If philosophy is philosophy of life, then the life of every culture and of every epoch of culture must have come to consciousness in its philosophies. Accordingly, the subject matter of comparative philosophy is histories and traditions of philosophy—histories of different philosophical traditions as they exist. What methods are we to adopt, then, for studying these histories, for studying life that has come to self-conscious reflection in them? If philosophy is for life and is necessarily philosophy of life, then life itself is the standpoint and criterion for comparing and estimating all philosophies. It is for this reason that Schweitzer's contentions have to be valued. But our knowledge of life, its phases, and their parts and problems, is deeper and wider in the twentieth century than before, and so also is our standard for judging them. The student of comparative philosophy is therefore not only equipped with greater knowledge than in the previous centuries but also has greater opportunities for broadening it. If in a given tradition certain aspects of life obtain lesser importance, they obtain higher importance in others. The student, therefore, has the opportunity to understand life fully and consistently and, with the conception thereby formed, can apply the standard with advantage. The standard itself thus gets richer and more adequate. The aim, hence, will be a metaphysics of humanism, a world-view of human life and for human life. The word humanism so far has received scant respect from academical philosophers, as they think that it is opposed to metaphysics and logical depths. But it need not and should not be. Comparative philosophy alone can lead to a humanism that can at the same time respect human life and give a corresponding metaphysical world-view, without eschewing the depths of logic.

Certainly, few of the philosophers who propounded world-views advanced them for their race, nation, or community alone. Each maintained that his philosophy was true for the whole world. But each worked within certain limits of time and space on his understanding of man and his world. Comparative philosophy, however, helps to break down the limits. In this century, whether one likes or not, the limits are breaking down. Comparative philosophy should prevent this process from resulting in conflict and chaos, and should place the cohesion of humanity and harmony of life as the ideal before men. What, then, should be its methods? They are those that are guided by the supreme principle of man and his life. It is in man that matter, mind, and spirit meet, and it is from him that they diverge. What are the methods for understanding man's conscious being? They are the methods of any and every true philosophy, and they should be the methods of comparative philosophy also. The approach to comparative philosophy is from philosophy, and its methods also have to be those of philosophy. If some philosophy or a tradition has, wittingly or unwittingly, avoided certain techniques, they have to be incorporated after study and evaluation.

This is, of course, the enunciation of a general principle, and is meant to point out that philosophy has its own autonomy and that its criterion cannot be and should not be derived from psychology, ethnology, anthropology, philology, sociology, or the like. These disciplines can only be helps, but when carried too far become hindrances. None of them can supply the criteria for philosophy. Man's being transcends the field of these sciences. Values are as important as facts are for philosophy. These sciences deal only with facts; each deals only with some of the facts, and even when it claims to deal with all of them, it deals with them from a limited standpoint. The integrality of life, even if assumed, cannot be made their standpoint. So they can only be helps to philosophy or checks when philosophy becomes too speculative and unrealistic. They can now and then pronounce judgment on philosophy if it commits excesses; but they cannot appropriate the function of philosophy. They cannot give a world-view, cannot raise the whole life of man to reflective consciousness.

J. Kwee Swan Liat enumerated eight approaches to comparative philosophy. The first is the philological approach. A study of the terms of the different philosophical traditions sometimes gives a clue to the interrelations among the concepts, particularly if the languages used belong to the same group. Max Müller, Bloomfield, and Jespersen did highly creditable work in this direction. But the root meanings may be misused in estimating the philosophies. For instance, Betty Heimann concludes, using the psychological method behind philology,[33] that Indian philosophy, even the Vedānta, is only transcendental materialism,[34] that it has no metaphysics but only physics,[35] and that it never had a conception of the beyond in its theology. One may be equally justified in saying that the Holy Spirit of Christianity is a materialistic conception, because originally spirit was conceived to be air or something like air.[36] However, philology is only a help, not the sole guide of comparative philosophy. Thought, like everything else in the world, has a growth. Sometimes concepts of material objects are raised to mean higher ethereal and spiritual objects; other times concepts with high ethereal and spiritual meanings are brought down to mean objects at the material level; the words are retained but the meanings are changed. As an example of the latter, we may refer to Varuṇa, who at one time was the custodian of moral right (*ṛta*) in the Vedas, but later became the god of material oceans. As an example of the former, we may refer to spirit itself, which first meant breath and air, but later acquired its spiritual meaning.

The second approach is the historical. Histories of the different traditions are reconstructed; and, in the development of ideas and problems, if there are mutual influences in the traditions they are noted. New ideas imported from another tradition give a fresh impetus to development, which will have a novelty because of the recognition of new aspects of life and new problems. It is usual to treat the

33 *Indian and Western Philosophy* (London: George Allen & Unwin Ltd., 1937), p. 13.

34 *Ibid.*, p. 61.

35 *Ibid.*, p. 29.

36 For a little more detailed criticism, see the author's article, "Research in Philosophy: A Review," *Journal of the Ganganatha Jha Oriental Research Institute* (Allahabad), published in three parts, February, May, and August, 1944.

Greek, Indian, and Chinese traditions as independent. Philosophically there is no harm in treating them in that manner, whatever may be the historical truth. Until Buddhism entered China, Chinese philosophy seems to have been independent of the Indian. But the Greek and the Indian could not have been so independent. First, the Greeks and the early Aryans who entered India belonged to the same stock; and their mythologies have much in common, as Max Müller demonstrated. Second, the Greeks of at least the second century A.D. admitted the influence of eastern ideas on their philosophies, and their admission was generally accepted even up to the time of Hegel, who spoke of the waltz of ideas from the East to the West. But now scholars want more convincing evidence. Even if they cannot discover it, the evidence is at least stronger in favor of the influence than against it. In fact, there is none against it; only that in favor of it is not strong and conclusive. No belief or opinion could have been formed without some basis. However, this point is of minor importance for comparative philosophy. If the subject matter of comparative philosophy is histories of the philosophical traditions, then reconstruction of their histories is of great importance. It is not necessary to say that this reconstruction itself is not comparative philosophy, the aim of which is the development of a world-perspective, which is at the same time the perfection of life in its completeness.

The third approach is the comparative approach. This is not really a new kind of approach, but a stage that follows the reconstruction of histories. After reconstruction, we have to see how the philosophies of the traditions framed and solved the problems of reflective life: logical, ethical, aesthetic, social, and metaphysical. Thereby we get comparative logic, comparative ethics, and so on. Yet, to get them is not the sole end of comparative philosophy, which has further work to do. Comparison involves the observation not only of similarities but also of differences. But what are the differences due to? Are they due to starting points, aims, or both? Or are they due to taking different aspects of life to be of basic importance? In answering the questions we enlarge our conception of life, and with the enlargement the way is cleared for a more comprehensive philosophy of life.

The fourth is the total integrative approach. This is the world-perspective. Whatever be the name by which it is called, it will be able to take into consideration all aspects of life as forming integral parts of man and will furnish the standard by which any tradition or philosophy can be judged. Attempts at constructing world-perspectives have already been begun by thinkers like Northrop,[37] Sheldon,[38] and others. But serious systematic work may have to wait for the completion of at least a major part of preparatory work.

The fifth approach is the formal-evaluative.[39] This would be the study of the consistency of the systems, without raising the question of their agreement with life. But if the test of any philosophy, as Bradley says, is consistency with itself and consistency with facts, and if philosophy is primarily philosophy of life, this will be a partial, though useful, approach. After all, any system has to be self-consistent. This approach may lead to classification of philosophies of the different traditions like that into materialism, realism, idealism, spiritualism, naturalism, and so on, which will have again to raise the question as to how, for instance, each materialistic philosophy tried to solve the problems of life and what kind of philosophy of life it succeeded in presenting.[40]

The sixth approach is the phenomenological approach. This also is a means to an end. Masson-Oursel, in a way, made this approach. With this method we may find out the correlation between a particular philosopher and his socio-cultural environment, between a concept and a system, or a system and the tradition, without caring to raise questions about philosophical foundations themselves. We may then say that Confucius and his philosophy are to his environment what Buddha and his philosophy are to his, and Socrates and his philosophy are to his. We may generalize further and find out some correlation between a philosophical trend and the geographical environment also, as Buckle, for instance, would do, though in doing so we may leave phenomenology behind. As we have noticed, the pressure of some socio-cultural context may pose the first philosophical problems for a tradition, though we cannot generalize and say that this holds true for all traditions. Schweitzer, for instance, noticed that Indian philosophy could not be explained in that way. Patañjali, the author of the

[37] *The Meeting of East and West.*

[38] *God and Polarity.*

[39] I am not following the order of Mr. Liat.

[40] I should place Northrop's *Logic of the Sciences and Humanities* (Macmillan: New York, 1947) under this class, for it discusses the logical forms of man's being. Such a study can be useful for the integrative approach also. But his attempt to separate intellect and intuition, as if they were separately used by the West and the East, is an epistemological oversimplification.

Yogasūtras, which is the most important work on Yoga in India, says that for one whose sensitivity is keen, even pleasures contain elements of pain.[41] As the most important work for yogic discipline, it gives the clue to how the problem of philosophy was posed for the spiritual philosophies of India. It was a keen and a highly eudaemonistic sense that must be responsible for the apparent pessimism and the intense inwardness of many of the Indian philosophies of life. Where and how can we have the pure, intense, unalloyed happiness? The answer they gave was: Inwardness.

Even when the first problems are brought to the focus of man's thought by some socio-cultural context, when once they are raised to the level of reason, they lose their particularity; and reason not only raises them to the level of universality but also interrelates them with other problems. Hence, the fact that the Chinese conditions of life raised certain problems, for instance, does not vitiate their universal application. Similarly, the view that the conception of the Absolute, first framed by Indian philosophy, got its inspiration from the vast expanses of the Indo-Gangetic plain—a geographical explanation sometimes given for the Upaniṣadic conception of the Brahman—even if the view is true, in no way decreases the value of the concept. The Germans may have formulated it under different stimuli and in another context. And whatever be the ways by which the Germans and the Indians arrived at the formulation of the concept of the Absolute, significant similarities are noticed between the two, and the differences, if they are properly understood, make the concept more valuable, not less. Philosophy of life is reason working on life, raising it to the level of universality, and the genesis of a concept or theory, however humble, does not detract from its value. As the Indian poets say, even the best of flowers, the lotus, is born in mud. Once the problem shapes itself, whatever be its genesis, reason will not be satisfied unless it traces the problem down to its foundations and universalizes it, and philosophy expands in the process. Thus the phenomenological approach is useful, but it is not itself the end of comparative philosophy.

The seventh and the eighth are the psychological and the socio-anthropological approaches. We have already noticed the defects of the psycho-philological approach when it appropriates to itself the right to pass judgment on philosophical traditions. And just as psy-

[41] See commentary on I, 5, *Yogasūtras.*

chologists are explaining the individual and social behavior, its abnormalities and perversities, they are explaining ethics and religion also. Work of this kind that has attracted the attention of the world is that of Freud, Jung, and Adler, and their followers. But theirs will be the explanation of the higher in terms of the lower; and often to give an explanation of divergences from the normal is supposed to be giving a justification and affirmation of the lower and falsification of the higher. Again, higher experiences, instead of being explained as higher, are explained away by being reduced to lower experiences, and rejected as individual and mass illusions or delusions; so much so that the higher values of life, which give dignity to man, are in danger of losing their importance. The result will be not "explaining" but "exposing" philosophy. Jung's attempts in this connection are noteworthy; but the higher realms of philosophy cannot be reached by ordinary psychology, but only by metaphysics or metapsychology, taking mind and matter as correlates. Otherwise, the result will not be comparative philosophy, but comparative psychological evaluation of philosophies and their traditions.

Again, a philosophy may be evaluated and explained in terms of the individual psychology of the philosopher who expounds it. Herzberg's *Psychology of Philosophers*[42] may enable us to explain only why a certain philosopher formulated certain concepts or took them as primary, why his mind developed the kind of outlook it did. But whatever be the genesis, once the concept is formulated, philosophy recognizes it and relates it to other concepts, and examines the truth and validity of all. For instance, Nietzsche's concept of the Superman, even if it is due to the perversion of his genius, has become an important concept of ethics, which has had to examine it and decide how far it is true or false. Schweitzer sees some truth in it, in that it is the result of one-sided life-affirmation. In India Aurobindo Ghose formulated the concept, but without the excesses. The concept has thus become important. But in this formulation, evaluation, and modification, the mentality of Nietzsche and Aurobindo Ghose, whether abnormal or normal, is left, and has to be left, in the background. The Superman of Aurobindo is like a yogi who affirms himself in affirming God through self-surrender.

The problem for philosophy is whether the concept is true or

[42] "International Library of Philosophy, Psychology, and Scientific Method" (London, Kegan Paul).

false; and its criteria are rational consistency and agreement with life. Only when it is absurdly or dangerously false, will it be of value to probe into the psychology of the philosopher; and even then the result will be of secondary importance for philosophy. It will only confirm the truth that philosophy is the result of a healthy mind, not an abnormal mind. However, to notice the shortcomings of the psychological approach is not to deny its usefulness. Philosophy is life become reflective; the laws of comparative philosophy are laws of life and laws of reflection. The laws of psychology also have a place in comparative philosophy; but they are not all its laws.

The socio-anthropological approach also has only ancillary value. It has the same merits and defects as the psychological approach. What has to be recognized is that philosophy has its own autonomy, its own field, ways, and methods, which are not exactly the same as the methods of particular disciplines, but are inclusive of them, and it gives them their significance from a total world-perspective, although in developing its world-view it may develop its own architectonic and divisions into logic, ethics, aesthetics, metaphysics, and so on. Comparative philosophy is valuable only because we have come to realize that none of the world-views of the traditions is self-sufficient, that is, full and adequate. In fact, the drive of comparative philosophy is towards a full and adequate world-view; and if all the traditions put together cannot offer it, and if we are able, with their help, to visualize the importance of unnoticed aspects of life, the world-perspective will be and will have to be expanded further.

The sociological approach will be useful in that it enables us to understand how the sociological conditions existing at the beginning of a tradition and its spurts of growth presented the philosophical problems. At later periods of its history, new changes may be added by changes in socio-cultural patterns. The patterns themselves may owe their change to the birth of a new religion. For instance, the social patterns of Europe were considerably changed by the introduction of Christianity. The Greek ways were also changed by the new religion. In its turn, Christian thought was markedly changed by the Renaissance and by the new confidence that the geographical and scientific discoveries infused into man, who had been pessimistic and despairing of his existence on earth throughout the Middle Ages. Man regained confidence in himself and in his reason and said that "knowledge is power." Whether this confidence is absolutely justified or not, it at least rectified the mistake of complete lack of confidence. In philosophy, the objectivity and universality of reason reasserted themselves.

Philosophy's main interest, however, does not lie in social conditions, but in the question whether this self-confidence of reason is really justifiable. Similarly in China, it is the socio-political conditions that posed the first problems; and the problems were solved with reference to the conditions. So man, society, and politics were taken as hard facts, the truth and necessity of which were not generally questioned. It is the duty of philosophy to examine whether they are the ultimate facts of the universe, or whether they get their significance from something else. Is or is not a wider and deeper world-view needed? So also, one may, if one likes, trace the main problems of Indian philosophy to sociological conditions; but his attempt will not be successful. Indeed, social conditions were of little concern to many of the ancient Indian philosophers. Their main questions were: Who am I, and where lies the highest and undiluted bliss? The conditions that gave rise to these questions could be the awakening of man to the discovery that he was not the physical body and to an extremely keen sensitivity to pleasure. But like the questions and answers of Chinese philosophers, the questions and answers of Indian philosophers also have a universal significance and are as important now as then for philosophy.

For the above reason, sociological evaluation of categories cannot take us very far. For instance, the elements according to Chinese philosophy are water, fire, wood, metal, and soil. But according to Indian philosophy, they are water, fire, air, ether, and earth. The Indian classification was to correspond to the five senses through which the material objects were known. But the Chinese classification was according to the things with which man worked and by which he lived. One may say that the Chinese were an agricultural people and agricultural life determined the classification of elements. But the Indian classification gives no clue to the social life of the people. All that we can say is that the classification is in terms of the forms of perception of material objects. But the Greeks also had a similar classification. In Greek philosophy we generally find four elements—earth, water, fire, and air. Some say that Anaximander's *apeiron* (the indefinite) corresponds to the Upaniṣadic *ākāśa* (ether). But the former is not the source of sound, perceived by the ear. It may better be compared to the Avyakta (Unmanifest) of the Upaniṣads. However, the Greek philosophers did not make the correlation between the five senses and the five elements as consistently and throughout as the Indians. We read that Democritus accepted this correlation, but the others seem to be indifferent and even averse.

Now, the acceptance of the same elements says nothing about the social conditions of the people. The Indians were an agricultural people like the Chinese, but they gave a different classification of elements. Fung says that, as compared with the Greeks, who were a commercial people, the Chinese were agriculturists and so less sophistic, self-centered, cunning, and reflective. This difference may explain the highly rationalistic element in Greek philosophy. But the Indians also were an agricultural people, and yet were as thoughtful, rationalistic, and sophisticated as the Greeks, though their philosophical interests differed. It is difficult, therefore, to rely much upon sociological explanations or evaluations of categories. And further, as we have said, whatever be the sociological conditions in which they originated, philosophy, and particularly comparative philosophy, has to ask, off and on, whether they are true and what should be the true set of categories.

A Comment on the View of Georg Misch

Georg Misch tells us that, in spite of diversity, all philosophy is a unity; in Greece it originated in wonder; in India in sacrifice; in China in political responsibility and the desire to hold on to the right way of life.[43] This view may be accepted with certain modifications. It is not true that philosophy could anywhere have started without some dissatisfaction, without some problem that conditions of life shape. Everywhere there must have been some curiosity or wonder, some curiosity even about death. And if Cornford is right, even the

[43] *The Dawn of Philosophy* (Eng. tr.; London: Kegan Paul, 1950), pp. 39, 47.

water of Thales is a theological or theistic concept, as water, heaven, fire, and the others are in the Veda. It is also safer to treat the pre-Sophist Greek philosophers as hylozoists than as materialists. The early Vedic thinkers also were hylozoists in that they did not draw a sharp distinction between matter and mind. Many gods are common to Greek and Indian mythologies, out of which philosophy grew. Therefore much is common between Greek and Indian philosophical beginnings. If the Greeks had the conception of *physis* as pure matter, the Indians also had it, particularly the non-Vedāntic schools like the Nyāya and the Vaiśeṣika. Of the two Vedic schools, the Mīmāmsā accepted matter as separate from spirit, though the Vedānta, on the whole, would treat it as a manifestation of spirit. If the distinction between spirit and matter is a later product in India, so also is it in Greece. So far Greece and India are alike.

Between Chinese and Indian philosophical beginnings also, there is a striking similarity which has so far been overlooked by scholars. Confucius was interested in establishing the *li* (manners, etiquette, good behavior, the how in social relationships); but the word *li,* we are told, originally meant sacrifice and still retains the meaning. If spiritual ideas are developed out of sacrifice (*yajña*) in India, then the laws of right living seem to be developed out of sacrifice (*li*) in China. What are we to conclude then? Sacrifice, whether of animals or of grain, was the method of social relationships, and the conception of society then must have included both gods and men. The question then is: What is true sacrifice? It may have been answered differently by the Chinese and the Indians. Of course, it meant for both: What are the true forms of right conduct? The Chinese said: The *li* of society. The Indians, if we take all of them, gave different answers. For some like Manu, the author of one of the ethical codes, it meant right conduct in society according to the four stages of life and the four castes. For Jaimini it meant action according to the injunctions of the Veda. Both Manu and Jaimini used the word *dharma.* But the Vedāntins drew another conclusion. What is a true sacrifice? It is surrendering, yielding. But surrendering of what? The whole universe in order to realize the Brahman. The word *dharma* does not play any great part in the philosophy of the Vedānta. But the question raised by Jaimini, What is *dharma?* was taken up philosophically by the Buddhists. It is very curious and interesting. It is Jaimini, the activist maintaining the ultimate reality of action, who raised the question about *dharma,* and said that it is action according to the Veda, including sacrificial action. And it is Buddhism, which denied the ultimate reality of action, that gave *dharma* the highest spiritual status. It is Tathatā, Thusness. Ultimately, *dharma* cannot be defined; it is just a way of the universe.

If *dharma* is the way of the world, then human conduct, if it is to be good and right, must conform to the way. The Mīmāmsā view that it should conform to the injunctions of the Veda is arbitrary. It must be said to the credit of the Mīmāmsā that it raised the question whether the Vedic injunctions are to be obeyed because they teach the good or the injunctions are good because they belong to the Veda. Kumarila accepted the first alternative and Prabhākara the second. Contemporary man will not be satisfied with the second. And even if he accepts the first, he will still ask: What is the good? To this the Mīmāmsā has no philosophical answer; but Buddhism gave it. The essence of the world is its Way, Tathatā, Thusness; and that is the good. The good of man lies in becoming one with the Way of the Universe. The difference then is: Confucius gave the answer in terms of society and state; Buddhism gave it in terms of the universe. We may generalize and say: The ramifications of Tathatā are the *li;* they are found in the material world, the human relationships and the relationships of men to divinity; to act according to them is right and good. Then there will be many significant similarities between the beginnings of Chinese and Indian thought, and both the beginnings are associated with sacrifice. The differences do not nullify the importance of similarity; they will help us in deepening and extending the meaning of the concept. The same will be the case with the eastern and western concepts of God and the Absolute. In spite of similarity, they may have different content. But the difference only helps the growth of the concept.

But the differences are important for comparative philosophy, because generally the central problem for a philosophical tradition is formulated at the beginning. I say generally, not necessarily, because in the western tradition the ancient, medieval, and modern periods present different pictures. Even Greek philosophy has been divided into two or more epochs, and the center of interest changes in each. But in Chinese and Indian philosophy, it does not change so often, although in order to suit the complexities of life it is differently conceived by the different schools. For instance, Confucius kept a balance between man, society, and state; Mo Tzu made society primary; Lao Tzu, man; and Hsün Tzu, state. Buddhism introduced individual and universal salvation also. In India the Mīmāmsā stressed man, ethics, and action; the Vedānta, transcendence of ethics, action, and finitude. Buddhism followed the Vedānta. But in both the Mīmāmsā and the Vedānta the recognition of the other person is not strong, and so even the Mīmāmsā did not develop a system of social ethics.

In Greek philosophy the transcendence of finitude and action is only indicated, but not made an active factor of the philosophies, and so we find a high development of social ethics. Its metaphysics, therefore, could not become a living religion. No temple seems to have been built for Plato's Idea of the Good or Aristotle's God. However, the problem once framed continued as such till the center of interest was changed by novel factors. The longer the problem continued to be central, the more detailed and critical was the study of the aspects of life that gave rise to it. If a tradition changes its central problem during certain periods, it will have better chances of studying a larger number of life's aspects. From this point of view, the value of different traditions does not lie merely in their being so many traditions, but in their elucidating different aspects of life in as consistent and thorough a manner as possible under the conditions. If a single tradition, during its many periods, elucidated all the aspects of life, the study of other traditions might be useless. But generally such has not been the case. A general continuity of interest may be traced even during the three periods of western philosophy, which is humanistic and epistemological. And everywhere there are periods of degeneration, which bring to the forefront the shortcomings and one-sidedness of philosophies through abuses, misapplications, and wrong emphases, necessitating changes in outlook. All these become data for comparative philosophy, if it is to be, and to lead to, an adequate philosophy of life. At the beginnings of traditions and at the beginnings of changes in them, we find brought forward the importance of new aspects of life and reality or a new importance to already accepted aspects of life and reality.

Standpoints of the Three Traditions

If we take all the three traditions together, we find three standpoints in philosophy: the inward, the outward, and the middle. As I have said, man's being has two dimensions or two directions, the inward and the outward. Mind is not static, nor does it look only outward; it looks inward also. Patañjali says that mind has five forms of activity: cognition, illusion, objectless verbal knowledge (*vikalpa*), sleep, and remembrance. It may be noted that sleep also is a form of mind's activity, not the absence of activity, nor even absence of mind. Outwards it can go back and forth in time and space, know objects as they are, create illusory objects, project nonexistent objects through words, and collect itself into an unconscious mass in deep sleep. These activities are all outward except in deep sleep, which is the usual inwardness attained by all men.

Indian philosophy, particularly the Vedānta and the highest forms of Buddhism, recognized the possibility of mind's collecting itself, not merely into an unconscious mass, but into a conscious unity, through which it can realize the grand conscious unity underlying the universe and extending far beyond it. It called the grand conscious unity by the name of God, Absolute, Brahman, Vijñāna, Tathatā, Nirvāṇa, and so on. In western philosophy also, the Neo-Platonists, the great Christian mystics, and some of the idealistic philosophers recognized its truth. Then the problem is posed for philosophy: How is that great unity, the One, the Advaita, to be related to the world of plurality? The unity is beyond time and space and is eternal; the plurality is in time and space and is transient. Transience is due to process, and its ultimate limit, so far recognized by science and philosophy, is matter constituted by evanescent events of energy, force. It is the limit of the outwardness of human life, man's conscious being. The great unity is the limit of inwardness and is a unity also of all the evanescent events of spatial and temporal extension.

Both the inward and the outward are the directions of man and point to something beyond him: the importance of this truth has not been properly recognized. On the whole, the outward limit is treated as objective and therefore as the objective basis for philosophical explanation, and the inward as merely subjective. This attitude results in materialistic philosophies, which contain only one aspect of the truth. In the West there are many; but India has its Cārvāka and China its Hsün Tzu and Lieh Tzu, though neither country developed its materialism well for lack of scientific development.[44] Some forms of idealism in the West, like that of Berkeley, tended to regard the innermost as real and the outermost as subjective. The mystics, both Neo-Platonist and Christian, adopted the same method in various ways. The Indian Vedānta, in a few of its extreme forms, did the same. From the point of view of our analysis, taking the world-view into consideration, it is of secondary importance whether a philosophy is realistic or idealistic in its epistemology. All philosophies are objectivistic, provided they offer some objective basis for philosophical construction of our world-view: the difference would be that, while some place the objective basis at the extreme limit of outwardness, the others place it at the extreme limit of inwardness. The fact that they accept such an objective basis implies that objectivity transcends man, whether outwardly or inwardly.

But in the process of tracking down the objective basis, the philosophies may forget and ignore man altogether. The attempt is made to reconstruct man in terms of the outward basis or the inward. In either case the tendency also is created to undervalue man, to whose being these dimensions really belong and in which they are exemplified. All such attempts prove to be ultimate failures in ethics. Spiritual and mystical philosophies like those of Śaṅkara and Plotinus can see little significance in the ethical struggle of man; and materialistic philosophies can see no significance in human life itself and can at the most exhort man to make the best of his life here by trying to live as harmonious and cooperative a life in society as material conditions allow. Chinese philosophy, on the whole, avoided both the extremes, but only by ignoring questions about the ultimate nature of the spirit within man and of the material world outside him. That is, it did not ask about the limits of inwardness or outwardness.

Human nature itself is a basic fact; and, if we wish to understand

[44] Fung Yu-lan, *A History of Chinese Philosophy,* I, 281; II, 190–94.

it, we have to look only at its manifestations in society. Thus there is outwardness; but the outwardness is limited to other men and to oneself with reference to other men. Even the idealist Mencius—who noticed the inward direction in man, mostly of an ethical and an emotional type, when he said that "the universe is within my mind"—did not mean by the universe any Supreme Spirit or the ultimate laws of the universe, but the affectional ethical constituents like sympathy, human-heartedness, rightness, and so on. If we do not extend the meaning of nature to cover the material world on the one side and the Divine Spirit on the other, then the dictum of Protagoras that man is the measure of all things can be found in Mencius also. This comparison may be unexpected, but it is not false. If "all things" are made to mean human relationships, then man finds them in himself, and he becomes the measure of their manifestation in society. Even if man is made the universal man, as by Socrates, Mencius' doctrine accords with the dictum. We can find the same even in Śaṅkara, who also asked man to look within to know the ultimate reality as the Upaniṣads conceived it. The difference lies here: the ultimate reality is different even from that of Mencius. If we are thus allowed to generalize and extend the meaning of Protagoras, then all idealists, whether they explain the ultimate in terms of man's reason, imagination, emotions, sentiments, cognitive activity, or any other mental form, are applying the dictum, "man is the measure of all things." The only difference will then be in how and how much they have understood man. Only those philosophers who take matter and the world as lying completely outside man and his being will be prevented from accepting the dictum.

But Chinese philosophy fails when ultimate questions are raised. It accepted man and his life as basic facts for philosophy, not because it came to such a conclusion in the light of answers to ultimate questions, but because it did not raise them and avoided them when raised, so that human life did not discover any foundation for its significance. All that can be said is that it found the foundation in itself. If it does not, there is no theory to condemn and prevent suicide. Further, it can lead only to self-sufficient humanism. Just as undiluted hedonism finds it difficult to avoid the conclusion of selfishness and self-aggrandizement, a self-sufficient humanism also finds it difficult to prevent them. Human-heartedness, sympathy, righteousness, and love are undoubtedly noble and good; they are the salt of life, the bonds of society, and make social life pleasant and worth living. But they need justification, which can be given only by recognizing the transcendence both within and without man. When, for instance, Mencius' doctrine that human nature is essentially good was challenged by Hsün Tzu, the followers of the former could not give a satisfactory reply, but only referred to normal men and their behavior. Chinese ethics is healthy and elemental, but without metaphysical foundations. Indeed, materialistic metaphysics also cannot offer a proper foundation for ethics. In this respect, it is a greater enemy of ethics than even some of the highest forms of spiritual Absolutism, which made man an utterly unimportant creature. They say at least that his ultimate nature is the value, though not his ethical struggle.

When the utmost limit of inwardness or outwardness is recognized, philosophy tries to rebuild, in terms of the limit, the various forms it takes. Modern scientific philosophers are impressed by the reality of outwardness, and so they start with matter (as Lloyd Morgan did)[45] or with space-time (as Samuel Alexander did)[46] or with events (as A. N. Whitehead did)[47] as constituting ultimate reality, and develop a method for explaining the forms of life and mind. But the idealistic and mystic philosophers are impressed by the reality of the limit of inwardness, and so they start with God (as theistic philosophers did) or with the Absolute or One (as the idealistic and mystic philosophers did) and develop a method for explaining the forms of mind, life, and matter. And there have been philosophers who fall in between the two extremes, starting from man and ending with the Absolute, but conceiving the Absolute in terms of man's reason, feeling, and so on, and sometimes even stopping short of the conception of a unified Absolute. Some of them attempt logically to deduce the multiplicity from the Absolute—which is called the explanation of multiplicity; but others whose conception of the Absolute is supralogical explain the multiplicity as an emanation, evolution, overflowing, play, and so on, of the Absolute. But when one starts with the inward or the outward limit, whatever be the way for reaching it, one has to make use of some form of evolution—the nature of which may be variously given as overflowing, emanation, or some emergent process—for explaining the opposite outward or inward limit. But on the whole, the

[45] *Emergent Evolution* (London: Williams and Norgate, 1923).
[46] *Space, Time, and Deity* (New York: The Humanities Press, 1950).
[47] *Process and Reality* (New York: The Social Science Book Store, 1941).

evolution from the outward to the inward has been more logically and scientifically demonstrated than the reverse. Evolution in the opposite direction, that is, from the inward to the outward, has only been psychologically and speculatively demonstrated.

If one starts with the outward limit, that is, matter, then life and mind are the two forms of inwardness which matter attains. Lloyd Morgan and Alexander call them emergent qualities. Alexander regards the Deity also as a new, but the highest, emergent quality. Thus Deity becomes a quality of space-time. For Lloyd Morgan, Deity supplies the nisus upwards. Whatever be the differences between these two philosophers, for both of them the appearance and deepening of inwardness is due to evolution; and every new emergent quality is higher than the preceding one. When we start with the limit of outwardness, this is how philosophical explanation has to proceed. Now, if the ultimate foundation of reality is matter or space-time, then is matter or space-time the highest value? Indeed, no. Matter or space-time has a value, but it is not the highest. Life is higher than matter, and mind higher than life. But why are they higher and why not lower? The only answer seems to be based on human sentiment, which is itself an evolute of matter, and so a traitor to its own mother, regarding itself as greater than its own creator.

With respect to value, philosophies that start from the inward limit fare better. The Supreme Spirit is higher than mind, mind higher than life, and life higher than matter. The higher the reality, the higher is its value; and if the highest is the only reality as in Śaṅkara, then it is the only value. Spiritual philosophies then can identify and equate reality and value; and this identity is the motif of the Platonic and Neo-Platonic traditions. But now the problem is: How does the multiplicity come out of the unity? Generally spiritual philosophies maintain that the One is above reason, beyond our powers of understanding. But like a mischief-maker reason demands a rational derivation of the world from what is beyond reason. Reason here is inconsistent with itself, in that, while accepting that the One is beyond reason, it asks for a rational derivation from the One. However, an explanation similar to the one given in deriving the higher from the lower is given also for deriving the lower from the higher. For this also the word evolution is often used. But evolution in the two directions will be intrinsically different. One is evolution of the higher from the lower, of the inward from the outward, of unity from the plurality; the other is the evolution of the lower from the higher, of the outward from the inward, of plurality from unity. If one is integration of plurality, the other is differentiation of unity. The plurality is an emanation, creation, manifestation out of the fulness of the One; just as the unity is an emergence, an evolution, a product, or even a resultant of the plurality. In the histories of the traditions, some philosopher or other has accepted one of these views.

But just as the approach from the limit of outwardness fails to do justice to the conception that ultimate reality is also ultimate value, the approach from the limit of inwardness fails to explain the rationality of the descending orders of being. In the history of philosophy the latter tended to lean towards, and encourage, supernaturalism and even superstition. Indeed, the universe is mysterious. But it is a rational and natural, not a supernatural and superstitious, mystery. Even if the scientist succeeds in creating life out of matter and mind out of life in his laboratory, the mystery of the process does not vanish. In high school classes our teacher may ask: How is water produced? The answer will be: By combining oxygen and hydrogen and introducing an electric spark. But if the teacher asks: Why should oxygen and hydrogen, when combined, become water? the students will be baffled. One may say: It is natural, Sir. But the mystery is not solved by using the word "natural." For we do not understand how the new quality of water comes in. It was not there before.

So the world at every stage is a mystery. Yet it is a natural and rational mystery. Only we cannot abandon all attempts to understand it rationally because it is a mystery. It is as much a mystery that unity evolves out of plurality as that plurality evolves out of unity. If the outward has really evolved out of the inward, we can understand the operation of evolution scientifically in its return process from the outward to the inward. For reason is more at home in the outward. The inward Spirit is beyond reason. But nothing can be rationally deduced from what is beyond reason. In this direction reason is not self-confident; and so it speaks of creation, emanation, manifestation, and evolution as mysterious. In the opposite direction it is self-confident and so speaks of natural evolution. There is no logical reason a priori for life evolving out of matter; yet the process is called natural evolution. Reason observes the multiplicity, its interrelations correlative to the involved unity, in explaining the higher in terms of the lower and considers such knowledge explanation; it observes also that elimination of one or more members of the multiplicity results in the disappearance of the involved unity. But it does not understand why and how the inward unity evolves the outward multiplicity. Such an experience is not normal. Reason works with the principle of order; and order implies a multiplicity in which it exists.

Matter answers the best to the principle of fixed order. Hence the contention of contemporary physicalism that we should rebuild our conception of the world in terms of physics. But the difficulty is that, unless we accept the higher realities beforehand, we cannot rebuild them simply with the help of the concepts of physics; much less can we rebuild with them the deeper inner experiences of man, which have an autonomy of their own. Yet, much of the rationality in the universe will be missed if we are content with the inward approach only. And the excesses of this approach are to be checked by the opposite approach and vice versa. In fact, in both the approaches, the scientist and the philosopher can only take note of what is happening in the universe; they cannot demand what should happen. If it is observation and correlations of observations that we can make, then the explanation that the outward evolves out of the inward can be made as rational as the explanation that the inward evolves from the outward.

Thus both the inward and the outward approaches can be made complementary to each other. The excesses and failures of each are checked and made up by the other. If the inward approach peoples the world with too many realities, the outward approach can distinguish between fantasies and realities and dismiss the former. If the outward approach fails to defend the reality of values and values of reality, the inward approach can come to its help. Further, both have a definite use for man. The inward approach can show the value and significance of his life; the outward can show the constituents of his life. In man matter and spirit meet. The inward shows how he is connected with spirit, and the outward with matter. If not only man's existence but also his value is to be preserved, then both the approaches are indispensable.

But as we have noted, either approach may forget man altogether. In deriving man from the Absolute, it may be forgotten that the Absolute is there as recognized by man. Similarly, in deriving man from matter, it may be forgotten that matter is conceived by man and is real for man's outward consciousness. Man needs matter as a foundation for his outwardness and God or the Absolute as a foundation for his inwardness. They are the two pole stars, which he postulates for guiding his thought and activity. The strength of Chinese philosophy lies in not forgetting the importance and centrality of man, its weakness in not caring for the inward and outward foundations. The greatness of Indian philosophy lies in revealing the inward foundation, its mistake in thinking that it could derive man's existence from the Absolute, and its defect in lessening the value of the individual. Plato started in the right way from man's reason and went up to the Idea of the Good, which he identified with God; but that God was the ultimate foundation of man's whole being, not merely of reason, was not as clearly brought out by Plato as by Plotinus, whose philosophy has the same merits and defects as those of the Vedānta. Christian philosophy tended in the same direction, until the Renaissance brought man and his reason again to the center, reassured man, and conferred utmost value on his thought and action. But later, thought, in its search for an objective basis, found it in matter, made man a purely subjective creature, deprived his mind of objectivity, turned his consciousness, knowledge, and perception into purely subjective affairs, and in the process made itself a subjective factor, without content (in the hands of logical positivists), forfeiting the right to say what the world and life are.

The self-confidence with which reason started in the history of western thought, ended in confidence in itself alone and not in the world around; and the certainty with which it started ended in the certainty of itself and not of the world. This is the latest result of philosophy, in which man finds himself completely alienated from his surroundings by his reason, so that he sees no significance in his life in terms of its foundations, and some of the world's leading thinkers perceive complete unbalance between man's knowledge and his ethics. The reason for the disparity between man's intellectual progress and ethical progress lies here. Plato could say that reason was the custodian of both the good and the true. Even many Indian thinkers said it. *Buddhi,* or reason, at its highest contained the attributes of the good, the true, and the beautiful.[48] But most of the contemporary thinkers of the West can hardly defend the statement.

The mistake of absolute idealists like Hegel was their inordinate

[48] *Sāṅkhyakārikās,* XXIII.

claim to deduce the world from the Absolute. Such an Absolute, whether materialistic or spiritual, led to totalitarianism in both China and Europe when the idea was applied to state and society. In this application the dignity and value of the individual was sacrificed, and he was made a mere instrument of the state. Thus the attempt to find ultimate significance for man's life and ethics ended in denying all. Hence arises the need for revaluing reason in terms of human life and ethics, and restoring man's essential connection with his inward and outward environment.

In the search for the ultimates in both the directions, philosophy should therefore start with the affirmation of man's life and of the value of human activity. It is here that philosophies like Aurobindo's also fall short of our requirement. He rejects Śaṅkara's Māyā, understanding it as unreality of the world. But he would do nothing better for ethics than Śaṅkara could. He writes: "We have to recognize, if we thus view the whole, not limiting ourselves to the human difficulty and the human standpoint, that we do not live in an ethical world." The supra-ethical "has no need for ethics." [49] We may accept, for argument's sake, all that Aurobindo says about the Absolute; we may accept that the Absolute is not bound by our ethical laws, because it is One and beyond the sphere of the plurality of persons. At the limits of inwardness and outwardness, there is no ethics. But if the Absolute is ultimately the creator, the evolver, of human life, it is the creator and evolver of ethics also. If every tiny speck of being has reality, then human life and ethics also have reality. If the former is real for the Absolute, the latter also must be real for it. It is difficult to see how Aurobindo can escape this conclusion. If the ethical nature of the world is unreal, then it is better to say that the world is unreal than to say that the Absolute created a real world for man to struggle ethically in, and yet treats the ethical struggle as unreal. But if man is real, then both the world and the ethical struggle must be real.

Besides, the inward and the outward limits are limits recognized by man for his thought and action. The recognition is purposive also, meant for his life, for expanding and deepening it. And so they are involved in his ethics. It may be that the Absolute has no ethical purpose; creation is a play (*līla*), a natural, unpurposive, unmotived process. But the philosopher will be mistaken if he thinks that, because man is essentially, at the limit of his inwardness, one with the

[49] *The Life Divine* (New York: The Greystone Press, 1949), pp. 90–91.

Absolute, he can behave like the Absolute in this world. Man cannot imagine that the Absolute has an ideal to be achieved. But he should not imagine that man also has no ideal to be achieved. The very process of the Absolute or even nature that works through him gives the lie to such belief. Ideal and purpose belong to man because he is transcended both inwardly and outwardly. Ethics with all the pressure of the "Ought" is as natural a discipline as that of matter or spirit. And the admission of the validity of ethics ought not to endanger the final position of Aurobindo.

The mistake of philosophies lies in viewing human life and activity as the life and activity of either limit, which of course is a limit of man's being and which has significance only to man's being. Man's activity is a struggle for depth and breadth of life. To say that this struggle has no value deprives man of all significance. To affirm the Absolute, we have to affirm man's life and activity first. If man is not affirmed, there can be no affirmation of the Absolute. To say that there is the Absolute gives direction to man's life and activity, but does not nullify them. The change that is needed in philosophy is, therefore, a change in standpoint. It is not from the Absolute or matter that philosophy, in its construction of the world-view, should start, but from man spread out in both directions. A study of both directions enables us to understand the content of his integrality. One mistake has not been noticed so far and ought to be noticed by philosophers: when we are unable to deduce the concept of matter from that of life or the concept of life from that of matter, it is presumptuous to think of deducing man from the Absolute or matter; in order to arrive at the Absolute or matter, we have to start with man.

Protagoras said that "man is the measure of all things"; but he did not ask what man is. So he was interpreted in different ways. Man was taken as the center of selfishness by some, as the rational norm of man by others. If Romero is correct, the West took man as the former. According to him, the symbol of destiny for India is "All"; for China "We"; and for the West "I." [50] For India the center of interest is cosmic or even supra-cosmic, for China social, and for the West selfish. In India man finds his being in the impersonal cosmos and beyond it, in China in society, and in the West in the individual self-centered man. I cannot think that the western man is so completely

[50] Hugo Rodriguez-Alcala, "Francisco Romero in Culture, East and West," *Philosophy: East and West,* July, 1952.

selfish. Even taking Romero's classification, we have to say that the three attitudes are complements of each other. None can be rejected. Philosophy has to show how the three attitudes are complementary. Thought works in man alone, not in anything impersonal; man and his experience are the starting points; the philosophy he develops is from them and for them.

From the standpoint thus formulated, we may attempt to answer one of the questions raised by C. A. Moore as the outcome of the deliberations of the East-West Philosophers Conference in 1949, namely, whether metaphysics is necessary as a foundation for ethics.[51] If the discussion has any truth, then the answer is in the affirmative. Ethics is humanistic, and no humanism that avoids metaphysics can give a complete theory. It can give no ethical answer to the question, Why should I not be selfish? Why should I not make other persons instruments to my end? Why is doing so unethical, if it can be done without punishment? If, in the language of Romero, Confucius said that the "We" is the standard and destiny of every man's conduct and life, he said it only because every man must first be saying "I." For the life of the "I" the life of the "We" becomes the destiny. If the argument is pressed further, the "We" also will be transcended and the "All" will take its place. Indian philosophers did not call it the "All," but the "That." However, it is then only that ethical striving will find its completion. One may call the awareness of the "That" religious consciousness.

Here there may be an apparent conflict between ethics and religion or at least some kinds of religion or spiritual philosophies. That the end is achieved through activity and struggle is the assumption of ethics; that it is eternally achieved, and that activity and ethics are therefore unnecessary, is the teaching of religion. But this opposition is only apparent. God or the Absolute is eternally present. He is within us always like a hidden treasure below the foundations of a house. But one who has not discovered God within himself is only as divine as the landlord who has not discovered the treasure is wealthy. Then how is God to be discovered? Not by annulling one's own self, but by expanding and deepening it, which is an ethical process.

It is here that mystic ways come into conflict with ethical activity. Distinct kinds of technique have been developed by the mystics for

[51] *Philosophy: East and West,* April, 1951, p. 70.

tactfully turning man's mind inwards until it reaches the Universal Spirit. But one who thinks that this method is easier to practice than ethical activity is mistaken. One out of ten thousand may attempt it; and out of those who make the attempt one out of ten thousand may have success. The strongest warning against it comes from the separation of knowing, feeling, willing, and acting at the human level. For an object to be known is not the same as its existing. Hence to depend on knowledge alone, whether it be mystic or ordinary, is to rely upon a vulnerable guide. What man thinks is Divine may be a fantasm. For man the check on knowledge is action, and that on action is knowledge; they are confirmatory of each other. Feeling confirms both and has to be confirmed by them. If man cannot be certain of the perceptual knowledge of even physical objects, he can be much less certain of the ethereal subtle entities of his inwardness. If activity helps in the former, ethics must help in the latter. The method of ethical activity is a safer guide to real inwardness than the method of mere knowledge. In either case, life and its value are not annulled, but enriched.

There are religions that preach only ethical activity and promise communion with God after death. Philosophically, we may say, they promise the infinity of inwardness after death. But man is an inquisitive animal and is not always content to wait until death in order to know what happens then. He will use his reason, imagination, and experience for picturing the state of existence after death. He may develop a philosophy in which death becomes a transitional phase of continuous life. Old ideas about heaven and hell may be discarded as superstitions; but the reality of death cannot be denied. One may ask what death has to do with philosophy; but it is a truth about human existence and a truth for philosophy of life, particularly for religious philosophy and philosophy of religion. Philosophy of life should include philosophy of death as well. Now, if man knows what existence he is destined to have after death, he will like to act now to avert it if it is evil and experience it if it is good. One of the greatest wonders, however, is that, though every man knows that he will die some day, only a few people care to give much thought to death. But without seeing through it, philosophy is not content. Man desires to have life even after death. He wants continually to affirm himself, whether in a finite or an infinite form. Spiritual philosophies say that the affirmation will be successful only in the infinite form. The finite form is not to be abandoned, but to be enlarged. Death gives a new chance and opportunity, as religious philosophies say, for this enlargement by enabling life to take better embodiment; but what is thus enlarged and revived should not be a Frankenstein's monster, but a Christ or Buddha. Hence the importance of ethical activity.

Further Evaluation of Standpoints

A few other points of evaluation may be noted here from the standpoint of man's inwardness and outwardness. What have generally been called degrees of reality ought actually to be called degrees of inwardness. Bradley wanted to construct them epistemologically with the help of the logical criterion of coherence: what is more coherent is more real. This view may be true so far as logical judgments go. But from our point of view, we would say that what is more inward is more valuable. If reality is the same as value, as it is for some spiritual and idealistic philosophies, then what is more real is more inward also, for the inward is higher than the outward. But here we have to be on our guard, lest we should deny value to man's existence, for man is not the most inward reality, but the meeting point of inwardness and outwardness. Then, instead of saying that matter has less reality than spirit, we have to say that it has less value. If we approach the same point from epistemology and adopt Bradley's method, we shall have to say that spirit has more reality than matter. The identification of the highest reality with the highest value or simply reality with value belongs to the grand Platonic tradition of western philosophy and the Vedāntic tradition of India. But if we accept the reality of man, then matter also, towards which his outwardness is directed, is real. Nature itself has given him some inwardness, but he has to struggle to attain more. And the more the inwardness attained, the greater is the value attained.

For a materialistic philosophy, which accepts the reality of outwardness only, value is an evanescent feature, absolutely accidental to reality. It may accept the distinction between higher and lower values, but the distinction can have no essential foundation in reality.

Another point of importance in the new relation between inwardness and outwardness is the relation between analysis and synthesis. The inward is the integrality of the outward; the outward is that into which the inward is split up; and the inward is the integral unity of the outward. Philosophies of outwardness explain the inward as due to the synthesis of elements; and the philosophies of inwardness explain the outward as due to the splitting up or diversification of the inward.

But as we have recognized, each explanation is complementary to the other. But here another important difference in method arises. If both the inward and the outward are given together, and man himself cannot produce the inward by combining the outward elements, two ways of explaining the situation are possible. These are called by Fung the positive and negative methods of explanation.[52] The positive method belongs to western philosophy and the negative method to some forms of eastern philosophy. The positive explanation will be that the inward is an integral unity of all the outward constituents. Life, for instance, is an integral unity of all the material particles. If it is asked: Can you produce life by combining all the material particles?, the answer will be: We can, if we understand the structural patterns also into which the constituents enter. The negative explanation will be that life is neither the same as matter, nor different from matter.

So far as science goes, the negative explanation is not helpful, though something can be said in its favor. The material particles that enter life are the correlates of life, not life itself, just as a particular wave length of light is a correlate of color, not color itself. Similarly we may accept that life is neither the same as matter, nor different from matter. But the positive method, and the confidence that we could understand the structure into which the material particles constituting life enter, enabled the West to make a given life full and healthy and gave much control over the constituents of life. As science has spread to the East, the advantage has been gained by the East also. But the negative method has its advantage in realizing the deeper spheres of inwardness, which are scarcely built up but revealed. By saying that the inward reality is not the same as the outward, man is warned that he cannot build up or manufacture the inward with the

[52] *A Short History of Chinese Philosophy*, p. 330.

outward; but by saying that the inward is not different from the outward, man is exhorted not to give up the outward but to realize the inward within the outward. Thus both the positive and negative methods are necessary for life; only we have to find out to which sphere each method is appropriate. The positive method is more useful to man in understanding and utilizing the reality that lies outwards to him; and the negative method is more useful in understanding and realizing the reality that is inward to him.

These methods are both the causes and effects of the general attitude to life in the West, China, and India. The positive method encourages and makes possible reconstruction, re-creation, reproduction, not merely logical but also physical. It is because of this method that a physician, for instance, is able to rebuild health, and the underlying principle of his science is reconstruction, rebuilding of life with the factors understood to be necessary. The negative method encourages and makes possible only recognition, acknowledgement, and acceptance of a reality. The positive method makes possible control of nature, which means reconstruction of nature, and control of society, which means reform of society. Certainly, both controls have their limits, for the ultimate constituents of even the material world cannot be created and changed, but have to be recognized as such. This limit is more patent in society, the constituents of which are human beings, whose essential nature, so far as our knowledge goes, cannot be completely changed. To alter it becomes an ethical question. For alteration of human nature will be alteration by us according to a preconceived mold based upon some philosophy, even if it is highly utopian in the good sense of the term. But if our philosophy is wrong, the mold will be unsuitable; and when we attempt to press man into it, either it will break or man will break. In either case, the result will be colossal human disaster, which is ethically unjustified. We have therefore to take facts as they are, study man as he is, the normal man, the rational, active, social, feeling, and emotional animal, as he is called, and recognize the limits imposed upon our reconstruction.

If the positive method helps and encourages reconstruction and control of the object, the negative method encourages self-control—control of man, his emotions, thoughts, feelings, and actions, by himself. The inward is not amenable to manipulation like the outward; it manipulates us more than we can manipulate it. We have to manipulate ourselves with reference to it rather than manipulate it with reference to us. Nature is of lower value than we; so we reconstruct nature with reference to us. Our activity bestows higher value on nature than it by itself possesses. But the inward is higher than we; and so when we mold our nature in accordance with it, we raise ourselves in value. Hence we find more self-control preached by philosophies and cultures of inwardness than by those of outwardness.

Here also we have to take a warning. The Chinese and Indian philosophies emphasize self-control more than western philosophy, particularly the contemporary. But this does not mean that they do not preach control of the "Other," whatever the "Other" may mean. For the Chinese philosophers the "Other" meant other human beings, who constitute society. Rigorists like Hsün Tzu rather overemphasized this control. Society was a complete "Other" to the person who was to control it. For the Vedāntins and the Buddhists in India the most inward, which is the essence in man, controls the rest in man, which is therefore an "Other" to it. The technique of this control developed by treating the rest as the "Other." As much intellectual energy was spent in analyzing and understanding this part of man as the West had spent in understanding physical nature. Analysis is present in Indian thought, but not to the degree to which the West developed and applied it, only because the inward is not amenable to alteration and reconstruction, but demands recognition.

Again, it may be useful in this context also to refer to the distinction that some philosophers have drawn between intellect and intuition, and identify each with the characteristics of the methods of the West and the East. But as we have seen, while the positive method insists on analyzing and reconstructing realities, it also recognizes its limits, and the limits are the realities accepted as given. So intuition is accepted, whether it is intellectual, perceptual, sensuous, or instinctive. This acceptance of intuition is also involved in the recognition that, whatever be the number of concepts utilized, no individual can be constructed with the concepts. It is involved also in the theory that life, mind, and Deity are new emergent qualities out of matter or space-time, but not resultants; for all qualities are intuited. If life is not a sensuous intuition, it is at least intellectual. Even in the case of universals, how is the universal man, for instance, known? It is not any of the particulars only or all of them put together; and so Plato said that it must have been known by reason previously; which means that it is an intuition by the intellect. Aristotle said that the universal exists in the particulars, but not separately. Even then, it is intuited by the intellect, not by sense. The universal man is not any of the common characteristics of men. It has an integrality, a qualitative uniqueness, which any of the common features of men do not possess; and as such it is recognized by the intellect.

Similarly, the negative method is not merely intuitive, but also intellectual. But intellectual analysis, even in the sphere of society, is greatly limited, when compared with the realm of nature. This is the reason for saying that Chinese philosophy also is intuitive in its method. The ethical and other qualities into which human nature is analyzed are cognized by observing one's psycho-social nature; and so it is thought that intuition alone is used. But taking the best of those constituents and reconstructing human nature at its best is again an intellectual attempt, not a mere intuitive attempt. Whether analysis and synthesis are carried on thoroughly or not is a different question. The Chinese show a lack of thoroughness in this respect, unlike the Indians, who developed elaborate and intricate logic. The Nyāya-Vaiśeṣika, Jainism, and early Buddhism cannot be accused of lack of analytic skill. But their aim was different; as philosophers of the inward, they were not interested in the control of nature. If spirit is the most inward reality of man, and man's being is rooted in matter also, then man's being has to be analyzed beginning from matter and ending with spirit; and these schools developed as much analysis as was possible in the light of the knowledge of the world at that time. But as the interest was overwhelmingly inward, and as the inward allows little alteration and reconstruction, the Indians may appear to have used mainly the intuitive method.

But epistemology is as important and great a part of Indian philosophy as of the western. Indeed, logic was not clearly separated from epistemology in India. But that was more or less also the case in the West up to about the seventeenth century. Boole, we may say, was the first to separate them, and he saw the relation between logic and algebra. The distinction between propositions and judgments was not clearly drawn by the earlier logicians, and the validity of a proposition apart from epistemic conditions was not distinguished from the truth of judgment till very recently. The whole of idealistic logic from Kant to Bradley and Bosanquet is based on the theory of judgment. The fact that the Indian logicians did not make the distinction between judgment and proposition does not prove that they used any intuitive method in logic. It shows only that the problem did not strike them. We have also to remember that Indian logic and epistemology have not had any development from the seventeenth century even till now, and that these remarkable developments took place in the West only after the seventeenth century.

In this connection, we may take up the problem of the relation between life of contemplation and life of activity. The East is generally said to be contemplative, and the West active; and eastern philosophies are said to preach a life of contemplation and the western a life of activity. The material backwardness of eastern civilization tends to support this distinction. But Schweitzer says that, though the West is instinctively activistic, it has not succeeded in building up a philosophy of activism and of life-affirmation. One need not think that the affirmation of the Absolute should necessarily be at the same time the life-negation of man. Nor should one conclude that the West failed to build up systems of activistic philosophy, whatever defects one may point out in them. At the same time it may be pointed out that Hsün Tzu and Li Ssu's condemnation of scholars as idlers producing nothing, and the destruction of Buddhist monasteries and the forcible conversion of monks and nuns to secular life show the activistic tendency in Chinese thought. In India also the Mīmāmsā may be referred to, which, from the beginning of the Vedas, not only emphasized the importance of action, but also gave what it considered to be ethical action—which we may call ethico-religious—a place equal to God's, and meant that God was unnecessary and right action (*dharma*) was self-sufficient. Whatever the Vedānta may have said about the philosophy of the Mīmāmsā and the ultimate ideal of life it presented to man, it never questioned the right of the system to guide the life of man in the mundane world. It was the opinion of India's wise men that the Mīmāmsā should guide the life of man during the first two stages of life and the Vedānta during the next two stages. In metaphysics they could not reconcile the two systems and said that they were meant for immature and mature minds, respectively.

It is therefore wrong to say that India and China preached only a life of contemplation. However, some forms of the Vedānta, Buddhism, and Jainism in India, and Taoism and Buddhism (particularly Chanism) in China extolled contemplative life, and these schools were held in high regard in both the countries, and influenced the outlook of the people. In addition, lack of scientific and technological development made the contemplative outlook conspicuous in the East. The recent changes, however, in the political and social outlook of the people of the East show that they are not averse to science and technology; but they did not think till recently that control of nature could solve many of the problems of man, which they thought self-control alone could solve.

But if control of nature and society cannot solve all the problems of men and many problems arise because of ethical shortcomings and failures, a life of mere activity also does not satisfy men. We have said that knowledge is a complement of activity and activity a complement of knowledge, and both keep man from diverging from reality. But if there is inwardness within man, which does not permit of much manipulation but only of realization, and if the deepening of inwardness is necessary for the fulness of man's life, then contemplation or meditation is also necessary. Aristotle placed before man the ideal of contemplation, calling it "thought of thought." Hegel interpreted it as thought's reflection on its own categories. The Marxists condemn it as an ideal of the aristocratic and bourgeois class. But no Indian philosopher would give it either the Hegelian or the Marxist interpretation. The West tends to understand consciousness as an ineffectual light playing on matter and contemplation as a thought of pale thought and so paler than the original. But contemplation is the conscious recollecting and integrating of the complete being of man spread outwardly and turning it inwards in order to catch the depths. Its perfection lies in attaining oneness with the universal consciousness that is one with universal matter, the universal inwardness that is one with universal outwardness. If reason has objective validity, then this universal consciousness also has objective validity. It is cosmic in the sense that, for it, the idea of an object is the existence of the object. We may note that, according to Plato, reason, which is part of the Logos, has cosmic significance; it is objective in the sense that what it knows is reality. Plato also hinted that there is something above the Logos, that is, more inward to the Logos. This cannot be realized unless man is ethically high, unless his consciousness is universalized and made to accord with the cosmos, that is, unless it becomes objective. Objectivity of consciousness is accord with the being of the cosmos. Consciousness of man, to start with, may be a subjective and erring entity; but it is his duty to make it cosmically objective and universal.

The misunderstanding of consciousness and contemplation by the

West is due to its general lack of interest in the inward reality. Even by Plato this inwardness is not clearly recognized as inwardness, but as merely rational consciousness. The Orphics and Plotinus had clearer insight. But Orphism was mixed up with much that was supernatural and mysterious, which philosophers rejected, and reason as understood by Plato was deprived of whatever inwardness it possessed. Plotinus offended both philosophers and Christianity, the former by the introduction of the supernatural, and the latter by his doctrine of man's ultimate oneness with the Divine Spirit and also by his doctrine of emanation, which conflicted with the Christian doctrine of creation out of nothing. It is interesting and relevant to note that mathematics, which Pythagoras supposed would lead man inwards, is now made the criterion of outward objectivity or externality. For the Greeks, reason was an inward entity also.

Contemplation is meant to keep man in touch with inward reality, to enable him to realize his inwardness and its freedom, and action is meant to keep man in touch with outward reality. The inward and outward realities, however, are not two, but the same spread out in two directions. In man this spreading out becomes aware of itself. Man's own being lies continuously and consciously in the two directions with an intensity and focus at the center and gradually fading out to the extremities. Outwardly he extends his consciousness through mind and senses, and inwardly through mind and reason. In both directions his mind may commit mistakes and create illusions. Ordinary action gives man the proper training for distinguishing realities from illusions, ethical activity produces in him the right inwardness and enables him to distinguish between what is truly universal in him and what is not by giving his feelings and emotions the right turn and habit, and contemplative activity makes him firm and steady by bringing him nearer and nearer the inward universal integrality, which is the Divine Spirit.

At certain depths of inwardness, intellect is absorbed by intuition, which is an integral experience. Only in this experience is the recognition of reality complete, without analysis and synthesis. This is the truth of mysticism to be philosophically understood. Here there is no epistemological synthesis of intellect and intuition, because intellect is already absorbed by those depths of intuition, and can do nothing else but assert and affirm the reality experienced. If at the level of pure logic, as in mathematical logic, nothing is affirmed or asserted, since intellect absorbs intuition completely at that level, at the level of man's innermost being intuition absorbs intellect completely and everything in experience is asserted as existent. This description of intellect and intuition is a description of what ought to be; for the assertions of those who are respected as having the experience of the inward reality are as divergent as the theories of mathematics and logic. So far as ordinary experience goes, man makes and ought to make intellect and intuition complements of each other.

Aspects in Need of Expansion

In conclusion we cannot but give a measure of general support to some, though not all, of the usual evaluations of the three traditions. The East was brooding when the West was active, only because the East confined its activity to man's life and what was inward to it and overlooked the truth that human life extends outwards also right into matter, the nature of which permits control and manipulation; not because it consistently spurned matter, but because it ignored its value for man, and became one-sided and unhealthy. The East now recognizes this, declaring that material backwardness is not the same as spirituality. India reached extremes and even committed excesses in this direction of inwardness. China committed fewer excesses, continued its traditional life for a very long time, but has realized the inadequacy of it all the same. But the West is still too proud of its activism, and some of its leaders have begun to realize that it is missing the meaning and significance of life. Even Schweitzer wants mysticism, though he wants ethical mysticism, not merely contemplative mysticism.[53] But we have seen the nature and value of contemplation for life. It is contemplation that brings to man's awareness his freedom from the determinism of matter, the divinity, spirituality, universality, and objectivity of his consciousness, its intrinsic value, not its

[53] *Civilization and Ethics,* p. 236. "Our great mistake, however, is thinking that without mysticism we can reach an ethical world- and life-view, which can satisfy thought."

instrumental value as a medium for knowing objects.[54] Contemplation need not be anti-ethical, for it is meant for the realization of the deeper intensity and expanse of life. Yet it is supra-ethical in that, if it is right, it touches the mystic unity, which is universal like reason and in which there is no distinction between "mine" and "thine" and the ethical reference to the other personality is transcended. Only when this transcendence is interpreted as anti-ethical or made the basis for justification of abuses, of intolerance, of disrespect for life, whether of one's own or of others, is contemplative life to be condemned. Such a contemplative life is not the true contemplative life.

What India, therefore, wants is a revival of its elemental activism of the early Vedas and the Mīmāmsā, a reinterpretation and reconciliation of the Mīmāmsā and the Vedānta, a wholehearted discarding of the philosophic outgrowth, which like a harmful parasite has weakened her general outlook on life in many of its parts. Starting with pure mysticism, a healthy respect for life cannot be cultivated; but starting with respect for life, a healthy mysticism can be developed: this is what Schweitzer seems to present as the basic requisite of a true philosophy of life.

What is further wanted in Indian philosophy is a metaphysical foundation for the social sense. The Upaniṣads made an individualistic approach by analyzing only the levels of man's inwardness. In this analysis we find little mention of other persons, other minds, so much so that the recognition of other persons, which is essential for ethics, is decidedly absent. The Pāñcarātra accepted a swarming hive of *ātmans;* but they are concerned only with God, not with each other.[55] The Sāṅkhya and the Nyāya accepted a plurality of *ātmans,* but they are absolutely unconcerned with each other. The Mīmāmsā treated action as itself the ruler and controller of the universe; but that action is not ethical in the sense of concern for others, but only for one's own future. Indeed, selfishness is not preached by any of these schools; but their doctrines savor of extreme individualism, which cannot be an adequate foundation for complete ethics. Buddhism developed the idea that the *bodhisattva* will not enter Nirvāṇa unless the whole world is saved; but this spiritual altruism was concerned with the sal-

[54] Russell W. Davenport in *The Dignity of Man* (New York: Harper & Brothers, 1955) has eloquently shown that the concept of the freedom of man in a deterministic world-view is meaningless without recognizing inwardness.

[55] See P. T. Raju, *Idealistic Thought of India,* p. 146.

vation of all living beings, and its full social implications were not worked out. While the Chinese used human-heartedness, sympathy, love, righteousness, and so on, as if they were ultimate metaphysical entities, similar virtues were certainly stressed by the Indian philosophers also, but without developing the social implications. We find only a psychological justification of the virtues as leading up to the highest yoga and Nirvāṇa.[56] Sympathy needs at least two persons, which philosophy has to recognize. If it is a conscious activity, then consciousness itself recognizes this duality. Whatever the modern epistemologist says about our knowledge of other minds, early philosophy, which was a philosophy of life, should have recognized the two terms and the bond between them, even if the duality and the bond were transcended and integrated in a mystic unity.

The West needs a more adequate recognition of the inward reaches of man's being, without which philosophy cannot justify spirituality and the freedom of spirit from deterministic matter. The West has had great saints, great ethical and spiritual leaders. But the self-certainty of inwardness has, on the whole, been confused with faith and therefore could not play its proper part in philosophy. Instinctive inwardness is not absent, but reason has been forbidden to explore its nature. If contemplation and higher forms of intuition are essential for deepening life, then philosophy has to say it in so many words, recognize their truth, and study their nature. Faith will not be enough. It can be misunderstood as simply external respect for a religious leader and even unreasonable adoration.

China needs a persistent effort to think out systematically to the extreme both the inward and the outward in order to discover the roots of man's being in both directions. Man belongs at the balancing point of the two directions. China was able to keep the balance, only because she was never enamored of either extreme. The sage-king has always been her ideal; saintliness within and kingliness without have been the characteristics of the ideal man. This saintliness, however, is not that which is the characteristic of the inward mystic, but at the most of the mystic of human nature, as in Taoism. One may not be far wrong in saying that the great Tao of the Taoists is the highly idealized nature of man, understood not as an abstraction, but as a concrete,

[56] See Rhys Davids, *Buddhist Psychology* (London: Luzac, 1924) and Tachibana, *Buddhist Psychological Ethics*.

creative dynamic force, constitutive of, and contributing to, the joy of life's being when life runs smoothly. Perhaps the founder of the idea had deeper experience; but it is not well clarified, and its relation with the rest of experience is not well worked out.

The advantage in working out the inward and outward limits of our being and discovering their relation is that we get an objectified view of the world and of the position of man in it. For man reality extends inwardly and outwardly from him. But when it is said that matter evolved out of spirit, it should not be meant that spirit first created man and through man matter. No natural science will accept that man was created prior to matter, for man himself possesses a material body. Matter must have been created prior to man, life must have evolved out of matter, and mind out of life. But this evolution, if it has any meaning, must be directed towards the very origin of the evolution of matter, namely, spirit. Man then must belong to this reciprocal phase of evolution away from matter. The two directions of inwardness and outwardness come to consciousness in man, and so man finds his being spread out in both directions. Our previous observation that matter and the Absolute are matter and the Absolute only for man has to be understood in this context. Otherwise, the assertion will sound subjectivistic or like a glorification of man and like self-sufficient humanism. The tinge of subjectivism is removed when the limits of inwardness and outwardness, which transcend man's being, are recognized. Chinese philosophy, by not caring for these transcending limits, lacks metaphysical objectivity, and is prone to be interpreted as subjective, though the Chinese philosophers will be surprised to hear of the criticism.

That the inward process is directed through man does not absolve man of his duty and ethical striving for inwardness. There are philosophers who believe that the cosmic upward process through man will naturally push man up to spiritual heights, whether he wants them or not. For this view we have had little or no evidence. On the other hand, whatever humanity has been able to achieve in its culture and civilization has been the result of conflict, struggle, and even blood and tears. The fact that the return process of evolution is working through man indicates that it will reach its consummation only through the activity of man. The occasional condemnation of epistemology is due to its averring that the eternally accomplished and established Absolute Spirit absolves man of all activity and is also due to the implication that for this realization man has only to remain inactive, to stop asserting and affirming himself. But if the upward process is real, it does not permit man to remain quiet. He may try to imitate the Supreme Spirit, which is eternally perfect; but so long as he remains man, he cannot be that Spirit. On the other hand, he may become an impostor and lose the sense of ethical objectivity. It is the mysticism of such people that is a danger to ethics and society.

Though man is a stage in the inward process of evolution, it is he who asks: Who am I? What is this world? What am I to do in it? He asks for the meaning of his existence. In this asking, he affirms his existence. Everything else, therefore, can have meaning for man with reference to his existence. But the meaning of his existence can be understood only with reference to everything else; but everything else exists only so far as he knows, infers, imagines, and accepts. Even to accept the existence of things not even imagined by me is an acceptance by me. Hence, the starting point of philosophy is man; the aim of philosophy is to tell man what he is to do and how to do it. Even reason is a function of man's being. It tried to work on spirit and found it to be not its proper field; it next turned to matter and mathematics and logic and said: Here are my realms. But then it forgot that it was a function of man's being. Humanism cannot be avoided in philosophy, if it is sincere to itself. But the mistake of humanism is that it forgets that man is not a self-sufficient being, that his existence belongs, with its ill-demarcated limits, to the continuous chain of being from matter below to Spirit above.

What is the lesson we derive from this limited and general comparison of the three traditions? If philosophy is necessarily a philosophy of life, then ethics should be given an autonomy of its own. This is the peculiar contribution that China can make to world-philosophy. For completeness ethics has to be based on some sound, true, and adequate world-view; but it need not wait to get a start till the world-view is completed. In fact, physics, biology, psychology, and every other science have to be founded on a world-view for completion; but they are not; and so, accepting that man is finite and has to begin with fragmentary knowledge, they developed independently. Then why should ethics also not be developed independently? The question of ultimate foundations of ethics may be left to the future, for man is not omniscient and goes on accumulating knowledge. The Chinese philosophers took the bold step of founding ethics on human nature as it appeared at its best; and as one can see, they developed idealism, realism, materialism, and even transcendentalism out of their observations of human nature. What are the factors of human life that work as bonds of society, conducive to harmonious social life? Whether the Chinese philosophers answered this question satisfactorily or not may be doubted. But they raised the question and started their ethics, which therefore took human life for granted, as the basic value, and affirmed it. Some empirical philosophers in the West also did similarly; but they were somewhat wavering, their method was not uniformly followed and was not accepted even by a considerable majority of ethical writers.

Likewise, spiritual life also must have its autonomy. Its reality does not depend upon our success or failure to explain the relation of spirit to mind, life, and matter. The recognition of its reality is prior to its explanation. This is the contribution of Indian philosophy. The child who does not know what it is to love one beloved may explain away the reality of the experience; but his explanation does not falsify the fact.

The contribution of the West lies in its teaching that life is not merely inward, not merely social, but also has its roots in physical nature, that material backwardness is not the same as spiritual greatness, and that we are to be sure of the method of our knowledge before we can be sure of the reality of the object. Because of the West's great contribution to our understanding of the outward, it has been wrongly called materialistic. But it has not lost its spiritual and ethical leaven, though its recent dominant philosophies keep that in the background and are puzzled to explain its relation to outwardness. But the West, on the whole, offers a more comprehensive view of life than China or India, though it often passed through periods of unbalance. Comparative philosophy should recognize the complementary nature of each of the three dominant attitudes; and there is much that is common to all the three, though developed in varying degrees. Each can learn much from the others and widen its scope. And they can be brought together and studied only as philosophies of life with man as the common denominator.

APPENDIXES

Chronological Table

The following chronology is given only to show the development of the world's thought in the three traditions. It is not detailed. Moreover, Indian chronology is not exact. Historical scholarship is not unanimous about many dates. In some cases there is a difference of centuries. The Indian column does not show as many names as the western and the Chinese, not because there were fewer philosophers up to the sixteenth century, but because many were continuers of the schools, writing commentaries on the texts of the original founders and their expositions, and the names of the continuers are not given. Many of the Chinese names also are those of continuers of schools, but each had some new idea to contribute. One can see from the table that after the sixteenth century there has been little new contribution to philosophy in either China or India.

Western Tradition	Chinese Tradition	Indian Tradition
		Mohenjo-daro culture and civilization, 4000–3000 B.C.
	HUANG TI, Yellow Emperor, *c.* 2697 B.C.	
	YAO, Emperor, *c.* 2357 B.C.	
	SHUN, Emperor, *c.* 2255 B.C.	
	YU, Emperor, *c.* 2205 B.C.	
		Ṛgvedic Hymns, *c.* 2000 B.C.
MOSES, 14th century B.C.		
	CHOU KUNG, Duke of Chou, *c.* 1200 B.C.	
		Bṛhadāraṇyaka Upaniṣad, 900 B.C.

WESTERN TRADITION	CHINESE TRADITION	INDIAN TRADITION
THALES, 7th century B.C. Hylozoism. Orphic and Apollonian religions, earlier than 6th century B.C.		
		MAHĀVĪRA, *c.* 600 B.C. Founder of Jainism.
	CONFUCIUS, *c.* 551 B.C. Interest in human relationships.	
ANAXIMANDER, 6th century B.C. Hylozoism.		
		BUDDHA, *c.* 600 B.C. Founder of Buddhism.
	YANG CHU, *c.* 500 B.C. Absolute affirmation of man.	
ANAXIMENES, 6th century B.C. Hylozoism.		
	LAO TZU, date uncertain Founder of Taoism.	
PYTHAGORAS, 6th century B.C. Mysticism of reason, philosophy of number.		
		MANU, author of *The Code of Manu*, *c.* 500 B.C.
HERACLITUS, 5th century B.C. Mysticism of reason, philosophy of becoming.		
		Mhābhārata, epic, *c.* 500 B.C.
	MO TZU, *c.* 479 B.C. Founder of Mohism.	
		Bhagavadgītā, *c.* 500 B.C. (part of the *Mahābhārata*).
ANAXAGORAS, 5th century B.C. Discoverer of Nous.		
		Rāmāyaṇa, epic, *c.* 400 B.C.
DEMOCRITUS, 5th century B.C. Atomism.		
PARMENIDES, 5th century B.C. Philosophy of being.		
Sophists, 5th century B.C. Change of interest		

WESTERN TRADITION	CHINESE TRADITION	INDIAN TRADITION
from cosmology to man.		
PROTAGORAS, 5th century B.C. Man as the measure of all things, subjectivism and relativism.		
SOCRATES, 5th century B.C. Founder of dialectic, rational universal man as the measure of all things, reason as the essence of soul.		
PLATO, 5th century B.C. Idealism, ideas as norms.		
ARISTIPPUS, 5th century B.C. Hedonism.		
ANTISTHENES, 4th century B.C. Cynicism.		
EPICURUS, 4th century B.C. Hedonism.	SHANG YANG, 4th century B.C. Legalism.	KAṆĀDA, author of *Vaiśeṣikasūtras*, *c.* 400 B.C.
		GAUTAMA, author of *Nyāyasūtras*, *c.* 400 B.C.
ARISTOTLE, 4th century B.C. Realistic idealism.	SHEN PU-HAI, 4th century B.C. Legalism.	PATAÑJALI, author of *Yogasūtras*, *c.* 400 B.C.
	SHEN TAO, 4th century B.C. Legalism.	JAIMINI, author of *Mīmāmsāsūtras*, *c.* 400 B.C.
PYRRHO, 4th century B.C. Skepticism.		
		BĀDARĀYAṆA, author of *Vedāntasūtras*, *c.* 400 B.C.
	MENCIUS, *c.* 372–289 B.C. Confucian ethical idealism.	

WESTERN TRADITION	CHINESE TRADITION	INDIAN TRADITION
	CHUANG TZU, *c.* 369–286 B.C. Taoism.	
	HSÜN TZU, *c.* 298–238 B.C. Confucian realism.	
	HAN FEI TZU, 3rd century B.C. Rigorism and legalism.	
	HUI SHIH, 3rd century B.C. Dialectician.	
	TSOU YEN, *c.* 3rd century B.C. Yin-Yang School.	
	LI SSU, 3rd century B.C. Rigorism and legalism. Burning of Books, 213 B.C.	
	TUNG CHUNG-SHU, 179–104 B.C. Confucian Old Text School.	
	LIU HSIN, *c.* 1st century B.C. Confucian Old Text School.	
PHILO, 25 B.C.–40 A.D. Platonic Judaism.		*Prajñāpāramītās*, source of the Mahāyāna, 100 B.C.–100 A.D.
	WANG CHUNG, *c.* 27–100 A.D. Naturalist and critic. Entry of Buddhism, 1st century.	
		VASUMITRA, 1st century Classifier of the Hīnayāna Schools.
		AŚVAGHOṢA, *c.* 100 Bhūtatathatā School.

WESTERN TRADITION	CHINESE TRADITION	INDIAN TRADITION
	MOU TZU, 2nd century Confucian admirer of Buddhism.	MAITREYANĀTHA, 1st and 2nd centuries Founder of Yogācāra or Vijñānavāda.
		NĀGĀRJUNA, 2nd century Founder of Mādhyamika.
PLOTINUS, born *c.* 204 Neo-Platonism.		
	HSIANG HSIU, 221–300 Rationalist Neo-Taoism.	
		UMĀSVĀTI, 3rd century Author of *Jainasūtras*.
	KUO HSIANG, died 312 Rationalist Neo-Taoism.	
		ASAṄGA, 4th century Yogācāra.
	CH'ING-T'AN movement, 314–366 Sentimental Neo-Taoism.	
		VASUBANDHU, 4th century Sarvāstivāda and Yogācāra.
ST. AUGUSTINE, 354–430 Christian Platonism.		
		PRAŚASTAPĀDA, 4th century Commentator on *Vaiśeṣikasūtras*.
	KUMĀRAJIVA, 344–413 Indian Buddhist in China.	
	BODHIDHARMA, 486–536 Indian Buddhist in China, founder of Chanism.	

WESTERN TRADITION	CHINESE TRADITION	INDIAN TRADITION
	SENG CHAO, 5th century Propagator of Buddhism.	
	HUI-YÜAN, 5th century Founder of Pure Land School, also called Lotus School.	
	TAO-HSÜAN, 5th century Liu (Vinaya) School.	
	TAO-SHENG, 5th century Chan School.	
	CHIH-KAI, born 531 T'ien-T'ai School.	
		GAUḌAPĀDA, 6th century Founder of the Advaita.
	HÜAN-TSANG, 596–664 Yogācāra and Chü-she (Kośa) Schools.	
		KUMĀRILA, between 7th and 8th centuries Follower of Jaimini.
		PRABHĀKARA, between 7th and 8th centuries Follower of Jaimini.
		JAYARĀŚI, between 7th and 8th centuries Expounder of Cārvāka.
		ŚAṄKARA, 8th century Protagonist of the Advaita.
	VAJRABODHI, 8th century Indian to introduce *tāntrik* Buddhism into	

WESTERN TRADITION	CHINESE TRADITION	INDIAN TRADITION
	China, Ch'ng-Yen (True Word) School.	
	AMOGHAVAJRA, 8th century Disciple of Vajra-bodhi.	
	HAN YU, 768–824, fore-runner of Neo-Confucianism.	
	LI AO, died *c.* 844, fore-runner of Neo-Confucianism.	BHĀSKARA, 9th century Vedāntin, Bhedābheda (identity in difference).
		VASUGUPTA, 9th century Kasmir Śaiva Advaita.
		ABHINAVAGUPTA, 10th century Kasmir Śaiva Advaita.
	NEO-CONFUCIANISM, 11th century	
	SHAO YANG, 1011–77 Neo-Confucianism.	
	CHOU TUN-YI, 1017–73 Neo-Confucianism.	
	CHANG TSAI, 1020–77 Neo-Confucianism.	RĀMĀNUJA, 11th century Vedāntin, Vaiṣṇava Viśiṣṭādvaita (soul-body relationship).
	CHENG HAO, 1032–85 Hsin Hsüeh School, or School of Mind.	
ST. ANSELM, 1035–1109 Ontological proof for the existence of God.	CHENG YI, 1033–85 Li Hsüeh School, or School of Laws or Principles.	
	CHU HSI, 1130–1200 Follower of Cheng Yi.	ŚRĪHARṢA, 12th century Advaita dialectician. Follower of Śaṅkara.

WESTERN TRADITION	CHINESE TRADITION	INDIAN TRADITION
	LU CHIU-YÜAN, 1139–93 Follower of Cheng Hao.	
		GAṄGEŚA, 12th–13th century Founder of Neo-Nyāya.
ST. THOMAS AQUINAS, 1227–74 Christian Aristotelianism.		MADHVA, 13th century Vedāntin, Vaiṣṇava Dvaita (dualism).
		NIMBĀRKA, 13th century Vedāntin, Vaiṣṇava Bhedābheda. (identity in difference).
		ŚRĪKAṆṬHA, 13th–14th century Vedāntin, Śaiva Viśiṣṭādvaita (soul-body relationship).
		VALLABHA, 15th century Vedāntin, Vaiṣṇava Śuddhādvaita (pure non-dualism).
	WANG SHOU JEN, 1473–1529 Confucian School of Mind.	
		BALADEVA, 15th century Vedāntin, Vaiṣṇava, Acintyabhedābheda (incomprehensible identity in difference).
		VIJÑĀNABHIKṢU, 15th century Sāṅkhya-Vedāntin.
		RAGHUNĀTHA, 15th–16th century Neo-Nyāya.

Western Tradition	Chinese Tradition	Indian Tradition
		ŚRĪPATI, 16th century Vedāntin, Śaiva Bhedābheda (identity in difference).
FRANCIS BACON, 1561–1626 Revolt against Aristotelian logic and founding of empiricism.		
RENÉ DESCARTES, 1596–1650 Rationalism and qualitative dualism.		
	WANG FU-CHIH, 1619–93 Ch'ing Neo-Confucianism.	
BARUCH (BENEDICTUS) SPINOZA, 1631–77 Monism of substance.		
JOHN LOCKE, 1632–1704 Empiricism.		
	YEN YÜAN, 1635–1704 Ch'ing Neo-Confucianism.	
GOTTFRIED WILHELM LEIBNIZ, 1646–1716 Monadology.		
	LI KUNG, 1659–1746 Ch'ing Neo-Confucianism.	
GEORGE BERKELEY, 1685–1753 Empirical idealism.		
DAVID HUME, 1711–76 Empiricism, criticism of universal laws.		

WESTERN TRADITION	CHINESE TRADITION	INDIAN TRADITION
	TAI CHEN, 1723–77 Ch'ing Neo-Confucianism.	
IMMANUEL KANT, 1724–1804 Critical philosophy, reconciliation of rationalism and empiricism.		
JOHANN GOTTLIEB FICHTE, 1762–1814 Voluntaristic idealism.		
	JÜAN YÜAN, 1764–1849 Ch'ing Neo-Confucianism.	
GEORG WILHELM FRIEDRICH HEGEL, 1770–1831 Absolute idealism of reason.		
FRIEDRICH VON SCHELLING, 1775–1854 Idealism of identity.		
ARTHUR SCHOPENHAUER, 1788–1860 Pessimism of the will.		
AUGUSTE COMTE 1797–1857 Positivism.		
CHARLES DARWIN, 1809–82 Natural evolution.		
SÖREN KIERKEGAARD, 1813–55 Existentialism.		
KARL MARX, 1818–83 Dialectical materialism.		

WESTERN TRADITION	CHINESE TRADITION	INDIAN TRADITION
THOMAS HILL GREEN, 1836–82 Neo-Kantianism.		
ERNST MACH, 1838–1916 Expedientism of scientific concepts.		
CHARLES PEIRCE, 1839–1914 Pragmatism (pragmaticism).		
WILLIAM JAMES, 1842–1910 Pragmatism.		
FRIEDRICH NIETZSCHE, 1844–1900 Doctrine of the superman.		
F. H. BRADLEY, 1846–1924 Absolute idealism, transcendence of reason.		
BERNARD BOSANQUET, 1848–1923 Hegelian idealism.		
HANS VAIHINGER, 1852–1933 Fictionalism.		
LLOYD MORGAN, 1852–1936 Emergent evolution.		
	YEN FU, 1853–1920 Introduces western philosophy into China.	
H. POINCARÉ, 1854–1912 Conventionalism.		
JOSIAH ROYCE, 1855–1916 Hegelian idealism.		
A. MEINONG, 1855–1921 New realism.		

WESTERN TRADITION	CHINESE TRADITION	INDIAN TRADITION
	K'ANG YU-WEI, 1858–1927 New Text School of Ch'ing dynasty.	
S. ALEXANDER, 1859–1941 Realism, emergent evolution.		
JOHN DEWEY, 1859–1954 Pragmatism, instrumentalism.		
A. N. WHITEHEAD, 1861–1947 Philosophy of organism, evolutionism.		RABĪNDRANĀTH TAGORE, 1861–1941 Personal idealism.
G. SANTAYANA, 1863–1952 Critical realism.		
F. C. S. SCHILLER, 1864–1937 Pragmatism, humanism.		
	TAN SSU-T'UNG, 1865–98 New Text School of Ch'ing dynasty.	
J. M. E. McTAGGART, 1866–1925 Pluralistic idealism.		
B. CROCE, 1866–1952 Neo-idealism.		BHAGAVAN DAS, 1869–1958 Realistic idealism.
BERTRAND RUSSELL, 1872—— Neutral monism, analysis.		
		AUROBINDO GHOSE, 1872–1950 Idealism, absolutism of integral experience.
G. E. MOORE, 1873—— Analysis.		
E. B. HOLT, 1873–1946 New realism.		

WESTERN TRADITION	CHINESE TRADITION	INDIAN TRADITION
A. O. LOVEJOY, 1873—— Critical realism.		
G. GENTILE, 1875–1944 Neo-idealism.		
R. B. PERRY, 1876—— New realism.	WANG KUO-WEI, 1877–1927 Introduces western philosophy into China.	
MORITZ SCHLICK, 1882–1936 Logical positivism.		
KARL JASPERS, 1883—— Existentialism.		
		S. RADHAKRISHNAN, 1888—— Non-dualistic Idealism.
M. HEIDEGGER, 1889—— Existentialism.		
L. WITTGENSTEIN, 1889–1951 Logical positivism, analysis.		
G. MARCEL, 1889—— Existentialism.		
R. CARNAP, 1891—— Logical positivism.		
J. P. SARTRE, 1903—— Existentialism.		
	MAO TSE-TUNG, 1893—— Marxism as interpreted by Lenin and Stalin.	
GILBERT RYLE, 1900—— Analysis.		
A. J. AYER, 1910—— Analysis, logical empiricism.		

Glossary of Indian and Chinese Terms

abheda. Non-difference.
adhijyotiṣam. Pertaining to the shining ones or deities.
adhikārin. Aspirant; one who is qualified; claimant.
adhilokam. Pertaining to the physical world, mundane, natural, empirical.
adhiprajam. Pertaining to the sexes.
adhividyam. Pertaining to sacrifices, invocations, and incantations.
adhyātmam. Pertaining to the Ātman.
Advaita. Nondual; nondualism.
ahaṁkāra. Ego.
ajīva. Inanimate; soulless; material substance.
artha. Wealth.
Arya Dharma. Religion of the Aryans; Aryan Way.
Arya Mata. Arya Dharma.
āśramas. Stages of life.
Ātman. Spirit; Supreme Universal Spirit; individual spirit; self; soul.
avayava. Step, or member, of a syllogism.
Avidyā. Ignorance, Nescience.
Avyakta. Indefinite; Unmanifest; unparticularized; undifferentiated; unarticulated.

bhakti. Devotion, love, adoration.
bhaktimārga. Way of devotion leading to salvation.
bhaktiyoga. *Bhaktimārga,* the yoga of devotion.
bhāva. Becoming; tendency to be born.
bheda. Difference.
bhedābheda. Difference-cum-identity; identity in difference.
bhūta. Element.
bhūtatathatā. Suchness of elements, thusness of elements; the way of elements; ultimate nature of things.
Brahman. The Absolute, the Universal Spirit.
buddhi. Reason; thought; cognition; knowledge; consciousness.

chala. Quibbling.
chang. The five constant virtues, *jen, yi, li, chih,* and *hsin.* These constitute ethics of the individual. See *Kang.*

cheng. Correct firmness.
ch'eng ming. Rectification of names.
ch'i. Gaseous ethereal matter; primeval matter.
chih. Wisdom.
chih. Universal concepts as opposed to *wu.*
ch'ing. Emotions and feelings; the affective nature of man.
chun tzu. Sons of princes.
chung. Doing to others what one wishes to be done by them to one; the mean.

Dharma. Duty; action according to the injunctions of the Veda; creative force of ethical activity; nature; principle; law; norm; quality; attribute; object; thing; category; the highest sustaining principle of the universe.
doṣa. Defect.
dṛṣṭānta. Example.
dvaita. Dual; dualism.

fa. Law, regulation.

gārhasthya. Householder's life; pertaining to the householder.
guṇas. Attributes; qualities; the three attributes of Prakṛti.

heng. Prosperous development.
hetvābhāsās. Fallacies; apparent or fallacious reasons.
ho. Harmony.
hsiao jen. Small men.
hsin. Good faith.
hsing. Nature; human nature.
hsing. Punishments.
hsüan. Mystery.
hsüan hsüeh. Dark learning; Neo-Taoism.

jāti. Birth.
jāti. Shifty argument.
jalpa. Wrangling.
jarā. Old age.
jen. Human-heartedness; love.
jīva. Soul; psycho-ethical personality distinguished from *ātman,* or self, by most of the Indian schools; animate substance.
jñāna. Knowledge; gnosis.
jñānamārga. Way of knowledge leading to salvation.
jñānayoga. See *jñānamārga.*

kāma. Desire, love.

kang. Major cord constituted by the relations of sovereign and subject, father and son, and husband and wife. These constitute the ethics of society. See *Chang.*

karma. Action, activity.

karmamārga. Way of action leading to salvation.

karmayoga. *Karmamārga.*

ko yi. The method of interpreting Buddhist ideas through Taoist and Confucian analogies.

Li. Form, universal, principle.

li. Profit making.

li. Sacrifice; sacrificial ritual; ceremony; courtesy; courtship; manners, etiquette; duty; moral code; unwritten code of honor.

Mahat. Cosmic Reason; Cosmic Person; Logos; the Great.

manas. Mind.

maraṇa. Death.

Māyā. World-illusion, the creative power of the Unconscious.

mīmāmsā. Inquiry; investigation; discussion; the name of the school of Jaimini expounding the philosophy of the first two parts of the Veda.

ming. The total existent conditions and forces of the universe; names of actualities as distinguished from *shih.*

ming-li. Terms and principles.

mokṣa. Liberation; salvation.

nāma. Name; mind.

nāma-rūpa. Name and form; mind and matter.

naya. Mode; standpoint.

nigrahasthāna. Ground of defeat; basis of disproof.

nirṇaya. Ascertainment; conclusion.

nirvāṇa. Quietude; nondisturbance; salvation.

pa. War lord.

Prakṛti. Primeval matter; nature.

pramāṇa. Valid means of cognition.

prameya. Object of cognition; the knowable.

prāṇa. Vital principle.

pratītyasamutpāda. Doctrine of cause as an occasion; dependent origination; dependent emergence; chain of conditioned effects.

prayojana. Purpose, aim.

pudgala. physical body; psychophysical individual.

Puruṣa. Ātman; self; spirit.

rūpa. Form; shape; matter.
rajas. The attribute of activity, one of the three *guṇas* of Prakṛti.

ṣaḍāyatana. Six fields of experience (of mind and the five senses).
Śakti. Energy; power; force; the creative force of the Universal Spirit; personification of such force as the consort of the Godhead.
samādhi. Trance; immersion in concentration.
sāmānya. Universal.
samjñā. Sensation, perception.
samsāra. World; becoming; change; flow.
samsaya. Doubt.
samskāra. Impression; instinct; urge; drive.
sannyāsa. Renunciation; life of the monk and nun.
sattva. The attribute of purity, one of the *guṇas* of Prakṛti.
shih. Power.
shih. Actualities as opposed to *ming*.
shu. Method of conducting affairs and handling men.
shu. Timelessness.
shu jen. Common men.
siddhānta. Doctrine, view, theory.
skandha. Aggregate.
smṛti. Memory; epic; ethical code; remembered text, as distinct from *śruti*, or heard text.
spanda. Vibration, activity.
sparśa. Touch; sense contact.
Śuddhādvaita. Pure nondualism as distinct from impure nondualism.
Śūnya. The Void, the Empty.
śūnyatā. Voidness, emptiness.
syādvāda. Doctrine of conditioned predication.

T'ai chi. Ultimate.
tamas. Darkness; the attribute of passivity, one of the three *guṇas* of Prakṛti.
Tao. Way.
tao. The way of each individual, as distinct from Tao, the Absolute Way.
tarka. Counterfactual conditional; indirect proof.
tathā. Such, thus.
Tathatā. Suchness, thusness.
Te. Nature of principle of individual things; inclinations; own nature.
Ti. God.
T'ien. Heaven; nature.
tṛṣṇā. Thirst; craving.

upādāna. Craving.
upādhi. Condition; limitation; proviso.

vāda. Discussion; controversy; debate.
vānaprasthya. Forest-dweller's life; retired life.
vāsanā. Perfume; impression; tendency; instinct.
vedanā. Sense experience; feeling; pain.
vihāra. Monastery.
vijñāna. Consciousness; mind; reason.
viśeṣa. Particular; ultimate differentiating principle of each object.
viśiṣṭādvaita. Nondualism of the qualified.
vitaṇḍā. Criticism without any position of one's own; frivolous argument.

wang. King.
wu chi. Ultimateless.
wu hsin. No mind, mindlessness.
wu hsing. Five elements.
wu-wei. Do nothing, nonaction.
wu yu. Effortless action.

Yang. The male principle in Chinese thought.
yi. Righteousness.
Yin. The female principle in Chinese thought.
Yoga. The practice uniting the individual and the Absolute Spirit.
yuan. Originating growth.
yüeh. Music.
yu-wei. Action.

INDEX

Index